LIFE
Before and
AFTER
MONTY
PYTHON

Also by

**KIM
"HOWARD"
JOHNSON:**

**THE FIRST 20~~0~~ YEARS OF MONTY PYTHON
AND NOW FOR SOMETHING COMPLETELY TRIV-IAL:**
The Monty Python Trivia and Quiz Book

LIFE
Before and
AFTER MONTY PYTHON

The Solo Flights of The Flying Circus

by
**KIM
"HOWARD"
JOHNSON**

ST. MARTIN'S PRESS NEW YORK, N.Y.

Once again, Monty Python's royalty from this book will go to the Rainforest Action Network, 301 Broadway, Suite A, San Francisco, CA 94133, to contribute toward the replenishment of rain forests cut down to produce this edition.

Production Editor: David Stanford Burr

Design by: A Good Thing Inc.

Library of Congress Cataloging–in–Publication Data

Johnson, Kim.
   Life (before and) after Monty Python: the solo flights of the flying circus/Kim "Howard" Johnson
       p.   cm.
    "A Thomas Dunne book."
    ISBN 0-312-08695-4 (pbk.)
    1. Monty Python (Comedy troupe) 2. Comedians—Great Britain—Biography. 3. Entertainers—Great Britain—Biography. I. Title.
PN2599.5. T54J645   1993
791.45'028'0922—dc20
[B]   92- 41315
                                                                    CIP

First Edition: April 1993

10 9 8 7 6 5 4 3 2 1

For John Tomiczek
and all of our adventures with Graham,
and Harvey Kurtzman, who had
the mad idea of introducing
Terry Gilliam and John Cleese

ACKNOWL-EDGMENTS

As with my other Monty Python books, *Life Before and After Monty Python* would not have been possible without the generous assistance of many people. Particular thanks are due to Alison and Terry Jones, Helen and Michael Palin, John Cleese, Tanya Kosevich and Eric Idle, Maggie and Terry Gilliam, David Sherlock, Neil Innes, Anne James, Roger Saunders, Alison Davies, Steve Abbott, Kath James, and all at Mayday Management.

On the American side, thanks to my parents, Ken and Marge Johnson, Dominick Abel, Laurie Bradach, Mike Carlin, Del Close, Max Allan Collins, Bob Faulkner, Sheila Gibson, Mike Gold, Charna Halpern, Simon Jones, Tim Kazurinski, Nancy Lewis, Jill and Michael McCarthy, Dave McDonnell and all at *Starlog*, Jim Steranko and *Prevue,* Tim Stouffer, George Wendt, Eric Zorn, and everyone at St. Martin's, all of whom must share some measure of complicity.

PREFACE

A few months ago a strange wild-looking man came up to me in a pub and started to ask me questions about Monty Python. He was weird, oddly dressed, and American. I assumed he was Terry Gilliam. I should have realized I was mistaken when he bought me a drink.

From then on this mysteriously insinuating fellow plied me with halves of bitter (a particularly intoxicating and revolting drink, much used in England as a substitute for foreplay), and when I was half gone he produced from underneath his grubby clothes a tiny tape recorder.

"This'll make another book," he said with a chortle as he snapped off a quick photo, "to save on expenses."

I kicked him in the balls and yelled bollocks, but the chap clearly had cast-iron testicles, for in one leap he was away, chortling manically, and was halfway to his publishers before I could recover.

Well, that's the story of this book. A sad indictment of our troubled times, when one man's moan is another man's miniseries. Some of what I said is not so very nice. But what can I tell you? I was drunk and I forgot to lie.

ERIC IDLE

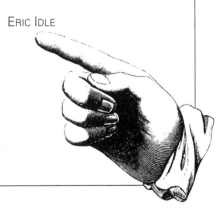

ix

AUTHOR'S NOTE

*A*fter I had finished my first book, *The First 20*☒
Years, Monty Python I was casting about for ideas for a follow-up
book. John Cleese was quite keen to have me write a book
chronicling the individual projects of the six members of Python.

John pointed out that all of them—Graham Chapman,
Terry Gilliam, Eric Idle, Terry Jones, Michael Palin, and himself—
had forged successful solo careers in film, television, theater, and
literature since they had set out on their own, and those projects
would make a terrific book.

So convinced was I that I immediately sat down and wrote
And Now for Something Completely Trivial, a Monty Python trivia
and quiz book, as a follow-up. (I would like to point out here that
John Cleese's performance in the quizzes was lackluster, at best.)

Still, I kept coming back to John's suggestion. Were there
really that many successful, interesting solo projects, enough to fill
an entire book? I started looking through my files for material, and I
thought, well, yes, maybe. I continued to compile information, and
it kept growing, and growing, and growing, and I realized it would
equal or surpass my first book in length. (And I thought the first one
was quite long enough, thank you.)

Along the way, I grew to realize the diverse talents that
made up Monty Python. I knew they'd all performed on stage in
comedy revues, but I'd almost lost sight of the fact that some of
them had also performed Shakespeare (Cleese in *Taming of*

the Shrew), operetta (Idle in Gilbert and Sullivan's *The Mikado*), and even lecture tours (Chapman).

All of them are talented writers, but their works range from award-winning children's books (Palin and Jones) and autobiography (*A Liar's Autobiography* by Chapman) to psychology (Cleese's *Families and How to Survive Them*), a scholarly treatise (*Chaucer's Knight* by Jones), and even a novel (Idle's *Hello, Sailor!*).

Most people who have read this far are familiar with television shows like Cleese's *Fawlty Towers*, but not many people know that members of Python have appeared on game shows (Chapman on *Hollywood Squares*), hosted talk shows (the BBC's *Paperbacks* with Terry Jones), and presented travelogues (Palin's *Great Railway Journeys* and the better-known *Around the World in 80 Days*, as well as the more recent *Pole to Pole*).

Since I wanted to make this book as comprehensive as possible, *Life Before and After Monty Python* also deals with the films, television, and stage shows before Monty Python.

I have included all the significant works they have created on their own to date. I haven't attempted to list all of their countless talk-show appearances or interviews, and I have also left out brief, minor, or more insignificant TV and film appearances as well as unreleased projects, such as Eric Idle's appearance in *Missing Pieces* (a film he hopes will *never* be released!). However, I've included all projects that are accessible to Americans as well as others that have interesting or amusing stories connected to them.

The dates and times are as accurate as possible, although running times in particular are variable. (Movie guides may list one running time for a film, the videocassette box may claim another, while a stopwatch can indicate yet another length.)

Of course, a film with the checkered history of *Brazil* actually has at least four different lengths. The European and American theatrical versions each include scenes not seen in the others, Universal prepared its own shorter version that subverts Gilliam's vision, and the networks have butchered the TV versions.

In addition, laser-disc releases now contain scenes not included in the original versions of such films as *The Adventures of Baron Munchausen* and *The Fisher King* as well as commentary by the director.

The writing of this volume was a long, grueling, wonderful experience that provided some delightful surprises. When Terry Jones opened his files to me, I discovered the pages of original notes he kept during the final meeting when the six of them selected the name "Monty Python." In a series of brand-new interviews done for this volume, each provided me with terrific stories and background information that has never seen print anywhere, supplemented by interviews I had conducted with all six of them going back to the mid-1970s.

Finally, when I was looking through all of my files, I discovered a lengthy interview with the late Graham Chapman that I had completely forgotten about. Most of it has never seen print in any form, and although a large portion of it involved *Yellowbeard*, which he had just completed, the conversation took a more philosophical turn. Graham discussed his feelings about life and about death, which came entirely too soon to suit him and his countless fans and friends. Although Graham had little use for such sentiment, these portions of the book were like visiting with a dear old friend one last time, and I hope readers will share that feeling.

Monty Python is a phenomenon unique in comedy, one that refuses to die. Although they made only three original films as a group and created only forty-five half-hour TV shows, their legend grows, as do the careers of the men who made up the group.

More than a dozen years after its release, the song "Always Look on the Bright Side of Life" (from *Life of Brian*) was released as a single after British football hooligans began singing it in the stands when their teams were losing. "It reached number one on the ITV charts, number one in Ireland, was number three for six weeks in Germany, and the album reached number twenty-one on the German album charts," says Eric Idle. "How many German comedy albums are up there in the American charts?"

Monty Python (to use the parrot metaphor one last time) may have ceased to be, at least as an active group, but as *Life Before and After Monty Python* attests, its members went on to forge new careers as varied and interesting as they are.

So, Cleesey, you were right, and here's your book. I'll let you—and the readers—decide how terrific it is. But at least this one doesn't have any quizzes for you to fail!

INTRO-DUCTION

*T*he Animals, The Birds, The Crickets, White Snake, The Penguins, The Jaguars, Three Dog Night, The Turtles, the Stray Cats, Mama Lion, Iron Butterfly, Country Joe and Fish, Wolfman Jack, the Robins, The Blue Jays, The Orioles, The Crows, The Boomtown Rats, The Flamingos, Adam Ant, Fontela Bass, The Bobcats, The YardBirds, Tyrannosaurs Rex, The Cardinals, The Sparrows, The Mighty Sparrows, The Stone Pines, The Monkees, The Thunder Birds, The Roaches, Mad Dogs and English Men, The Beastie Boys, The Buzz Cocks, Elephants' Memory, A Flock of Seagulls, The Flock, Rhinoceros, Screaming Jay Hawkins, Bonzo Dog Doo Da Band, Los Lobos, Moon Dog, Gil Scott Heron, The Eagles, The Lounge Lizzard, The Harmonicats, The Silver Swans, Impalas, Toad and The Wet Sprocket, Sopwith Camel, The Beatles and then there were "The Pythons."

As much about Rock and Roll as any other Band, "The Pythons" were to comedic Art what The Beatles were to music. They were special men at a very special time doing very special things and shaping a form of Comedy like their predecessors—Chaplin, Laurel and Hardy, The Marx Brothers, and Lenny Bruce—breaking new ground with "Monty Python's Flying Circus"—and one day the tent was folded by the untimely death of Graham Chapman, first on the alphabetic roll at the end of each "Python Show."

As Artists they were complete—but what happened next? Tonight Michael Palin will still be circling the Globe and tonight there will be T.V. shows not worthy of mention but for the interruptions provided by John Cleese standing up for Magnavox, and oh yes, "Yellow Beard" will be shown again tonight, and oh yes again, Terry Gilliam's "Fisher King" for which I sang "How About You" will appear on a movie channel. But what are the others doing now post "Python?" This wonderful book by Kim "Howard" Johnson, who also took us through the other two "Python" books, will inform, delight, and entertain you with Terry Jones's entertaining of children and Eric Idle—a nifty and suspiciously kind guy and you will have been lifted to yet another plane which dissects the Group even more by their forced separation and the larger magnifying glass that Howard Johnson uses on each individual. No more rabble-rousing collective snake-like venom, in the form of the "Pythons'" looking glass panning for pomposity at any level and gunning for hypocrisy as one six - or seven-headed Hydra—instead, one by one, each member who when seen alone appears naked— but in the group a battle dress of armor and aprons and silly things. George Harrison went on stage with them in New York—I went on stage, with my intrepid and loving wife, and promptly fell eight feet into the orchestra pit, breaking my right hand. I am so happy to be able to say the "That's tight! Broke the frigin' metacarples, clean through." You mean, "What are they really like...? Well...You mean Now?"

Love,

Harry Nilsson

Part One

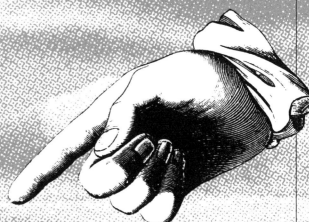

BEFORE MONTY PYTHON

HUMBLE BEGINNINGS

*T*he six individuals who would become Monty Python honed their talents at college, though there appear to have been occasional indications of their potential during their youth.

John Cleese theorizes that he began making people laugh as a defense mechanism; he was six feet tall when he was twelve years old, and made jokes in order to feel less of an outsider. Michael Palin often tells of his debut on stage when he was five years old; while playing Martha Cratchit in *A Christmas Carol,* he fell off the stage.

Eventually Cleese, Graham Chapman, and Eric Idle gravitated toward Cambridge University. There the Footlights society, famed for producing David Frost and *Beyond the Fringe,* held a strong attraction for the three of them. Palin and Terry Jones likewise wound up at Oxford and became involved with the theatrical world there. On the other side of the ocean, Terry Gilliam continued cartooning when he arrived at Occidental College in California, but there was little promise of what was to come.

Cambridge University

GRAHAM CHAPMAN, JOHN CLEESE, ERIC IDLE

Cambridge University held a certain allure for would-be actors, writers, and humorists in the early 1960s. Although the school's Footlights society had been in existence since 1883, the club had just mounted its most successful revue to date.

The 1960 Footlights show, *Beyond the Fringe,* was written and performed by Peter Cook, Dudley Moore, Alan Bennett, and Jonathan Miller; the show ran for years in London's West End and on Broadway, and revitalized satire in Great Britain. Its creators, like the future Pythons, were all fans of Spike Milligan's *The Goon Show,* which was presented during the 1950s on BBC-Radio. Created and performed by Spike Milligan, Harry Secombe, and Peter Sellers, its anarchic, unconventional humor and wordplay provided a heavy influence on the then-teenage Pythons.

Chapman, Cleese, and Idle did not attend Cambridge primarily for the Footlights, however. Chapman was going to study medicine, Cleese was a law student, and Idle planned to study English. Their plans took a detour, this time by way of a circus that was not yet flying.

Graham Chapman was the first of the future Pythons to arrive at Cambridge, where he continued his medical studies at Emmanuel College. Although he didn't make it into the Footlights during his first year (he was turned down by the club's secretary, David Frost, who explained that aspiring members had to be invited to audition), he teamed up with another student and they put on their own smoker.

"There were only twenty-five undergraduate performers of this club [the Footlights] each year, and in order to join it, you had to be asked to do an audition," explained Chapman many years later. "In other words, you had to be noticed somewhere around the place doing something funny, performing or something. Then you were asked to audition in front of a few members of the committee, and if you were good enough for them, you were allowed to audition at a smoking concert.

"Now, a smoking concert is a strange thing. It originated when the gentlemen retired after dinner and were entertained—in various ways, I imagine, but this was not like that," he laughed. "None of that stuff, none of that at all! This was not your nude ladies, this was nothing at all to do with them.

"This was really a group of people trying to be entertaining to their fellow members of the club. If the auditionees at one of these smoking concerts entertained the people sufficiently, they were then allowed to join the club. And that was done on a strict voting basis, so you could really keep out a lot of people! It was possible to keep it down to about six members a year, by which you would ensure yourself a place in the annual revue."

Footlights members who saw their show invited them to audition, and Chapman became a member his second year at Cambridge, inducted at the same time as first-year law student Cleese. For them both—and the other Footlights members—the annual revue was the highlight of the year.

"The annual revue had quite a professional standard of budget, so it was a worthwhile thing to be in. There were a lot of little extras," noted Chapman. "Because of the smoking concerts—and we had about two of those every term, and we had all these people auditioning—that meant

A very young John Cleese with father Reg and mother Muriel. Photo from The Collection of John Cleese, used by permission

John Cleese (left) participates in Sports Day at St. Peters School, Weaston-super-Mare, May 30th, 1953. Photo from The Collection of John Cleese, used by permission

there was a lot of material being produced, a lot of material being written, and a lot of people forming in all sorts of different ways to try to get into this damned revue each year. That meant that the actual revue itself had quite a reasonable standard. It was a semiprofessional sort of thing, and a lot of people went on from that into entertainment. It was like a separate college, in a way."

John Cleese had finished up at Clifton College and then passed the entrance exam for Cambridge's Downing College, but it was two years before he was able to enroll. In a move that calls to mind his Monty Python schoolmaster character, he went back and taught at his old prep school during that period.

"I completed public school at the age of eighteen and then taught for two years without a thought of a career in comedy, except that when I'd done a house entertainment at Clifton in my last year, somebody said `Oh, when you go to Cambridge, you must join the Footlights.' I said `Oh, must I? Who are they?'"

In view of this encouragement, Cleese indeed decided to try to join the Footlights, but like Chapman, he was also rejected the first time.

"When I went up to Cambridge over two years later, I did stop at the Footlights desk and ask about the club. They said `Do you sing?' I was worst singer in Europe, fourteen years in a row. So I said `No,' and they said `Oh, never mind. Do you dance?' My jaw dropped and I went red, and said `No.' They said `Well, what do you do?' and I said `I suppose I try to make people laugh.' And I said something else, and just retired in confusion."

Fortunately, a friend of his had been asked to write some pieces for the club, and he asked Cleese to collaborate with him. When the pair presented the sketches to the group, the law student found himself elected to the Footlights.

"Nothing happened at all until Alan Hutchinson—he's my closest friend now, we met my second day at Cambridge—came up to me halfway through the year and said `I've bumped into an old school friend who helps to run the Footlights. Would you like to do a sketch with me, and we can both get in it?' We wrote something together and performed it, and we were both elected. Subsequently I did some sketches and gradually began to get the hang of it, although it took me several attempts to write—I didn't have the slightest idea what I was doing.

"It was a friendly enough club. By the time I was halfway through my second year, I was beginning to show one or two glimmerings of talent. By the time I got to my third year, I was writing some sketches that were really quite good."

Graham Chapman had been at Cambridge a year before John Cleese enrolled, and the future writing partners met through the Footlights.

"I think the two of us met at the end of my first year, so I suppose I'd been in the Footlights for about a term, and didn't really know anyone yet," recalls Cleese.

"I vaguely remember my first meeting with Graham, and funny enough, my main impression was I didn't like him much! I think we met at some sort of audition, and we went out afterwards and had a cup of coffee and a tea cake together. I didn't feel very comfortable with him,

A twelve-year-old Terry Gilliam works a simpler kind of magic during Christmas, 1952. Photo from The Collection of Terry Gilliam, used by permission

and I didn't find him likable. But I seemed just to forget that, and as we started to see each other on a more regular basis, we were just sort of drawn to write together. I don't ever remember whether he suggested it to me, or I to him, but we became a regular writing partnership to the extent when, if anybody came into my room and saw a pad of paper and a pencil and an open Bible, they would say accusingly, 'You've been writing a sketch with Graham again!'

"I suppose all together, we probably wrote a dozen top-drawer sketches while we were at Cambridge. We did start writing in 'sixty-two. We wrote a mountaineering sketch for the *Footlights Revue* of that year, and several other things with other people, with three or four people writing some of those sketches. Then Graham went off, having finished a year earlier than me, and did medicine at Bart's while performing cabaret in the evening with a guy called Tony Hendra.*"

Neither Cleese nor Chapman were cast in the revue their first year, but they appeared together onstage for the first time in mid-1962 in *Double Take*, which also featured Tim Brooke-Taylor, Humphrey Barclay, and Tony Hendra. This was also the first year in the Footlights for an English student named Eric Idle, who, like Chapman, was invited to audition after he staged a smoker for the club; he would not appear on stage with Chapman and Cleese for a few more years, however.

Idle began appearing with other actors in Cambridge revues, including an appearance at the 1963 Edinburgh Festival. Ironically, Terry Jones was featured in the Oxford Theatre Group's show there at the same time. One critic, Harold Hobson, writing in the August 22 *Edinburgh Evening News*, called their two shows among the best in the festival:

if any section of the official dramatic Festival achieved its aims as completely as the Cambridge University Footlights '63 and the Oxford Theatre Group's * * * * achieve theirs, then this Festival would not only be—what it is—good, but unrivalled.

Yet these Oxford and Cambridge late night revues are given in makeshift halls, down sinis-

The Clifton College football team; John Cleese is in the front row, second from right. Coincidentally, the boy sitting next to him was named Andrew Parrott. Photo from The Collection of John Cleese, used by permission

ter streets and crooked alleys. Their chairs are uncomfortable, their stages look as if they have been run up by amateurs when they were thinking of something else; and one might almost guess, from the appearance of the Oxford troupe, that they have no running water ...

[The halls] suit the Oxford team, who, apart from a ravishing girl, are, it must be admitted, a shabby lot, supremely well; and to Cambridge, suave, civilised, soigne, brushed and bourgeois, they afford a setting of illustrating contrast.

The Cambridge quartet—Richard Eyre, David Gooderson, Eric Idle and Humphrey Barclay—have the stronger personalities. They give pleasure by what they are, by the irresistible efflorescence of their spontaneity. They attract admiration as effortlessly as the sun attracts the flowers. Oxford, on the other hand, compel it. What they do is diabolically clever. Every one of them—Ian Davidson, Jane Brayshaw, Douglas Fisher, Robin Grove-White and Terry Jones—is a first-class mimic; they are superb, all the time, as someone else, whether it be the creator of the tattoo, the Prime Minister, or a pro-hyphen, anti-peerage Labour M.P. Most people here unaccountably describe the Oxford revue as an escape from satire. It is, in fact, satirical from beginning to end. What throws people out must be the fact that it is funny.

While Idle was performing *Footlights '63* at the 1963 Edinburgh Festival, Chapman was using his sabbatical from performing after *Double Take* to study at St. Bart's Hospital. Cleese kept at it,

---

* Hendra later became the editor of the *National Lampoon* from 1971 through 1978, and co-created the British TV series *Spitting Image*

though, and appeared in *A Clump of Plinths* during the summer of 1963. The show proved exceedingly popular, and apparently through the efforts of Humphrey Barclay, it was mounted in London's West End after its initial run at the university, and its title was changed to *Cambridge Circus*.

"I had no idea that *Cambridge Circus* was a success at the beginning, until two things happened," notes Cleese. "First of all, two extremely nice men in gray suits, Peter Titheradge and Ted Taylor, came into the Footlights club room one evening and said something like would I ever consider starting a career writing comedy for BBC-Radio, which, after a little bit of thought, and a slight hesitation about not doing something respectable like being a solicitor, which is what I was being lined up to do—with a little bit of thought, I was able to let go of the legal world rather easily. Being the BBC, it had other aspects of the civil service which reassured my parents, because of the apparent stability of working for the BBC.

"The other thing that happened was an impresario called Michael White arrived in the club room somewhere around the same time as my two friends from the BBC. Michael said he wanted to send us to the West End, which was quite a thrill, and gave us a little bit of a launching pad. He managed to get us into a West End theater and get us Equity cards. There we were, performing in the West End not so long after leaving Cambridge!

"That had two effects. First of all, it was a thrill, because people actually came to see us. I also remember it was incredibly useful for me, because I'd left Cambridge with the dearth of six

The Oscar Wilde sketch in **Cambridge Circus** *with Jonathan Lynn (left), John Cleese (center), and David Hatch (right). Photo from The Collection of John Cleese, used by permission*

hundred pounds. This was simply the sum of money that my father was supposed to have made up over and above the state scholarship in science that I'd got from the Bristol council, but he wasn't able to give me any money. As that was exactly what he was supposed to give me, although he guaranteed it at the bank—whatever that means—I was six hundred in the red the day I left Cambridge. The wonderful thing about Cambridge was that after about two months in the West End, maybe a little more, I'd actually paid off the entire debt! So, something that I was expecting to carry around my neck for two and a half years as a solicitor's clerk was gone, and I was back to zero. That was an *incredible* help."

Cleese's BBC career, which had begun by contributing sketches to Frost's *That Was the Week That Was* while still in school, grew into a regular writing position at the BBC. He wrote jokes for *The Dick Emery Show* and other BBC-Radio shows, including a Christmas special called *Yule Be Surprised*, the memory of which still embarrasses him.

"It's quite true—the first script they ever gave me was called *Yule Be Surprised*. It was written by a man called Eddie McGuire. I was given the script and told to take some of the jokes out," Cleese says with a laugh.

"After a short pause, another guy, whose name I have sadly forgotten, was introduced to me. He was going to write most of the sketches. That was my first experience at any sort of regular work in those days—four months out of Cambridge and about a month out of *Cambridge Circus*. There I was, sitting at my desk writing this one sketch a week. I based it on an archetype of a Peter Cook sketch which I had never seen but had always been told about. I remember Trevor Nunn telling me about it when he directed the 'sixty-two revue—it was called 'Interesting Facts.' I subsequently had the very great joy and privilege of performing that sketch with Peter Cook in an Amnesty show."

Cambridge Circus ran for five months at the Lyric Theatre in the West End, beginning August 16, 1963. Chapman was not with the show when it opened, but joined the cast when one of the actors, Tony Buffery, dropped out; the cast also included Tim Brooke-Taylor, Bill Oddie, Jo Kendall, and David Hatch. Cleese was writing for the BBC during the day, while Chapman found himself making hospital rounds at St. Bart's and thrashing around on the Lyric stage every night.

A 24-year-old John Cleese "with my Maurice Chevalier grin" on top of the Aeolian Hall, which housed BBC-Radio Light Entertainment. Cleese says he caused a minor commotion by not wearing a jacket and a tie when he first began working for the BBC. Photo by Jo Kendall

"The success of *Cambridge Circus* meant that I had a job at the BBC, a steady job which I then did until about June or July of the following year, 1964, when Michael White suddenly suggested we should take the show out of the deep freeze, warm it up and take it to New Zealand, with the possibility of America. We weren't confirmed vis-à-vis New York until we were towards the end of the New Zealand trip. But, the whole point was, it was a jaunt, a little bit of excitement, a bit of money, and a chance to see the world. I don't think any of us thought of it very much in terms of where it would lead, and I think we were very doubtful whether the show would work on Broadway, a doubt which proved to be a very accurate assessment of the situation!" Cleese declares.

So Cleese took leave from the BBC, and Chapman decided to take a year off from his medical studies, but he didn't quite know how to explain it to his parents.

Around this time, a number of medical students were invited to have tea with the Queen Mother, and Chapman was among those selected. While he was speaking to her, he happened to mention that he had the opportunity to tour New Zealand.

"It's a beautiful place," she told him. "You must go."

"I told my parents about it," Chapman later explained, "only I phrased it as though I had been given a royal command which I couldn't refuse."

His parents, properly respectful of the Royals, allowed him to give up his studies for the duration of the tour, and Chapman, Cleese, and the rest of the cast were off to New Zealand for six weeks.

"The tour was mainly chaotic because New Zealand, in those days, was more or less another planet," notes Cleese. "I remember standing on a beach, staring across the sea, thinking `Only three thousand miles to Chile!'"

One of the stranger moments occurred when Chapman had difficulty ordering a three-egg omelette. He was finally served three fried eggs that were sitting on top of an omelette.

"The New Zealanders, in those days, were a little bit out to lunch and almost nothing in New Zealand worked. The only thing was, because they were New Zealanders, they'd never been anywhere where things *did* work. So, if you criticized them, they thought you were mad!" Cleese says with a laugh.

Still, some of Cleese's favorite moments in the Footlights occurred on the New Zealand tour.

"The man in charge of the show did not realize that he had to not only get the flats* *in* at the beginning of sketches, but he had to get them *out* at the end. I remember Graham coming on to do a solo towards the end of the first half, and he could hardly get on, because there were so many of these flats that had been flown in, and just left there," explains Cleese.

The Custard Pie sketch, as performed in Cambridge Circus: *originally written by Terry Jones and performed at Oxford, they borrowed it when the show began its West End run. From left are David Hatch, Bill Oddie, Tim Brooke-Taylor, and Jonathan Lynn. John Cleese Photo, used by permission*

*Large canvas covered wooden frames painted for use as scenery in theatrical productions

"I remember him picking his way through these flats eventually, one of them bumping him on the shoulder while he was doing his routine. He never registered the fact that it was bumping him on the shoulder from behind.

"When he got off, I said 'Didn't you realize you were being bumped? The audience could see you were being bumped—why didn't you react to it?' And he said 'Well, I assumed you'd gotten behind me with a broom and was poking me with it!' Which shows what passed for a norm in those days...."

At the conclusion of the tour, the cast traveled to New York, where *Cambridge Circus* opened on Broadway on October 6, 1964. It ran for twenty-three performances (including an appearance on *The Ed Sullivan Show)* and was then transferred off-Broadway, where it ran until early 1965, and an American cast took over. (A soundtrack album was released featuring the original British cast, however.)

"The American show was a bit of a blur, really. We got there and started rehearsing the show, and strange shadowy men sat halfway back in the stalls without us really knowing who they were. Then messages came that material in the show wasn't right. At first, we reacted in a defiant way, and then realized that they probably knew a bit more about American audiences than we did," Cleese recalls.

"We managed to get a couple of extra items and fit them in the show at short notice. One was a number Graham did, a parody of the Marc Antony death speech. He actually carried the body, but found it progressively harder to carry the body satisfactorily. The body started as dead, but then became more alive as it tried to help Graham carry it. I think there was also some Beatles' takeoff based on the music of the 'Hallelujah Chorus.' We did that as a Beatles' number, and it was a great success.

"We got very good reviews, except for one former sportswriter on *The New York Times* called Howard Taubman. He gave us a bad review, and it killed us. Walter Kerr, who was a proper critic and knew what he was talking about, loved the show, and in fact wrote twice about us in an attempt to keep it alive. But we came off before we'd even started. I think we'd been on for three weeks, and we just weren't in a routine. We always knew we were in trouble, so we never sort of settled. It was all a bit strange and temporary."

It was during *Cambridge Circus* in New York that another significant event occurred in the history of Monty Python. John Cleese was selected to appear in a photo-feature for *Help!* magazine, and found himself working with a young assistant editor called Terry Gilliam. It was a meeting that would have unique repercussions.

After *Cambridge Circus*, Cleese opted to stay in the United States, while most of the others returned to Britain, Chapman going back to medical studies.

Meanwhile, back at Cambridge, Eric Idle was busy with the Footlights. Following in the

Cleese relaxes just before **Cambridge Circus** *goes off on its tour of New Zealand. Photo by Jo Kendall*

footsteps of *A Clump of Plinths* was intimidating, but Idle wrote, directed, and appeared in the 1964 Footlights revue at Edinburgh, where he first met Michael Palin.

For Idle, 1965 proved to be the breakthrough year. He was elected president of the Footlights and was responsible for changing the bylaws to allow women to become full members. One of the first female members of the Footlights was, in fact, feminist author Germaine Greer.

(Strangely enough, America's most famous feminist also has a Python connection. Gloria Steinem served as Harvey Kurtzman's first assistant editor on *Help!* magazine, a job later taken by Terry Gilliam.)

Idle wrote for and appeared in the 1965 Footlights revue *My Girl Herbert*. He claims the show itself was not outstanding, though it toured Britain and ran for three weeks at the Lyric Hammersmith in London. With the end of *Herbert*, Idle had also ended his days at Cambridge, and set out to make his way in cabaret, repertory theater, and the BBC.

CAMBRIDGE CIRCUS

FEATURING JOHN CLEESE.

(1963) Odeon PPMC 1208, (1965) Odeon PCS 3046

SIDE ONE

Green Line Bus

Patients For the Use Of

Boring Sexy Song

Great Moments in British Theatre (How Green Was My Buttonhole?)*

Pride and Joy

B.B.C.B.C.*

Sing Sing*

SIDE TWO

Boring Straight Song

Swap a Jest

Those Were the Days

O.H.M.S.*

Judge Not*

The original soundtrack album from the show with the original cast. John Cleese–related highlights include "B.B.C.B.C.," a reading of the evening news if the BBC were broadcasting in Old Testament times, with Cleese giving the weather; and "Judge Not," a courtroom sketch in which Cleese plays the prosecutor.

THAT WAS THE WEEK THAT WAS

WITH WRITTEN CONTRIBUTIONS BY JOHN CLEESE.

Featuring David Frost, Millicent Martin, Lance Percival, Roy Kinnear, William Rushton, Kennth Cope, and David Kernan. Written by Christopher Booker, Caryl Brahms, John Cleese, Quentin Crewe, Peter Dobreiner, David Frost, Ron Grainer, Willis Hall, Richard Ingrams, Dave Lee, Peter Lewis, Leslie Mallory, Bill Oddie, Ned Sherrin, Steven Vinaver, Keith Waterson. Produced by Ned Sherrin; recording supervised by George Martin. (1963) ODEON PMC 1197 PCS 3040

SIDE ONE

That Was the Week That Was

I've Heard of Politics But This Is Ridiculous

326098 L/Cpl. Wallace A.J. Royal Signals

Emergency Call

Lawrence of Arabia

Regella

Salvation Army

Dixon

Peter Cadbury

SIDE TWO

Engagement

If You're Game, Baby

Safe Comedian

Stop Press

Ad Nauseum

Skybolt

Faith in This Nuclear Age

Fly Buttons

Well I Must Admit, Sir

Closing Titles

*John Cleese performs on these tracks.

The soundtrack album of the original TV series that marked John Cleese's introduction to BBC-TV also features writing contributions by Cleese and fifteen other writers.

Cleese had become friendly with David Frost during their days together in the Footlights, and when Frost's fortunes started to rise in the BBC after he had left Cambridge, he wisely began to bring up talented friends he had known at the university to work for him (including Bill Oddie, who also contributed to *TW3*).

The show marked Cleese's first important professional work in television. Although his contributions were sporadic, as he was still preoccupied with his studies and the ongoing *Cambridge Circus*, it did provide a foot in the door.

Cleese wrote one of the cuts on this album, "Regella," which originally appeared in one of the Footlights shows, and submitted it to *TW3*, where Frost bought it.

"'Regella' is a little solo about the stupid use of statistics in astronomical programs, like 'Regella is so far away from the sun that it would take an ordinary white rhinoceros running at 16 miles an hour over 1,600,000 years to get there,' and 'If the Royal Albert Hall was the size of an orange, then Regella is 139,000,000 times as big as a pomegranate.' It's that kind of stuff," explains Cleese.

"I only wrote about three sketches for *That Was the Week That Was*, and then sent in a couple more, and didn't try after that. A lot of people think I was in it, because that was fronted by David Frost, who was very welcoming toward my attempts to send in material. Frost also fronted *The Frost Report*, so I'm often accused of being in *TW3*. In fact I was only a student at the time."

Oxford University

TERRY JONES, MICHAEL PALIN

A young Terry Jones, before he began his comedy career at Oxford, in the Haymakers production of **Time Remembered.** *Photo from The Collection of Terry Jones, used by permission*

Oxford had no equivalent of the Footlights, which was fine with Terry Jones, who had no theatrical ambitions at the time. A native of Colwyn Bay, Wales, he was accepted at both Oxford and Cambridge. Though he actually hoped to attend the latter, he decided to pursue his history studies at Oxford's St. Edmund Hall because that school was the first to accept him.

Jones's classmates and one of his instructors were responsible for his interest in theater, and he began performing with the Experimental Theater Company (or ETC) during his first year. The turning point came during his second year, however, when he encountered a first-year student named Michael Palin, who was studying history at Oxford's Brasenose College.

Palin, a native of Sheffield in Yorkshire, had been writing and performing comedy with Robert Hewison. Jones had seen the pair perform, and he and Palin ended up writing a sketch together for a show called *Loitering Within Tent.*

Amazingly enough, this very first Palin-Jones collaboration was subsequently used in the Monty Python stage shows, and appears in *Monty Python Live at the Hollywood Bowl.* It is the famed "Slapstick/Custard Pie Sketch," in which a

professorial type discusses the history and evolution of comedy, while a trio of assistants demonstrate the throwing of custard pies, slipping on banana peels, and hitting each other with boards. It was so admired by their peers at Cambridge that they gave Chapman, Cleese, and company permission to perform it in *Cambridge Circus.*

"The idea for it came from a guy called Chris Braden, who was the son of Bernard Braden, who started a show over here called *That's Life,*" notes Jones. He explains that he never planned any extensive collaboration with Palin.

"It was just for that revue, *Loitering Within Tent,*" reveals Jones. "He had started doing cabaret with Robert Hewison. That's where I first saw Michael—he was doing this revue with Robert Hewison, who is now a theater critic. They did these rather existential sketches, like a tape recorder in a bucket. Mike and I then wrote the 'Slapstick Sketch,' we worked on that together."

After *Loitering Within Tent* in late spring, 1963, Palin and Jones went their separate ways. Palin was busy doing plays and cabaret during his first year at Oxford. The theatrical career of upper-classman Jones, however, got a significant boost due to an obscure British pop song.

"The first revue I did for Oxford was in Edinburgh with Doug Fisher, Ian Davidson, and Robin Grove-White," states Jones. "They had done the revue in Edinburgh the year before, and they were going to do the revue again that year, my second year. The fourth member of their team, a guy called Paul McDowell, had just made a hit record with a group called the Temperance Seven. They had just made a record called 'You're Driving Me Crazy' that had become number one, and he was the vocalist, so he couldn't go with the group to Edinburgh.

"I had just done *Loitering Within Tent,* when I got a phone call. Ian Davidson said 'Come and do the revue in Edinburgh,' so I got up and filled in for Paul McDowell. That was really a turning point in my life, that phone call from Ian Davidson, and I got into the revue."

The revue, * * * * was very well received. The August 22, 1963, *Glasgow Herald* reported:

Whether the title is intended as a censored fashionable word or an automobile organisation rating, this Oxonian late-night revue is a scintillating success.

Largesse in talent, wit, and execution is distributed with infectious offhand abandon. Conversational gamesmanship with tennis scoring, door-to-door sales of 'You, too, can be the life of the party' skit, anarchic Tory women, a modern English civil war documentary, songs, excellent music, and visual knockabout make a memorable hour.

Ian Davidson, Jane Brayshaw, Doug Fisher, Robin Grove-White, and Terry Jones are all quite brilliant in this effervescent nocturnal whoop-up.

After Edinburgh, * * * * transferred to the Phoenix Theatre for a brief run in 1964; Graham Chapman and John Cleese were performing *Cambridge Circus* in London's West End at approximately the same time. *Cambridge Circus* continued to receive positive notices for its production there, although reviews for the London production of * * * * were more mixed. Critic David Nathan wrote "There are one or two, perhaps even three or four, good things in it.... One of the young men, Douglas Fisher, shows a great deal of promise, but generally speaking they project an air of bumbling amateurism which ensures that most of the points are lost in a theatre far too large." However, Christopher Driver wrote:

*To judge from * * * *, which has come from Oxford to the Phoenix Theatre via Edinburgh, the Oxbridge joke-engine has changed gear again. * * * *, despite the brashness of the title, is distinguished by a certain economy in humour, a relaxation of the hectic phut-phutting of laughs that has categorised earlier models. Several models are unusually long for revue and until one has accustomed oneself to the cast's demure observance of the speed limit, some of them even appear slow. But by the end of the evening the trick has worked.*

*Is it only coincidence that two of the most successful sketches are not only of several min-utes duration but also explore the concept of the meta-joke, the joke about joke-making? In one, a university lecturer expounds with the assistance of three impassive laboratory demonstrators the origin and construction of various simple japes like the banana skin and the custard pie. In another, two joke salesmen fit out a simple fellow with a few appropriate spiels. . . . * * * * goes back to first principles, allowing mime and fancy full rein. Mr. Davidson, ably assisted by the crisp and sly Douglas Fisher, plays it sweet and cool. Vaut le voyage."*

After * * * *, Jones returned for his third year at Oxford with the distinction of having performed in the West End, and was much in demand. He decided to work on a new production for the ETC called *Hang Down Your Head and Die*, set in a circus ring, with capital punishment as its theme. The show, which also featured Michael Palin, ran briefly in the West End as well and was lauded by critics.

Don Chapman, writing about the original production in the February 12, 1964, *Oxford Mail*, cited:

The kaleidoscopic brilliance with which it presents its almost encyclopaedic view of the subject, and the astonishing adroitness with which it rings the changes on it with everything from farce to pathos is unique in my theatrical experience.... Left trampled under the feet of the other performers is the white-faced auguste, an exquisite mime in the form of Terry Jones, who is destined to play the part of the victim and to be carried screaming to the gallows as the rest of the company belt breezily down to the footlights to take their final bow. It is this figure . . . which gives the evening its dramatic unity. . . . I don't suppose . . . anyone . . . expected such professional and intelligent entertainment from amateurs.

Other newspapers were just as effusive in their praise, and Terry Jones, playing the condemned man, was singled out by several critics. Writing in the February 19, 1964, *Cherwell, the Oxford University Newspaper*, Rudman calls the show "bloody marvellous," and says "the quiet authority and graceful talent of Terry Jones gives the show a core of sympathy that no audience can fail to dig."

And Daphne Levens, writing in the February 20, 1964, *Oxford Magazine*, calls Jones the star, and says "Pathos, scorn, sweet-sour foolery, horror, hearty indignation are glancing moods round a bitter hard centre, deftly expressed in stage terms and collated with cool intelligence.... Terry Jones is an accomplished actor and a delicate mime—he can even borrow from Marcel Marceau without need for apology."

Perhaps the most prestigious review of *Hang Down Your Head and Die* was written by Harold Hobson and appeared in the February 16, 1964, *Sunday Times*:

> . . . They offer a programme which is both horrible and beautiful. If the last inexorable progression towards an execution, made the more awful by its grotesque and bitter caricature of a Punch and Judy show, proved too strong for the nerves of some of the audience, it also had in it things which even my theories admit to manifest theatrical value. I am thinking particularly of the pantomime choruses about the hangman which the audience has been cunningly inveigled into singing, and of the heart-shaking and pathetic moment when the condemned man goes on singing alone after everyone else has stopped. His voice falters and he too falls into silence. . . . This moment of appalling discovery is magnificently revealed by Robert Hewison, David Wood, and Terry Jones.

> Lay [sic] Down Your Head and Die *transcends its purely forensic values. . . . In any case, these are considerable. There is as much curious*

Micheal Palin (left) and Terry Jones in the Oxford Revue in 1964, the first major collaboration of a team that would survive Monty Python. Photo from the collection of Terry Jones, used by permission

information here as in `The Anatomy of Melancholy'. . . At Oxford, you will find out these things, and others besides. They are imparted with the cold disgust of those who have gone too far to argue any more, and have moved from debate into faith. . . .

When Jones returned to Oxford for his final year, he began working on *The Oxford Revue* with Palin, Doug Fisher, Annabel Leventon, and Nigel Pegram. Although Palin and Jones had been working together on occasional shows, their real collaboration began with this revue. Jones feels the show's nontraditional approach to comedy was instrumental in the development of Monty Python.

"It was an escape from satire," explains Jones. "Mike and Doug and I all felt that the show we did was nonsatirical, it was fantasy. In a way, looking back on it, I can see the kind of material we were doing had a Python feel to it."

The Oxford Revue, directed by Doug Fisher, was presented in Edinburgh in the summer of 1964, as Jones was finishing his final year at Oxford. Although the show then moved to London, its venue was less than prestigious.

"We got an offer to perform it in London at a club called The Establishment, which had been started by Peter Cook and that lot," Jones recalls.

"It was started as `the' satirical club in London, but by this time, around 'sixty-four, it was a bit run-down—I think it had gangster connections," he laughs. "It was pretty sleazy by the time we did our show there. Most of the time we outnumbered the audience. Mike was in that show, but he couldn't come down because he was back at university, so we had to replace him with a guy called David Walsh.

"We did that for about six weeks at The Establishment, usually, as I say, outnumbering the audience. Occasionally the croupier from upstairs—it was really a gambling place by then—would come and sit at the front of the audience and laugh and clap very determinedly, and look around very threateningly at the rest of the audience.

"I did that for about six months, then I did another little thing at another club called the Poor Millionaire with a guy called Noel Carter. We wrote this pantomime takeoff one weekend. I was just getting going a bit then," notes Jones.

While he was trying to survive life after Oxford, Palin was continuing on with his final year at the school. Still collaborating with Robert Hewison—his partnership with Jones was an on-again, off-again situation—Palin co-wrote, produced, and directed *The Oxford Line,* which opened on August 23. He and Hewison were also featured performers in the review, along with Diana Quick, Mick Sadler, and David Wood. Palin's written contributions to the show (many of them co-scripted) included the "Opener," "Vicar," "English," "Getting to Know You," "Jean-Paul Overe," "Restoration Box," "Battle of Wits," "Brassomania," "Bananas," and "How Wintrop Spudes Saved the World from Total Destruction"; "Tinpally" saw Terry Jones share a writing credit with Palin and three others (the cast biography of the then-twenty-two-year-old Palin notes that "Michael aims to take up a career as a script-writer"). Graduating in 1965 and with his university

From left, Douglas Fisher, Terry Jones, and Michael Palin in a scene from 1964's Oxford Revue. *Photo from the Collection of Terry Jones, used by permission*

days behind him, Palin headed to London to join up with Jones, who had found a home with the BBC.

SEVEN-A-SIDE

FEATURING TERRY JONES AND MICHAEL PALIN.

(1964) MJB Recording and Transcription Service.

SIDE ONE

All That Gas (David Wood) performed by Dick Durden-Smith, with Wood and Bob Scott

Grin (Michael Palin/John Gould) Palin

Song About a Toad (Terry Jones/Gould) Adele Weston

Birds Are All the Same (Wood) Wood

Forgive Me (Jones/Gould) Nigel Rees

The English Way to Die (Wood) Wood, Durden-Smith

Vocal Gems from "The Proctors' Memorandum on the Conduct and Discipline of Junior Members of the University" (The Proctors/Gould) Scott

SIDE TWO

More on the Moor (Roddy MacRae) Wood, with Jane Sommerville, Susan Solomon and Weston

The Spanish Main of England (Gould) Scott

The Hanging Gardens of Babylon (Gould) Michael Sadler

Song of British Nosh (Palin/Gould) Palin, Wood, and Scott

Baby, I'm Addicted to You (Wood) Weston

I've Invented a Long-Range Telescope (Palin/Gould) Palin

Last One Home's a Custard (or, Six Characters in Search of a Song) (Doug Fisher/Palin/Jones/Gould) Solomon, Sadler, Sommerville, Palin, Wood, Weston, and Scott

This rare, very early recording by the Oxford University Experimental Theatre Club and Oxford Theatre Group contains selections from several successful 1964 university shows.

"It was made during Mike's year, when he was doing the revue. There were a couple of my songs there, but it wasn't me singing it because

I'd already gone to London," says Terry Jones. "It was privately made by the Experimental Theatre Club and had a limited release in Oxford."

From *Hang Down Your Head and Die* are "All That Gas" (originally sung by Terry Jones), "The English Way to Die," and "More on the Moor."

Several songs are from the *Oxford Revue*—"Song About a Toad," "Forgive Me," "Song of British Nosh," "I've Invented a Long-Range Telescope," and "Last One Home's a Custard."

From the ETC summer musical revue, *Keep This to Yourself*, are "Grin" and "The Hanging Gardens of Babylon."

"The Proctors' Memorandum" was a cabaret standby, while the remaining songs are from *Etcetera, Etcetera*, produced by the ETC's Etceteras.

Highlights include "Grin," performed by an over-ingratiating Palin; the romantic "Song About a Toad"; "Song of British Nosh," which compares foreign foods with British snacks; and the absurd, Pythonesque "I've Invented a Long-Range Telescope." A superior version of "Forgive Me" is performed by Terry Jones in the *Mermaid Frolics* stage show.

Occidental College

TERRY GILLIAM

Strangely enough, Terry Gilliam entered Occidental College in California as a physics major. Not so strangely, he didn't last long in the science department.

"After six weeks in physics, I decided 'It's the arts for me!' I was an arts major for a bit, and couldn't stand the art history professors, so I became a political science major, and that's how I graduated." Gilliam laughs.

The crew-cutted Gilliam's interests were not solely in politics, however, and he even joined a fraternity, but he soon became bored with most of the rituals. He had developed an interest in cartooning several years before, and began honing those skills with his work on *Fang*, the school's humor magazine.

A very presentable Terry Gilliam at age 19, during his years at Occidental College. Photo from The Collection of Terry Gilliam, used by permission

"There was a gang of us, and we were always looking for outlets, and I suppose the college humor magazine seemed to have potential as an outlet. So, we took it over and turned it from what was basically a literary poetry-oriented magazine into a humor magazine. We started lowering the tone early, and we continued to do so.

"I was editor of that my senior year," Gilliam recalls. "One of the people we were ripping off was Harvey Kurtzman with *Help!* magazine."

Academics bored him, and despite his abilities, he barely graduated. One of the more important influences on Gilliam in the early 1950s was *Mad* (founded by Harvey Kurtzman), the comic book–turned–magazine. During his last years at Occidental, Gilliam had been sending some of his work from *Fang* to Kurtzman, who at that time was in New York editing *Help!*

"I was hoping for some kind of approval, and he did send a really nice letter back saying he liked what we were doing, so after college, with nothing better to do, I decided to go to New York and meet Harvey. I just walked into this job—it was waiting for me!" reveals Gilliam, even though Kurtzman had tried to frighten him off.

Gilliam says he had always been a cartoonist, though he never had any artistic ambitions.

"I had no ambitions, really," he says with a laugh. "I never knew what I was doing. I always just did what I liked. The only thing I wanted ever to do was to be a film director, although there was one point in college where I thought I was going to be an architect. But I worked at an architect's office one summer, and that was the end of my architectural career. I didn't like all the bullshit that went with it. I really had no ability to work within normal systems, I suppose. . . ."

THE ODD JOBS

*U*pon graduation from their various universities, the Pythons-to-be embarked on what were still not clearly defined careers. Most, though not all, of these were related to show business—John Cleese briefly wrote on international affairs for *Newsweek* magazine, while Terry Gilliam had an equally unpleasant, brief career working for an advertising agency.

By way of their university shows, each of the Oxbridge group already had some measure of success behind him, and they all naturally gravitated toward performing and television work. (Terry Gilliam continued to write and draw, though he never displayed inclinations toward animation.) In the process, they wrote and performed on a wide variety of TV (and radio) programs.

Their contributions to some of these were minimal—a joke here, a witty ad lib there—and some of them have faded from memory. Others were much more important. Writing for *The Frost Report* brought together Cleese, Graham Chapman, Eric Idle, Terry Jones, and Michael Palin for the first time; although they made up only a small percentage of the show's staff, they became familiar with each other's writing styles.

Still, no matter how insignificant or unimportant some of their early work may seem, it all played a part in the molding and shaping that eventually resulted in Monty Python.

I'M SORRY, I'LL READ THAT AGAIN

JOHN CLEESE, GRAHAM CHAPMAN.
ADDITIONAL WRITING CONTRIBUTIONS BY ERIC IDLE. 1964–74

One of John Cleese's earliest BBC enterprises also proved to be his longest-running. During the West End run of *Cambridge Circus*, Humphrey Barclay, who had gotten a job as a BBC radio producer, assembled the cast members to perform three programs in 1964.

"When we'd done the stage show in the West End for a time, Humphrey Barclay and I were offered jobs with the BBC. 'Writer-producer' they were called, but I only wrote, and Humphrey only produced. I can't remember when David Hatch came into the BBC, but [it was] not long after. So, it was kind of inevitable that the material from the *Cambridge Circus* show would finish up on the radio. We did three half-hour shows based on it, which I quite liked," explains Cleese.

The cast members, who included Cleese, Chapman, Tim Brooke-Taylor, David Hatch, Jo Kendall, and Bill Oddie, had grown up listening to *The Goon Show* during the 1950s and were eager to attempt a similar radio show for the '60s. They called it *I'm Sorry, I'll Read That Again*. The initial three shows were so successful that the performers were soon awarded a regular series.

But there were some changes when the show resumed in October 1965. Graham Chapman had left the group and was replaced by Graeme Garden. (Brooke-Taylor, Garden, and Oddie went on to create *The Goodies* for BBC-TV a few years after.) John Cleese was in the United States at the time; he didn't rejoin the show until the second series in 1966, but appeared throughout the entire run of the show.

"When I got back from America, I found all my *Cambridge Circus* crowd, plus Graeme Garden, who had not been in the original cast were back in England. I was still in America doing *Half a Sixpence* and *Newsweek*, so they did a number of *I'm Sorry, I'll Read That Again*s without me. When I got back, I found that they'd already done one series, and Graham had, in a sense, filled in for me. They sort of opened up and made a space for me, and I came in," recalls Cleese.

And it became one of the longest-running programs in BBC history. There were eight series that ran from 1965 to 1974—the show began years prior to and did not end until after the final series of *Monty Python's Flying Circus*.

Barclay produced the first half of the eight-series run, and the program was acclaimed by audiences and critics. The *Sunday Times* called it "Radio scatterdemalion . . . deliberate irreverence . . . and terrific verbal agility."

ISIRTA gave Cleese a chance to grow as a writer and performer, and he developed an appreciation of the medium of radio, even though he eventually tired of the routine and stock characters in the show.

"At the beginning, I enjoyed it a lot, because it was wonderful practice for me to get in front of an audience with that script. I was still learning how to work an audience, still figuring out how to time things, still trying different ways of doing it. I hadn't acquired that almost automatic, gut understanding of how to do things, which you do when you've been doing it for twenty years. In those days I was still experimenting and learning every day. I also felt that I kept my violin tuned, so to speak, by doing this once a week. It kept me in practice for my television work," reveals Cleese.

"However, by and large, I began very rapidly to tire of *I'm Sorry, I'll Read That Again*. Its material was very much to do with bad puns, which the audience laughed, but mainly groaned at. There was a lot of reliance on catchphrases, and although it was okay and the atmosphere was terrific, and the audience was wonderful and people liked the show, and we produced something with an extraordinary individual sound to it, I never ultimately respected the material enough. It worked, but it didn't get the adrenaline going. I didn't very often get sketches which I thought 'Oh, that will be fun to perform.' Whereas on most of the television work I was doing, whether it was *Frost* or the *1948 Show*, I really did love most of the material and was excited about doing it.

"*I'm Sorry, I'll Read That Again* went on and on and on, and in the end I think I did over one hundred shows. In retrospect, I'm not sure why. I think I should have bowed out gracefully

Graham Chapman, Tim Brooke-Taylor, and John Cleese in the recording studio performing "I've Got a Ferret Sticking Up My Nose." Photo from the Collection of John Cleese, used by permission

earlier on, but in those days, I probably didn't know how to gracefully leave a group. I got better at that later on," Cleese says, laughing.

"And I probably didn't want to be left out. I probably felt I needed the money and the exposure, although at thirty-two pounds an evening, it was hardly highly paid work. And, considering it was radio, it was a bit funny to think I thought of it in terms of useful exposure. But I did. When the show finished, I must say I never missed it, and my enthusiasm for it, which waned rather early, just went on gently waning. It was helped by the fact that I was fond of the people I was working with. I always got on well with Tim, and I was particularly fond of David Hatch, who stayed a good friend. Like Graham, who respected him, he was a wonderful voice man and could do any accent he liked. I always enjoyed performing with Jo, because I thought she had good timing. But it just didn't ever turn me on."

Eric Idle also became involved with *I'm Sorry, I'll Read That Again* after leaving Cambridge, and the show was his first writing job after graduation.

"I went to do cabaret after the university revue, which came to London. I did cabaret at the Blue Angel and the Rehearsal Room," relates Idle. "Then I went to rep [repertory theater] at Leicester, did *Oh, What a Lovely War.* Hated rep, hated being rep, and so I started to write backstage for *I'm Sorry, I'll Read That Again.* I was busy writing one day, and another actor came up to me and said `Going well, is it?' and I said `Yes.' He said `Do you mind joining me on stage?' So I realized then that I wasn't actually cut out to be totally an actor!"

The shows were sometimes reminiscent of *The Goon Shows* with their quick wordplay and puns, and there were often recurring characters. The second half of each show would usually feature a longer sketch, often the "Prune Play of the Week." (Angus Prune was one of the recurring characters, and the *I'm Sorry, I'll Read That Again* theme song was called "The Angus Prune Tune.") Cleese's participation in the shows became increasingly sporadic, and he seldom wrote material for the series.

"I did write a little bit of material for it right at the start. Certainly I wrote a lot of those first three, before we went to New Zealand and America. When I got back, I wrote the odd sketch, but I was normally too busy with the TV writing. I really functioned as an actor, but did a few rewrites on the day [of the performance]," recalls Cleese.

Despite his eventual boredom with *ISIRTA*, though, Cleese still retains a fondness for the medium of radio, and he continues to write and perform radio commercials today.

"The tremendous, tremendous advantage of radio is that there are not too many things that can go wrong between the script and the listener," explains Cleese. "It's as though there are fifteen different stages where something can come between a film script and the end product, and in television there are about seven or eight. In radio, there are about two.

"For example, in *Fawlty Towers,* it's frightening to hear how many funny lines are lost by sound. You'd think it was very simple to get the sound on the track, but a lot of lines are partly covered by audience laughter, or the mike isn't in the right place. There are very funny lines that are missed as a result of that. You'd never get that happening in radio. If you do a good performance on radio, unless the sound controller actually dies, it works. That's the nice thing about radio.

"It's tremendous fun to go into a studio for a day and play with a script. Very simple, and it's not very technical. You don't have to do hundreds of rehearsals over so the cameraman knows where to put his shots and the sound man knows where to put the boom. It's simple."

Cleese is still proud of some of his work on *I'm Sorry, I'll Read That Again.* At one point, he grew fond of rodents, particularly ferrets. (Several of their publicity photos picture the cast all holding stuffed ferrets.) During the Monty Python stage shows, he always wanted to perform one of his songs from ISIRTA but was overruled. Pity. What Python fan could resist John Cleese singing "I've Got a Ferret Sticking Up My Nose?"

I'M SORRY, I'LL READ THAT AGAIN

WITH JOHN CLEESE.

Featuring John Cleese, Tim Brooke-Taylor, Graeme Garden, David Hatch, Jo Kendall and Bill Oddie; highlights of the series. (1967) EMI M-11634

SIDE ONE

The Auctioneer

The Day After Tomorrow's World

The Doctor (Oddie/Cleese)

Blimpht

John and Mary (Oddie/Cleese)

Robin Hood (Garden/Cleese)

SIDE TWO

Identikit Gal

Baby Talk

Family Favorites

The Curse of the Flying Wombat

Closing/Angus Prune Tune

I'M SORRY, I'LL READ THAT AGAIN

WITH JOHN CLEESE.

Featuring John Cleese, Tim Brooke-Taylor, Graeme Garden, David Hatch, Jo Kendall, and Bill Oddie. (1978) BBC Records REH 342

SIDE ONE

Opening Credits

Full Frontal Radio, Prune Manifesto, Buffers

Critics

Motoring Flash

Quickie (Cleese/Hatch)

Honours List, News in Welsh, Minority Programmes

Home This Afternoon a Go Go (Cleese, Garden, Hatch, Oddie, David Lee Group)

News Flash

Listening to the Flowers

SIDE TWO

Opening (Cleese, Hatch, the David Lee Group)

Talent Contest

Eddie Waring Impersonation

Sickman's Blues

Taming of the Shrew, Closing Credits

I'M SORRY, I'LL READ THAT AGAIN

WITH JOHN CLEESE.

Featuring John Cleese, Tim Brooke-Taylor, Graeme Garden, David Hatch, Jo Kendall, and Bill Oddie. (1989) BBC Radio Collection ISBN 0-563-22717-6.

A two-cassette collection of some of the complete, original radio shows; scripts by Graeme Garden and Bill Oddie (with Tim Brooke-Taylor).

SIDE ONE (originally broadcast June 9, 1968)

Postal Announcement

The Kevin Mousetrap Show (David Frost Parody)

Wonderful World (Scratchy Throat)

Doctor's Office

Melody Farm (song)

Favorite Stories From Shakespeare/Macbeth

SIDE TWO (originally broadcast March 22, 1970—without Cleese)

Offensive Announcement

Full Frontal Radio Prune

The Rolf Harris Dirty Songbook

Babies

Is This Your Life?

Stuffing the Gibbon (song)

Prune Play of the Week (James Bond parody)

SIDE THREE (originally broadcast April 5, 1970)

Show Tune Medley

Common Market/Radio Prune Goes International

Censored Tom Jones

It's a Washout

Thud Bang Bang (song)

Prune Play of the Week

SIDE FOUR (originally broadcast December 23, 1973)

Ministerial Broadcast to the Nation

Radio Terrapin

Childhood Remembered

Just My Bill (Eddie Waring)

Brian Clough (song)

The Colditz Story

THE LOVE SHOW

TERRY JONES AND MICHAEL PALIN 1964–65

After graduating from Oxford in 1964, a less-than-affluent Terry Jones moved to London while Michael Palin was finishing up his last year at the university. The two were friends and had worked together while still in school, but it was by no means a certainty that the team would continue beyond graduation. Jones was looking around for occasional writing assignments, sometimes writing with Miles Kington, when a bigger opportunity arose.

"A guy called Willie Donaldson, who had produced or put up the money for *Beyond the Fringe*, gave me fifty pounds to write this thing called *The Love Show*. He just had the title. Basically, he intended it to be sort of like *Hang Down Your Head and Die* and *Oh, What a Lovely War*. I decided it was going to be about sex. So, I started researching," Jones recalls with a laugh.

As he was working, Jones decided he could use another hand on the project, and contacted Palin at Oxford.

"Terry had been doing some work on a thing called *The Love Show*, which was like a theatrical documentary about sex and attitudes about sex throughout the ages," explains Palin. " This fit in very well with Terry's twin interests, sex and theater. He had got to a certain point and needed someone to bounce ideas off.

"*The Love Show* was really a way of looking at and examining these attitudes, but not in a stuffy way. So, when I came down from Oxford, I really had nothing to do at all. I didn't know what I was going to do, and he said would I help him rewrite it?

"He took me to see a man called Willie Donaldson, who is a very funny, humorous man, but dodgy as an impresario. He was the man who had financial control over the thing. We went to a pub in Sloane Square, I remember very well. We sat and discussed it, and Willie Donaldson said that he would pay me fifty pounds. That was the

first money I ever earned! There and then in that pub in Sloane Square, he sat down and wrote a check for fifty pounds to help Terry write *The Love Show*. Which was my first paycheck ever," notes Palin.

"We worked on it at Terry's home in Esher, and in the end, I don't think it ever got done. It was the first time that Terry and I had collaborated outside of Oxford."

The writing process for *The Love Show* stretched on and on. The script was ultimately never produced, though they continued work on it after Jones had been hired by the BBC and Palin began performing after Oxford.

HIRED BY THE BBC

TERRY JONES

While Terry Jones was working on *The Love Show*, with its £50 paycheck, he also started writing another abortive project.

"Somebody gave me a commission to write a TV thing for 200 pounds. It was called *The Present*, and it was never seen—I wrote it, but we never shot it. But that 250 pounds really kept me going my first year," relates Jones.

His financial problems only contributed to his general discouragement at the end of his first year in London, and he began to consider seriously packing it all in and going back to Oxford. At any rate, Jones was ready for a change.

"I decided I needed to get a job," he recalls. "So, my second year, I canvassed around. I remember I was having trouble with my then-girlfriend, and thinking I was going to go back to Oxford—she was still at Oxford—and I'd just had this terrible phone call. It was really all over with, and I thought 'I've just got to be near her.' I was walking over Lambeth Bridge—I was living in Lambeth at the time—and I suddenly thought 'This is a deciding moment. I either go back to Oxford and mooch around and get visible, or else I go back and get a job. I've got to do one or the other.' So I watched the water going under the bridge for a long time, and decided to go back to London and get a job."

Aware of the symbolism of crossing the bridge, Terry Jones chose to utilize his Oxford experience and try his luck at television writing.

"Eventually I was offered a job as a copywriter for Anglia Television, which I had accepted. Then I was contacted by Frank Muir at the BBC. I went to see him and he offered me a job in a very small office, with two desks and two typewriters and a telephone. I was meant to be a trainee, to have a look around and see what was happening."

His job responsibilities were not well defined, and after a few months, his employment became a bit more tenuous.

"I was there about six months, I suppose, being a script editor and seeing what kind of material came in," he explains. "I was occasionally writing for programs like *The Billy Cotton Bandshow* and *The Kathy Kirby Show*, just being around. I had carte blanche to wander over and watch shows being made. It was very educational. There were several of us that used to sit there writing jokes."

The apprenticeship came to a less-than-triumphant conclusion, though Jones managed to make it through without being fired.

"After about six months in this strange job where I didn't know quite what I was doing, I went on a six-month director's course, to train as a director. My friend Ian Davidson, who directed the first revue I did at Edinburgh, was in the same course. Unfortunately, I got peritonitis halfway through and didn't manage to finish it," reveals Jones.

"At the end of the course, I then became a production assistant in the BBC. I was *absolutely* unqualified for this. I'd gone on this course teaching me how to direct, but I didn't know how you went about being an assistant. I was the world's worst. I was shouted at by a director once on the street. So, I did that for about six months, until it looked like I didn't have much of a future at it, and it might not go on much longer!"

NOW!

MICHAEL PALIN
1965–66

While Terry Jones was serving his shaky apprenticeship at the BBC, Michael Palin had graduated from Oxford and gotten his first job in television. It wasn't strictly comedy, however—instead, the fresh-faced, amiable Palin found himself hosting a teenage pop music show in Bristol called *Now!* for the now-defunct Television West Wales.

The show's producers were apparently hoping for the British equivalent of Dick Clark, but wound up with a young Python. Palin remembers that the exclamation mark in *Now!* was a very important part of the show's name.

"*Now!* exclamation mark is what I remember about that program. It was very important—that gave the show the feeling of excitement and immediacy that we all were led to believe was important at that time," he recalls, laughing.

"I have really ambivalent feelings about it. The standards of the shows were not great. What I had to do was fairly humiliating, like walk around Bristol dressed in a long Edwardian swimsuit and huge boots on, miming to Nancy Sinatra's 'These Boots Are Made for Walkin'.' I'd just come out of Oxford with a history degree! I mean, this didn't seem to be the natural logic of things. . . ."

Sophomoric as much of it was, the show provided Palin with valuable on-camera experience and was also financially useful.

"When I did *Now!* from about October of 1965 to May or June of '66, it paid me enough to be able to write scripts with Terry Jones, which were in the end much more useful to us. That put us on the road to working with the other Pythons.

So it was, in its way, just what was needed—a fairly easy way to earn quite good money."

Now! was Palin's first regular TV work, though he had been involved in a few previous projects.

"Terry and I did *The Oxford Revue* with three others at the Edinburgh Festival in 1964, and a television crew up in Edinburgh did a little program about us. We were mucking around and running about, being filmed—that was really our first television job.

"Then, in 1965, just before I started *Now!* Terry and I made another film for a program called *The Late Show*, which our friend Ian Davidson directed. That was done right about the same time as *Now!* but *Now!* was regular work. We'd go up to Bristol Tuesday and shoot some film, and Wednesday the show was recorded," notes Palin.

"I met a great load of people—Tom Jones, Englebert Humperdinck, who was then called Gerry Dorsey. . . . He and I shared a dressing room, that's how low we both were in the order of things. [I met] Pete and Dud [Peter Cook and Dudley Moore], the Scaffold, and occasionally a really good band, like the Animals, but we couldn't afford the best."

Palin finally developed a method to get him through the madness, a secret he is finally ready to reveal to the public.

"I always did it with two pints of Guinness in me. I'd go down to the local pub and have two pints of Guinness—it was the only way I could tape the show," he laughs.

THE KEN DODD SHOW

TERRY JONES AND MICHAEL PALIN

When Terry Jones was working for the BBC, Michael Palin began to assist him in some of his television writing. At that time, a former music-hall comic named Ken Dodd became enormously popular. He was starring in his own TV series, which offered the opportunity for young writers to break in.

"Ken Dodd wouldn't be known in America, but he was a very well known character here," explains Palin. "He started in the music halls and was a stage actor and northern comic; he became very popular across the country in the mid-1960s. He was profiled in the quality papers and thought to be mainstream, good bourgeois middle-class fare. Terry and I were asked to do some writing for his show, since Terry was working at the BBC, where Ken Dodd was doing his shows.

"We went down to see him at the Palladium, which is the really big theater to play in London," recalls Palin. "It was quite a thing then to be able to get near someone like Ken Dodd, who was a very popular, famous, celebrated figure. So, it was quite a bit of star points for us.

"We went into his dressing room, and Terry started to whistle. Ken Dodd, because he's very, very strong on all the theatrical traditions, said to Terry 'Outside! Get out!' Terry just whistled away, thinking nothing of it. 'Get out, turn around three times, and come back in again!' He had to explain to Terry that whistling in a dressing room is bad luck, just like quoting lines from *Macbeth* is supposed to be very bad luck for actors." He laughs.

"So, it was a very bizarre evening! We did get a glimpse of the Ken Dodd Joke Book—it wasn't a book, it was a whole huge filing system with millions of jokes."

Python trivia fans should note that *The Ken Dodd Show* holds a significant place in the career of Terry Jones.

"The first television I ever wrote was a thing for Ken Dodd," reveals Jones.

"It was a visual gag, based on a suggestion from Miles Kington, about police sports. I remember having to go up to Ken Dodd and show him this visual joke. We had all these policemen in full uniforms and hats for a policeman's walking race. All the policemen were walking about," he says, demonstrating the typical policeman's saunter that follows the starter's gun.

"I had to go up to his office at the BBC and show Ken Dodd and his producer and director this joke, and persuade them to do it. We had a lot of other things about police sports, running around a race track and catching a car.... But that was the first joke I ever wrote [for the BBC].

"That was actually Ken Dodd's year. He became very well known and hit the public limelight, staged a one-man show at the Palladium, that sort of thing. The funny thing was, when they mentioned that it was Ken Dodd's year in the 'Review of the Year,' they showed that clip of my little joke of the policemen's walking race," Jones laughs. "I never got any credit for it!"

THE BILLY COTTON BANDSHOW

TERRY JONES AND MICHAEL PALIN

By late 1965, Terry Jones and Michael Palin had established themselves as a writing team, and Jones's contacts at the BBC aided them in submitting sketches for a variety of shows. Although the pair had worked together at Oxford, both writing and performing, Palin had actually been doing most

of his work with longtime friend Robert Hewison. When Jones offered him the opportunity to write with him for the BBC, Palin had to make a difficult choice.

"I think one of Mike's hardest decisions when he left Oxford was not to go on writing with

Robert," reveals Jones. "They'd always been a partnership at university. Michael wouldn't have done anything if it hadn't been for Robert Hewison—I think Michael would have gone into advertising or steel or something. He'd never even thought of doing comedy. He'd thought of acting, but not comedy.

"It was Robert Hewison who was very keen to do cabaret, and Robert really got him going. So, it was a very difficult moment for both of them when Mike decided he was going to do something else. In fact, when Mike came back from doing this show in Wales [*Now!*], he started writing with me. So, I stepped into Robert's shoes as Michael's partner."

During their formative years as a professional team, Palin and Jones contributed jokes to numerous BBC shows.

"*The Billy Cotton Bandshow* wasn't much—it was just something Terry and I wrote sketches for," explains Palin. "One of Terry's jobs at the BBC was to help supply all the variety shows with link material. If any comedian came along who didn't have enough material to introduce the next act, they would ring Terry up, and he'd have to rush out and write a few lines. Terry and I made use of his office at the BBC to write other stuff. We wrote a thing called 'The Body,' a five-minute piece that was Terry's first production as a director—it featured an early version of Pither.* While Terry was there, sometimes we had to do what we were expected to do, which was write a joke. That was *The Billy Cotton Bandshow*!"

ADVENTURES IN AMERICA

JOHN CLEESE

Cambridge Circus opened on Broadway in September 1964 and ran for three weeks. During the Broadway run of *Cambridge Circus*, the troupe appeared on *The Ed Sullivan Show*, and Cleese had been selected to appear in the previously mentioned *Help!* magazine photo strip about a man who falls in love with his daughter's Barbie doll (under the direction of then–assistant editor Terry Gilliam).

A negative review in *The New York Times* caused the *Cambridge Circus* to close in less than a month, but the cast rapidly agreed to an offer to appear off-Broadway, where it played until February 1965.

"Some nice people came along, and said 'We've got a little theater off Washington Square. Would you like to do the show there?' We went, and I was happier there,' recalls John Cleese. "It was a smaller place, where you didn't have to project, you didn't have to do makeup, and you could roll up ten minutes before the start of the show. I thoroughly enjoyed performing there. I'd rather do small acting than opera acting, and in a small house like that you could do subtler stuff. Maybe that's why I always worked better on television and film than I ever did on stage. Anyway, we stayed there for months, and then they suggested we should do

a second show, which we did—some new material and a bit of old stuff polished up."

Graham Chapman returned to London and resumed his medical classes after *Cambridge Circus* ended its run on Broadway. This time around, he completed his studies and became a qualified physician with no further intervention by the Queen Mother. Although his TV work during this time was minimal, he did do some scripting for *The Illustrated Weekly Hudd*, later explaining that he wanted to do some writing on his own, without collaborating with Cleese.

John Cleese, on the other hand, was trying his luck in the United States. While he was performing off-Broadway, Tommy Steele came to the show and liked Cleese.

"The next thing I knew, I was being asked to audition for *Half a Sixpence*," he recalls.

"I went along as a joke, because I'm the most unmusical man in Europe, and thought it would be very funny to tell my grandchildren I'd once auditioned for a Broadway musical. Of course, they gave me the part."

*Reg Pither, from the "Cycling Tour" episode of Monty Python's Flying Circus.

"Then the director was fired and another director came in, a guy called Gene Sachs, who became very famous. I didn't really know what was coming. Originally, I'd been told I might write a bit of the book, and I did. Some of the people liked it, but it was one of those Hollywood situations. You didn't quite know who was in charge, and the producers were around in twos and threes, with none of them really working together. So, none of my stuff got on. When the director was fired, we went back to the original book. But it went reasonably well in Boston and Toronto, and when it got on Broadway, it got very good reviews."

Half a Sixpence was a learning experience for the young John Cleese, in a great many ways.

"I enjoyed doing it—it was amazing!" notes Cleese. "I'd never spent my time with a lot of gay guys before, who were, incidentally, the singers. The dancers were straight—it's usually the other way around. I got very used to it and formed some good friendships. I was extremely fond of a lot of people in the cast, but lost contact with almost all of them, unfortunately."

Opening on Broadway in February 1965, Cleese played a man who embezzles money from Tommy Steele. Evidently, his acting skills were enough to overcome his lack of musical ability, and the director allowed him to stand in the back and mouth the words while the rest of the chorus sang. Still, the production had its problems prior to opening night.

"What I remember about *Half a Sixpence* is a complete sense of bewilderment, not knowing what was going on where. There were lots of different people, singers, actors, dancers, all rehearsing in different rooms—I didn't quite know what was going on, but assumed that it was all normal," relates Cleese.

"Then I ever-so-slowly realized that there was a bit of a panic. Although I loved our little director, called Word Baker, who had directed *The Fantasticks*, I suddenly realized it just wasn't happening. It was just not being pulled together. Then Gene Sachs came in with a short amount of time, very businesslike. The first few days he was almost like a sergeant-major. I think he needed to be that to give us a sense that things were under control and somebody was in charge, somebody knew what direction we were going in.

"The main problem I had with Gene was that I had no idea how loud you had to speak in a musical, and he kept at me, saying `Louder, John!' Eventually I went on stage in Boston at a dress rehearsal, and I did it so loudly, just to annoy him, that he would say `Not *that* loud!' To my astonishment, he said `That's it! That's the level you need!'

"I had never realized that if you go on after a big dance number, you practically have to shout for anybody to even notice you standing there."

Cleese says he admired all of the people in the production, including its star, Tommy Steele.

"I enjoyed the show a lot, liked all the people in it. I only had a small part, a few lines here and there, one scene with Tommy, who would always take my wrist and try and lock it and shove me gently into the orchestra pit—I don't mean he really tried, but I had to be on my toes in order to avoid getting a shove," he laughs. "I enjoyed that, I thought he was very professional. A lot of fun, but he was very tough on anyone who was unprofessional in a way the audience would notice. I admired that, I thought he created a good atmosphere. [There was] a very good team spirit, although there was a lot of cast changes at the beginning—I had three mothers in about eight weeks!"

After spending nearly six months in *Half a Sixpence*, Cleese began a brief tenure at *Newsweek* magazine in July 1965, a job for which he says he was "spectacularly unqualified." Although initially hired by the International Affairs Department, he ended up writing the obituaries for people who were still alive.

"I attempted to get out of show business by becoming an international journalist with *Newsweek*," he explains. "I failed after a month because my mentor was sent off to cover some upset in the Dominican Republic, and I didn't know how to write *Newsweek* style—or probably any style.

"At *Newsweek*, I just remember going into these meetings where all these very well informed people were having ideas about what we should be writing about. I was given the lighter items to write, and I thought I did one or two of them quite well," he says, but notes that it was difficult to translate some of this humor to the magazine's style.

"The trouble is, a lot of humor which is based in fact has got to use ellipses. They could never dare to allow ellipses to occur, because it meant that one or two of the readers might have to make a mental effort to understand something.

So, they did tend to explain my jokes by putting in the one sentence that I'd left out in order to make it funny.

"But they were nice people. If my mentor had not disappeared, I might have picked it up. I certainly thought it was a very good magazine, and I was very respectful of the professionalism that people there showed. Eventually I realized they were going to let me go, so I wrote a letter of resignation, saying 'Thanks very much but I know I can't do it.'"

John Cleese was not out of work for long, however. Deciding to stay in the States awhile longer, he immediately joined The Establishment (a group founded by Peter Cook), which was then touring the country.

"I got involved in The Establishment because I knew John Morris, who had the rights to the old Establishment show. When I was about to resign from *Newsweek*, he said 'Do you want to be in the show?' I said 'Sure.' I left *Newsweek* on Friday, and on Sunday afternoon I started to rehearse. I was quite proud—I don't think I've ever been out of work for a day in my life. Lucky!"

The Establishment began performing in Chicago in September and a few weeks later traveled to Washington, D.C. Toward the end of the year, Cleese received a phone call from David Frost, who was trying to organize a new TV show to be called *The Frost Report*.

"I was intending to come back to London and perhaps marry Connie, when Frost said 'Would you like to be in a TV show?' He just rang me up from the airport, as he so often did. I said 'Yes, please.' He said 'There are two people, both called Ronnie, who no one's heard of, but they're both very good. When are you going to come over?' I told him and he said 'I'll see you in the New Year.'"

LATE NIGHT LINE-UP

TERRY JONES AND MICHAEL PALIN

One of the lesser moments in the careers of Palin and Jones, *Late Night Line-Up* came about during Jones's recuperation from peritonitis, toward the end of his apprenticeship at the BBC. The pair were writing jokes for a number of other shows when this opportunity knocked.

"*Late Night Line-Up* was an another-job-for-the-boys kind of enterprise," explains Palin. "Although Terry was salaried at the BBC, I hadn't had a salary from anybody since I started out in the business. Terry had gotten to know various people, including a guy called Rowan Ayres. Rowan was very much wise with these . . . distinguished, urbane sorts that ran *Late Night Line-Up.* This was a rather serious program, with serious people dealing with the problems of the day."

"*Late Night Line-Up* was run by the Presentation Department of the BBC," Jones relates. "Basically, the Presentation Department just introduced programs and ran the logo. They got the show together in a tiny little studio which was just meant for the weatherman. They put on a show in which they would review that day's programs. It was a great idea, actually. It was the last thing on at night, so even if you missed something, you could get home and watch *Late Night Line-Up* at eleven and see people discussing the big play or documentary that had just been on. I came on to jazz up the Friday show."

Although Jones only wrote for the program, he recruited Palin and two other friends to perform the sketches on the air every week.

"They decided that they would have a thing called 'Line-Up Revue' on Friday night, when they would let what they had of their hair down," explains Palin. "They asked Terry to get together a little team of people, and Terry of course went to his mates and friends, namely myself, Robert Hewison, and Barry Cryer. We wrote and performed these sketches without an audience, so we had no way of knowing whether they worked or not.

"One was very, very aware that this was a serious arts program, trying to be funny. It was a very strained atmosphere. At the end, we'd do our little silly sketches—I remember once jumping off chairs doing Batman and Robin. The linkman* would look as though he'd just swallowed a really extremely unpleasant mouthful of pins: `Well, that was our resident comedy team . . .' We lasted, I think, three or four weeks, and eventually were given the sack. We really were shown out!" He laughs.

Terry Jones remembers the low point of the show more vividly.

"It fell apart. One of the presenters had been away, and when he came back, he didn't like introducing this flippant material into *Late Night Line-Up*," recalls Jones.

"Dennis Potter, the playwright, was on one evening. He suddenly had this outburst and said `I didn't come all the way from Gloucestershire to appear on a podium with rubbish like that!' And so that was the end of our career at *Late Night Line-Up*."

Despite their lack of success on the show, Palin tries to be philosophical about it all, saying the experience wasn't a complete loss.

"When we did the Python shows, we had a number of arts programs as our basis for *It's the Arts*, and *Is There?* which are all based on the *Line-Up* kind of approach of a program that takes itself very seriously indeed. So, I suppose all experience, somewhere along the line, is useful."

A CORPORATE AMERICAN IN EUROPE

TERRY GILLIAM

While Terry Gilliam was working with Harvey Kurtzman on *Help!* magazine, he met John Cleese in a well-documented collaboration when Cleese posed for a photo comic strip for the magazine called "Christopher's Punctured Romance." The two promised to keep in touch.

"When *Help!* folded, I went off to Europe for six months of checking out. I decided I'd better come back to the States to decide whether Europe was the place for me or not," explains Gilliam.

"I was back in New York for a bit, where I lived in Harvey's attic for a couple of months. Then I moved back to L.A. and was working as a freelance illustrator, doing comic books and things. I actually did a book called *The Cocktail People* with Joel Siegel."**

Gilliam did work for comic magazines, such as *Surftoons*, but found it tough to make ends meet.

"The whole business of freelance illustrating was proving to be pretty rough. I was broke again, and at that point, Joel was working at this advertising agency called Carson Roberts. He got me a job there. The interesting thing was, the guy

I went to work for used to be Stan Freeberg's writing partner, and so he had a soft spot for funny folk," he notes.

"I had long hair at the time, and I think the agency thought `This is really groovy, a guy with long hair.' I was basically hired as both copywriter and art director, so I was able to do everything myself."

Before long, though, Gilliam started tiring of the rat race.

"I was getting disillusioned, but what finally broke the camel's back was that they had the account for Universal Pictures. At the time, Universal was just doing really shitty B movies, and Joel and I had to spend our time doing ads for Universal Pictures. I lasted at the agency for eleven months. I just got fed up with it. I can't remember whether they fired me before I quit or not—it was a neck-and-neck affair," he recalls with a laugh.

The advertising agency marked Gilliam's last brush with corporate America, but the experience proved useful years later.

"Several of the things in *Brazil*, like the offices pulling the desk back and forth—all that came from working in the ad agency, my few months of corporate bureaucratic life. You get a lot of information very quickly in those surroundings." He laughs.

It was time for a change, and Europe beckoned once again.

---

*British slang for the announcer or moderator who would link segments of a show together.

**Siegel is now the film critic of ABC-TV's *Good Morning, America.*

"The girl I was living with was English, and she was keen to come back to England. I was keen to leave the country, so I came to England!" he recalls, noting that when he arrived in 1967, he began doing more freelance drawing.

"I was doing illustrations for magazines and newspapers, ad agencies, and cartoons for magazines back in the States. She got a job as editor at a magazine called *London Life* and I started working with her as art director on the thing.

"The one connection I really had in London that was my own connection was Cleese, who I'd met in New York when we were doing *Help!* John was very successful in television, and I said `I've got to get out of magazines. Can you introduce me to somebody?'" Gilliam reveals.

Cleese introduced Gilliam to Humphrey Barclay, who was producing a new show called *Do Not Adjust Your Set*, and Barclay introduced him to Eric Idle, Michael Palin, and Terry Jones.

PAYING THEIR DUES: THE FROST REPORT

WRITTEN CONTRIBUTIONS BY GRAHAM CHAPMAN, JOHN CLEESE, ERIC IDLE, TERRY JONES, AND MICHAEL PALIN. FEATURING JOHN CLEESE. FIRST SHOW MARCH 10, 1966.

The Pythons have endured a love-hate relationship with David Frost over the years, but his influence on their careers was certainly significant.

In many ways, Frost is a modern-day Renaissance man adept in using the media, and the Pythons mercilessly skewered their former boss at several points during *Monty Python's Flying Circus*.

In "Timmy Williams' Coffee Time," a man who is devastated at a number of personal misfortunes, including the death of his wife, goes to have a heart-to-heart talk with his old friend "Timmy" (who more than resembles Frost), but he is constantly interrupted by reporters, a documentary film crew, and numerous fans, all of whom are glad-handed and offered jobs. The closing credits attribute the writing to "Timmy Williams" in large letters, with the "additional writing by" credits containing dozens of names as they whiz past.

Frost is also caricatured as a block of wood on the talk show sendup "It's a Tree," uttering "Super, super" at every inane moment. Even though several of the Pythons' memories of the incident have faded, Frost's home telephone number ended up in the "Mouse Problem" sketch early in the *Flying Circus*. And, a few years later, Eric Idle did a deadly accurate version of Frost in a sendup of the Frost-Nixon interviews for *Saturday Night Live*.

David Frost was a member of the Cambridge Footlights shortly before John Cleese and Graham Chapman. He starred in their revue and immediately afterward went on to do TV and night-club work. In November of 1962, however, he leaped into the public eye in *That Was the Week That Was*, a live, satiric, political, musical variety program that was a forerunner of shows like *Monty Python's Flying Circus* and *Saturday Night Live*. The series, which came in the wake of *Beyond the Fringe*, received great acclaim and made a star of Frost. An American version of *TW3* was short-lived, but Frost nevertheless established himself in the States as well.

Among the legions of contributing writers for *TW3* was a very young John Cleese. In fact, his occasional sketches and jokes marked Cleese's first professional work in show business, and so when Frost began work for another series in early 1966, he contacted Cleese and other members of the Oxbridge group that had drifted into television writing.

When Cleese returned from the United States, he brought in Graham Chapman to write for the series, and the pair resumed their writing partnership.

"When I got back, it seemed the most natural thing in the world for Graham and I to link up together. So, as I arrived back in England with the invitation from David Frost to do *The Frost Report*, I simply said yes, and more or less without thinking or checking with anyone brought in Graham," explains Cleese.

Scripting *The Frost Report*, under head-writer Marty Feldman, were Barry Cryer, Dick Vosburgh, Peter Vincent, David McKellar, and Cleese, Chapman, Idle, Palin, and Jones. The show brought the future Pythons into closer contact, even though the five of them had known, or at least been aware of, each other as a result of their university work.

"We met Eric at Edinburgh in 1965. He'd been doing the Cambridge revue while I was doing the Oxford revue, so we'd met up," relates Palin, but admits that *The Frost Report* was the first close encounter with the Cleese-Chapman team for Jones and him.

"It was my first contact with Graham and really the first time I spent much time with John. I knew that he was a successful Cambridge writer, brilliantly funny, and had written a piece about a man watching stones. That was the first time we had ever worked together, and we cemented that relationship the following year, in sixty-seven."

Although he usually wrote alone during the Python years, Idle recalls that he sometimes worked with partners during *The Frost Report*.

"I used to write with Tim Brooke-Taylor a bit and with Graham for a little tiny bit. [I was] writing sketches for that for several years, and we won the Golden Rose of Montreux. So that's where everybody came together—Mike, Terry, Cleese, Chapman, me—all meeting every week at the writers' meeting, discussing ideas. That's where we first became accustomed to working together, just thinking along the same lines.

"It was a very big success—Cleese was a big star," says Idle. "I mean, John is four years older than me—people tend to forget. Now I'm very, very thrilled to find that he is four years older than me!"

Monty Python's Flying Circus was only three years in the future, but at this point, most of its creators were still considered inexperienced rookies when they got the call from Frost.

"Terry and I were contacted while we were working together in 1966," explains Palin. "I think we were working on *The Love Show* at the time at Terry's parents' house in Esher, with their wonderful cat Geronimo, when the phone rang. It was a guy called Jimmy Gilbert asking Terry and me if we could write sketches for this new series starting up, *The Frost Report*.

"We eventually found that we were two of many, many writers, but it was my first introduction to the real comedy-writing world of television. I remember going to a script meeting—we had a meeting every week where ideas would come up, a bit like *Saturday Night Live*—and this meeting was held in a church hall. We'd go along, very junior—very junior, indeed.

"I remember going on one day without Terry and thinking 'Nobody will know who I am now.' I walked into the room sort of timidly, and the two people who came up and introduced themselves to me and made me feel welcome were Marty Feldman and Barry Cryer. I've never forgotten that. They actually bothered to come along and say hello and introduce me to some of the others. That was spring of 1966, when I was also doing *Now!*"

John Cleese was the only future Python who would be a regular performer on the show. Making the adjustment from small American stages to national TV in Britain wasn't difficult in itself, but the prospect of performing on live TV before millions made him very nervous.

"The transition from playing small clubs in Washington to being on prime time in English television was completely painless. There was a great deal of terror, because it was a live show. I can still remember not being able to sleep the night before. I had this thing called the autocue [electronic cue cards], but I had never used it before. I wanted to try and remember [my lines]," he reveals.

"I just remember lying awake for hours, running lines again and again, occasionally forgetting them, and then increasing my state of panic. So, those first few shows live—I don't imagine that a matador going to the arena could have felt much more nervous, and I remember thinking that once before a show. But anyway, we got through it, and of course they were successful."

Cleese was actually very good at memorizing lines throughout the series, partly due to his cabaret training, but he did have one catastrophic moment on national television.

"There was one sketch I was doing where they kept cutting four lines, and they'd put it back in, they'd cut it again and put it back in—when I actually got to that moment on the taping, live, I suddenly realized I couldn't remember whether the lines were in or not," relates Cleese. "They'd been taken in and out every day that week, and I couldn't remember whether they were in or out!

"During the time it took me to think of that, I realized I didn't know where I was in the sketch anyway. At that point, I was supposed to say to Ronnie Corbett `You know, you must be one of the smallest men I've ever met,' and I managed to say to him `You know, I think you must be one of the tallest men I've ever met.' I remember he looked pretty startled at that. I somehow got through it, I don't know who—somebody inside my skin got through it for me.

"At the end, I had a sort of battle fatigue reaction to it. I went home, laid out on the bed, and I just cried for about an hour out of sheer fright. What I'd been frightened about for a series and a half, forgetting my lines badly on the air, had finally happened. Of course, the next day I discovered nobody'd noticed!" He laughs.

"It was a major discovery for me. I also realized that if you did forget your lines, the only thing to do is to look very determined and interestedly at another actor!"

Aside from such terrifying moments, Cleese found *The Frost Report* a very good experience.

"There was a very calm, pleasant, orderly Scot in charge called Jimmy Gilbert, whom I remain very fond of. There was a very, very good panel of writers who were good judges of material. On the whole, the good stuff was selected and the bad stuff wasn't. There were so many people writing, you were never short of material. In fact, I was instrumental in getting one or two of my sketches cut! We usually found we were overlength on certain days, and when I had a sketch I didn't have much faith in, I used to try and talk it out of the show, usually successfully, partly because I was very scared doing it all live in front of this very big audience—we used to get fourteen million."

Cleese's fellow performers were also very talented; he notes that he learned a great deal from "The Two Ronnies."*

"I was very lucky to learn with Barker and Corbett, because they were very relaxed but hugely professional. You could always rely on them. Ronnie Corbett's timing was extraordinary. I felt he could do some bits of timing that almost nobody I knew could carry off. Whereas Ronnie Barker just played any character that you liked—it didn't matter whether it was an effete, upper-class Englishman or an Albanian peasant, he would play it and it would be believable and funny. It was great to have such a high degree of friendly professionalism around me, and they took the strain from all my nerves."

The Frost Report, which debuted on March 10, 1966, consisted of eight shows in the first series and seven the following year, with a Christmas special at the end of 1967. Each of the programs dealt with a theme; these included love, money, authority, elections, education, and class. One recurring scene featured Cleese, Ronnie Barker, and Ronnie Corbett as representatives of the upper, middle, and lower classes; Cleese, naturally, was the upper-class gentleman, while the lower class was always the butt of the jokes. (Cleese would occasionally appear a few years later to reprise his role on *The Two Ronnies*, where Corbett and Barker revived the sketch.) In between the two series of *Frost Reports* was *The Frost Programme* for the now defunct Rediffusion television company, featuring Cleese; it began appearing October 19, 1966, and ran through the following January 4.

"It was entirely sketch comedy. You either wrote sketches—by and large John and Graham wrote one very funny sketch each week—or you wrote link material, which Frost read off the autocue, jokes and such. I used to write pages of that," reveals Idle.

Palin and Jones also found their own niche on the show.

"We wrote little jokes for David—he had a long monologue at the beginning and little jokes throughout the show, so we'd write little one-liners for him," notes Palin. "We'd try to break into sketch-writing, but that was pretty well sewn up by the likes of Cleese and Chapman, and Barry [Cryer] and Marty [Feldman] and the regulars.

"The ad libs were written by the likes of us. We did actually get to write one or two little sketches, minisketches—quickies, I suppose you'd call them, one of which was in the show that won the Montreux Golden Rose Award in 1966. So, if we weren't writing much and we were getting paid absolutely nothing, we were in a show that was very prestigious."

Graham Chapman explained that despite the prestige attached to *The Frost Report*, it was actually a fairly conventional show, and the frustrations Cleese, Idle, Jones, Palin, and he developed doing

*Ronnie Barker and Ronnie Corbett would star in their own TV comedy series, *The Two Ronnies*, a few years later.

shows like *The Frost Report* would eventually lead to *Monty Python's Flying Circus*.

"It *posed* as a satirical show on a weekly basis, but it was really just a compilation of sketches, and those sketches always seemed to follow a similar format. They had to have a beginning to let people know what was going on, a middle, and an end—a tag which was often very artificially introduced, just to let the audience know it's ended." Chapman laughed. "In a way, it was almost infantile in its approach to what we expected the audience's intelligence to be able to take.

"We felt they were a little brighter than that on the whole, and didn't have to be spoonfed—so much so that I think a lot of comedy then was spoiled because it was overexplained. You could see what was going to happen. If you were even averagely bright, you could see what was going to happen seconds before it did, which in some cases can be satisfying, but a lot of the time in comedy, gets away from the surprise element. Consequently, you lose your audience."

Frost and his producers were aware that their writers were paid very little. As a result, even though Cleese was the only one of the future Pythons to perform as a part of Frost's stock company, Palin, Jones, and some of the others were allowed to appear in small roles, in order to collect paychecks for acting.

"In the second series we wrote much more. We ended up writing short films, like `Judges in a Playground,' what judges do after they leave the court—they go out to this playground and muck about, go down slides and on swings, and then go back to court. We began to write one or two sketches, and I think that's how our humor really came to the notice of John and Graham, who were writing superb sketches at the time," notes Palin.

As *The Frost Report* was drawing to a close, two of the performers received an offer from Frost himself.

"Frost came to me and Tim Brooke-Taylor individually and said `How about doing a show each?' We said we'd like to do one *together*. We pulled in Graham; then, after very little thought, Marty [Feldman], and then we of course had *At Last the 1948 Show*," explains Cleese.

At Last the 1948 Show would prove to be another valuable stepping-stone in their collective careers, although *The Frost Report* was the most important program to date for Cleese, Chapman, Idle, Jones, and Palin. While they were also doing some occasional writing and performing for a variety of other TV shows, all five were forming the bonds that would develop into Monty Python.

THE FROST REPORT ON BRITAIN

FEATURING JOHN CLEESE. WRITTEN BY JOHN CLEESE, GRAHAM CHAPMAN, TERRY JONES, DAVID FROST, TIM BROOKE-TAYLOR, BARRY CRYER, TONY HENDRA, HERBERT KRETZNER, PETER LEWIS AND PETER DOBEREINER, DAVID NOBBS, BILL ODDIE, AND LUDWIG VAN BEETHOVEN. (1966) PARLOPHONE PMC 7005

SIDE ONE

Matter of Taste*

Schoolmaster*

SIDE TWO

Scrapbook*

Adventure*

*Features John Cleese.

Just Four Just Men*

Internal Combustion

Deck of Cards

Top of the Form*

Unknown Soldier*

Bulletin*

Hilton

Zookeeper*

Numbers

"Matter of Taste," in which Frost attempts to guess the vintage of the drinks served by Cleese, may have been the inspiration of the infamous "Wee-wee Sketch" that never made it into *Monty Python*. "Top of the Form" is a grammar-school quiz show, but not the same as the "Top of the Form" sketch presented in *Secret Policeman's Other Ball*. "Adventure" is a sketch that was revived occasionally as well; Cleese is an interviewer who expects to be talking to a deep-sea diver but actually faces an insurance salesman (Frost).

THE FROST REPORT ON EVERYTHING

FEATURING JOHN CLEESE, RONNIE BARKER, RONNIE CORBETT, DAVID FROST, AND SHEILA STEAFEL. WRITERS INCLUDE ERIC IDLE, TERRY JONES, MICHAEL PALIN, GRAHAM CHAPMAN, AND JOHN CLEESE (MISSPELLED "CLEASE"). (1967) JANUS JLS-3005

SIDE ONE

The State of England

Theatre Critic*

Frost, What People Really Mean

Three Classes of People*

Narcissus Complex*

SIDE TWO

Frost on Agriculture, Speech

The Secretary*

Frost on Commercials

Selling String

Executive and the Teaman

Three Classes*

"Three Classes" became an ongoing gag on *The Frost Report* and, later, on *The Two Ronnies*. John Cleese was featured as the upper-class gent, Ronnie Barker as the middle class, and Ronnie Corbett represented the lower class, as they each commented on a variety of topics.

*Features John Cleese.

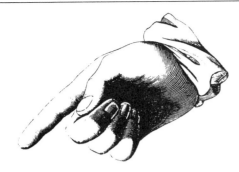

MISCELLANEOUS TELEVISION, THEATER, AND FILM

*J*ones, Palin, Idle, Chapman, and Cleese were doing so much writing—and occasional performing—for so many programs that they have trouble remembering some of them. In fact, there are no surviving copies of some of these shows; the BBC and ITV didn't begin keeping film and tapes of most of their TV shows until late in the 1960s.

After *The Frost Report* ended, the future Pythons worked on only three TV series that were important to the development of *Monty Python's Flying Circus* in 1969: *At Last the 1948 Show* (1967) with Chapman and Cleese; *Do Not Adjust Your Set* (1968–69) with Idle, Jones, Palin, and Gilliam; and *The Complete and Utter History of Britain* (1969), a Jones and Palin production. They all wrote for a variety of other shows around this time, though, often overlapping with each other.

As insignificant as some of these may be, they all had their place in the careers of the future Pythons and are thus worthy of at least a brief mention.

THE LATE SHOW

The Jones and Palin team was continuing to branch out with its writing and performing in the wake of the success of *The Frost Report*, and were becoming in demand. Terry Jones's shaky apprenticeship at the BBC had ended by this time, but he and his partner were writing more TV sketches than ever on a freelance basis.

One of the shows that the pair contributed to was *The Late Show*, a series first broadcast October 15, 1966. In addition to sketch-writing, the team also had the opportunity to do a bit more performing than they had been allowed previously.

"We both got involved in *The Late Show*,

but I think I did perhaps more than Terry," explains Palin.

"*The Late Show* was a little more acting—I did quite a few parts in some of the *Late Show* pieces, as did Terry. It was a program by some of the same team that had done *That Was the Week That Was* and that sort of early groundbreaking show. It was a late-night satire show on Saturday; I remember doing one or two sketches with the likes of Barry Humphries and John Bird. It was actually quite interesting, because the parts were not entirely comic—we had to do some serious roles to get the humor over."

THE ILLUSTRATED WEEKLY HUDD

The Illustrated Weekly Hudd was another program that Jones and Palin contributed to on occasion. As previously mentioned, Graham Chapman also did some individual writing for the show as well, just to prove to himself that he could still write on his own, without John Cleese.

"I've still got one of the films we wrote for

that, a sixteen mill. film of the whole show, actually," reveals Jones. "Somebody gave it to us just for one little bit that Mike and I did. It was directed by Ian Davidson, who got us in to do it—he directed the first revue that I was in at Oxford. In fact, that's probably the first thing on TV that Mike and I ever appeared in."

A SERIES OF BIRDS

As their writing continued, Jones and Palin worked on an assortment of shows for old friends, including John Bird. To their surprise, they found themselves credited as "script editors" by the time *A Series of Birds* first appeared on October 3, 1967.

"I don't quite know what that meant," Jones recalls with a smile. "There was never any script to edit! It all used to arrive at the last minute, I mean, actually on the day that they were going to record it. It was a nightmare. We were just there as sounding boards for John Bird, really."

Michael Palin says he was just as puzzled to be given the "script editor" title for *A Series of Birds*.

"I don't know why we were given that role. We were all rather fond of John Bird—he was very good at satire, and a good actor too," relates Palin. "He was doing this series in which each half hour was a story in itself. They were good stories—one was about the British Revolution, a present-day revolution in Britain, with a group of people who thought their symbol of the revolution was Nelson's Column. They were going to pull it down with a tractor and a rope, and the rope breaks. It's all very silly, but it mixed fantasy with a certain amount of good satire and observation. I think John found it hard to write them all on his own, so Terry and I did quite a bit of rewriting."

TWICE A FORTNIGHT

Since Terry Jones and Michael Palin were apparently doing such a good job as script editors on *A Series of Birds*—even though they didn't really understand what it meant—they were appointed to the same position on *Twice a Fortnight*, which first aired October 21, 1967.

"*Twice a Fortnight* was directed by Tony Palmer," notes Jones. "We made film inserts for him. It was basically done as a live show in front of a tanked-up audience—we gave them wine and everything. It was Tim Brooke-Taylor and Graeme Garden—Mike and I just made these little film inserts, like 'The Battle of Hastings,' which was a surreal film about the Battle of Hastings. Upon see-

In "The Door," a short, surreal film by Michael Palin and Terry Jones for Twice a Fortnight, *the two play workmen who carry the door across a skyline and discover a whole new world on the other side. Photo from the collection of Terry Jones, used by permission*

ing that film, my brother said 'How about doing that as a series?' and we went into a long thing that became *The Complete and Utter History of Britain*."

Many shows around that era were done on videotape and subsequently erased by the BBC, but the film inserts survive, as was the case with *Twice a Fortnight*. Fortunately, Terry Jones was determined to obtain copies of their work, since so many of their earliest TV shows were lost or wiped out by the BBC.

"I was determined not to lose track of everything we'd done, so I used to make myself *so* unpleasant at the BBC." He laughs. "I was *constantly* nattering away at these people. Poor Tony Palmer used to try to get the film out of *Twice a Fortnight*. Eventually I got it, but it took me six months of badgering to get these things."

Jones managed to amass many of the early films that he did with Palin, and it's a good thing he did. He may have the only existing copies of some of the material.

One example of their work for *Twice a Fortnight* was a short film called "The Door." Like much of their work around this era, it was slightly surrealistic and largely visual.

"'The Door' started with two men carrying a door across the skyline," Jones explains. "They put the door down and say they're going to have some sandwiches. A milk truck drives up, and the milkman happens to leave some milk at the door. Somebody opens the door and takes the milk in, so the two workmen go into this other world. . . ."

NO, THAT'S ME OVER HERE

This sitcom, starring *The Frost Report*'s Ronnie Corbett, featured episodes written by Eric Idle, Graham Chapman, and Barry Cryer. The first show aired November 14, 1967, and Idle even did a bit of acting in one program.

"That was another Frost enterprise—he set that up as a series for Ronnie," explains Idle. "I only wrote the first series—there were six or

seven of them. I was in one too. I played Ronnie's hippie nephew with long hair who came to stay, and 'How does it feel to be one of the beautiful people,' the Beatles' song [was playing in the background]. I came in, spaced out, saying 'Hey, man' to frighten Ronnie Corbett. I dropped out of that largely to work on *Do Not Adjust Your Set*."

LOOK HERE NOW

This little-known series starred Ronnie Corbett, and was shown on Canadian TV; the writing was by Graham Chapman and Barry Cryer.

THE TWO RONNIES

When longtime Frost regulars Ronnie Barker and Ronnie Corbett got their own series, they recruited some of their old colleagues to write sketches and monologues for the half-hour shows, and earlier John Cleese came in to portray the upper-class gentleman.

Terry Jones, Michael Palin, Eric Idle, and Graham Chapman all contributed jokes and sketches for the pair as well, even though they were busy with their own shows at this time.

"This was post–*Frost Report*, and people knew we were around to write sketches," explains Palin. "This was all 'sixty-seven, 'sixty-eight, while we were doing *Do Not Adjust Your Set*. I mean, we just wrote. We'd write twenty-two hours a day if we had to, to get the stuff in."

BROADEN YOUR MIND

After *At Last the 1948 Show*, Graeme Garden and Tim Brooke-Taylor had an opportunity to do their own BBC series; *Broaden Your Mind* premiered October 28, 1968. Colleagues Graham Chapman, John Cleese, Eric Idle, Terry Jones, and Michael Palin all contributed sketches to the series, which enjoyed a brief run that autumn. (Garden and Brooke-Taylor would later join with Bill Oddie to create the more successful, better known *The Goodies*.)

MARTY

THE MARTY FELDMAN COMEDY MACHINE

Marty Feldman had done a great deal of writing through the 1960s with David Frost and the various Pythons, but Frost had always been reluctant to feature the comedian on-camera because of his strange, pop-eyed appearance.

But when the other creators of *At Last the 1948 Show*, including John Cleese and Graham Chapman, insisted, Feldman became a part of the performing ensemble and a star was born.

He got his own BBC series, *Marty*, which began on April 29, 1968, and then did a follow-up series later that year; Cleese, Chapman, Terry Jones, and Michael Palin all contributed sketches to it, even though they were gearing up for Monty Python.

Terry Gilliam's animations on *Do Not Adjust Your Set* got immediate response from Marty Feldman, however, and he did one or two animations for Feldman's series around that period.

Feldman became popular enough to receive another series about three years later, produced in Britain and shown there, and then edited and turned into his own American television series. None of the Pythons contributed sketches for ABC-TV's *Marty Feldman Comedy Machine*, but Terry Gilliam furnished several animated sequences for the show, which was broadcast in Britain (beginning October 8, 1971) and in America that same fall.

"The Marty Feldman's Comedy Machine was done over here (in Britain)," reveals Gilliam. "It was Marty Feldman's show, and Larry [M*A*S*H] Gelbart produced it; I got to work in color, because there was more money.

"None of the British writers would write for it, because the producers were working Hollywood-style, where you come in to work nine-to-five at the studio. They had to bring in all these blackleg*

American comedy writers, like Rudy DeLuca and Pat McCormick and Barry Levinson—that's who did the writing way back when! It's amazing at how comedy spawns all of these incredible talents. . . . When you look around and see all of the incredible people who have come out of comedy, television writers who have gone on—Garry Marshall, Barry Levinson, Steve Martin—the list goes on and on and on."

Fans who would like to see Gilliam's animated titles for Feldman's show are in luck—numerous stills are included in his book, *Animations of Mortality.*

DOCTOR IN THE HOUSE

When London Weekend Television decided to create a TV series based on the book *Doctor in the House* (which had already been responsible for a successful series of films in the 1950s), they could not have chosen a better candidate to write the first program. Graham Chapman was a successful comedy writer and a fully qualified medical doctor, and based on the July 12, 1969, episode he wrote with John Cleese, called "Why Do You Want to Be A Doctor?" he set the pattern for the show's lengthy run.

Chapman and Cleese were about to plunge into *Monty Python's Flying Circus* at the time, and so they didn't write more than the initial episode

together. Through the years, however, each of them would write several shows for the ongoing series, Chapman often collaborating with Barry Cryer, Bernard McKenna, or David Sherlock. Chapman actually co-wrote eight more episodes in 1969; an episode written by Cleese (called "No Ill Feelings") that aired February 3, 1973, featured an early forerunner of the Basil Fawlty character. In addition, Graham Chapman appeared as Roddy in 1970's *Doctor in Trouble*, the seventh feature in the film series.

*Writers who slipped in and wrote illegally.

ALADDIN

BEAUTY AND THE BEAST

One of the longtime traditions of British theater, particularly around the holidays, is the children's pantomime show. Unlike the American connotations of the word, an English pantomime is not a silent, mimed scene but a broadly played, vocal story. (The performers often speak directly to and interact with the audience.)

In 1968 Terry Jones and Michael Palin were asked to write a pantomime for a theater on the edge of London, the Watford Civic Theatre. The pair had not been doing much writing for the stage at

this point, but decided to pick up the challenge and give the form a twist with their version of "Aladdin."

"We wrote what was a traditional pantomime, but trying to introduce a few characters who were fresher and more original," explains Palin. "So, we had the most boring man in the world. We had a prince called Prince Fong who had the world's most boring song, which sent everybody to sleep: `My name is Fong, This is my song . . .' Anyway, this song was stupendously boring. . . . We introduced a few new characters, but basically it was writing the *Aladdin* story. It was very successful, actually, it did very well."

The following year the same theater asked them to follow up their success with another pantomime. They decided to do their version of *Beauty and the Beast*.

"That was more demanding. I don't think it was quite as successful, and proved to be the end of our career as panto writers—until we wrote the Fegg panto, *Aladdin and His Terrible Problem*," says Palin, referring to the peculiar pantomime published in *Bert Fegg's Nasty Book for Boys and Girls*.

"*Beauty and the Beast* had much less story, really. Basically, the prince turns into a beast, comes back, kisses her, and turns into a prince again, and they go off into the sunset. This has to be stretched out over three and a half hours to get all the ice cream sold."

THE MAGIC CHRISTIAN

SCREENPLAY CO-WRITTEN BY AND CO-STARRING JOHN CLEESE AND GRAHAM CHAPMAN. (1969) 101 MINUTES

Sir Guy Grand	Peter Sellers
Youngman Grand	Ringo Starr
Dame Agnes Grand	Isabel Jeans
Hon. Esther Grand	Caroline Blakiston
Capt. Reginald K. Klaus	Wilfred Hyde-White
Oxford Coach	Richard Attenborough
Laurence Faggot	Leonard Frey
Hamlet	Laurence Harvey
Ship's Vampire	Christopher Lee
Traffic Warden 27	Spike Milligan
Solitary Drinker	Roman Polanski
Priestess of the Whip	Raquel Welch
Director in Sotheby's	John Cleese
Oxford Team Member	Graham Chapman

Screenplay by Terry Southern and Joseph McGrath, from the novel by Terry Southern. Additional Material by Graham Chapman, John Cleese, and Peter Sellers. Executive Producers Henry T. Weinstein and Anthony B. Unger. Produced by Denis O'Dell. Directed by Joseph McGrath. Produced by Grand Films Ltd./videocassette release by Republic Pictures Home Video (2548). (Note: Running time is listed on the videocassette box as 101 min. but is actually closer to 93 min.)

Sir Guy wakes up in his mansion, while a disheveled young man sleeping in a park is chased off by a policeman. Several short vignettes follow to contrast their mornings, and when the young man is feeding ducks in the park, Sir Guy approaches and decides to adopt him, calling him Youngman Grand. He gives him a suit and explains that they are going to observe the effects of money on the arts.

Upon arriving at the theater and sitting with Sir Guy's two sisters, they are just in time to see Hamlet deliver the "To be or not to be" speech; he accompanies it with a striptease.

During a board meeting at Grand and Son Holdings, Ltd., Sir Guy chastises the members and says they are becoming a nation of tiny cars. He shows his plans for the British Zeus, accompanied by an animated film of the gigantic car. He also introduces Youngman to the board, and we discover that the board room is actually in a railroad car.

Sir Guy and son arrive at their destination, a country estate, and go on a hunting expedition the next day. Their group breaks out machine guns and tanks to dispatch pheasants, finishing one off with a flamethrower.

Sir Guy takes Youngman to his new home and introduces him to the extensive staff. Afterward, Sir Guy and Youngman play war games with guns that fire on model cathedrals.

Sir Guy and Youngman watch the Oxford rowing team practicing for their race against Cambridge and bribe the Oxford coach. When they return to their car, they've just received a parking ticket. Sir Guy argues with the traffic warden, while Youngman sits in the car doing isometric exercises. Sir Guy offers the traffic warden £500 if he will eat the parking ticket, and the warden happily complies.

Youngman reads about a luxury liner called *The Magic Christian* as he and Sir Guy arrive at Sotheby's for an art auction. They study a Rembrandt, which a director says has not been authenticated. Regardless, they offer him £30,000 for the painting, which he accepts. Sir Guy then cuts out the nose and gives it to Youngman, while the flabbergasted director looks on. During the auction itself, Sir Guy and Youngman make bids by harmonica, dart guns, air horn, guns, and semaphore flags.

At the Oxford-Cambridge boat race, Sir Guy offers to make one team a deal. One of the crew laughs at the thought of a bribe, until Sir Guy opens a briefcase full of money. During the race, Oxford is behind, but the team cuts the rudder on the Cambridge boat and then rams it, breaking the Cambridge ship in two.

Sir Guy and Youngman board the *Magic Christian*, while the captain addresses the passengers via TV monitor.

In another cabin, a lady passenger is served her tea by a waiter who is actually a vampire. The vampire roams the halls, and the passengers panic. Some of them try to escape through the engine room, where they discover a priestess whipping topless slaves as they row in the galley.

The group escapes, only to find that they're still docked in London. Sir Guy and Youngman call them back with promises of free money. Youngman has blood, urine, and manure delivered to a swimming pool and throws money into it. The upper-class gents climb into it and dive for pound notes. Sir Guy joins Youngman sleeping in the park, and Sir Guy bribes the police to let them stay.

 NOTES

John Cleese and Graham Chapman became more heavily involved in writing and performing in films than Eric Idle, Terry Jones, and Michael Palin, particularly after they had finished *At Last the 1948 Show* (1967).

The best-known of these films is undoubtedly *The Magic Christian*. A vehicle for Peter Sellers, who starred as the richest man in the world, the film co-starred Ringo Starr and featured a soundtrack by Badfinger that included the top-ten hit "Come and Get It."

Graham Chapman and John Cleese were brought in to rewrite one of the many drafts that had been prepared for the film.

"John and I were writing one day, or wondering what to write, and we got a phone call from Peter Sellers. We didn't know him, but we thought a Peter Sellers movie script would be interesting. He said would we do some rewrites on the script? When he mentioned a figure of five hundred pounds a week, that seemed a lot to us at the time, so we thought yes, we'll have a look at it and see whether we will or not," explained Chapman.

"We did look at the script, and we also read the Terry Southern book. I liked the book quite a lot. It was, by its very nature, episodic, but there's some very funny stuff in it. The film was not a good as the book, and it was all over the place as a screenplay. There were not very many pieces of it that really worked, we felt, but we did think we could certainly make it as good as the book, and we might even improve on that."

"The Terry Southern script had been through thirteen drafts by the time it got to us. We read one that contained the most elegant and verbose stage directions I have ever come across in my life, but quite hopeless dialogue, I'm afraid," notes Cleese.

"Graham and I managed to put this script into shape in three or four weeks until we got it to the point where they were able to raise money on it, at which point Terry Southern arrived and was laid to rest in a nest of bourbon crates. They went back to a script that was more or less as terrible as the one that Peter had refused to finance in the first place."

Graham Chapman explained that their script had indeed ensured that *The Magic Christian* would be made.

"The producers could find the money on the basis of the script that we wrote. We also did the rewrite to help get the money to include Ringo Starr in the role opposite Peter. So, the movie was set up," explained Chapman.

John Cleese, Ringo Starr, and Peter Sellers have fun between takes during the filming of The Magic Christian. *Photo from the Collection of John Cleese, used by permission*

"On the first day of principal photography, they went right back to the original script. That was the decision of Peter, and a very annoying one to us. Certain bits that we wrote were kept in, but not a great deal really. The film was a bit of a mess—there were some funny sections, but it was a disappointment."

John Cleese appeared in one of the best sketches in the entire film, not coincidentally written by Chapman and him, and shot on the first day.

"I was lucky enough to get to play quite a good sketch that Graham and I wrote, which was set in a Sotheby's showroom. It was about Guy Grand buying a portrait and then cutting the noses out because he was only interested in noses. It was what he collected. It was about greed as opposed to aesthetic morality, whether you'd sell a Rembrandt to someone who was only going to cut the noses out. It was a good sketch, and I enjoyed playing it, but basically, the film was a complete mess," relates Cleese. "It was done by a very nice man who had no idea of comedy structure, and it finished up as a series of celebrity walk-ons."

Chapman recalled another interesting aspect of the first day's shooting, which revealed how Ringo's part (as Sellers's son) was diminished due to Sellers; it involved the scene that Cleese appeared in.

"Ringo was still in it, but not very much. One curious thing occurred on the first day of filming. It was characteristic of Peter, although I didn't know it at the time.

"Guy Grand and his son were wandering around Sotheby's, the auction room, collecting valuable articles of art. As soon as they had paid for them, they would throw them into a shopping trolley—really very valuable articles that they then treated as though they were nothing; the whole film really was about money and what you can do with it. That was quite a nice sequence by the end of the day," explained Chapman.

"That was shot again the second day. Peter claimed that he hadn't quite got his character right, but the real reason was that Ringo Starr got a lot of laughs."

American Python fans will note that *The Magic Christian* provides a relatively rare opportunity for them to see Cleese and Chapman performing in their pre-Python days; they both performed in sketches that they wrote, and Chapman can be seen as the leader of a rowing team (although he isn't listed in the closing credits).

There is another interesting sidelight to the film for Python fans. The "Mouse Problem" sketch, a documentary parody about men who enjoy dressing up as mice, was originally written for *The Magic Christian*. Peter Sellers was quite happy with the sketch, but when he returned the next morning, he decided not to include it in the film. The reason? His milkman didn't care for it.

 ## CRITICAL COMMENTS

"Fiendishly funny adaptation of Terry Southern's insane novel."

—Leonard Maltin

Critical milkmen aside, Cleese and Chapman continued to dabble in films shortly before Python began.

Chapman appeared without Cleese in 1970's *Doctor in Trouble* (which also featured *The Goon Show's* Harry Secombe), while John Cleese in particular found himself in demand as a performer in a number of largely undistinguished films as he became better known.

"Some of those films were just a question of somebody ringing me up and telling me about the part, sending me a few pages through the post, and my saying `Yes, I'd like to do it,'" notes Cleese. "I would turn up somewhere and do a day or two days—usually not knowing really what the film was about or what I was doing—but everyone was always very nice. Several of the small bits I got seemed to have been written by Dennis Norden, who I think had spotted me and often used to suggest me for the parts."

INTERLUDE

In 1967's *Interlude*, Cleese is featured as a television executive in the story of a symphony conductor and a reporter who have an affair; the film stars Oskar Werner, Barbara Ferris, and Donald Sutherland.

"The director, Kevin Billington, asked me in to do a very nice little part as a greasy, vain P.R. officer at a television company. I got to play one or two scenes with Oskar Werner, who was very interesting, I liked him a lot. I also had some scenes with Barbara Ferris in the canteen," recalls Cleese.

"I can only remember in my naive filmic state how astounded I was at the number of people standing around in the canteen when I was shooting a couple of scenes with Barbara. I couldn't believe that so many people were required. I was still green at that point!"

THE BLISS OF MRS. BLOSSOM

Cleese has a small part in this 1968 Shirley MacLaine–Richard Attenborough comedy, the story of the wife of a brassiere manufacturer who keeps a lover in the attic. Cleese plays an often-befuddled shopkeeper.

"*The Bliss of Mrs. Blossom* was a very nice part—half a day, probably the first thing I ever did, playing with Freddie Jones. Didn't know what I was doing, and didn't realize that one or two other people didn't know either—it takes a bit of time to

THE BEST HOUSE IN LONDON

Cleese makes a brief appearance in this 1969 film, which stars David Hemmings and George Sanders in the story of a group of government officials in Victorian London who sponsor an official brothel.

"I turned up to be a plantation messenger," relates Cleese, "and got a message that I had to wear these very considerable muttonchop whiskers. Then I got another message—did I mind playing it Indian? As I sat there in Indian makeup and muttonchop whiskers, I remember thinking `Why did they cast me?' It lasted about a day.

"I shot a scene with George Sanders, and remember him being very professional. We were in a scene where people were supposed to be firing rifles into the room where we were having dinner, and he was being very British. In fact, the effects themselves were a bit dangerous—little bits flying past our eyeballs. At one point, I had to hold a glass and have it shot out of my hand by a man with a .22 rifle, and although he was resting the rifle on a chair only about three feet away, I was quite pleased when the shot was over!"

THE LOVE BAN/ IT'S A 2' 6" ABOVE THE GROUND WORLD

Cleese has a small role in this comedy about a Catholic couple going on the pill, which starred Hwyel Bennett and Nanette Newman.

"The Love Ban was called It's a 2' 6" Above the Ground World. I had a tiny scene directed by a man called Ralph Thomas, who had a reputation for always being finished at twenty past five.* I had a long speech written by Bryan Forbes. It was very witty, but Bryan was very happy to let me make a couple of changes.

"I did the speech once, not very well, and did it again, and dried** right in the middle, quite badly. But, I remembered what the line was, and picked it up and went on, and at the end, Ralph Thomas said `Fine, that's it, we'll print that. Now,

the next setup is—' and I said `Ralph, I dried quite badly.' `Did you?' `Yes, Ralph, quite major.' `Didn't notice.' `What?' I said. `No, it looked quite natural, just as though you were thinking of the next line.' I said `Are you sure?' He said `Absolutely. It was fine, trust me. Now, the next setup—'

"A couple of weeks later, I was called in to do the voice-over on this film. There I was on the screen, drying. The most blatant dry I've ever seen on a cinema screen in my life! Well, I managed to get the shot out of the film, use a reverse angle, and re-record the dialogue over and put it on the reverse, but it shook my confidence. More than that, I realized why he always finished at twenty past five!"

THE STATUE

John Cleese is also featured in 1970's The Statue, the story of a professor whose wife sculpts an eighteen-foot-tall statue of him; he says he enjoyed working with its star, David Niven. "What a sweet

man he was, he was as nice as anyone. My part didn't even exist in the original movie. When they cut the film together, they discovered that it didn't make any sense, nobody could follow the plot. So

Dennis Norden, who's a great craftsman, wrote another week's worth of scenes. I played a psychiatrist, a friend of David Niven. He came to me every ten minutes in the movie and said `Well, what I've just been doing is this, and what I'm going to do next is that. . . .' And I would say `Good idea.' This enabled people to understand the plot!" Cleese laughs.

THE RISE AND RISE OF MICHAEL RIMMER

Graham Chapman and John Cleese collaborated in the writing of 1969's *The Rise and Rise of Michael Rimmer*, which starred Vanessa Redgrave, Peter Cook, Denholm Elliot, and featured Cleese in a small role as an advertising executive. The plot involves an efficiency expert who takes over an advertising agency and eventually rises to become prime minister. David Frost had gotten the pair involved in the production, and they had actually co-written the script (with Cook and director Kevin Billington) several years before its eventual release.

"Frost wanted Graham Chapman and myself to write a movie, which we wrote the summer after we'd finished the first series of *Frost Reports*. We came out to Ibiza and we went through the story with him. He made some suggestions and then we went ahead! Graham and I were excited at earning so much money—I can't quite remember, but it was something like a thousand or five hundred pounds, split between the two of us. For us, in those days, it was quite major money!" relates Cleese, who recalled that it was during this time that Chapman met longtime companion David Sherlock. Cleese and Chapman had developed their own unique collaborative style by this point as well.

"It was the summer holiday in Ibiza where Graham met and fell in love with David," recalls Cleese. "I remember being slightly surprised that I would be working inside at the desk in the shadows in the cool, and Gray would be lying with a very small bathing costume outside on the balcony shouting suggestions in to me in the gloom. I found it was all right to work with Gray like that, because to be perfectly honest, I did most of the work. Graham was a great embroiderer, so I would take the brunt of the story on. He would always be around with interesting, offbeat ideas which

stopped it from getting too predictable, which was my danger."

This method suited both of them quite well, even throughout Python.

"Gray was not a hard worker in terms of how much effort he put in when he was actually in the room, although there were times when he was turning out an amazing amount of comedy in different writing partnerships with two or three people. He would write on three different scripts during the course of a day, for example. But he was not a hardworking man and not very good at applying himself—he was much better if somebody else was doing that, and then he would come in with wonderful, off-the-wall suggestions, little bits of imagination. Which suited me fine, because I quite liked controlling the general direction of it. Then Gray would come in and put me in a more interesting direction than the one I had thought of," reveals Cleese.

"Anyway, it wasn't a bad script, and after a time, we decided we'd get Peter Cook to play the lead. So, Peter came in. We all agreed Kevin Billington would make a very good director, so the four of us worked on the script for some time.

"I do remember Kevin Billington saying rather quietly to me after about four days, `Does Graham ever say anything?' I realized that if you weren't used to him, he *did* seem a bit on the quiet side," he laughs.

Several years passed before *The Rise and Rise of Michael Rimmer* was shot and released.

"It was made eventually, and it had some very funny things in it, but none of us understood much about story. It doesn't work at all as a good story. The management at Warner's changed while the film was being made, so the new lot came in with no interest in it, and they never bothered to push it. It is actually worth watching, because there are a few very funny minutes in it, surrounded by a certain amount of very poor story."

*He always finished early, at exactly the same time every day.
**His mouth dried while he was speaking.

RENTADICK

The Cleese-Chapman team also collaborated on the script in the late sixties for a film that was eventually released in 1972 under the unfortunate title *Rentadick*, directed by Jim Clark and produced by Ned Sherrin. Starring James Booth, Richard Briers, Michael Bentine, and Spike Milligan, the plot of the spoof involves a detective agency called Rentadick, Inc., that is hired to find a stolen nerve gas that paralyzes its victims from the waist down.

Cleese considers *Rentadick* one of his worst experiences in film. Very early on, Cleese, Chapman, Frost, and the original producers were planning to use Charles Crichton as director (who directed *A Fish Called Wanda* more than twenty years later), but ran into problems.

"It was a script developed for David Frost. We went ahead and figured it out, got a plot we quite liked, looked around for a director, and found Charlie Crichton. We sat down with the old man, slightly embarrassed because we'd knicked the ending of *Lavender Hill Mob*, and we realized Charlie'd directed that. But, Charlie being Charlie, he didn't notice—or had forgotten what it was, anyway.

"His expertise was breathtaking to us guys. He would leave us in the evening, and by the time he saw us in the morning, he'd push a piece of paper toward us and say `I had a few thoughts last night, but I don't think they're any good.' And you realized he'd solved the problem, put in two jokes, and taken out half a page. He was just that expert on a level that Gray and I had never encountered before. We just loved him.

"But then, a funny thing happened. David Frost sold the rights to Ned Sherrin. We were not told that he sold the rights to Ned Sherrin—only that he'd been brought in as a producer, so we still thought that David had the ultimate say-so. Then Sherrin said he didn't want to work with Charlie. We just didn't know why, and we never quite got an answer out of him. He just didn't want to. We said we didn't want to do it without Charlie, because he worked on the thing and he's the best," relates Cleese.

"Then Sherrin said `In any case, I can't pay you what you're due in the contract, you'll have to take a cut.' We said `We'll take a cut if you'll use Charlie,' and he said no, he wouldn't use Charlie.

He showed us a film by the guy he wanted, called Jim Clark. He is a very good editor who worked with John Schlesinger a lot. The difficult thing here was, we didn't think Jim showed much understanding of how to direct comedy, except for pastiche—he did pastiche very well, because he was an editor with a wonderful eye. But he just didn't have a sense of how to work with actors on an original comedy.

"We said that, but Ned just didn't want to listen. He wouldn't use Charlie, so we said goodbye, and as a result, Tim Brooke-Taylor and Marty and the two Ronnies just dropped out. They said `Well, if you're not in, we're not interested,' and Ned went ahead with a completely new crew.

"He wrote about this in the papers a few years ago, and remembered most of it quite wrongly—there were none of the future Pythons going to be in it in those days, because it was before we'd really gotten to know each other very well, although the Python grouping got together shortly after that. However, neither Michael nor Terry nor Eric nor Terry G were in any way involved in the film. They made it eventually, and Alexander Walker called it `another nail in the coffin of the British film industry,' which indeed it was."

Cleese remains upset more than twenty-five years later about his experiences with Sherrin on the film.

"I'm afraid Ned had absolutely no talent at all for this type of comedy—in fact, he did a series of French farces for the television which more or less put the nail in that genre too. He had absolutely no ability to direct or produce comedy. I resented him very much, first of all for not using Charlie, and secondly for behaving very badly.

"He behaved badly twice, first of all when we said we wouldn't take a cut if he didn't use Charlie—I know this, because an accountant who worked for him worked for us, and told me this was happening—he was setting up two companies so that we would have a percentage of royalties in a company that was set up in such a way that we couldn't possibly make a profit. I don't know if Sherrin ever actually set up the company in this way—there wasn't any need to, really, because the film was such a disaster that there was no possibility do so. As far as I was concerned, that was the single meanest thought I'd ever suffered or have suffered since at the hands of anyone in show business, and for that reason, I would never consider getting involved with him in any other professional endeavor. It's not just that I don't trust him, I don't think he's any good either." *Rentadick* proved to be just as bad as Cleese and Chapman had feared, and the two of them decided to disassociate themselves with it.

"Eventually Graham and I got to see the film, because we wanted to see whether we wanted to keep our names on it. We saw it and it was exactly the disaster that we had predicted. We asked for our names to be removed from the script, and Sherrin refused, at which point we went to the Writer's Guild and had them removed. I don't know quite what the Guild did, but they threatened him with some kind of sanction, and he then removed the names, which is why, in the film, there's no credit for script, there's only a credit for additional material. Nevertheless, whenever the film appears on television, our names are always sadly associated with it, which is scarcely fair under the circumstances."

DITTO

While Cleese and Chapman did not want *Rentadick* to be filmed, another screenplay that they hoped would be shot in the late sixties, *Ditto*, did not pan out.

"Carlo Ponti contacted us while we were doing these different scripts for Peter Sellers," relates Cleese.

"Of course, he was a huge name in those days, Sophia Loren's husband. Sophia Loren and Peter Sellers were huge together on account of a film called *The Millionairess*—I don't know how big it was internationally, but certainly in England, they were about as big as you get. So, to be called in by Carlo Ponti, with an invitation to write for those two, was pretty amazing.

"He had a short story about a man who'd gotten a duplicating machine that could duplicate people. Graham and I wrote what I thought was a very interesting script about the psychological responses to this situation. The Sellers character duplicated his wife, whom he was a little tired of, and of course the new one becomes the very sexy one, although she's exactly the same as the old one—they are duplicates.

"Then, of course, two wives get together and duplicate the husbands. Another husband is duplicated and he starts to go mad, so he duplicates himself about forty times so that he can tackle the others, and we finished up with a kind of native American scene!" reveals Cleese.

"I thought it was a really interesting script, but we never heard a word. Carlo Ponti had three disasters in a row. One was called *Sunflowers* with Marcello Mastroianni—they were all absolute turkeys, and he kind of disappeared. We never heard another word. We had a copy of the script, but he had all the rights."

Graham Chapman always claimed that *Ditto* was ready to be shot, when an extramarital affair put an end to it. Nevertheless, Chapman revived the project shortly before he died, rewriting the script with David Sherlock. He had planned to shoot it in Canada, and was considering directing it himself. Unfortunately, it never happened.

MORE MISCELLANEOUS MINOR MOVIES

During this same period in the mid-to-late sixties, Eric Idle, Terry Gilliam, Terry Jones, and Michael Palin were concentrating most of their efforts on television writing. They did make occasional forays into film, though.

ISADORA: THE BIGGEST DANCER IN THE WORLD

GUEST APPEARANCES BY ERIC IDLE AND MICHAEL PALIN. FIRST BROADCAST SEPTEMBER 22, 1966, ON BBC-1. PRODUCED AND DIRECTED BY KEN RUSSELL.

Vivian Pickles played the title role in this version of the life of dancer Isadora Duncan; Eric Idle played the "Death Chauffeur" while Michael Palin and Idle were part of a jazz band playing on the roof of a hearse.

"I had just come down from university, and I was looking for any work at all that involved getting near a camera and getting BBC-Television exposure," explains Palin. "I heard that Ken Russell was making a film, *Isadora*. A guy called Tony Palmer who's a film director now—does long films about Wagner and opera—was a friend of a friend of mine, and said `Oh, yes, I'm helping assistant produce this film with Ken Russell, would you like to come and be in it?'

"So, I played the part of an undertaker. There were four of us playing musical instruments on top of a hearse as it drove through London. I don't quite know why we were doing it, but with Ken Russell, ours was not to reason why—we just went ahead and did it. Both Eric and I were on top of the roof."

Eric Idle got his comedy career off to a successful start with Ken Russell as well.

"I played the chauffeur of Isadora Duncan, and I drowned her two children," relates Idle. "It's a sad and gruesome story which is based on the truth. He stalled his car on the banks of the Seine in Paris and got out to hand-crank it. But he'd left it in reverse, and it went backwards into the Seine, drowning her two children. It was my first professional acting role. Ken Russell took one look at me and said `Death's chauffeur for him!'"

ALICE IN WONDERLAND

GUEST APPEARANCE BY ERIC IDLE. FIRST BROADCAST DECEMBER 28, 1966, ON BBC-1. PRODUCED AND DIRECTED BY JONATHAN MILLER.

This adaptation by Jonathan Miller starred Alan Bennett, John Bird, Peter Cook, Sir John Gielgud, Sir Michael Redgrave, and Peter Sellers.

"It was a wonderful production, and rather bizarre. Jonathan Miller had done it all with these Freudian archetypes, in black-and-white with a Ravi Shankar soundtrack. It's a very strange *Alice in Wonderland*," recalls Idle, who plays one of the Caucus.

"I played a very strange thin man with a top hat, and drowned in a pool of tears."

CRY OF THE BANSHEE

ANIMATED TITLES BY TERRY GILLIAM. (1970) 87 MINUTES

As Terry Gilliam recalls, "Everything started breaking at the same time!" as he began to get animation job offers. "All these things started happening after Python became successful."

This Hammer horror film, starring Vincent Price, features animated titles by Gilliam, which he did just after the first series of *Monty Python's Flying Circus*.

"I used a lot of Albrecht Dürer engravings," he recalls, "and Vincent Price's head was cracking open and demons were pouring out, lots of blood and nice medieval stuff."

WILLIAM

ANIMATED TITLES BY TERRY GILLIAM. FIRST BROADCAST JANUARY 3, 1973, ON ABC-TV.

This ABC-TV *After-School Special* on Shakespeare featured titles by Terry Gilliam, though his memory is unclear with the details.

"It was just some silly cartoons with William Shakespeare," he explains. "I can't even remember what I did on it—I don't even know what happened on these title scenes."

"They just approached me [to do the titles]," Gilliam says, explaining that once Python became popular, he began to receive numerous offers for animation jobs.

"I never approach anybody. I just sit and keep people at bay. It's quite an extraordinary thing—when you're doing something like *Python*, all the people in the media love it. My cartoons were things that always looked pretty extraordinary, and useful to the advertising business. They just approached me. I never hunt for work!"

Breakthroughs

AT LAST THE 1948 SHOW

GRAHAM CHAPMAN, JOHN CLEESE. ADDITIONAL APPEARANCES BY ERIC IDLE. FIRST SERIES BEGAN AIRING FEBRUARY 15, 1967 (REDIFFUSION). SECOND SERIES BEGAN AIRING SEPTEMBER 26, 1967. FEATURING TIM BROOKE-TAYLOR, GRAHAM CHAPMAN, JOHN CLEESE, MARTY FELDMAN, AND AIMI MACDONALD. WRITTEN BY TIM BROOKE-TAYLOR, GRAHAM CHAPMAN, JOHN CLEESE, AND MARTY FELDMAN. PRODUCED BY DAVID FROST. DIRECTED BY IAN FORDYCE.

At Last the 1948 Show was, for Graham Chapman and John Cleese, the immediate predecessor to *Monty Python's Flying Circus*. It was the show that allowed them to experiment with comedic ideas and concepts that they later perfected in Python. Certainly, credit must be given to David Frost, who offered his co-workers the opportunity to create their own show. It's safe to say that without the freedom they were given in *The 1948 Show*, *Monty Python* would have been quite different, and may not have even come into existence at all.

". . . *The 1948 Show* was where, for the first time, we got a little bit of freedom," recalled Graham Chapman. "We were the actors as well as the writers for *The 1948 Show*, and that removed an element of control—no interpretation by the actor of what you write. Also, no egos in the way that 'I'm not going to do that, because that would ruin my reputation with my public.' That was no concern to us, we didn't worry about that. No reputations to lose, I suppose, at that point!" he laughed.

"So, we *were* able to do *sillier* things because we were a little more in control—to do things that were a little more risky, too, that were not so conventional. I think we felt a little bit stifled sometimes, particularly writing for *The Frost Report*, which was a fairly conventional sketch show. We'd take material along to script meetings, and the cast would laugh at it a great deal, but then say we couldn't possibly do it, because it was wrong for their image, or they felt a little bit too infantile—it might make them look silly."

Graham said that doing their own shows after *The Frost Report* was very emancipating.

"When we first did our own show, and when we had even more control with Python, it

The cast of At Last the 1948 Show. *(Clockwise from top: Aimi Mac-Donald, Graham Chapman, Tim Brooke-Taylor, John Cleese, and Marty Feldman). Rediffusion photo from the collection of John Cleese, used by permission*

freed us from all those constraints. Half our comedy shows before that used to have songs and dance routines in the middle—it was a hangover from the days of variety," noted Graham.

"It was almost as though they were afraid to have a whole half hour of solid comedy. *We* were, in a way, because it took a lot more writing—harder than `And now so-and-so sings this song!' We thought it was a little bit lazy, even though we were lazy ourselves. Being lazy ourselves, I suppose that's why we were overjoyed when we were joined by Michael Palin, Terry Jones, Eric Idle, and Terry Gilliam—that meant we had much less writing to do.

"We were a little annoyed at how conventional comedy had become, and wanted it to break free of that and change things. If it worked, fine, if it didn't, then no matter—it was a worthwhile experiment. The initial experiment for John and myself was . . . *The 1948 Show*. That seemed to work, but

even in that, we often felt obliged to have an end to a sketch, where often it was not necessary, and to put more structure in than we really needed. But we did take some risks, and we were able to do that more so with Python," related Chapman.

Even Cleese, who is often overly critical of his early work, still enthuses about *At Last the 1948 Show*.

"It was terrific. That was the first chance I ever had, when I was given my head by David Frost," he recalls. "He offered Tim Brooke-Taylor and myself shows. We didn't want shows separately, so we decided we'd do one together. We brought Graham in automatically, because obviously he was going to be the third, and we looked around, and suddenly decided that we would ask Marty [Feldman], who was only known as a writer. So, Marty's first screen appearances were in the '*48 Show*.

"I can still remember David when we said we wanted Marty to be one of the four performers. Dear David said [sotto voce] `But won't the audience be a little uncomfortable about the way he looks?' And of course, it's so funny, because the way he looked was his fortune."

First broadcast February 15, 1967, the cast also featured "the lovely Aimi MacDonald." One of the running gags in the series centered on MacDonald's believing that she was the centerpiece of the show; one program featured the "Make the lovely Aimi MacDonald a Rich Lady Appeal." There were two series of *At Last the 1948 Show* and a total of thirteen shows, which had been thought lost for many years.

"They've mainly been wiped,* but we recently discovered that Swedish television has some in their vaults. They're in black and white, and not of very good quality, but it's fascinating to see Marty's first screen stuff," explains Cleese.

At Last the 1948 Show broke new ground because it was one of the first shows to use the medium of television to send itself up, utilizing state-of-the-art 1967 technology, according to Chapman. They attempted to ignore or flout the conventions of the typical TV variety show, and bend the formats with the same anarchic point of view as their hero, Spike Milligan. The result, though not perfect, was a large step forward.

*Wiped out or erased.

"It was a very happy show, because we started to do a wilder type of humor than I'd ever been allowed to do before, and that's always marvelous," recalls Cleese. "We were allowed suddenly to do something that we'd been held back from. But it was also a bit of a nightmare, because we weren't very experienced. We did it in a great rush.

"I remember being up at half-past ten at night trying to write sketches that we were going to have to put on tape in three days' time. The pressure on us was pretty tremendous, and I got used to that terrible feeling of panic and slight depression as you're writing late at night, because the other things you've written the previous days aren't working, andyou've got to come up with something new. You're feeling tired and depressed, which makes it even harder. A lot of young comedians will recognize that feeling. Well, that's when I went through it."

The show also gave Eric Idle a chance to perform in some small roles. *Do Not Adjust Your Set* had not yet come about, so Idle was the only one of the future Pythons to appear in both of these ground-breaking series.

"I used to play small bits in it," recalls Idle. "I'd come to be the dead body. The first time, I was the defense counselor in a courtroom sketch, and they used to use me every week just to play the odd bits. It was my first real experience doing TV after Cambridge, in a professional sense, with people, and not being nervous. I never had much to do, and yet I was around this comedy show. It was a very funny show!"

At Last the 1948 Show was the first TV project to offer him great personal satisfaction, says Cleese, who remembers it fondly. "There was a kind of terror and excitement at doing . . . *the 1948 Show*, the first time I ever had a really major stake in a television thing. There was terror and excitement at doing TV comedy for the very first time under pressure, not enough time, not enough resources, and I think I shall always remember that as a sort of good young person's experience, an interesting first blooding as to what it was all about."

DO NOT ADJUST YOUR SET

WRITTEN BY AND STARRING ERIC IDLE, TERRY JONES, MICHAEL PALIN, AND TERRY GILLIAM. FIRST BROADCAST OF SERIES ONE JANUARY 4, 1968, ON REDIFFUSION. FIRST BROADCAST OF SERIES TWO FEBRUARY 19, 1969, ON THAMES TV. DO NOT ADJUST YOUR STOCKING BROADCAST DECEMBER 26, 1968. FEATURING DENISE COFFEY, ERIC IDLE, DAVID JASON, TERRY JONES, MICHAEL PALIN, AND THE BONZO DOG (DOO-DAH) BAND. WRITTEN BY ERIC IDLE, TERRY JONES, AND MICHAEL PALIN. ADDITIONAL MATERIAL AND ANIMATION BY TERRY GILLIAM. PRODUCED BY HUMPHREY BARCLAY (SERIES 1), IAN DAVIDSON (2). DIRECTED BY DAPHNE SHADWELL (SERIES 1), ADRIAN COOPER (2). MUSIC BY THE BONZO DOG (DOO-DAH) BAND.

"*Do Not Adjust Your Set* was really the first major, indeed most important thing that I was to do," notes Michael Palin of his early years.

Several of his collaborators on the show could say the same. *Do Not Adjust Your Set* was as vital to the development of *Monty Python's Flying Circus* for Eric Idle, Terry Gilliam, Terry Jones, and Michael Palin as *At Last the 1948 Show* was for John Cleese and Graham Chapman.

Do Not Adjust Your Set actually began as a children's show, but soon developed a cult following with adults. BBC-Radio producer Humphrey Barclay, who had worked on *I'm Sorry, I'll Read That Again*, first approached Eric Idle with an idea for the series.

"Humphrey Barclay came to me and said `I want to do a kid's show,' and he asked me to write it and be in it," recalls Idle. "I knew him at Cambridge—we'd done Footlights together, shows at Edinburgh. He said `Will you write for me?' and I said `Yes, but I want to work with Mike and Terry.' He thought that would be a good idea, so we got Mike and Terry in to write and perform it too. Then he brought in David Jason, who is now the biggest thing in English comedy, and Denise Coffey, and the Bonzo Dog Doo Dah Band."

Michael Palin recalls that he joined the team as part of a Palin-Jones package.

"*Do Not Adjust Your Set* was very important, really, because it was the first time we were given a free hand as writers and performers," relates Palin. "Humphrey Barclay had asked Eric and Terry to do something with him. He hadn't asked me, and Terry said `Uh, well, I'm not doing this unless my friend Michael comes along,' and he said `All right.' So they asked me along, and it turned into a very nice team."

As Terry Jones explains, the allure for most of them was the chance to perform their own material on a regular basis.

"Our agent was saying `What do you want to do a children's show for? Why don't you write

The cast of Do Not Adjust Your Set. *Clockwise from upper left: Eric Idle, Michael Palin, David Jason, Denise Coffey, and Terry Jones. Photo from the Collection of Terry Jones, used by permission*

a stage show for someone that you can make money out of?' We wanted to do it, obviously, because it was performing," reveals Jones.

The group did two series of thirteen shows each for *Do Not Adjust Your Set* as well as a Christmas special titled *Do Not Adjust Your Stocking.* The first series was for Rediffusion Television, but after they went out of business, the second series was picked up by Thames Television.

"We became a cult hit," notes Idle. "We were the biggest thing on the TV before the *Ten O'Clock News.* It went very well. We won an award early on for children's TV excellence: the Silver Bear of Berlin, or Munich, or somewhere."

Do Not Adjust Your Set was also responsible for yet another addition to Python personnel. Michael Palin says that since it was a children's show, it was broadcast from about five-fifteen till a quarter to six, including five minutes of ads.

"We had to supply about twenty-five minutes of material, but then we also had the Bonzo Dog [Doo Dah] Band, with Viv Stanshall and Neil Innes," relates Palin. "It was the first time we met Neil. They were the resident music act on the show, so that cut our time down to—we could get away with about twenty minutes or so of written material."

Neil Innes was an art student and musician, and the band was mostly made up of other art students. Their live performances were highly theatrical, and their approach to music and performing was Pythonesque even before Monty Python existed. The Bonzos released a number of albums in the late 1960s and early '70s, and even had a hit single, "I'm the Urban Spaceman," which was produced by Paul McCartney (under the name Apollo C. Vermouth). The Bonzo Dog (Doo-Dah) Band even appeared in the Beatles' *Magical Mystery Tour,* singing "Death Camp for Cutie" while a stripper performed in the foreground.

After meeting the ensemble on *Do Not Adjust Your Set,* Innes went on to do occasional audience warmups for *Monty Python's Flying Circus* and even performed a bit in the fourth series of shows. But Innes is probably best known among Python fans for his roles in the films and stage shows, beginning with *Monty Python and the Holy Grail.*

During the middle of the first series, the final, significant ingredient was added. Terry Gilliam had returned to London earlier in the year and found himself unemployed. Cleese provided him with an introduction to Humphrey Barclay,

One of Cleese's favorite photos from Rediffusion's **At Last the 1948 Show.** *(from left: John Cleese, Marty Feldman, Graham Chapman, and Tim Brooke-Taylor) Rediffusion photo from the Collection of John Cleese, used by permission*

who was producing *Do Not Adjust Your Set* at the time, but Gilliam found it difficult to make contact with Barclay.

"I caught him on the phone," explains Gilliam. "For a month I'd been trying to get through to him and I was getting nowhere. One day I called and he picked up the phone, so I got a chance to see him. I had some written material and some cartoons, and it turns out he was an amateur cartoonist. He liked the cartoons a lot, and he liked a couple of the writing things, and bought two, which then got forced on Mike, Terry, and Eric. I can't even remember what they were —they were really more conceptual than dialogue-oriented."

Gilliam recalls that Jones and Palin were not particularly pleased at having this American writer foisted on them at first, though Idle warmed up to him more quickly.

"It was the first time they used something from someone outside the group. They didn't really like it, but fortunately they decided to be nice and give me a break," he recalls. The American joined *Do Not Adjust Your Set* midway through the first series, though his contributions were minimal at first. He attempted to write sketches, but never quite found his niche. It was not until after the first series that Gilliam found himself doing animation for the very first time.

Glimpses of Python could be seen in *Do Not Adjust Your Set,* and it was certainly not an ordinary children's show.

"We'd do a little sort of cold opening, and then sketches, some of them very quick. There'd be regular features—I played a chef who cooked silly things, and Denise Coffey played Mrs. Black. Then there was a character called Captain Fantastic, who was a little man in a shabby mac who went around, having slightly magical powers, but not quite enough," reveals Palin.

"Other things were very much what became mainstream Python. We'd do a sketch about shop assistants trying to sell a suit which manifestly doesn't fit—I'd do all this spiel, `The jacket is lovely,' `But there's a sleeve missing,' `Ah, that's how they're wearing it this year.' Things like that. There was the man who is called to rescue someone who has fallen off a cliff and is hanging on by his fingernails, and the man who is sent to rescue him recognizes him from television, so he has this long talk about what programs he's been in, and all that, while the man's life is ebbing away. . . . Fairly run-of-the-mill stuff—we had to write them fairly fast."

Each of them was also involved with other projects while working on *Do Not Adjust Your Set.* Between the first and second series, Eric Idle and Terry Gilliam were involved with a fascinating failure of a show called *We Have Ways of Making You Laugh.* While Terry Jones and Michael Palin were doing the second series of *Do Not Adjust Your Set,* they were also collaborating on *The Complete and Utter History of Britain.* In addition, they were continuing to write sketches for a variety of other programs.

"That was our phase of being script doctors, open all hours, which really continued until just before Python," says Palin of the writing sessions with Jones.

"We had a break suddenly in 1969, when the second series of *Do Not Adjust Your Set* had finished, *The Two Ronnies* had finished, *The Complete and Utter History of Britain* had been done. We'd worked ourselves flat out, and it was just suddenly nice to have a bit of a breather. And then after the breather, Python came along!"

Do Not Adjust Your Set had prepared its writers for *Monty Python* better than they had realized. On January 28, 1968, Michael Palin told the *Sunday Times,* "Every time we write a sketch which we can't use on the programme because it offends one of those taboos, we just file it away. Very thrifty. We should be able to flog the lot to one of those adult comedy shows." Little did he realize at the time that they would soon be using some of that material in "one of those adult comedy shows" called *Monty Python's Flying Circus*.

 ## CRITICAL COMMENTS

"*Do Not Adjust Your Set*, Rediffusion's Thursday evening children's comedy series . . . has been running hitchless, each week proving itself one of the best children's comedy shows and also one of the funniest shows on television. Billed as 'grownup comedy for children,' it is consistently funnier than BBC-1's childish comedies for grownups like *At the Eleventh Hour* or *Twice a Fortnight*—or, for that matter, Rediffusion's own *At Last, the 1948 Show* . . . Producer Humphrey Barclay and writers Eric Idle, TerryJones, and Michael Palin have been able to build a steady following relying on word of mouth. And in one month, a sort of underground cult of adult viewers has developed. . . .

"Undoubtedly what strikes one most about the show is its professionalism. The slapstick routines have a merciful slickness. 'Captain Fantastic' is an uncanny pastiche of the comic-book heroes done in 'Perils of Pauline' silent picture style. . . . Beyond all of this technique, of course, it is funny. Humour is the art of surprise, and sketch after sketch ends with a surprise which is a delightful surprise in itself."

—Stanley Reynolds, *The Guardian*, January 26, 1968

"It's adult in a way that those late-night satirical shows never manage to be adult."

—*Sunday Times*, January 28, 1968

"One of the few inventive programmes on any channel was *Do Not Adjust Your Stocking*. The predominantly young cast of this cheerful, inconsequential show have an endearing undergraduate amateurishness and get away with the most appalling visual puns. They have, too, some original ideas. There was a delightful sequence in which many of the cliche Christmas cards . . . suddenly became animated in a frenetic chase. The documentaries about army training were pleasantly satirised in Father Christmas College where trainee Santa Clauses were shown practicing their chimney-pot drill under the instruction of regimental gnomes."

—Sylvia Clayton, *Daily Telegraph*, December 27, 1968

". . . Yesterday, the show included a new feature, some really clever animated cartoons done by Terry Gilliam. These cartoons were as good as you would get at any hour on television, the equal of cinema cartoons."

—Stanley Reynolds, *The Times*, April 3, 1969

WE HAVE WAYS OF MAKING YOU LAUGH

ERIC IDLE, TERRY GILLIAM. FIRST SHOW AUGUST 23, 1968.

"*We Have Ways of Making You Laugh* was very unfunny. We didn't have any ways of making them laugh!" recalls Eric Idle.

After the first series of *Do Not Adjust Your Set*, Humphrey Barclay set about creating a new show for a new network. Perhaps in a mood to experiment, he decided to develop a talk show that would include several comedy sketches, in addition to a house cartoonist who would do funny drawings of the guest panelists. From *Do Not Adjust Your Set*, he brought along Eric Idle to write and perform sketches and Terry Gilliam to do cartoons. "Humphrey went over to London Weekend Television and produced *We Have Ways of Making You Laugh*, with Frank Muir hosting," explains Gilliam. "Humphrey dragged me along to do cartoon sketches of the guest stars. Everybody would be sitting around making witty comments—the team was Frank Muir, Dick Vosburgh, Dennis Greene, and Eric—and the camera would look over my shoulder as I was drawing a cartoon of the person."

"It was the first show on London Weekend Television. It won the franchise, and it was the first show actually on the air," notes Idle.

When they performed the first show live, Idle says it worked perfectly. "It was very funny, the audience roared out in laughter. Strangely enough, Humphrey Barclay came back and said 'Well, congratulations, but unfortunately, it didn't go out—the unions pulled the plug.' We'd done this thing, so we said 'Why didn't you tell us?' 'We didn't want you to stop in case they put the plugs back in!' So after that, the show never really went as well again.*

"Gilliam used to sit around drawing sketches. I used to be a performer, and Frank would sit around with some guests—it was sort of a loose half chat, half comedy. People are always trying to combine chat and comedy, which never works," says Idle.

We Have Ways of Making You Laugh may be best remembered for giving the world Terry Gilliam's first animation. He had never done an animated film before, but the opportunity arose one week when the show featured a disc jockey who was notorious for terrible puns.

"He was obsessed with connecting links to records with one pun after another," notes Gilliam. "Dick Vosburgh collected three months' worth of this material, and he didn't know what to do with it, and I suggested an animated film. I had two weeks and four hundred pounds to do it, and so the only way I could do it was with cutouts. It was in black and white.

"It went out, and people had never seen anything like that. It was just amazing, the effect of going out to millions of people watching television. The immediate effect was all these people going 'Wow, this is incredible,' and they said 'Can you do another one for us?'"

That was the beginning of it all. Gilliam then followed it up with another film called *Beware the Elephant*. One of his earliest creations was visible during the Python stage shows, which featured a short cartoon titled "Christmas Cards." Consisting of figures and symbols from Christmas cards that come to life in typical Gilliam fashion, the film was originally done for *Do Not Adjust Your Stocking*, a holiday version of the series. So, from humble beginnings on *We Have Ways of Making You Laugh*, Terry Gilliam had established a niche for himself as an artist who could produce wonderful little cartoons.

*Even though Terry Jones and Michael Palin weren't involved with *We Have Ways of Making You Laugh*, they still managed to get caught up in the disastrous opening days of London Weekend Television.

"I had been signed up as an actor to work with the Two Ronnies on *Frost on Saturday*, which was a variety show with sketches and interviews and all that. I was a sort of fall guy for the Two Ronnies, so although I wasn't on the first night of London Weekend Television, which opened with *We Have Ways of Making You Laugh*, I was there on the second night with *Frost on Saturday*," reveals Palin.

"There was a strike, as happens when new television companies are on the air. They're a bit vulnerable, so they will call a strike. We carried on and produced this strike-breaking show, with heads of drama working the cameras. I remember Frank Muir, who was head of light entertainment, working as floor manager—it was like troupers carrying on while the shells were exploding above us. And it was just extraordinary that we got this show done!"

HOW TO IRRITATE PEOPLE

GRAHAM CHAPMAN, JOHN CLEESE, MICHAEL PALIN

After *At Last the 1948 Show*, Graham Chapman and John Cleese were writing and appearing in a number of TV and film projects. Cleese wasn't quite certain what he wanted to do. He knew he wanted to involve Connie Booth, who had recently moved to London from America, and he had also become interested in working with Michael Palin.

It was David Frost who stepped in again and suggested they develop the special that became *How to Irritate People*.

"David asked me to do it," explains Cleese. "Connie and I got married after our three-and-a-half-year courtship, a lot of which was conducted across the Atlantic, and it was the first thing I did when I got back, because I wanted her to be in it. I wrote some stuff, mainly with Graham Chapman

"Graham, Connie, and Michael Palin were the main actors, though I think Eric did some of it, and I think Barry Cryer was involved. I have no idea what it's like. When David told me that he wanted to put it out on video, I said to him `Look, I don't have time to go back and look at stuff I did twenty-five years ago—I don't have time to write the stuff I want to write today!' But one day I will go back and look at it and find out what it's like. Michael did. He said some of it stands up very well, some of it doesn't."

The video of *How to Irritate People* was released in Britain in early 1990 by David Frost, who was the executive producer, says Palin. "I had a look, and thought it had strengths and weaknesses, so we made a few cuts here and there and we put it out.

"Frost was quite important to things at that time. He had Cleese and Chapman under contract to write films and all that. He had a contract with Westinghouse Systems in America, and he wanted to break British humor in the States.

"He got Graham and John to write *How to Irritate People* for him, which was a number of sketches about getting into situations where people irritate you, such as waiters in restaurants being terribly fawning. One of them involved a husband sitting around the home and company coming around for dinner; the wife is getting him to tell a joke, and

he doesn't want to tell it, but as soon as he starts, she keeps correcting him. There were lots of nice things in it," relates Palin.

Another sketch was inspired by a real-life incident involving Michael Palin. He had bought a car, but when he started having problems with it, the salesman refused to accept that there was anything wrong. When he complained that the brakes were going out, the salesman told him "Oh, well, it's a new car, bound to happen."

Cleese and Chapman were both so taken by the story that they wrote a sketch around it for *How to Irritate People*, in which Palin played the car salesman. When the group was looking for old material to rewrite for *Monty Python's Flying Circus*, Chapman suggested substituting a dead parrot for a defective car, and it became a classic.

Chapman and Cleese wrote the script themselves. Palin and the rest of the cast were simply brought on as actors, as most of them were involved in other projects.

"The show was done in 1968, but things overlapped. We'd rehearse *Do Not Adjust Your Set* in the morning and do this in the afternoon—we'd just work all the hours God gave," Palin recalls.

"But it was very good. The script was the funniest thing, the most impressive selection of sketches I'd seen in a long while—intelligent and also very silly—all of the hallmarks of Cleese and Chapman's stuff. I was just asked to act in it, and I was very flattered to be asked—myself and Tim Brooke-Taylor and Connie Booth, John and Graham. . . . It was a wonderful thing to work on, but it all fell apart at the recording stage.

"Although we'd gotten the rehearsal done very smoothly, the actual shooting and recording was done very badly. John, who was doing the links, had to come out of character each time—he'd dress up as the linkman, do his one link, go into the next sketch, come out, take his clothes off, get dressed as the linkman, do that, change again. . . . Why they didn't do all the links together, God only knows, but it meant it went on for a very long time and put considerable pressure on all the cast. In the end, the audience was just leaving to catch their last buses home . . ." notes Palin.

"Unfortunately, it was not nearly as successful as I think it should have been, but it has some wonderful things in it, including some of the best work that Graham's ever done—very funny sketches. So it's worth it from that point alone"

How to Irritate People was also worth it in that it allowed Palin to collaborate with Cleese and Chapman to a significant extent. They would be working together again soon.

THE COMPLETE AND UTTER HISTORY OF BRITAIN

WRITTEN BY AND STARRING TERRY JONES AND MICHAEL PALIN. FIRST BROADCAST JANUARY 12, 1969, ON LONDON WEEKEND TELEVISION. FEATURING TERRY JONES, MICHAEL PALIN, WALLACE EATON, COLIN GORDON, RODDY MAUDE-ROXBY, DIANA QUICK, AND MELINDA MAYE. PRODUCED BY HUMPHREY BARCLAY. WRITTEN BY TERRY JONES AND MICHAEL PALIN. DIRECTED BY MAURICE MURPHY.

Terry Jones as a court jester, one of many roles played by him and Palin in **The Complete and Utter History Of Britain.** *Photo from the Collection of Terry Jones, used by permission*

While Terry Jones and Michael Palin were getting the second series of *Do Not Adjust Your Set* underway, they were asked to do *The Complete and Utter History of Britain*. Work on the two projects overlapped, and the sixth and final episode of the latter was broadcast just days before the first episode of the second series of *DNAYS*. Originally,

there were seven different *Complete and Utter Histories*, but the seven were eventually edited down to six when they were broadcast.

"Humphrey Barclay was again involved," notes Palin. "He'd been the man behind *Do Not Adjust Your Set*, and he was providing programs for the new London Weekend Television. He asked Terry and I what we'd ideally like to write, so we came up with this idea.

"The show's about history as if there had been television facilities around at that time, so we could have people interviewed on television, in the showers, after the Battle of Hastings. We had Samuel Pepys doing a chat show, and things like that. It was a nice format, but it didn't work nearly as well as it probably should have done."

Although *The Complete and Utter History of Britain* was the last major project that Palin and Jones would embark on before Monty Python, they still had to labor under the usual constraints of television before they could start breaking all the rules.

"*Complete and Utter History* was pre-Python in the sense that we were controlled in some way by the format," Palin explains. "We had to use whatever actors we could get rather than do the roles ourselves. I think the difference shows.

"People say sometimes that we were very selfish in Python, but at least we did it the way we wanted to, and it was much more indicative of what was really needed then than what we did before, which was to get guest actors in and hope that they would understand our humor, which they did not always do. And that's really what happened on

Complete and Utter History—we didn't get people who quite knew what we were on about. It had some nice stuff."

Terry Jones agrees with his partner's assessment of the series. "They weren't terribly successful, in my opinion. I think the scripts are really funny. In fact, somebody from Columbia Television was suggesting redoing the scripts, and there's some smashing material. We just didn't have control over it, and the actual casting wasn't very good.

"Mike and I were doing mostly anonymous subsidiary roles, and I personally think the people they had doing some of the other things were a bit heavy. They weren't quite in the spirit of the thing, though they were quite good performers."

Unfortunately, there is no real way to judge because, like so much British television in the 1960s, most of the shows have been lost. The programs combined film and video segments, and although Jones was enough of an archivist toobtain copies of the films, even he couldn't find the videotapes.

"In those days, there was no video, I couldn't get a hold of it. *The Complete and Utter Histories* themselves have disappeared; all that remains are the film inserts," reports Jones. It is frightening to think that if the same policy had been in effect at the BBC a few months later, *Monty Python's Flying Circus* might have been lost as well. *The Complete and Utter Histories* provided the last important link in the chain that led to *Monty Python*. John Cleese and Graham Chapman had finished *At Last the 1948 Show* and were writing and performing TV and films. Palin, Jones, Idle, and Gilliam had finished *Do Not Adjust Your Set* (and, in the case of Palin and Jones, *The Complete and Utter History of Britain*), and were similarly writing and performing in various projects in 1969.

"I think it was really the *Complete and Utter Histories* that got John saying `Why don't we do something together?'" explains Jones. "John particularly wanted to work with Mike, and Mike said `I write with Terry, can Terry come along too?' We just came as a package, and John and Graham said `Eric and Terry Gilliam can come along as well.' So in the end, Python was *At Last the 1948 Show* meets *Do Not Adjust Your Set.*"

Part Two

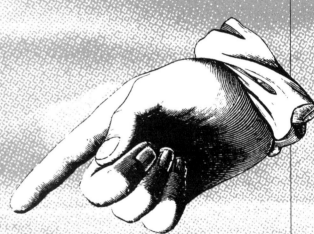

THE PYTHON YEARS

THE ROAD TO MONTY PYTHON

*B*y 1969 Graham Chapman, John Cleese, Terry Gilliam, Eric Idle, Terry Jones, and Michael Palin were all in demand.

As a result of their recent successes, the television networks were eager to work with them all, in whatever partnerships or teams they chose. Cleese had a virtual standing offer to do his own BBC series, while Thames Television was eager to continue working with the group from *Do Not Adjust Your Set* when that series ended.

"Thames wanted us to do a grown-up show, and we were talking about that when this BBC opportunity came up," explains Idle.

In fact, Idle says they were very close to creating a new Monty Python–like show for Thames when they were contacted by Cleese and Chapman; that effectively ended talks with the independent network and was the official beginning of *Monty Python's Flying Circus*. Thames has always regretted the loss.

"The controller of Thames, Jeremy Isaacs, who was head of Channel Four till recently, still kicks himself that they didn't get us," according to Idle. "I think we actually had a slot, and then they came back to us and said `No, we can't put you in that slot, but we do want you to continue to develop the show.' Meanwhile, Michael had been talking to John, I think, and so that all happened very quickly. Suddenly we were on with thirteen [shows], so Of wesaid to Thames `Sorry.' They still think they missed out on Python!"

Of course, any series the group would have developed for Thames would have been distinctly different from Python. At that stage, Thames was hoping for a grown-up version of *Do Not Adjust Your Set,* and it would not have involved Cleese and Chapman.

"At that point, it was more like David [Jason], Mike, Terry, me, and whatever we could develop as an adult show," reveals Idle. "It was a longer slot—I think three-quarters of an hour was talked about at one stage. And then it suddenly happened very quickly. Mike had been talking to John and done a show with John called *How to Irritate People.* So, John and Graham were a pair, and he was interested in Mike. Mike, Terry, and I were sort of put together, and I guess we dragged along Terry Gilliam for that, too."

The birth and growth of *Monty Python's Flying Circus* has been well documented in many interviews and books (including this author's *The First 20Ø Years of Monty Python*). Essentially, Barry Took, a producer and father figure to many of the younger writers and performers at the BBC, felt

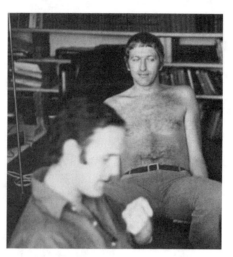

Rare, never-before-seen photos of the first Monty Python writing sessions, taken by Terry Jones at his London home. This shot shows a shirtless Graham Chapman in what Jones calls a typical pose, with a blurred John Cleese in the foreground . Photo copyright Terry Jones, used by permission

that combining the Cleese-Chapman team with Palin and Jones would be a worthy experiment. Cleese had always wanted to work with Palin, and a phone call to Palin one evening by Cleese laid the groundwork. They each brought along additional ingredients in the forms of Chapman, Idle, Jones, and, in an inspired touch, Gilliam. At their very first meeting with the BBC (arranged by Took), they were given a commitment for thirteen episodes.

During much of this time, Cleese had been under contract to David Frost; when he began to get interested in Python, Frost excused Cleese from the contract. That was the final obstacle, and *Monty Python's Flying Circus* was at last off the ground.

What followed were forty-five shows that revolutionized television comedy, five films, a series of stage shows, numerous books and records, and a rich legacy of individual projects that came after Monty Python. Again, the Python accomplishments have been detailed elsewhere. The rest of this volume concentrates on those solo projects.

Arthur Megapode's Flying Circus

Before skipping over the *Flying Circus* years, one aspect of its creation deserves further comment. Choosing a title for the series was a rather lengthy, frustrating process, and Chapman, Cleese, Gilliam, Idle, Jones, and Palin found they could never agree. Each had favorites, including *Owl Stretching Time; A Horse, a Spoon, and a Basin; Sex and Violence;* and *Bunn, Wackett, Buzzard, Stubble, and Boot.*

Python fans are familiar with many of these alternate titles, and the Pythons have spoken of many of them throughout the years. What those fans may not realize is that a lengthy list of titles was made at one point, most of them long forgotten—until now.

While researching this book, Terry Jones was kind enough to open his files to me. As I eagerly perused the various clippings, notes, and scripts, I encountered five pages of lined notebook paper filled with strange titles.

Terry casually explained that when the BBC insisted that they absolutely must decide on a name for the series immediately, they had a meeting (held at three-thirty on Thursday, according to the notes). It was a brainstorming session at which Terry acted as secretary, writing down all the possible suggestions for their new show. Terry favored using the name Arthur Megapode in one form or another, and each of the others had favorites as well. There were also many "Flying Circus" variations listed with the possibilities.

But, enough talk. Listed below, and revealed for the first time since 1969, are the alternative titles (as listed in Jones's notes) for the series that came to be known as *Monty Python's Flying Circus.*

This rare shot of the Pythons taking a break from one of their early writing sessions was taken by Terry Jones in the backyard of his London home. Michael Palin (left) apparently prefers to do his writing on the ground here, as Graham Chapman, John Cleese, and Eric Idle watch him pose for Jones's camera. Photo copyright Terry Jones, used by permission

1 2 3

Megapode's Flying Circus

Arthur Megapode's Flying Circus

Admiral Megapode's Flying Circus

The Sparkling Music and Stars Interview

The Political Satire Show

Ow! It's Megapode's Flying Circus!

Owl Stretching Time

Them

It's Them!

Gwen Dibley's Flying Circus

It's T.H.E.M.

Arthur Megapode's Cheap Show

The Horrible Earnest Megapode

Megapode's Cheap Show

Megapode's Panic Show

The Panic Show

The Plastic Mac Show

The Venus De Milo Panic Show

El Megapode's Flying Circus

Noris Heaven's Flying Circus

The Amazing Flying Circus

The 37 Foot Flying Circus

The Flying Circus

The Fly Circus

Vaseline Review

Vaseline Parade

The Keen Show

B B Circus

El Thompson's Flying Circus

Megapode's Flying Circus

Megapode's Atomic Circus

The Whizzo Easishow! (Guaranteed to last 1/2 hour! Money back if not!)

Human Circus

The Zoo Show [crossed out]

Arthur Megapode's Flying Circus

Arthur Buzzard's Flying Circus

Myrtle Buzzard's Flying Circus

The People Zoo [crossed out]

Arthur Megapode's Zoo

Charles IInd's Flying Circus

The Laughing Zoo [crossed out]

The Comedy Zoo [crossed out]

El Trotsky's Flying Circus

The Joke Zoo [crossed out]

El Megapode's Flying Circus

Nigel's Flying Circus [crossed out]

Brian's Flying Circus [crossed out]

Brian Stalin's Flying Circus

The Year of the Stoat

Limb's Flying Circus

The Plastic Mac Show

The Nose Show

El Moist's Flying Circus

Sydney Moist's Flying Circus

Stephen Furry's Flying Circus

Will Strangler's Flying Circus

Cynthia Fellatio's Flying Circus

El Turbot's Flying Circus

Norman Python's Flying Circus

Bob Python's Flying Circus

Ken

Monty Python's Flying Circus [the eventual winner]

O

The Down Show

Owl Stretching Time

The Full Moon Show [crossed out]

Ow! It's Colin Plint!

A rare shot of the Pythons with Steve Martin, performing in their last sketch together in September of 1989 for a Showtime 20th anniversary special. Graham Chapman was too ill to participate; the sketch was not used in the TV special because the Pythons were dissatisfied with the result. Photo from the Collection of Terry Jones and copyright Python Productions

The Beginning and the End

After the show's title was finally chosen, the first episode of *Monty Python's Flying Circus* aired October 5, 1969. The forty-fifth and final show was broadcast December 5, 1974. The end of the TV shows marked the end of Monty Python as a close-knit working ensemble, and each man began concentrating on his own solo career after 1974, although the group still reassembled for occasional movies and stage shows after that.

The year 1989 marked Monty Python's final appearance as a team. The six of them had not worked together since *The Meaning of Life* in 1983. There had been very casual discussions of another movie, and for a brief time, it looked as if the group members might perform their stage show again, this time in Russia. As John Cleese explained it, he didn't know—nor was he overly worried—whether their jokes would be understood; he just wanted to go to Russia.

None of these materialized, however. In fact, the final reunion of the Pythons took place during the taping of a twentieth anniversary special produced for the Showtime network in the United States. The retrospective was hosted by Steve Martin; at the conclusion of the hour, Martin opens a cabinet to reveal all six of the Pythons in hiding for a quick visual joke.

The original intention was quite different, however. The show was to feature an original sketch in which the Pythons portrayed schoolchildren, with Martin lecturing to them. Each former Python had been led to believe that the sketch had been written, or at least approved, by one of the others. Instead, they found themselves performing someone else's material, which they had always said they'd never do. The footage was unusable.

More important, by this time Graham Chapman's health was poor. When they gathered for the filming in early September 1989, Graham thought he had begun his recovery from the cancer that was soon to take his life. Although he was in good spirits, he was quite weak and his appearance was very gaunt, and he was confined to a wheelchair. The others buoyed Graham's spirits with talk of another Python film, and his morale was high for weeks afterward. Any opportunities for new Monty Python projects ended with his death on October 4, 1989, one day shy of the twentieth anniversary of the first broadcast. Terry Jones called it "the worst case of party-pooping I've ever seen."

Part Three

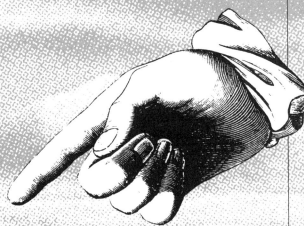

AFTER MONTY PYTHON

TAKING
OFF

*E*ven while all six cast members were working on *Monty Python's Flying Circus,* they continued writing and performing for TV and films.

John Cleese and Graham Chapman each wrote separately for Ronnie Barker and for the *Doctor* series. Cleese picked up occasional acting assignments; and at one point, Chapman was simultaneously writing for *The Two Ronnies, Doctor,* and *Monty Python,* literally working morning, noon, and night. Eric Idle was producing his own series, *Radio Five on Radio One,* a radio show in which he wrote and performed virtually every role. (In many ways, it was a precursor to his *Rutland Weekend Television.*) Terry Gilliam was producing animation for Marty Feldman.

Michael Palin and Terry Jones also did occasional TV writing, including a play called *Secrets,* which aired on BBC-2 in August 1973. Fifteen years later, it was turned into a film titled *Consuming Passions*; the story involves a chocolate factory that discovers a huge new demand for their product after a workman falls into one of their vats. Palin and Jones also appeared on a sports-oriented comedy album called *Funny Game, Football* during Python, but all of them stayed committed to the show until after the third series.

John Cleese was the first to leave *Monty Python's Flying Circus.* He claims he became restless late in the second series, though he didn't actually quit until after the third series ended. The others did the final six shows without him. Most of the Pythons agree that even though some of the material was very good, it was probably a mistake to do the fourth series without Cleese.

Although Cleese says he only intended to quit the TV series and always planned to continue with Python films, the others dispute his claim. What they cannot dispute, however, is that John Cleese pursued his solo career with a vengeance. Less than two years after he left *Monty Python,* he began the television series *Fawlty Towers,* which would remain his biggest success until the movie *A Fish Called Wanda.* The others were not long in following, and before long, their talents manifested themselves in a wide variety of projects.

This section is organized chronologically, followed by an alphabetical listing of its contents with the year of release.

Michael Palin is shown here in Jamaica during the writing of Meaning of Life, 1982. Photos Copyright Terry Jones

The Seventies

FUNNY GAME, FOOTBALL

INCLUDES TERRY JONES AND MICHAEL PALIN. FEATURES "THE GROUP" (TERRY JONES, MICHAEL PALIN, ARTHUR MULLARD, BRYAN PRINGLE, BILL TIDY, JOE STEEPLES, MICHAEL WALE). WRITTEN BY JOE STEEPLES, BILL TIDY, MICHAEL WALE. MUSIC BY NEIL INNES. (1972) CHARISMA PERSPECTIVE CS4, (1972) EP CHARISMA CB 197

SIDE ONE

Piraeus Football Club (song)

Crunch!

Rangers Abroad

An Open Letter to George Best

The Missionary

Sir Alf Speaks

World War III

Newsnight With Coleman

Soccer Laureate

Bovver Boys (song)

SIDE TWO

Scilly Season

Government Policies

I Remember It Well

Floor's the Limit

Director's Song

Blackbury Town

A Joke

Michael Palin and Terry Jones are featured throughout this (English) football-oriented comedy album; much of the humor may be challenging to people not familiar with English football. Highlights include Jones portraying a Pepperpot visited by "The Missionary," who tries to convert her to football; "I Remember It Well" features Palin and Jones reminiscing. "Floor's the Limit" is a Pythonesque quiz show with Palin as host and Jones as the unfortunate contestant answering questions on football.

"I've totally forgotten about it," admits Terry Jones. "Bill Tidy is a very good cartoonist, and Michael Wale is a radio commentator nowadays. And Michael and Joe were a couple of journalists. I think Mike and I were just keen to do a bit of work, but I really have no idea!"

SECRETS

A PLAY BY TERRY JONES AND MICHAEL PALIN. FIRST BROADCAST AUGUST 14, 1973, ON BBC-2. WRITTEN BY TERRY JONES AND MICHAEL PALIN. PRODUCED BY MARK SHIVAS. DIRECTED BY JAMES CELLAN JONES.

A young man goes to work at an old, traditional chocolate factory that has been taken over by a conglomerate. Several men accidentally fall into a vat of chocolate, and before anyone can prevent it, the chocolates are shipped out and sold. Customer response to this new flavor is highly favorable, and so after unsuccessfully attempting to reproduce the same results with beef and pork, the company tries to find available bodies for their recipe.

(For a more detailed synopsis, see 1988's *Consuming Passions*.)

 ## NOTES

This black comedy was penned by the Jones and Palin team for a BBC-2 series called *Black and Blue*; while they were doing *Monty Python*, they were still doing outside writing like this.

"It was a TV play commissioned in 1973 by a guy called Mark Shivas," explains Palin. "He commissioned drama at the BBC, he's quite a well-known producer. He had an idea for a series for BBC-2 called *Black and Blue*; it was going to be what it says, stories that were supposed to be quite tough and unconventional, emphasizing black humor—and I suppose blue humor as well, though the blue didn't come out as well as the black.

"They asked Terry and I if we would like to write one of them in 'seventy-three, just after Python. It was quite a compliment to be asked to do something in a mainstream drama series that had a comedy intent as well. So, we came up with this story about the people falling into the vat at a chocolate factory!"

Palin says they tried to inject a more thoughtful element to the story too.

"It was really intended to be more than anything else—apart from a good farce, there was supposed to be farce in it as well—something that had an element of truth or insight into the way that modern companies operated. Once the most dreadful damage had happened, they couldn't stop it because of their modern methods, so the implication of these people falling in went all the way through," he relates.

In 1988 the teleplay was adapted for the big screen as *Consuming Passions*, and expanded to allow for more elaborate sets and locations and also to expand some characters.

ROMANCE WITH A DOUBLE BASS

STARRING JOHN CLEESE AND CONNIE BOOTH. (1974) 40 MINUTES

Princess Constanza..Connie Booth
Musician Smychkov..John Cleese
Count Alexei ....Graham Crowden
Musician Razmakhaikin ....Desmond Jones
Maestro Lakeyich...Freddie Jones
Leader of the Orchestra ....Jonathan Lynn
Major Domo ....John Moffatt
Musician Zhuchkov..Andrew Sachs

Screenplay adapted by John Cleese, Robert Young, and Connie Booth. From an original screenplay by Bill Owen. Adapted from a short story by Anton Chekhov. Produced by Ian Gordon and David King. Directed by Robert Young. Produced by the Pacific Arts Corp. Inc./Presented by Anton Films.

Smychkov carries his double bass through the woods, formally dressed with a top hat. At the castle ahead, a betrothal party is being planned for the princess, and the orchestra is set to play that evening.

When Smychkov arrives, he is sent off and told to come back later. He goes down to the river and decides to go swimming, wearing only his top hat. As he swims along, he spies the beautiful princess asleep on the shore. When she wakes, she thinks she is alone, and goes for a swim. A thief watches her and runs off with her clothes, and Smychkov discovers his clothes have been stolen as well. He hides from the princess, who stumbles onto him, and, hiding from each other's sight, he promises to get her back to her castle.

The princess hides inside the bass case, and he takes turns carrying the case and doubling back to carry his bass. During a swim, they discuss music, and the princess reveals her fears about her upcoming wedding.

Later the maestro and another musician spot Smychkov dashing through the woods with his case. They insist on carrying the bass case to the castle for him, despite his protestations, as he can't reveal the princess is inside naked. He covers himself with the bass, he makes his way into the castle through the kitchen. He finds some ill-fitting clothes and rushes to rehearsal, where his case—with the princess hiding inside—is waiting. He suddenly leaves the rehearsal and sneaks up to the princess's bedroom for a gown and shoes.

Smychkov arrives again to begin rehearsing, but they are ordered to begin playing when the count arrives early. While they are playing, Smychkov is apprehended for stealing the princess's gown and shoes. Before they take him away, the princess arrives, fully dressed, and meets the count. At her request, Smychkov and the orchestra resume playing, and he is exonerated.

 ## NOTES

Based on a Chekhov short story and adapted for film by John Cleese and Connie Booth, this film short (actually, it could probably be considered a four-reeler, since it runs about forty minutes) marked their first major collaboration following Python. In terms of their professional collaboration, it paved the way for *Fawlty Towers* the following year, although there are few visible similarities in the two projects.

Romance With a Double Bass lies somewhere between a short subject and a feature, which is one reason it is not always easy to track down. (The extensive nudity by both Cleese and Booth also limits its venues.) Movie theaters in Britain often run shorts before the main features (an uncommon practice in America today), which is where *Romance With a Double Bass* was usually presented.

The short was shot on location during October 1974 in Wiltshire at Wilton House and Somerley Estate.

"Connie and I had split up, but a very nice actor called Bill Owen came to me with this lovely little Chekhov short story, and he and I discussed it. I then worked on the story, along with Connie. We brought in Robert Young, and we eventually shot it in the autumn of seventy-four. It was shot in color and with sound and it lasted forty-five minutes, and the whole thing cost 16,000 pounds, of which I put up a thousand and a fellow called David King put up the other fifteen. It was put out in England with *The Eiger Sanction,* and was quite politely and nicely reviewed in passing. Over the years, we've gotten the odd hundred pounds coming back in royalties."

Cleese recalls the filming as an enjoyable experience.

"It was an extraordinarily happy collaboration. Like all things that are small, cheap, and done in a good spirit because people want to do it, rather than in terms of money, it was a success. It was a very happy collaboration, and directed by a very good guy, Robert Young," Cleese enthuses.

The film came close to never being completed, and the unit was actually lucky to finish it.

"It was hair-raising in retrospect, because I think we had a ten-day schedule, and if we'd lost another hour with rain, we wouldn't have been able to finish the film," he recalls with a laugh.

"We did it by the skin of our teeth, and it's really quite good. If we'd had time for about five more setups in the ballroom in the final scene, it would be that much better, but for the money, I think it's pretty amazing. It was a very happy little endeavor.

"As far as I remember, we paid the technicians, but the thirteen principals, including Henry Herbert, who loaned his house for the purpose of the making of the film, shared royalties and didn't take any fees. A very happy occasion, and the first time I worked with Robert Young, but certainly not the last—he directed a lot of my commercials, and I intend to make features with him!"

BERT FEGG'S NASTY BOOK FOR BOYS AND GIRLS

BY TERRY JONES AND MICHAEL PALIN. PUBLISHED BY EYRE METHUEN (1974). (PUBLISHED AS DR. FEGG'S NASTY BOOK OF KNOWLEDGE *IN THE U.S. IN 1976; RE-RELEASED WITH ADDITIONAL MATERIAL IN 1985 AS* DR. FEGG'S ENCYCLOPAEDIA OF *ALL* WORLD KNOWLEDGE *BY PETER BEDRICK BOOKS—HARPER & ROW; ISBN 0-87226-005-4/0-413-56430-4)*

The book includes a variety of material, profusely illustrated, and is ostensibly a children's book hosted by a rather unsavory, violent hulk known as Dr. Bert Fegg. The contents, arranged alphabetically, range from "Alcoholic Dogs" to "Zero-Rated, I Was Hitler's Double."

Some of the highlights include "Anatomy," an advertisement for Dr. Fegg's Permanent Head Restorer, "Cookery," "The Famous Five Go

The original British edition of the **Fegg** *book*

Pillaging," "Learn to Speak French in Four Minutes," a board game called Plaguo!, "The National Geographical Magazine," "Across the Andes by Frog," a one-page History of the World, "Make Your Own 747," magic tricks performed by The Great Feggo, a pantomime entitled "Aladdin and His Terrible Problem" by George Bernard Fegg, "Soccer—My Way by the Supremes," a Captain Fegg comic strip, and "A Cowboy Story."

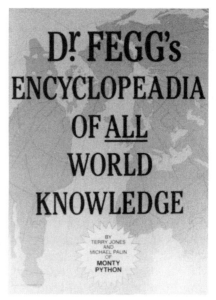

The first American edition

The most recent version

 ## NOTES

A great deal of the material that Terry Jones and Michael Palin were creating during the Monty Python years couldn't be used on the TV show, and they decided some of it could best be presented in a book. They had previously been involved in the production of the Monty Python books, and came up with the idea of a parody of children's books, with "Bert Fegg" as a framing device for the material.

"Bert Fegg was a character I used to draw in school," explains Jones, "one of the comics that I used to draw in math lessons. Bert Fegg was this terribly, incredibly violent character that I invented and drew comics about to while away tedious math lessons which I never listened to—I don't know how I managed to pass the exams.

"I just suggested that it might be interesting to write a book. The idea behind it was to write a children's book that adults would like as well, like *Do Not Adjust Your Set* was a children's television show that adults got hooked into. That was the original idea, and I was terribly angry that it got sold in the humor section rather than the children's section!"

 ## CRITICAL COMMENTS

". . . If the truth were known, Dr. Fegg is just a wee bit disappointed with the way in which the book has turned out. He wanted his book to give readers a really `Nasty shock' . . . Unfortunately, several articles had to be deleted on legal advice. . . . Despite these unfortunate losses, Dr. Fegg still thinks the book is worth 1-pound 50—of anybody's money."

—Anna Pavord, *The Observer Magazine*, October 20, 1974

RUTLAND WEEKEND TELEVISION

CONCEIVED, WRITTEN, AND PERFORMED BY ERIC IDLE WITH NEIL INNES. FIRST SERIES OF SIX SHOWS BEGAN AIRING MAY 12, 1975. SECOND SERIES OF SEVEN SHOWS BEGAN AIRING NOVEMBER 12, 1976. CHRISTMAS WITH RUTLAND WEEKEND TELEVISION HOLIDAY SPECIAL (WITH SPECIAL GUEST GEORGE HARRISON) AIRED DECEMBER 26, 1975.

By the end of the third season of *Monty Python's Flying Circus*, John Cleese felt it was time to leave; after the fourth series of six shows, Eric Idle knew it was time to bow out, and the remaining Pythons reluctantly agreed. Idle was ready to strike out on his own, and a radio project he had been working on during *Python* gave him an idea for a TV series.

"I'd done a radio show somewhere in the middle of *Python*," says Idle. "There were four radio stations in England, so I did a show called *Radio Five*. Now there *is* a Radio Five, but in those days, that was a joke. I used to come on to Radio One, which was the pop music station, about as hip as Dick Clark, and do an hour's show a week. I had lots of different voices which I'd prerecord, with rock music playing in between. It would take me hours—it would take me ten hours to record one hour's worth of material, because I had to play all of the voices, and in those days the technology was really primitive, and we didn't have anything like dubbing. If you were doing both voices in a sketch, you had to lay all that voice down and time yourself back and forth.

"That was what sort of set me thinking about independent stations. So, *Rutland Weekend Television* seemed to be a good takeoff on it. *Rutland Weekend Television* was actually a title suggested by John Cleese. I paid him a pound for it. I'd been doing one or two appearances on what was called *Up Sunday*, a late-night Sunday satire show on BBC-2, which was put on not by the Light Entertainment Department but by Presentation, which would just make announcements and say 'Here on BBC-2 . . .'"

A series based on a very small TV station was later used in America by SCTV, but Idle says his show came first.

"Let's get the order straight!" he laughs. "No, *SCTV* is the same idea—you just use a minor television station as a comedy device."

Rutland Weekend Television was done on an extremely tight budget, and Idle was forced to make do with what they had available. Although he wrote all the scripts himself, Neil Innes was along to perform original music in each show, most of it comedic, and both of them struggled with the budget offered them by the Presentation Department.

"We did the only comedy show Presentation's ever done, and we did it in a *tiny* little studio about the size of the weather forecast studio next door on the fourth floor of the BBC. We did a series for about 30,000 quid," Idle laughs. "It shows a bit, but it's really very ingenious if you know how little was spent on it. We'd run on tape, there was never an audience participating. I was just looking at some of the highlights last week—I'd selected some highlights at one stage, and [there are] some really very respectable sketches.

"The second series was slightly difficult, we went back and discovered that they'd put us in a studio in Bristol! Neil Innes would do a song or two a week, and he'd be in the sketches. It was pretending to be a TV station, and we had dramas and documentaries. It seems to have gotten quite a cult following now. I hear a lot about it more and more these days, but because there was no audience laughter, I never quite knew how funny it was, I could never tell, and now there's all these pressures to re-release it."

Unlike *Fawlty Towers* and *Ripping Yarns*, *Rutland Weekend Television* was never shown on American television or available on videocassette.

"It's never run in the States because I always had the American rights," he explains. "They wouldn't pay me any money, so I insisted I had the American rights, and I wouldn't let them use it."

Between the two series, Idle did a *Christmas with Rutland Weekend Television* special that featured a friend he had made earlier in the year—George Harrison.

"There's a *terrific* gag in that Christmas special. We had a wonderful time, we'd never been so legless doing that show. We were pissed through most of it. It's not that funny a show, but there's a wonderful moment where I keep trying to say `Our special guest, George Harrison,' and he keeps saying no, he wants to sing a pirate song. `No, no, we want you to be George Harrison, come on,' and so right at the end of the show `And now, ladies and gentlemen, George Harrison,' and he comes on with his white things, his Bangla Desh robes, and plays [intro to *My Sweet Lord*] [sings] `I want to be a pirate, a pirate's life for

me, all my friends are pirates and we sail the BBC. I've got a Jolly Roger, it's black and wide and vast, so get out of your skull and crossbones and I'll run it up your mast,' and we go `Stop, stop!'

"I'm glad to say that's an Idle-Harrison composition and it's actually in *Songs by George Harrison,* the illustrated book. `The Pirate Song.' It's a very funny gag, because you just do not expect him to launch into— he looks *so good*, you know, he looks the same, with the full band and everything. It's a very good gag. . . ."

THE RUTLAND WEEKEND SONGBOOK

BY ERIC IDLE AND NEIL INNES. (1975) BBC RECORDS REB 233 (U.K.), (1976) ABC/PASSPORT RECORDS PPSD-98018 (U.S.).

SIDE ONE

L'Amour Perdue

Gibberish

Wash with Mother/Front Loader

Say Sorry Again

The Rutles in "Rutles for Sale" ("I Must Be in Love")

24 Hours in Tunbridge Wells

The Fabulous Bingo Brothers

In Concrete—Concrete Jungle Boy

The Children of Rock and Roll

Startime—Stoop Solo

Song O' the Insurance Men

Closedown

SIDE TWO

I Give Myself to You

Communist Cooking/Johnny Cash Live at Mrs. Fletcher's

The Old Gay Whistle Test

Accountancy Shanty

Football/Boring

Good Afternoon/L'Amour Perdue Cha Cha Cha

Disco—the Hard to Get

Closedown—the Song O' the Continuity Announcers

This soundtrack of the TV series contains plenty of highlights from the shows, including "I Must Be in Love," the song that started the Rutles (although it doesn't contain the Idle and Harrison "Pirate Song"). The songs are by Neil Innes (though several are co-written with Eric Idle), while the comedic bits are by Eric Idle.

RUTLAND DIRTY WEEKEND BOOK

BY ERIC IDLE. PUBLISHED BY METHUEN/TWO CONTINENTS (1976), ISBN 0-846-70185-5/0-413-36570-0. CONTAINS MATERIAL INSPIRED BY THE TV SERIES, WITH NEIL INNES, AND A GUEST PAGE BY MICHAEL PALIN.

The book includes

"The Vatican Sex Manual,"

"A History of *Rutland Weekend Television* from 1300,"

"The Rutland *TV Times*,"

"Saturday *RWT* World of Sport Listings,"

"Sunday Listings—Misprint Theatre presents `The Wife of Christ,'"

"*Rutland Stone*,"

"The Wonderful World of Sex,"

"New Publications from Rutland University Press," . . . and much more.

 ## NOTES

"The *Rutland Dirty Weekend Book* expanded the sketches on the series," explains Idle, "and a lot of the photographs were from the series."

One section of the book, "*The Vatican Sex Manual*," was excerpted and featured in Playboy when the book was released in America; it sold well, even though the series hadn't come out in the U.S.

"I wrote lots of new material altogether [for the book]—elaborate parodies of *Rolling Stone*, *Who's Had Who in Television*, phony biographies of fictitious people, `The Vatican Sex Manual'—I just spent a lot of time writing new stuff. It sold very well indeed, and still has a lot of good laughs. . . ."

FAWLTY TOWERS

CONCEIVED, WRITTEN, AND PERFORMED BY JOHN CLEESE AND CONNIE BOOTH. FIRST SERIES OF SIX SHOWS BEGAN AIRING SEPTEMBER 19, 1975. SECOND SERIES OF SIX SHOWS BEGAN AIRING FEBRUARY 19, 1979.

Basil Fawlty	John Cleese
Sybil Fawlty	Prunella Scales
Manuel	Andrew Sachs
Polly	Connie Booth
Major Gowen	Ballard Berkeley
Miss Tibbs	Gilly Flower
Miss Gatsby	Renee Roberts
Terry	Brian Hall

Written by John Cleese and Connie Booth. Produced and directed by John Howard Davies, Bob Spiers, and Douglas Argent.

SHOW 1:

"A Touch of Class" As Sybil reminds Basil to hang a picture, he reprimands Manuel for putting too much butter on the trays for the guests. Basil tries to hang the picture, but has to prepare the bill for a couple who are checking out in a hurry, because they didn't get their wake-up call.

Basil gives the newspaper to the major and complains about the class of guests the hotel has been getting. Basil has placed an expensive ad in a magazine to attract a higher class of clientele. After arguing with Sybil, he reluctantly signs in the very nonaristocratic Danny Brown, and goes back to hanging the picture.

In the dining room, Basil reluctantly assists Manuel and Polly. He is called to the reception desk where he testily signs in a guest. When he finds out the guest is Lord Melbury, he fawns all over him, and deposits Melbury's valuables in the hotel safe. He then orders the Wareing family from their table in the middle of a meal in order to give the table to the unimpressed Melbury.

After accidentally pulling a chair out from under Lord Melbury, Basil happily agrees to cash a £200 check for him, unbeknownst to Sybil. Basil sends Polly to the bank in town, where she runs into Danny Brown, who shows her a badge and points out Lord Melbury entering a jewelry store.

Later, in the hotel bar, Lord Melbury admires Basil's coin collection, and offers to take it and have it appraised, while Mr. Wareing tries to order a drink. Polly takes Basil aside and says she's learned that Melbury is a con man, and Basil refuses to believe it. While Basil forbids her, Sybil opens the hotel safe and discovers bricks in Melbury's bag.

Furious, Basil steps out to the reception desk to find new guests Sir Richard and Lady Morris. When Melbury suddenly appears, Basil launches into a tirade. As he screams, Melbury runs off, pursued by policemen, and Basil kicks him. Frightened, Sir Richard and Lady Morris leave, despite shouts by Basil. He returns sullenly to hang the picture when Mr. Wareing appears, still asking about his drinks.

Also featuring:

Lord Melbury	Michael Gwynn
Danny Brown	Robin Ellis
Sir Richard Morris	Martin Wyldeck
Mr. Watson	Lionel Wheeler
Mr. Wareing	Terence Conoley
Mr. Mackenzie	David Simeon

SHOW 2:

"The Builders" As Polly works behind the desk and Manuel practices his English, Basil and Sybil prepare to depart for a weekend holiday in Paignton. Basil warns Miss Tibbs and Miss Gatsby there are builders coming, and criticizes one of Polly's drawings.

Basil receives a phone call from O'Reilly, the builder he has hired to put a door through to the kitchen; he cautions that his wife thinks he is using another builder, Stubbs, as Sybil doesn't like O'Reilly. Basil also warns Polly, and they leave.

Later that day, while Polly naps, Manuel takes charge behind the desk. A garden gnome is delivered, and when the builders arrive, Manuel takes charge. Naturally, the job is done wrong, and Basil has a fit when he arrives back the next morn-

John Cleese as Basil Fawlty and Andrew Sachs as Manuel in a classic moment from episode two, "The Builders." Photo Copyright BBC

ing. He calls O'Reilly, who has to come over and correct the job before Sybil arrives back at noon.

Unfortunately, Sybil arrives back early and spots the mess. Basil tries to blame it on Stubbs, but Sybil learns the truth. She launches into a tirade against O'Reilly and orders him to leave, then goes off for her golf game. Basil asks him to stay and complete the job, despite Sybil.

The next morning, the work has been completed. Sybil, who had already called Stubbs, is amazed. When Stubbs arrives, he is impressed, until he finds out that a wooden lintel was used for the supporting wall, and it could give way at any moment. As Sybil shouts at him, Basil runs off, thinking of going to Canada.

Also featuring:

O'Reilly	David Kelly
Lurphy	Michael Cronin
Jones	Michael Halsey
Kerr	Barney Dorman
Stubbs	James Appleby
Delivery Man	George Lee

SHOW 3:

"The Wedding Party" Basil sits at the bar with the major, as Mrs. Peignoir, an attractive French antique dealer, flirts with him; Manuel has been given the night off for his birthday.

Basil walks in as Polly is kissing her boy-friend good-bye, and he looks through her sketchbook, disapproving. When a young couple, Alan and Jean, arrive to check in, Basil insists on separate rooms because they aren't married. Sybil enters and offers them adjacent rooms while Manuel tries to deliver a thank-you speech for his birthday present, an umbrella.

Upstairs, Polly runs into her old friends Alan and Jean, who have arrived for a wedding. Alan tries to find a place where he can buy batteries for his razor, but Basil naturally misconstrues the matter.

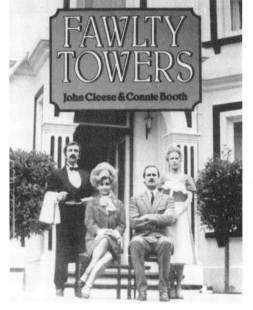

Later, Basil gets out of bed to answer the door, finding a tipsy Mrs. Peignoir. When he picks up her purse and she inadvertently sits on his back, Alan and Jean enter, and Basil tries in vain to cover his embarrassment. He finally gets up again and ends up grappling on the floor with a drunken Manuel, and Alan stumbles onto the scene.

At breakfast the next morning, Manuel is hung over, while Basil serves Mrs. Peignoir, who asks him to fix the window in her room. Mean-while, Jean's parents, Mr. and Mrs. Lloyd, are registering with Sybil, and plan to go to the wedding that afternoon. As Basil carries their bags upstairs to their room, he looks inside to see Jean hugging Mr. Lloyd and misunderstands. He prevents Mrs. Lloyd from going to her room and a few minutes later sees Polly embracing him as well.

Basil stands outside of Alan's room, where Alan massages Jean as Polly tries on a dress; he is horrified at the sounds coming from inside. A few minutes later he tells them all to leave and fires Polly, until Sybil explains his mistake, and he has to apologize to everyone, blaming Sybil for it all.

Later that night Sybil has gone off to stay with her friend Audrey. Basil promises to fix Mrs.

Peignoir's window, but as he works on it, Sybil enters downstairs. Mrs. Peignoir flirts with him, but when he finishes, he locks himself in his bedroom. Downstairs, Sybil hears a noise, but when she knocks on the bedroom door, Basil thinks it is Mrs. Peignoir, and tries to get her to leave. He finally discovers it is actually Sybil, and she makes him go downstairs to check on the noise.

In the darkened lobby, Basil hits Manuel with a frying pan, and Jean, Alan, and the Lloyds enter unexpectedly, as Basil, in shirt and underpants, sits across the prone Manuel.

Also featuring:

Alan ....Trevor Adams
Jean ....April Walker
Mrs. Peignoir...Yvonne Gilan
Mr. Lloyd ....Conrad Phillips
Rachel Lloyd..Diana King
Customer ....Jay Neill

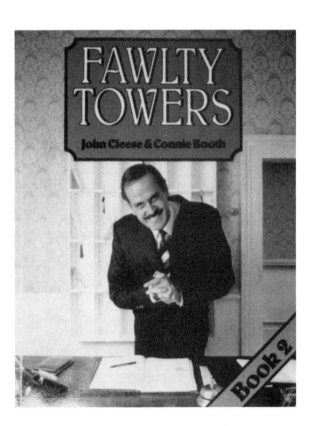

SHOW 4:

"The Hotel Inspectors" One of the guests, Mr. Hutchison, asks Basil to call him a taxi for the afternoon and draw him a map to his destination, which increasingly irritates Basil. Sybil checks in Mr. Walt, another guest, and Basil's irritation grows.

Sybil says that her friend Audrey has heard that there is a group of three hotel inspectors in the area, warns Basil to exercise a little courtesy. As Basil tries to use the phone, Mr. Hutchison approaches and asks him to reserve the television that evening so that he can watch a documentary. Basil refuses, but as he starts to get angry, he suddenly connects Mr. Hutchison with the hotel inspectors and becomes very servile.

During lunch, Basil grovels over the demanding Mr. Hutchison, at the expense of Mr. Walt. Mr. Hutchison complains about the food, his drink, and the wine, while Basil continues to fawn. Sybil calls him away and informs him that Mr. Hutchison is actually a spoon salesman. Basil angrily serves him, although the orders are mixed up.

Basil, suddenly suspecting that Mr. Walt is actually the hotel inspector, redirects his fawning. When Mr. Hutchison complains about being served an omelette that he didn't order, Basil accidentally knocks him out while trying to stop his loud protests. They carry Hutchison to the bar, where he revives enough to take a swing at Basil and then storms upstairs. Mr. Walt is making a phone call and observes the incident, and Basil tries to bribe him not to mention it in his book. Mr. Walt says he is an outboard motor salesman, and Basil runs to the kitchen.

Three men, the real inspectors, enter the lobby. As Hutchison tries to leave, Basil emerges and throws a pie at his face, then fills his briefcase with cream. He throws Hutchison out, kisses Manuel gratefully, and spots the three men.

Also featuring:

Mr. Hutchison	Bernard Cribbins
Mr. Walt	James Cossins
John	Geoffrey Morris
Brian	Peter Brett

SHOW 5:

"Gourmet Night" Basil is in front of the hotel trying to fix his car, when Manuel calls him to the telephone. Just before Basil can finally pick it up, Sybil grabs it. It is Andre, a restauranteur, and Sybil thanks him for recommending Kurt, their new chef. She invites Andre and Kurt to dinner on Sunday, then orders Basil to take the car in for repairs; Polly is pleased that she has sold a sketch—Kurt has bought her portrait of Manuel.

At Sunday dinner, the guests include Andre and the Heaths, with their eleven-year-old son Ronald, who complains about the food. Sybil decides to hold a Gourmet Night. Andre says hello to Kurt in the kitchen and warns him about his drinking; Kurt introduces him to his friend Manuel and kisses Manuel on top of the head.

Basil fidgets as the Gourmet Night is about to begin; due to cancellations (and Basil including "No Riff-Raff" in the ad), there are only four guests, Colonel and Mrs. Hall and the Twitchens. Mr. Twitchen is one of Torquay's leading Rotarians. After chasing Miss Tibbs and Miss Gatsby to their room, Basil fawns over the guests. Polly interrupts him to let him know that Kurt has gotten drunk, because he's in love with Manuel and Manuel has rejected him. Basil finds Kurt unable to function, so Polly suggests that he call Andre's restaurant to prepare the food and pick it up with his car. Andre agrees, though all he can cook is the duck.

In the dining room, the unctuous Basil explains to his guests that the revised menu consists only of duck. In the kitchen, they work to prepare the vegetables, while Manuel attempts to serve the guests. Mr. Twitchen finds a hair in his mousse, while Mrs. Hall's mullet is raw.

Basil drives over and picks up the duck and sauces, but when he returns, he drops it, and Manuel accidentally steps in it and walks, ruining it. Basil makes Sybil call Andre for another one, and drives over. Basil takes the wrong tray, while back at the restaurant, Manuel plays the guitar, and Polly does some singing in order to entertain the guests. Basil's car won't start, and he beats on it furiously with a tree branch.

Finally, Basil runs back to the hotel, places the platter on the serving trolley, and wheels it proudly into the dining room, where he unveils a dessert instead of a duck before their astonished eyes.

Also featuring:

Andre	Andre Maranne
Kurt	Steve Plytas
Colonel Hall	Allan Cuthbertson
Mrs. Hall	Ann Way
Mr. Twitchen	Richard Caldicot
Mrs. Twitchen	Betty Huntley-Wright
Mr. Heath	Jeffrey Segal
Mrs. Heath	Elizabeth Beson
Master Heath	Tony Page

SHOW 6:

"The Germans" Basil visits Sybil in the hospital, where she is being operated on for an ingrown toenail. She reminds Basil of the fire drill the next day, of German guests arriving, and to hang a moose head on the wall. The doctor tells Basil that it is a simple operation but will be quite painful afterward, and Basil rubs his hands in satisfaction.

At the hotel, Basil and the major discuss women, while Polly gets her German book to study: Basil and the major reveal their mutual distaste for Germans. Basil tries to hang the moose head, and Manuel enters. When he practices his English, the major thinks it is the moose head talking and is perplexed.

The next morning Basil tries once again to mount the moose head, while he and Polly warn the guests about the fire drill. He accidentally sets off the burglar alarm on the hotel safe; he has to explain to the guests that the fire drill hasn't started yet, and demonstrates the fire bell. He explains that the actual fire drill will begin in thirty seconds, at which time the guests leave. Meanwhile, Manuel sets the kitchen on fire, but Basil won't believe it when Manuel tells him. When the guests return, complaining, Basil has to tell them all that the hotel actually is on fire, but he can't work the fire extinguisher.

Basil wakes up in the hospital, because he had suffered a concussion. He insults the sister and tries to go back to the hotel; the doctor puts him in bed, but Basil sneaks away. At the hotel, the Germans have arrived, and Basil attempts to deal with them, cautioning Polly not to mention the war. While Polly calls the doctor, Basil ushers the Germans into the dining room, and inadvertently manages to work the war into nearly every sentence. By the time he does his Hitler impression, the women are in tears and the men are outraged. The doctor enters and Basil runs off, while the moose head lands on top of Manuel, confusing the major once again.

Also featuring:

Sister	Brenda Collins
Doctor	Louis Mahoney
Mr. Sharp	John Lawrence
Mrs. Sharp	Iris Fry
Large Woman	Claire Davenport
German Guests	Nick Lane, Lisa Bergmayr, Willy Bowman, Dan Gillan

SHOW 7:

"Communication Problems" Guests are checking in, including the overbearing Mrs. Richards. When she becomes impatient while waiting, Polly turns her over to Manuel, which serves her right. Mr. Firkins checks out, and he gives Basil a tip on a racehorse named Dragonfly. As Sybil warns Basil against betting, Manuel reports that Mrs. Richards is unhappy. She tells Basil that she wants her room rate reduced, and explains that she doesn't like to turn her hearing aid on because it runs down the battery; Basil refers her to Sybil.

Basil sends Manuel to the betting shop for him that afternoon, and later that evening Basil returns with his winnings, which Polly hides from Sybil. Mrs. Richards complains she is out of toilet paper and gets into an argument with Basil. After she leaves, Polly gives Basil his winnings, which puts him in a good mood. He tells Terry, the cook, about his luck, but Sybil is suspicious because of his good mood. Manuel almost gives it away, but Basil urges him to say nothing about the horse.

Mrs. Richards reports that she has had some money stolen from her room. Sybil, who saw Polly counting money earlier, asks about it, and Polly says she won it on a horse. Sybil still suspects Basil, but Basil asks the major to hold his money for him until morning.

The next day Mrs. Richards demands they call the police, and as the major returns Basil's money, she catches them. The major says that he has found the money, and Sybil grabs it and returns it to Mrs. Richards before a horrified Basil. Basil says it's his money, but the major doesn't remember too clearly, and Manuel, according to his instructions, knows nothing about the horse.

A deliveryman brings a vase Mrs. Richards bought the night before, and also her purse, which she had left. Basil keeps the money from the purse but when Sybil appears, Polly covers for him, saying he's holding the money she won on a horse. The major suddenly recalls Basil winning the money on a horse, and as Sybil grabs the bills, Basil drops the vase, and Sybil gives Mrs. Richards Basil's winnings.

Also featuring:

Mr. Yardley	Mervyn Pascoe
Mr. Thurston	Robert Lankesheer
Mrs. Richards	Joan Sanderson
Mr. Firkins	Johnny Shannon
Mr. Mackintosh	Bill Bradley
Mr. Kerr	George Lee

SHOW 8:

"The Psychiatrist" Basil is irritated at Mr. Johnson, a guest Sybil finds attractive, while Basil remarks to Sybil that Johnson looks like a monkey. Dr. and Mrs. Abbott check in as Basil does a monkey impression, but Basil is horrified to learn that Abbott and his wife are both doctors, and becomes very deferential. Sybil tells Mr. Johnson that they don't have an extra room for his mother, so he says she'll have to stay in his room, and Sybil chats as he phones a friend.

Basil returns, highly impressed with the Abbotts. He insults Johnson and, as he does a monkey walk, the Abbotts suddenly appear. They go into the dining room, while Sybil recommends a local restaurant to Mr. Johnson.

After dinner, Mrs. Abbott says she's a pediatrician, while her husband is a psychiatrist. Basil becomes manic when he hears he is a psychiatrist, convinced that they are all obsessed with sex. Basil misunderstands their innocent questions, and when they go for a walk, Basil checks in a very attractive Australian girl, Raylene Miles. When Basil and Sybil have their backs turned, Johnson smuggles a girl up to his room.

Basil shows Raylene to her room and promises to fix her light switch. As he reaches for the switch, he accidentally grabs her breast just as Sybil walks in; he tries to explain, but Sybil blames it on male menopause. Basil hears a girl in Johnson's room, but Johnson denies it and orders champagne. Basil listens outside his door and Johnson catches him, so Basil enters the Abbotts' room, which is adjacent, and listens through the wall. When the Abbotts walk in, he pretends to be "checking the walls." He leaves and is caught listening at Johnson's door again, and Basil blames Manuel for dropping the champagne tray. When he delivers the bottle, he fails to catch Johnson doing anything wrong.

Entering Raylene's room on the other side of Johnson's to listen in, Basil and Raylene are both surprised to find the other is there, and Dr. Abbott responds to her surprised scream. Naturally, Sybil sees Basil coming from Raylene's room, but she explains that Basil was just "checking the wall."

Basil recruits Manuel to help him with the ladder and peer into Johnson's room, but he winds up at the wrong window, and the Abbotts spot him just before the ladder falls. Sybil goes to get him, and Manuel's attempts at an explanation don't help. She hits Basil, and Basil takes it out on Manuel, until Mrs. Abbott spots them.

Early the next morning, Basil is sitting outside Johnson's room. Basil tries to tell Sybil that Johnson had a girl in his room, but she doesn't believe him. Mrs. Abbott returns a guidebook to Johnson, and Basil makes a fool of himself when she leaves. Basil's greasy hand again grabs Raylene's breast by accident, and he rushes to explain to Sybil.

Basil finally loses his temper and screams at Sybil that he'll prove Johnson has a girl in there. He shouts outside his door, and Johnson explains that he does have a woman in his room—his mother. Basil, enjoying himself in front of the crowd that has gathered, is ready for his moment of triumph, until Johnson's elderly mother does come out of the room, and Basil is in agony.

Also featuring:

Mr. Johnson	Nicky Henson
Dr. Abbott	Basil Henson
Mrs. Abbott	Elspet Gray
Raylene Miles	Luan Peters
Mrs. Johnson	Aimee Delamain
Girlfriend	Imogen Bickford-Smith

SHOW 9:

"Waldorf Salad" In the busy hotel dining room, Basil is dealing with customer complaints, Sybil is boring a customer, and Manuel is mixing up orders. While trying to serve the guests, Basil greets two late arrivals, the Hamiltons—a British woman and her obnoxious American husband. Mr. Hamilton complains about England and demands a hot dinner. Even though the kitchen is supposed to be closing, he gives Basil money to bribe the chef to keep it open.

Terry the chef has to leave, even though Basil tries to bribe him to stay, and Manuel and Polly leave as well.

Later the Hamiltons come down to the dining room; Sybil makes conversation with them while Basil tries to prepare their drinks. Mr. Hamilton orders Waldorf salad and steak, and Basil, who hasn't told them that the chef has left for the evening, reacts. He looks frantically around the kitchen for the ingredients to the salad. When he can't find them, he begins telling Mr. Hamilton how the delivery man broke his arm. Basil then returns to the kitchen to threaten the absent chef, as Sybil comes out with the salads prepared.

Basil screams in the kitchen—supposedly at the chef—and after he puts the steaks on and shouts some more, he brings Mr. Hamilton a note of apology from the "chef." He rushes back to the kitchen when he sees the smoke, and as he shouts at the empty air, Mr. Hamilton walks into the kitchen.

The Hamiltons go upstairs to pack, but Basil stops them. Mr. Hamilton tells him off in the lobby for keeping their money but letting the chef go, and they poll the guests who have assembled in the lobby as to whether they're satisfied with the hotel. After several of them complain, Basil erupts and orders all of the guests out of the hotel. Mr. Hamilton orders them taxis, and Basil tells Sybil it's them or him.

Basil leaves instead, but after walking out into the rain, he comes back in to register for a room.

Also featuring:

Mr. Libson ....Anthony Dawes
Mrs. Johnstone...June Ellis
Mr. Johnstone ....Terence Conoley
Miss Hare ....Dorothy Frere
Miss Gurke ....Beatrice Shaw
Mr. Arrad...Norman Bird
Mrs. Arrad..Stella Tanner
Mrs. Hamilton ....Claire Nielson
Mr. Hamilton..Bruce Boa

SHOW 10:

"The Kipper and the Corpse" In the crowded hotel bar, the major sits with Mrs. Chase, who is holding her dog. When Dr. Price enters, Basil agrees to fix him sandwiches. Four business associates enter. One says he feels ill and, on his way upstairs, asks Basil to bring his breakfast to his room in the morning.

In the dining room the following morning, Mrs. Chase complains to Manuel, and her dog tries to bite Polly and Manuel. Polly adds tabasco sauce to the dog's sausages, and Basil carries breakfast up to the sick man, noting that the expiration date for the kippers has passed. The guest, Mr. Leeman, is dead, although Basil doesn't notice as he delivers breakfast and keeps up a one-sided conversation.

Shortly after, Polly runs downstairs and informs the kitchen that Mr. Leeman is dead. They take Dr. Price up to the room. Basil is afraid he's poisoned him with the kippers, but when Dr. Price says he'd been dead for hours, Basil is joyous. They call the coroner.

Basil and Manuel try quietly to move the body from the room, but when Miss Tibbs sees them, she screams and faints. They drag her into Mr. and Mrs. White's room with the body, just as the couple are returning from breakfast. Basil hides Leeman and Miss Tibbs in the closet and lets the Whites in. They hear moaning from the closet and bring out a very shaken Miss Tibbs, then lead her to her own room while the Whites book a room elsewhere. Sybil comforts the elderly lady, while the Whites book a room elsewhere.

Manuel and Basil carry the body downstairs into the office. Basil goes to the kitchen to cook Dr. Price's sausages, and Miss Tibbs faints in the lobby when she accidentally spots the corpse. As Basil and Manuel carry the corpse into the kitchen the Whites are driving off, but when they spot the procession, they crash. Basil and Manuel also encounter Mrs. Chase, who reports that her dog is ill.

Dr. Price is horrified to find that they put the body in the kitchen, so Basil and Manuel put the body in a laundry basket and carry it out. The Whites go back upstairs, while Sybil registers a new guest, Mr. Ingram. When Mr. Leeman's business associates arrive for breakfast, they tell Basil they're there to collect him, and Basil assumes they're from the coroner's office. When Basil looks inside the laundry basket, it is empty. He and Manuel drag the body off the laundry van and back upstairs. They carry the body into one room and find Mr. Ingram; then they carry it into another room and discover the Whites have returned.

Basil and Manuel carry the body downstairs again; they argue, and Manuel climbs into the basket, so Basil places the body beside the hat rack and stands in front of it. Sybil brings Mr. Leeman's three associates out of the office after telling them the bad news. One of them has hung his hat on the rack and wants to retrieve it before they leave, so Basil has Manuel get out of the basket to hand him his hat; when Miss Tibbs, Mrs. Chase, and Dr. Price join the scene, Basil climbs into the basket himself and is driven away.

Also featuring:

Mrs. Chase..Mavis Pugh
Dr. Price ....Geoffrey Palmer
Guest...Len Marten
Mr. Leeman ....Derek Royle
Mr. Xerxes..Robert McBain
Mr. Zebedee ....Raymond Mason
Miss Young ....Pamela Buchner
Mr. White ....Richard Davies
Mrs. White ....Elizabeth Benson
Mr. Ingrams ....Charles McKeown

SHOW 11:

"The Anniversary" Polly, Terry, and Manuel talk in the kitchen, when Sybil comes in, angry that Basil has forgotten their fifteenth anniversary. Basil enters humming, and after she drops a few broad hints, Sybil leaves. Basil assures the others that he's throwing a surprise anniversary party for her, and Manuel is cooking paella. Polly asks Basil if he's decided about the car loan she asked him about weeks ago, and he puts her off.

Sybil confronts Basil again, and when he plays dumb, she stomps off. Terry asks Basil why Manuel is cooking, and while they argue, Sybil leaves angrily and drives away. Basil tries chasing her, but as she drives out of sight, two party guests, Roger and Alice, pull up.

When the couple enters, Basil explains that Sybil is ill upstairs and adds that she had lost her voice. Roger is suspicious and whispers that they must have had a fight. Basil fixes them drinks. More guests, Arthur and Virginia, arrive and bring a cake. Basil's story becomes more elaborate as Reg and Kitty come in, and Kitty says she just saw Sybil downtown. Basil claims it's just a local woman who looks like Sybil and his wife is really ill upstairs, too ill to have company. He gets more and more upset, and finally challenges them to come upstairs. They hesitate, and Basil asks Polly upstairs to help him for a moment.

Basil gives her the £100 loan for her car to impersonate Sybil, and steps outside. Manue claims Terry won't leave his cooking alone, and Basil brushes him aside to call the guests upstairs. He goes for an ashtray, then grabs a bottle from the bar, but Manuel accidentally spills it on him as he complains about Terry.

The guests stand outside Sybil's door as Basil offers nuts and crisps,* then introduces them to the major as he walks by. When Basil finally leads them in, the curtains are closed and the room is very dark. They wish her happy anniversary and she waves to them. When Basil shows her the cake, he sees Sybil's car pulling up outside. He leaves the guests upstairs while he runs down and sees the real Sybil, who has just come back for her golf clubs. When he doesn't try to talk her into staying, she leaves, hurt and angry.

Upstairs, Basil offers more drinks, but the guests say they have to get going. Outside, Sybil sits crying with Audrey, and Basil leads the guests downstairs into the lobby. When Sybil suddenly appears, Basil pretends she is only the local woman who resembles Sybil, and ushers her into the kitchen, past the fighting Terry and Manuel, and shuts her in a closet. The speechless guests walk out, as Basil prepares to face Sybil.

*Potato chips

Also featuring:

Roger ....Ken Campbell
Alice...Una Stubbs
Virginia ....Pat Keen
Arthur...Robert Arnold
Reg ....Roger Hume
Kitty...Denyse Alexander
Audrey ....Christine Shaw

SHOW 12:

"Basil the Rat" As Basil and Sybil arrive back at the hotel, they quarrel over a party that Basil doesn't want to go to that evening. In the kitchen, Basil discovers Mr. Carnegie, from the Public Health Department, who delivers a lengthy list of complaints and gives them twenty-four hours to fix them. They all get to work, and Polly puts the cat out.

Basil goes to Manuel's room to have him take the dead pigeons from the water tank, when he spots Manuel's "Siberian hamster" in a cage. Basil says it is a rat, and takes it away before the health inspector comes back. One of Polly's friends agrees to take it, and Manuel sadly agrees.

Later, they continue cleaning, Manuel wearing a black armband. He sneaks away later to a nearby building with food, calling for the rat, named Basil, but he returns and tells Polly that the rat has escaped. The major sits alone in the bar and spots the rat next to him; he goes for his shotgun, but when he returns there is no sign of the rat. He tells Basil that the rat is on the premises, and they all begin hunting for it. Basil sprinkles rat poison on a veal fillet and places it on the floor.

When Mr. Carnegie arrives, Sybil is about to show him around when they hear gunfire and find Basil wrestling the gun from the major. In the kitchen, the plate of veal falls to the floor, and

Terry picks it up before the inspector comes back. There Basil sees the cat nibbling on the plate of veal, and puts the cat and a piece of veal outside; he then realizes that the veal may be poisoned and retrieves it from all of the guests who have been served.

Mr. Carnegie says they've passed the inspection and decides to stay for lunch, specifically ordering the veal. Basil, Sybil, Terry and Manuel realize that the cat is still alive, and so decide to fix him the piece the cat had been chewing on. Just as Mr. Carnegie is about to eat his meal, though, Basil sees the cat throwing up, and snatches the plate away. He finds another piece of veal to serve him, but then finds out the cat was just coughing up a hairball, so the first piece might have been okay after all, and Basil has to switch plates again.

Meanwhile Manuel, who is taking the order of another couple, spots his rat at their feet. They complain and decide to leave, but the rat is in the woman's handbag. Basil reaches in for it, claiming there has been a bomb scare, and drops the bag quickly as the rat runs off. Manuel recaptures it and puts it in a biscuit tin, where Mr. Carnegie comes face to face with it. He is in shock, and Basil passes out.

Also featuring:

Mr. Carnegie...John Quarmby
Guest..Stuart Sherwin
Mr. Taylor ....James Taylor
Mrs. Taylor ....Melody Lang
Ronald ....David Neville
Quentina ....Sabina Franklyn

Critics constantly cite *Fawlty Towers* as one of the finest TV shows ever, and its popularity rivals *Monty Python*. Although a total of only twelve shows were made, all indications are that *Fawlty Towers*—with its universal characters and well-crafted stories—is funny enough to stand the test of time.

Basil Fawlty is the harried husband and irascible innkeeper who would undoubtedly be running a first-class hotel if he didn't have to deal with guests. His other obstacle to happiness and contentment is his wife and worthy opponent, Sybil, who can hold her own against his rages and fits. Polly, their maid, is the quiet voice of reason in the eye of the storm, yet she manages to be drawn into Basil's schemes more often than she would like. Their Spanish bellboy/waiter, Manuel, is still the most consistent, constant irritant to Basil, however; his slavish devotion to his employer and his less-than-perfect English combined with a substandard intelligence are guaranteed to incur Basil's wrath. The cast is rounded out with several resident guests, including the scatter-brained major, and Miss Tibbs and Miss Gatsby, with an assortment of guests coming and going each show.

Fawlty Towers seemed to be almost a natural progression in the careers of its creators. John Cleese and Connie Booth had been wanting to work together for several years, and John's departure from *Monty Python* after the third series of TV shows gave them the opportunity. They had written sketches together previously, as well as writing and starring in *Romance With a Double Bass*. The pair also wrote a sketch for the second of the German *Monty Python* specials.

"We did a prolonged fairy tale, a sendup of a medieval fairy tale, which Connie and I wrote," reveals Cleese. "It was actually well liked at the time, and we used it in the stage show at Drury Lane. Terry Jones actually wanted to base a feature on it! But that was the first thing that Connie and I wrote together.

"The BBC wanted me to do something else. When they knew I wasn't doing Python any more, they said `Well, what do you want to do?' and I said `Well, I'm not sure, but I'd like to write

something with Connie,' so they said fine. I sat down with Connie, and within an hour we knew what we were doing. We were able to discard certain of our options.

"We thought about doing some man-woman sketches, sort of like Nichols and May in America. But Nichols and May have done it so wonderfully well, and Eleanor Bron and John Fortune have done it very well in England, so we thought `Someone else has done it.'

"Then we suddenly thought about a hotel, and it felt very right. It was based on a hotel I'd stayed at when I was filming Python back in seventy-one," says Cleese.

During filming for the Python shows, the group was booked into a hotel called the Gleneagles [which is actually referred to briefly in "The Builders"] in Torquay where, according to Michael Palin, "the proprietor seemed to view us from the start as a colossal inconvenience." After the first night, they decided to move out.

"The manager was just wonderfully rude," notes Cleese. "He was like Basil, except he was very much smaller, a little skinny guy about five feet four, with a large wife who dominated him. Well, that couldn't be possible, so we reversed the sizes."

Cleese had actually used the idea of this hotel before, when he had to do some writing after a financial setback. "I'd lost some money in an investment—I put some money into a gym and set a man up, and about three months later he died. Most extraordinary! I'd lost quite a bit of money on that, so I wrote some *Doctor in the House* shows," he says.

"I'd set one of the episodes at a hotel that had been based on this one. An old friend of mine said to me `You know, there's a series in that hotel,' and I thought `Bloody television producer, can't see a program without thinking about a series.' The extraordinary thing was, he was absolutely right. It did make a series, but at the time he suggested it, I didn't take him seriously. Three years later, when Connie and I sat down, it was the second or third idea that came into our minds."

The *Doctor in the House* script, called "No Ill Feelings," aired in early 1973. When they looked back on the possibilities, they realized the potential for such a series.

"You can have almost anyone you want walk in, and you don't have to try and find an explanation, plus the fact that you've got your basic regulars," Cleese explains.

"Also, you've got a situation which almost everyone understands. If you have a series set in an undertakers, as they had in English television, not everyone has walked into an undertakers, so you don't quite know what your feelings are, what goes through people's minds.

"If you're in a hotel, everyone knows what it's like to walk up to a front desk, everyone knows what it's like if someone's casual or rude or overattentive. Everyone's ordered meals in restaurants, everyone's come out the door of their room and wondered where the bathroom is—this sort of thing. Everybody knows what's going on, you don't have to set anything up, you don't have to explain anything. It's all very sensible and straightforward and conventional. And then, you can start straightaway with the jokes."

The acting ensemble—Prunella Scales, Andrew Sachs, Cleese, Booth, and the other supporting players—is superb, and each character is clearly delineated, but Cleese says he is proudest of the writing. "The acting is extremely good, but I'm primarily proud of the plots that Connie and I cobbled together, because they do work very well, and there's a lot of skillful writing in there," he declares.

Although the writing took time, which is one of the primary reasons for the quality of *Fawlty Towers*, the pair didn't find it extraordinarily hard to write.

"It was difficult in the sense that it took a lot of time—it wasn't difficult in that we nearly always got it in the end. But I'm the only person in history to have put six weeks aside to writing an episode, and *that's* why it has three times more good stuff in it than the average good television episode," says Cleese. "The average good television episode is written in two weeks, so we spent three times as long as that and there's three times as much material in it.

"If you watch the shows chronologically, there's quite a development in the style. It becomes, in a sense, more and more realistic, it becomes a little less Alan Ayckbourn. Towards the end, we're exploring character much more, while at the same time not losing the humor that comes from the farce. I think you'll find that the characters are filled out, inevitably, by the end."

Character development was one of the many things that was sharpened in the second series, which was—and had to be—better than the first six shows, according to Cleese.

"The first show, for example, if you look at it is a little bit crude, because we were learning the art. Oddly enough, the first series is pretty good. I think the second series is quite a lot better. In a sense, it's more ambitious and it achieves more, but it needed to, because people's recollections of a successful series are usually that it's better than it was, which means that the second series has got to be better to be seen to be as good.

"Writing *Fawlty Towers*, which I enjoyed enormously, was very hard and very frightening. I knew once we had done the first series that we had set a very high standard. I knew nothing but the best would do, so there was a lot of pressure, but nevertheless, a great sense of satisfaction when I began to realize that Connie and I'd gotten the scripts right—not so much in performing, because there was never enough time. Somebody asked me if I'd enjoyed *Fawlty Towers*, and I said `There wasn't enough time to enjoy it!' And that was absolutely spot on. There was a great satisfaction with the end product, after spending twenty hours editing each show with the director, a real satisfaction there."

After the first series had ended, it was several years before Cleese and Booth began working together on the second series of six shows, and much had changed in the intervening years. Most significantly, the two of them had gotten divorced, and it says a great deal about their character that they were not only able to remain friends but to work together for lengthy periods of time on the second six shows. Writing on the second series commenced after the *Life of Brian* script had been finished, and Booth even visited Cleese in Tunisia during the filming of that movie to finish hammering out the six plots.

When the shows aired early in 1979, audience reaction was enthusiastic, although some critics said the new shows weren't quite as good as the first series, just as Cleese predicted. In the years that have passed, the second series has come to be accepted as every bit as good as the original, if not better. In fact, when Cleese analyzes his favorite shows, he notes that the best ones are from the second series.

"I have two or three favorites," he says. "I'm very fond of the dead body, very fond of the rat, and I also very much like that uncomfortable episode when they have the anniversary and Polly has to pretend she's Sybil. I'm very fond of that one, because I think a lot of the humor in it's very unusual, and a little unlike what the rest of the show was.

"Funny enough, I don't think the German episode is as good as people think—but I love the fire drill bit—because the two halves of the show are not integrated particularly well."

Of course, *Fawlty Towers* became a spectacular success in countries around the world. American producers tried to imitate its success with two regrettable U.S. versions. One was a 1978 pilot called *Snavely* with Harvey Korman in the Basil Fawlty role, while *Amanda's*, starring Bea Arthur, had a six-show run on ABC-TV beginning February 10, 1983. The latter show in particular baffled Cleese.

"I asked the American company how the adaptation was looking, and they told me `It's looking good—we've only made one change.' They wrote out Basil Fawlty, which I found incomprehensible," exclaims Cleese.

Even before the second series had been written, the team had been approached about doing a Christmas special or a *Fawlty Towers* movie. They briefly considered the idea and developed a couple of possible plots. Booth wanted to send Basil and Sybil on holiday to a Spanish hotel, which he finds just as bad as his own. Their other thought involved Basil's plane waiting on the ground for sixteen hours at Heathrow, so when the plane is hijacked, Basil overcomes the hijackers single-handedly out of sheer anger; Basil is a hero, until the captain says they have to return to Heathrow, and Basil hijacks the plane to Spain himself. Ultimately, the pair decided against a *Fawlty Towers* movie.

"Neither of us feel very fired by the idea," Cleese noted in 1978. "It's just what I talk about

with Python. We've done twelve *Fawlty Towers* and spent over a month on each of them, so we think, well, let's do something a bit different. It's rather like flogging a dead horse."

Cleese's lack of interest in repeating himself and the personal though amicable separation with Connie Booth make it highly unlikely that there will be more *Fawlty Towers*. Booth has gone on to her own film and stage career (with roles in such films as *High Spirits* and Michael Palin's *American Friends*). Although Cleese has kept busy with a variety of projects, he agrees that, until *A Fish Called Wanda*, *Fawlty Towers* was easily his most successful post-Python achievement.

"In terms of viewers, it overtook Python, which amazed me. I think it probably would have gotten more attention in the States than Python, except there were no movies, because instead of being concerned with ideas, it was concerned with human behavior and emotions. It was much more accessible," notes Cleese at his London home. "I was surprised at how successful it was everywhere, including this country.

"When Connie and I wrote it, we didn't have the slightest idea that it was going to amuse anything other than two or three million people on BBC-2, and it finished with audiences that were comfortably bigger than Python ever got. We really thought it was almost a private little joke, and I'm still astounded to find that it plays in Hong Kong in Cantonese! I don't understand it—Basil must be some kind of an archetype."

Like Python before it, Cleese says he co-wrote *Fawlty Towers* using the "private joke" approach, and all of his comedy writing is primarily designed to amuse himself.

"I think it's the only way to write comedy," he reveals. "Whenever I've come across people who consciously write down [to an audience]—write things they don't think are funny, but they think the audience will—I never thought that worked at all. I think the people on *Cheers*, for example, would agree. When they think of something funny, if they don't laugh at it themselves, they don't put it in."

 ## CRITICAL COMMENTS

"*Fawlty Towers* is a perfect showcase for the manic talents of actor John Cleese. . . . Lovable eccentricity is always good for a laugh; Basil's convincing display of paranoia more often than not demands that a team of kind men in white coats should come along and take him away."

— Pamela Cunninghame, *New Zealand Herald*, September 8, 1980

". . . It is one of those broad comedies that only the British seem to be able to pull off.... Cleese doesn't just *star* in the series, he takes it over.... The comedic timing is superb, the dialogue rapid-fire and crisp.... Although the farce does get a bit out of hand sometimes, Cleese, the master of mugging, is always ready to follow it up with still-another hilarious exercise in outrageousness. A worthy antidote for prime-time pap. . . ."

— Clifford Terry, *Chicago Tribune*, October 8, 1989

Fawlty Towers: The Albums, Books, and Videos

THE ALBUMS*

FAWLTY TOWERS

BY JOHN CLEESE AND CONNIE BOOTH. (1979) BBC RECORDS REB 377

Features the soundtrack to the TV shows "The Hotel Inspectors" and "Communication Problems."

FAWLTY TOWERS: SECOND SITTING

BY JOHN CLEESE AND CONNIE BOOTH. (1981) BBC RECORDS REB 405

Features the soundtrack to the TV shows "The Builders" and "Basil the Rat."

Note: The *Fawlty Towers* albums include narration by Andrew Sachs as Manuel to describe the more visual scenes.

FAWLTY TOWERS: AT YOUR SERVICE

BY JOHN CLEESE AND CONNIE BOOTH. (1982) BBC RECORDS REB 449

Features the soundtracks to the TV shows "The Germans" and
"The Kipper and the Corpse."

FAWLTY TOWERS: A LA CARTE

BY JOHN CLEESE AND CONNIE BOOTH. BBC RECORDS REB 484

Features the soundtracks to the TV shows "Waldorf Salad" and
"Gourmet Night."

 *THE BOOKS*

FAWLTY TOWERS

BY JOHN CLEESE AND CONNIE BOOTH.

Published by Futura/Contact Publications (1977), ISBN 0-8600-7598-2 (paperback) (U.K.).

Features the scripts of "The Builders," "The Hotel Inspectors,"
and "Gourmet Night," profusely illustrated with photos from the
TV shows.

JOHN CLEESE & CONNIE BOOTH

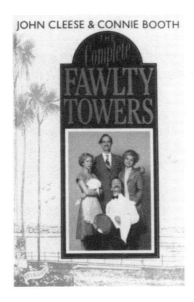

FAWLTY TOWERS TWO

BY JOHN CLEESE AND CONNIE BOOTH.

Published by Weidenfeld and Nicolson (1979), ISBN 0-7088-1547-2 (paperback) (U.K.).

Features the scripts of "The Wedding Party," "A Touch of Class," and "The Germans."

THE COMPLETE FAWLTY TOWERS

BY JOHN CLEESE AND CONNIE BOOTH.

Published by Methuen (U.K.) (1988), ISBN 0-413-18390-4 (hardback),
Published by Pantheon (U.S.) (1989), ISBN 0-679-72127-4 (paperback).

Contains the scripts from all twelve shows, including a brief photo insert.

 ## THE VIDEOS

Fawlty Towers (CBS/Fox Video 3719): "A Touch of Class," "The Hotel Inspectors," and "The Germans."

Fawlty Towers (CBS/Fox Video 3720): "The Builders," "The Wedding Party," and "The Psychiatrist."

Fawlty Towers (CBS/Fox Video 3721): "Gourmet Night," "Waldorf Salad," and "The Kipper and the Corpse."

Fawlty Towers (CBS/Fox Video 3722): "Communication Problems," "The Anniversary," and "Basil the Rat."

HELLO, SAILOR

BY ERIC IDLE. PUBLISHED BY FUTURA PUBLICATIONS (1975), ISBN 0-8600-7235-5 (U.K.).

The prime minister, reluctantly elected, keeps his secretaries waiting while he sits in a steam bath with a young blond boy. Jonathan Beech is trying to break the record for seducing the daughters of every minister in the cabinet. The foreign secretary has been dead for four months, but the public isn't aware of it because he's been stuffed, while astronaut Jim Sickert is upset because he's the only member of his crew who will remain in orbit while the others walk on the moon. The president plans to extend the Vietnam War to Europe by liberating France, an invasion financed by Warner Brothers.

While in Harrod's looking for another daughter, Jonathan sees his friend Cecil, who is scattering a friend's ashes throughout the store. The president phones the prime minister and asks if they can bomb Cambridge, because of their deal with Warner's. While the prime minister plays with his young friend Bobo, his cabinet argues about selling tanks to South Africa, and they decide to let America occupy Cambridge for a few days.

In Southeast Asia, General Atkinson can't find any communists, so he has to hire some. Splendiman accompanies the prime minister and Bobo on a trip to Istanbul, where they hope to placate the Commonwealth Conference over the tank sales to South Africa, while all England is excited over the royal divorce. In the harbor is the British aircraft carrier *Triumphant,* which had run aground and gotten stuck years before, and British sailors had turned into a huge, legendary brothel; the conference is being held on board.

General Atkinson and his men finally invade Cambridge but he is irritated when he can't find any of the enemy. At the conference, Seaman Beal reports to the prime minister that while he was trying to photograph the foreign secretary with a hook-

er, he discovered that the foreign secretary was actually dead and stuffed; he is going to blackmail the government. Vice-Admiral Haugh and his ship are ordered to Istanbul. While Astronaut Sickert orbits the far side of the moon alone, he tests out a condom for a British company. Wingco "Fatty" Warwick leads the RAF in a raid to bomb the Suez Canal, and the Royal Navy is accused of fishing.

Seaman Beal almost makes the prime minister jealous with a picture of Bobo and Splendiman, who have been forced to share a room. Just as the conference is voting to expel Britain, the prime minister stops the vote by announcing the foreign secretary is dead. They compromise by agreeing Britain can sell them tanks but not ammunition.

The RAF squad has to land in Noman, as they are low on fuel, and are held prisoner by Arabs there. Astronaut Sickert blackmails Mission Control and refuses to dock with the lunar crew until they pay him $2 million, though he later decides he wants a job in the administration. On a live broadcast, the president offers Sickert a job in his administration. The RAF squad tunnels to freedom, dressing in drag to divert their captors.

The prime minister is horrified to hear that Bobo has left for Noman with another man, and has to return to London without him. The president ups his offer to Sickert, who becomes the new vice president.

Jonathan joins the victory celebration at the Albert Hall, where he meets Lady Candida, and she seduces him during the ceremony. The ceremony is disrupted by Lord Bishop, Bobo's father, who accuses the prime minister of corrupting his son. The home secretary strips down to a superhero costume, and a riot breaks out before the heavily censored ending.

 ## NOTES

Hello, Sailor! was the first—and to date, the only—full-length novel of adult fiction written by a Python.

Eric Idle, always one of the more verbal members of the team, says it was the result of an

illness during the early years of Python.

"I just had flu, and the first line came to me," he states. "This line came into my head, and as soon as I felt a bit better, I sat down and wrote it, and kept writing. I wrote it out by hand. It just came on out—sometimes things do that."

Although the writing itself came very quickly, it was several years before the results saw print.

"I wrote *Hello, Sailor* in 1970, and it was published in 1975. It took a long time to get out. A scurrilous book." He laughs. "I nearly got it published right away toward the beginning. There was this publisher that was really keen to publish it, and I went to their office, and they said 'We'd like to make you an offer, but we have to wait until the one o'clock from Chepstow,' the racetrack. He said 'Do you mind coming across to the pub?' We went across to the pub, and we had a drink, and he's watching this race, knuckles gripped on the table, and he's going 'Aarghhh!'

"The horse came in, and he went 'Right, now I'm prepared to make you an offer.'" Idle

laughs. "I thought 'Hang on a minute—if their entire business was on this horse, tomorrow the offer could just as easily be rescinded.' I decided not to go with them."

When it was eventually published, it ended up doing well, Idle recalls happily. "It's always sweet when a book's published. It didn't do big in hardback, but it did over 20,000 in paperback, which in those days was quite a lot for a first novel."

Although Idle briefly considered doing a novelization of his *Splitting Heirs* screenplay ("It's first-person narrative, and it lends itself very much to book form. . . . the novel form is a good way to learn about your characters"), he changed his mind when the screenplay became less narrative and more dramatic.

So, even though he doesn't completely rule out a return to the novel form, *Hello, Sailor* stands as the only original, full-length novel by a Python.

Video Arts Training Films

WRITTEN BY AND STARRING JOHN CLEESE. FIRST FILMS PRODUCED 1975

 ### PARTIAL LISTING OF VIDEO ARTS FILMS FEATURING JOHN CLEESE

Decisions, Decisions (28 min.) John Cleese plays a manager who has been put in charge of his organization's move into a new building, and every decision he has made seems to have gone wrong. While sitting alone and despondent in his office one evening, he is confronted by Great Decision Makers of the Past—Field Marshal Montgomery, Queen Elizabeth I, Brutus, and Sir Winston Churchill. Written by Jonathan Lynn. Directed by Peter Robinson. Featuring John Cleese, Prunella Scales, and Nigel Hawthorne.

The Importance of Mistakes (33 min.) A taped speech by John Cleese on the role of mistakes in the creative process.

Meetings, Bloody Meetings (30 min.) John Cleese plays a manager who is put on trial for negligent conduct of meetings, before a courtroom run according to his haphazard regard to rules. Written by John Cleese and Antony Jay. Directed by Peter Robinson. Featuring John Cleese and Timothy West.

More Bloody Meetings (27 min.) A follow-up to the last film, John Cleese again plays the manager. During a trip to the dentist, he dreams that the office has become an interrogation room, and the dentist is trying to extract a confession from him. Written by Antony Jay. Directed by Charles Crichton. Featuring John Cleese and Graeme Garden.

The Unorganized Manager This four-part series deals with the way managers organize their time and need to delegate authority.

> *Damnation*, Part 1 (24 min.), sees manager Richard Lewis confronting St. Peter (played by Cleese), who restores him to life and sends him back to Earth with a list of his eleven deadly organizational sins.
>
> *Salvation,* Part 2 (26 min.), sees St. Peter show Richard how to organize himself and allocate his time.
>
> *Lamentations*, Part 3 (20 min.), sees Richard blame all of his mistakes on his subordinates.
>
> *Revelations*, Part 4 (29 min.), finds Richard recognizing and accepting the error of his ways.

Written by Jonathan Lynn (Parts 1 and 2), and Andrew Marshall and David Renwick (Parts 3 and 4). Directed by Charles Crichton. Featuring John Cleese and James Bolam.

Man Hunt (31 min.) A film for managers who conduct occasional, but important, selection interviews. John Cleese portrays three types of managers: Ethelred the Unready, who has not prepared for the interview; Ivan the Terrible, who overwhelms the candidate; and William the Silent, who fails to put forth the direct questions. Written by John Cleese and Antony Jay. Directed by Peter Robinson. Featuring John Cleese.

How Am I Doing? (26 min.) In this film on the appraisal interview, John Cleese plays three different managers: Ethelred the Unready, who never prepares; Ivan the Terrible, who shouts but seldom listens; and William the Silent, who hates to face up to unpleasant facts. Written by Jonathan Lynn. Directed by Peter Robinson. Featuring John Cleese.

I'd Like a Word With You (27 min.) How to conduct a disciplinary interview is the subject of this film, which also features John Cleese as Ethelred the Unready, Ivan the Terrible, and William the Silent. Written by Jonathan Lynn. Directed by Peter Robinson. Starring John Cleese.

This brochure from Video Arts details information on releases, rentals, and corporate campaigns, with John Cleese prominently displayed on the cover. Photo Copyright Video Arts

The Balance Sheet Barrier (30 min.) John Cleese is Julian Carruthers, a sophisticated manager who wants someone to explain business finance in simple language, while Ronnie Corbett plays Ron Scroggs, a very successful small businessman who watches every penny like a hawk. Written by Antony Jay. Directed by Peter Robinson. Featuring John Cleese and Ronnie Corbett.

The Control of Working Capital (26 min.) Julian Carruthers (John Cleese) calls upon the help of his small businessman friend Ron Scroggs (Ronnie Corbett) to learn how to use working capital to keep a company afloat and show him where cash is locked up in his business. Written by Antony Jay. Directed by Peter Robinson. Featuring John Cleese and Ronnie Corbett.

Cost, Profit, and Break-Even (23 min.) Another member of the Scroggs family initiates Julian Carruthers into the mysteries of fixed and variable costs, break-even points, and depreciation.

Written by Antony Jay. Directed by Peter Robinson. Featuring John Cleese and John Bird.

Depreciation and Inflation (17 min.) Scroggs teaches Carruthers that he is running his business into the ground by valuing stock at the original purchase price, rather than the new buy-in price. Written by Antony Jay. Directed by Peter Robinson. Featuring John Cleese and John Bird.

Budgeting (30 min.) Scroggs shows Carruthers what a budget is for and how Carruthers could have used it to prevent disaster. Written by Graeme Garden. Directed by Peter Robinson. Featuring John Cleese and John Bird.

Return on Investment (20 min.) Carruthers inherits money on his birthday that he plans to invest in his business, but after Scroggs advises him, he begins to have doubts. Written by Graeme Garden. Directed by Peter Robinson. Featuring John Cleese and John Bird.

Can We Please Have That the Right Way Round? (22 min.) John Cleese demonstrates the importance of planning, designing, and familiarizing yourself with equipment before a slide presentation. Written by Denis Norden. Directed by Peter Robinson. Featuring John Cleese and James Cossins.

Who Sold You This, Then? (23 min.) John Cleese is Charlie Jenkins, a service engineer and master

in the art of "unselling" products; he winds up a deranged customer himself when his hi-fi has quit working during the last bar of a Sibelius symphony. Written by Antony Jay and John Cleese. Directed by Peter Robinson. Featuring John Cleese and Jonathan Lynn.

Awkward Customers and *More Awkward Customers* (24 min., 31 min.) A number of "special" customer types and methods of dealing with them are explained, including Mr. Tiger (the angry customer), Mrs. Camel (the snooty customer), and Mrs. Ferret (the suspicious customer). Written by Antony Jay and John Cleese. Directed by Peter Robinson. Featuring John Cleese.

The Cold Call (24 min.) John Cleese plays a telephone salesman who learns the rules of telephone sales from his colleagues ("You lift this bit and speak in there, don't you?"). Written by Jonathan Lynn and Antony Jay. Directed by Peter Robinson. Featuring John Cleese, Jonathan Lynn, and Linda James.

In Two Minds and *The Meeting of Minds* (18 min., 15 min.) These films deal with misunderstandings that can develop whenever a salesman doesn't know what the customer needs, and the barriers that can be built between the salesman and customer. Written by John Cleese and Antony Jay. Directed by Peter Robinson. Featuring John Cleese, Tim Brooke-Taylor, and Connie Booth.

 NOTES

Toward the end of the *Monty Python* years, John Cleese had the opportunity to invest in a fledgling company that would produce and distribute industrial training films. Until that time, most of the films designed for businesses were rather dull, uninspiring, and ineffective corporate tools, but Video Arts set out to change all that.

After investing in the company, John Cleese studied effective business skills and, using his early training as a schoolteacher, determined that the best way to communicate and teach those skills was with humor. Cleese and some of his colleagues set out to write and perform films that would teach through entertaining. Today Video Arts has a catalog of over eighty different films marketed to corporate clients, with more being added every year.

John Cleese looks very regal as Queen Elizabeth in Decisions, Decisions, **which sees famous decision-makers through history. Copyright Video Arts**

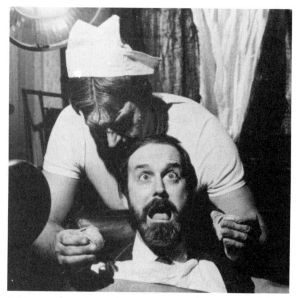

This sequel to the first "Meetings" film sees Dave Prowse as Bonzo the Nurse treating the Meeting Chairman in More Bloody Meetings (Prowse also played Darth Vader in the Star Wars films) Copyright Video Arts

Cleese as Julian Carruthers discusses his budget with Ron Scroggs, played by John Bird, in Budgeting. Copyright Video Arts

Video Arts' success surprised even Cleese.

"For five years, it ticked along predictably," relates Cleese. "The product was very good, better than the product of the competitors. We organized it efficiently and marketed it intelligently, so I suppose it was all predictable, all foreseeable. Then suddenly the curve just started to go up and up and up in a way that none of us had anticipated at all.

"Our films, without any question at all, were much better than anything else on the market. Our main rival had to buck up a lot, and they started hiring a couple of top people in British comedy and started making better films. The fact was, the whole standard of industrial training films went up so sharply that I suspect more and more people started using them, because they began to say 'Well, if they're this good, we'll use them.' Whereas, the old market used to be a few not frightfully good films coming from two or three British companies, and a lot of American films that weren't awfully inspired. I think we increased the market by increasing the quality of the product."

About 90 percent of the films are humorous, says Cleese, and the comedy makes them more effective.

"We've discovered that, on the whole, you want about five major points in each film that need to be explored and explained, and the audience needs to be persuaded that they are right. We don't tell them, we put in scenes which will persuade them that this is the way to handle a particular situation, and which demonstrate what happens in that situation when you don't handle it properly. So, we have about five very serious and important lessons which are recapitulated, not only when they've just been taught, but also at the end," Cleese explains.

"And we probably have an almost innumerable number of other, smaller lessons which may be absolutely nonverbal. In the 'Interview' film, the guy who's being interviewed has a clock on the wall behind him, so the man who's interviewing him can look at the time without making it apparent to the interviewee that he's checking how much longer he's got. Now that's a point that doesn't appear in the script—it's just there for the people who spot it. There's lots of small points like that, the nonverbals, but five key points are spelled out at great length and then recapitulated in caption form at the end."

Cleese says the comedy is integrated into each film.

"The jokes, on the whole, go all the way through. They're very easy in the scenes where we

With Ronnie Corbett in **Control of Working Capital.**
Copyright Video Arts

show people doing it wrong, particularly because the audience watching it is very specialized and immediately knows—I mean, if you spent your time sitting behind the reception desk of a hotel, and you start watching a scene set behind the reception desk of a hotel, you immediately know when a guy isn't getting it right," says Cleese.

"So, the scenes where the man gets it wrong are always funny. The hard thing is making the scenes where he gets it right funny. Sometimes those scenes have quite a bit less humor, but then they're usually pretty short. I would be very surprised in our films if a minute passed without some humor. And a lot of the time, it's almost throughout."

Although many of the films are rather straightforward, some of the others involve seemingly silly moments, such as Cleese (with mustache intact) portraying Queen Elizabeth I.

"That didn't strike me as silly, actually," says Cleese, straightfaced. "In Python, we had some things that were just sheer silliness, like the `Fish-Slapping Dance'—just joie de vivre absurdity. You never have that in the training films, because everything is in there for a point.

"I think the most absurd scene—which I wasn't in—was a girl playing a sales assistant who couldn't stop a character called Mrs. Rabbit from talking. So she produced a megaphone from behind the counter and shouted at her over the megaphone. That was the most bizarre image I can remember, because most of the comedy in the training films is set very strongly in reality. It's comedy of observation."

The lessons learned by his Video Arts research even profited Monty Python. According to Cleese, the group's meetings used to be long, rambling, unorganized, and inefficient, but after his work on such films as *Meetings, Bloody Meetings,* they were able to accomplish their goals in a fraction of their previous time.

Cleese appears in many, but not all, of the company's films, and says he almost invariably portrays the person who gets things wrong, with a few exceptions.

"We did a film on time management and delegation where I play St. Peter up in Heaven, who actually told the guy who was getting it wrong how to do it right, which was quite fun. It was all in a Heaven set, with the gates and the mist—a little like *Heaven Can Wait.*"

Although none of the other Pythons have been involved in the films, Cleese has featured some of his *Fawlty Towers* colleagues (including Connie Booth, Prunella Scales, and Andrew Sachs) and other English comedians, such as Jonathan Lynn, John Bird, Alan Bennett (of *Beyond the Fringe*), Tim Brooke-Taylor, Graeme Garden, and Rowan Atkinson; several films were even directed by Charles Crichton, who of course collaborated with Cleese on *A Fish Called Wanda.*

Cleese's association with Video Arts continues, though he has since sold his share of the company, and he still writes and performs in new films. Unfortunately for most Python fans, the short films are designed for and marketed to business customers, so few of his fans outside the corporate world have had a chance to view them. (More information on Video Arts films is available by phoning the U.S. office at 708-291-1008.)

John Cleese seems to be having trouble holding the attention of his colleagues in **Meetings, Bloody Meetings.** *Copyright Video Arts*

THREE MEN IN A BOAT

BASED ON THE JEROME K. JEROME STORY. STARRING MICHAEL PALIN, TIM CURRY, AND STEPHEN MOORE. FIRST BROADCAST DECEMBER 31, 1975, ON BBC-2. SCREENPLAY BY TOM STOPPARD. PRODUCED BY ROSEMARY HILL. DIRECTED BY STEPHEN FREARS.

The film is an adaptation of Jerome's classic story of three holiday-makers (Michael Palin, Tim Curry, and Stephen Moore) and their misadventures when they decide to row up the Thames.

 NOTES

Three Men in a Boat involved Michael Palin strictly as an actor; the script of the adaptation was by Tom Stoppard, who would later collaborate with Terry Gilliam on the *Brazil* screenplay.

"Yeah, that was an acting job—and it was very nice to be asked," says Palin. "It was one of those things that come out of the blue—I was asked by Stephen Frears. It was a great story and a book I've always enjoyed, and so to be able to play one of those characters was lovely.

"It also coincided with one of the most marvelous summers, so we just mucked about on the Thames and enjoyed a wonderful sunny summer. Although it looks very idyllic, the Thames, it's full of motor launches, and it's a very popular holiday place, so we could very rarely do a take without the motorboats somewhere in the distance. We had to postsync the entire show, which was my first experience with the world of revoicing!"

OUT OF THE TREES

STARRING GRAHAM CHAPMAN. FIRST BROADCAST JANUARY 10, 1976, ON BBC-2. WRITTEN BY GRAHAM CHAPMAN, BERNARD MCKENNA, AND DOUGLAS ADAMS.

A series of fast-paced, Pythonesque sketches featuring Graham Chapman and an assortment of players, including Simon Jones, Mark Wing-Davey, and Roger Brierley (who is featured with Chapman as Genghis Khan and son).

 NOTES

The Cleese-Chapman writing partnership began drifting apart later during Python, and when Cleese left Python at the end of the third series, Graham Chapman began to look around for another collaborator. Although he ultimately wrote most of his material in the fourth series by himself or with the other Pythons, he did begin to do some writing with Douglas Adams. In fact, Adams co-wrote a sketch that was used in one of the final shows. (Terry Jones plays a patient bleeding to death in an emergency room, and Graham Chapman, as the doctor, refuses to treat him until he completes the admission form correctly.)

Neil Innes also co-wrote a couple of sketches with Chapman, and Innes and Adams are the only two non-Pythons to receive writing credits for the TV series.

Adams and Chapman had been collaborating at the end of Python (in fact, Adams co-wrote a few passages from Graham's *A Liar's Autobiography*), before Adams began his *Hitchhiker's Guide to the Galaxy* radio series.

Bernard McKenna had also begun collaborating with Graham Chapman; they would later write the screenplay for *The Odd Job*, and McKenna's work as an actor includes numerous roles as one of the repertory company members in *Life of Brian*.

Together, Chapman, Adams, and McKenna created the fast-paced, Pythonesque *Out of the Trees*, which marked Graham's first—and only—TV special. It was intended to be a pilot for a comedy series, a series that didn't happen because of Graham's increasing involvement with Monty Python and *Life of Brian*. Adams recalls that there was some very good material in it, but the show "didn't hang together properly" and the structure hadn't really been found; he says it was shown only once, late on a Saturday night opposite *Match of the Day*. He noted "I don't think it even got reviewed, it was that insignificant."

The Amnesty International Benefit Shows

FIRST PRESENTED 1976

PLEASURE AT HER MAJESTY'S APRIL 1-3, 1976

With Graham Chapman, John Cleese, Terry Gilliam, Terry Jones, Michael Palin, Carol Cleveland, Neil Innes, Alan Bennett, John Bird, Eleanor Bron, Tim Brooke-Taylor, Peter Cook, Graeme Garden, Barry Humphries, Jonathan Lynn, Jonathan Miller, and Bill Oddie. Stage show directed by Jonathan Miller at Her Majesty's Theatre, London; film directed by Roger Graef.

Highlights of the film include a brief introduction by John Cleese; the "Dead Parrot" sketch; "The Last Supper" with John Cleese and Jonathan Lynn; a Python courtroom sketch with Peter Cook sitting in for Eric Idle; the "History of Slapstick" lecture by Graham Chapman, with help from Palin, Jones, and Gilliam; and "So That's the Way You Like It," the Shakespearean *Beyond the Fringe* sketch with Terry Jones sitting in for Dudley Moore; ending with "The Lumberjack Song" by Michael Palin and the cast.

A TV documentary narrated by Dudley Moore was released in America, as was an unauthorized film titled *Monty Python Meets Beyond the Fringe*; this consisted of the TV documentary with the backstage scenes edited out, which an unscrupulous impresario in Washington tried to pass off as a new Monty Python film.

Cast members from the very first Amnesty International benefit included (back row, from left) Alan Bennett, John Cleese, Jonathan Lynn, Michael Palin, Bill Oddie, Graham Chapman, John Fortune, Jonathan Miller, Des Jones, and Graeme Garden, with (front row) Carol Cleveland, Terry Jones, Neil Innes, Peter Cook, Eleanor Bron, and John Bird. Photo from the Collection of John Cleese, used by permission

CRITICAL COMMENTS

(*Pleasure at Her Majesty's*—film version)
"A competition which arose by chance this week for the funniest
film in London was won by a short margin by the aptly-titled
Pleasure at Her Majesty's. . . . The collection consists only of comic
gems. . . ."

—Patrick Gibbs, *Daily Telegraph*, March 18, 1977

Soundtrack album: *A Poke in the Eye (With a Sharp Stick)*, Transatlantic/TRA 331 (1976) (U.K.). *The Complete A Poke in the Eye (With a Sharp Stick)*, Castle Communications ESDCD 153 (1991) (U.K.).

Late in 1991, Castle Communications released a double CD-version of the show, with additional material by Monty Python, Neil Innes, and other previously unreleased performances.

AN EVENING WITHOUT SIR BERNARD MILES MAY 8, 1977

With John Cleese, Terry Jones, Connie Booth, Peter Cook, Dudley Moore, Julie Covington, Jonathan Miller, Peter Ustinov, John Williams. Directed by Terry Jones and Jonathan Miller at the Mermaid Theatre.

Soundtrack album: *The Mermaid Frolics*, Polydor/ 2384101 (1977) (U.K.).
One side of the album contains music, the

other includes comedy sketches as well as a song, "Forgive Me," sung by Terry Jones (which dates back to his Oxford days).

THE SECRET POLICEMAN'S BALL JUNE 27-30, 1979

With John Cleese, Terry Jones, Michael Palin, Neil Innes, Rowan Atkinson, Eleanor Bron, Ken Campbell, Billy Connolly, Peter Cook, John Fortune, and the Tom Robinson Band, plus Pete Townshend and John Williams (including an acoustic guitar duet on "Won't Get Fooled Again"); special appearances by Anna Ford and Mike Brearley. Stage show directed by John Cleese at Her Majesty's Theatre. Film directed by Roger Graef.

Highlights from the show include John Cleese and Peter Cook performing "Interesting Facts"; Terry Jones and Michael Palin in "How Do You Do It?"; John Cleese and Terry Jones in "The Name's the Game"; Michael Palin and Rowan Atkinson in

"Stake Your Claim" (performed on *Another Monty Python Record*); Cleese and Palin in "Cheese Shop," Cleese, Jones, Palin, and Atkinson doing "Four Yorkshiremen"; and Peter Cook and the entire cast with "The End of the World."

 ## CRITICAL COMMENTS

". . . I could have done with more satire and less deadpan zaniness. We get rather too many surrealistic spoofs of the inane participation games, the pompous interviews, and the solemn

lectures which bore us on television. It is curious to see how much these comics depend on absurdist humour, now quite out of date in the theatre."

—John Barber, *Daily Telegraph*, June 29, 1979

"This is a straight-forward, no frills compilation which packs so much into its running time that it is undoubtedly a bargain package for all fans of the various and varied stars."

—*Screen*

Performing "The Name's the Game" from The Secret Policeman's Ball, *as the celebrity guest, cricketer Mike Brearley (left) prepares to assault Mrs. Yettie Goose-Creature (Terry Jones), under the beaming eyes of John Cleese. Paul Cox/LFI Photo from the Collection of John Cleese, used by permission*

Soundtrack album: *The Secret Policeman's Ball*, Island ILPS/9601 (1979) (U.K.).

Two albums were released following the shows, one containing comedy material, the other containing the music.

SECRET POLICEMAN'S OTHER BALL SEPTEMBER 9-12, 1981

With John Cleese, Graham Chapman, Neil Innes, Rowan Atkinson, Jeff Beck, Alan Bennett, John Bird, Tim Brooke-Taylor, Eric Clapton, Phil Collins, Billy Connolly, Donovan, John Fortune, Bob Geldof, Chris Langham, Griff Rhys Jones, David Rappaport, Alexei Sayle, Pamela Stephenson, Sting, John Wells, Victoria Wood, and a special appearance by Michael Palin (in the film version, to promote Secret Policeman merchandise). Stage show co-directed by John Cleese and Ronald Eyres at the Theatre Royal, Drury Lane; film directed by Julien Temple (1982) and released by United International Pictures.

Includes "Clothes Off!" (from At Last the 1948 Show) with John Cleese, Pamela Stephenson, and Graham Chapman; as well as "Beekeeping" (also from the 1948 Show) with John Cleese and Rowan Atkinson; and "Top of the Form," a young person's quiz show with John Cleese, Graham Chapman, Rowan Atkinson, John Bird, Tim Brooke-Taylor, John Fortune, and Griff Rhys Jones. The U.S. version of the film of Secret Policeman's Other Ball actually includes material from the first two shows, edited together.

 **CRITICAL COMMENTS**

(*Secret Policeman's Other Ball* —British release)

"Get ready to sample the best and worst of British satirical comedy talent. . . . Cleese appears in a number of sketches ranging from the corny to the faintly amusing."

—Arthur Thirkell, *Daily Mirror,* March 19, 1982

Soundtrack album: *The Secret Policeman's Other Ball,* Island/HAHA 6003 (1981) (U.K.)

Two albums were actually released following the shows, one containing the comedy material, the other containing the music.

The Complete Secret Policeman's Other Ball. Castle Communications, ESDCD 152 (1991) (U.K.)

Late in 1991, Castle Communications released a double CD, containing much material that had never been released, including Python-related and Neil Innes performances.

Book: *The Secret Policeman's Other Ball* Methuen Trade Paperback (1981), ISBN 0-413-50080-2 (U.K. only).

A selection of scripts and photos from the show, with handwritten program notes by Terry Jones and Michael Palin.

THE SECRET POLICEMAN'S OTHER BALL

(1982) (101 MINUTES). AMERICAN THEATRICAL RELEASE BY MIRAMAX FILMS; U.S. VIDEOCASSETTE COMPILATION RELEASE BY MGM/UA HOME VIDEO/ MIRAMAX FILMS MV800175

With John Cleese, Graham Chapman, Terry Jones, Michael Palin, Rowan Atkinson, Eleanor Bron, Tim Brooke-Taylor, Barry Humphries, Chris Langham, Alexei Sayle, Victoria Wood and many more; musical guests include Jeff Beck, Eric Clapton, Phil Collins, Donovan, Sting, and Pete Townshend. Directed by Roger Graef and Julien Temple.

The American release includes material from the first two "Secret Policeman" shows, including Cleese and Cook in "Interesting Facts"; Cleese and Palin in "Cheese Shop"; "Four Yorkshiremen" with Cleese, Jones, Palin, and Atkinson; the cast in "The End of the World." The second half, from the "Secret Policeman's Other Ball," begins with Cleese and the cast in "Introduction"; Cleese and Atkinson in "Beekeeping"; "Top of the Form" with Cleese, Chapman, and several others; Cleese and Chapman in "Fan Dancing"; and in "Clothes Off!" with Pamela Stephenson.

CRITICAL COMMENTS

"*The Secret Policeman's Other Ball* contains some of the funniest sequences to be found in any first-run movie at the minute . . . lunacy is well-served."

—Vincent Canby, *New York Times,* May 21, 1982

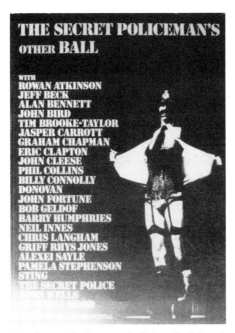

THE SECRET POLICEMAN'S
OTHER BALL

WITH
ROWAN ATKINSON
JEFF BECK
ALAN BENNETT
JOHN BIRD
TIM BROOKE-TAYLOR
JASPER CARROTT
GRAHAM CHAPMAN
ERIC CLAPTON
JOHN CLEESE
PHIL COLLINS
BILLY CONNOLLY
DONOVAN
JOHN FORTUNE
BOB GELDOF
BARRY HUMPHRIES
NEIL INNES
CHRIS LANGHAM
GRIFF RHYS JONES
ALEXEI SAYLE
PAMELA STEPHENSON
STING
THE SECRET POLICE

The Secret Policeman's Other Ball *book*

THE SECRET POLICEMAN'S PRIVATE PARTS

(1984) (77 MINUTES) VIDEOCASSETTE COMPILATION RELEASE MIRAMAX FILMS/MEDIA HOME ENTERTAINMENT M295

With John Cleese, Graham Chapman, Terry Gilliam, Terry Jones, Michael Palin, Carol Cleveland, Neil Innes, Connie Booth, Phil Collins, Donovan, Pete Townshend, and many more.
Directed by Roger Graef and Julien Temple.

Includes selections from the first four Amnesty International benefits, edited together for American videocassette, including a running Python courtroom sketch (with Peter Cook as the defendant), "Dead Parrot," "Slapstick Lecture," "Bookshop" (with Cleese and Booth), "The Last Supper," Terry Jones singing "Forgive Me," Cleese and Jones in "The Name's the Game," and even Terry Gilliam singing "Two Legs," concluding with Michael Palin singing "The Lumberjack Song."

SECRET POLICEMAN'S THIRD BALL MARCH 1987

With Joan Armatrading, Chet Atkins, Jackson Browne, Kate Bush, Robbie Coltrane, Duran Duran, Ben Elton, Stephen Fry, Peter Gabriel, Bob Geldof, David Gilmour, Lenny Henry, Mark Knopfler, Emo Phillips, Lou Reed, Spitting Image, and John Cleese. Stage show directed by Paul Jackson; film directed by Ken O'Neill for Virgin Films/Elephant House.

Includes a brief appearance by John Cleese in a sketch with Stephen Fry and Hugh Laurie in which he accepts the "Silver Dick" award, which spoofs his refusal to participate in that year's show.

Book: *The Secret Policeman's Third Ball.* Sidgwick and Jackson trade paperback (1987), ISBN 0-283-99530-0.
Contains the scripts, performance photos, and portraits of the cast.

and video.

THE SECRET POLICEMAN'S BIGGEST BALL
AUGUST 30–SEPTEMBER 22, 1989

With John Cleese, Michael Palin, Peter Cook, Dudley Moore, Jeff Beck, Eleanor Bron, Robbie Coltrane, Ben Elton, Dawn French, Stephen Fry, Lenny Henry, Hugh Laurie, Griff Rhys Jones, Mel Smith, Spitting Image, and John Williams. Directed by John Cleese and Jennifer Saunders at the Cambridge Theatre; film broadcast in Britain on ITV October 1989 and in America in June 1991 on Arts and Entertainment cable.

The ten-year anniversary Secret Policeman's show includes a Peter Cook–Dudley Moore reunion, and John Cleese and Michael Palin in a new version of the "Dead Parrot" sketch reworked for Margaret Thatcher, plus Cleese in "The Last Supper," Cleese and Palin in "Argument Clinic," a cast finale, plus Cleese as a "Spitting Image" puppet.

 ## CRITICAL COMMENTS

"Although there are a couple of duds among the collection of old and new sketches, the zingers more than make up for the stinkers. . . . On the whole, *The Secret Policeman's Biggest Ball* resembles nothing so much as video vaudeville, where the props are minimal, the jokes are uneven, and the comics sweat for their supper. In fact, it's enough to make you wish for the good old days of comedy. . . ."

—Ginny Holbert, *Chicago Sun-Times*, June 7, 1991

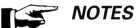

The first Amnesty International benefit was actually a reunion of the Oxbridge regulars who had carved out some success in TV and films, and by all accounts, it was a delight for the participants. The members of Python and *Beyond the Fringe* had worked together in the past and become friends, and the performers were playful and relaxed for the first benefits. The shows were relaxed, and managed to garner money and publicity for Amnesty International.

Cleese recalls the first shows as "great. They were quick in-and-outs, three or four nights performing. You didn't have to do immense amounts of preparation because it was a charity show done late at night," he says.

"Everybody knew that it was going to be a little bit rough. That was almost the point of it, that was part of the deal. That just meant it could be fun, and it could just be about doing the material as well as you could for three or four nights, and then forget it. That was a good experience."

By 1979 Amnesty International became more ambitious, and when it asked John Cleese to organize a

The Secret Policeman's Third Ball *book*

show that year, pop stars such as Pete Townshend were included. Although Townshend performed acoustically, the shows were beginning to draw rock-and-roll audiences, and the mixture of rock and comedy sketches was becoming more difficult.

The Secret Policeman's Other Ball in 1981 saw a flood of pop stars, such as Phil Collins, Sting, and Eric Clapton, join the cast of comedy performers. As a result, John Cleese lost his interest in the Amnesty shows, citing the pop stars and their entourages as a contributing factor; Cleese was much more comfortable getting together with the cream of Britain's comedy crop than organizing rock concerts.

"That one wasn't so much fun, just from a selfish point of view. The first few shows consisted of old friends and acquaintances getting together

and doing bits. It was a very cooperative and friendly feeling. That show, pop people arrived in large numbers, all of them traveling with entourages, like Elizabeth Taylor and Richard Burton used to do. So, instead of being surrounded backstage by people whom you knew, and whom you could josh, there were hundreds of strangers standing around, and you didn't know who they were or who they were with," says Cleese.

"Some of the younger comics were using their elbows unacceptably to get more time on stage, and they started using it for self-publicity. What was so nice about the first shows was that you'd say to someone like John Fortune 'Would you mind cutting your sketch on Tuesday and I'll cut mine on Wednesday?' and everybody would say 'Yeah, sure.' I remember one particular guy on the first night, Alexei Sayle, who ran overtime. I asked him if he'd take a few minutes out, and on the second night he did longer than he did on the first night, quite obviously deliberately."

After his experiences during *The Secret Policeman's Other Ball*, Cleese said he wouldn't get involved with any more of the Amnesty shows unless the focus changed.

"I would only do another one under certain conditions," he said. "I would say to them 'Look, you want to do a show with all the pop people, that's terrific. Good luck, I hope you make a fortune. But that's not the one that I want to be in. If you'd like me to organize one for you next year, well, I'll do that, but it'll be the sort of show that I want to enjoy doing.'"

As a result, his participation with the third *Secret Policeman* show several years later was minimal, and none of the other Pythons participated at all. By the time of the fourth *Secret Policeman* in 1989, however, the emphasis was again on comedy, and Cleese and many of the original performers were back.

THEIR FINEST HOURS

TWO ONE-ACT PLAYS WRITTEN BY TERRY JONES AND MICHAEL PALIN.

BUCHANAN'S FINEST HOUR AND UNDERWOOD'S FINEST HOUR

OPENED MAY 20, 1976, AT THE CRUCIBLE THEATRE, SHEFFIELD. DIRECTED BY DAVID LELAND.

Buchanan's Finest Hour opens with a large packing crate on stage. Suddenly a voice from inside reveals itself to be Sir Clive Henshaw, a candidate for Parliament, under the assumption that he is being delivered to address the press as part of a carefully orchestrated publicity stunt. Unfortunately, Harrington, the man in charge of moving the box, reveals that he is trapped inside with him, as is a French escape artist and his fiancée, attempting to break out of the unbreakable box. As they all realize something has gone horribly wrong, another smaller box is delivered onstage, this one containing the Pope and his handler, who are under the assumption that they are about to be carried onto the Vatican balcony. Gradually, they all realize things have gone horribly wrong, and they are being used

in a promotion by an international packaging firm.

The Box: Buchanan's Finest Hour is the film version of the play, directed by Mickey Dolenz of the Monkees. Richard Vernon was the voice of Henshaw, Terry Jones portrayed Harrington, Michael Palin was Dobre Elapso (the French escapologist), and Charles McKeown portrayed the Italian.

Underwood's Finest Hour involves a maternity ward doctor who would rather listen to the cricket test match commentary than deliver babies. One unfortunate patient goes into labor as England needs sixty-seven runs to win in forty minutes. The last man, Derek Underwood, comes on and starts hitting wholly uncharacteristic "sixes," so that England wins on the last ball and the husband has to deliver the baby.

 NOTES

The two one-act plays were performed on the same bill at the Crucible Theatre, which approached Jones and Palin. "They were already written," says Jones of the two plays. "We said 'We've got these things, *Underwood's Finest Hour* and *Buchanan's Finest Hour.*"

Buchanan's Finest Hour was actually scripted as part of a writing exercise by Jones and Palin. "We wanted to see if we could write a play where the audience never saw the actors," explains Palin, "and we nearly succeeded." Still, the show saw audiences staring at two large boxes on stage for nearly an hour.

When *Buchanan's Finest Hour* was revived in October 1990 in Chicago for its American premiere

at the Second City (directed by Kim "Howard" Johnson), reviews ranged from positive to enthusiastic, though audience reaction was widely mixed.

"There's a point about halfway through the show where the audience realizes that they're never going to see the actors, and I could feel the energy in the room drop," said Jones. Therefore, for the American premiere, he suggested changes that involved a foot and the Pope's fist breaking through their respective boxes. This not only gave the audiences hope that they might eventually see the actors inside, but proved to the crowds that there were actually people inside these boxes—and many people still could not believe they were watching boxes filled with actors!

CRITICAL COMMENTS

"The reason for the play's neglect is hard to fathom, given not only the popularity of all things Python-related, but also the fact that *Buchanan's Finest Hour* is a screaming laugh riot. . . . What's refreshingly different from Jones and Palin's often hyperactive TV work is the visual simplicity, even minimalism, of this play. . . . Every new burst of verbal activity brings more laughter from the audience; the laughter grows louder as the characters' desperation grows greater. If the description makes it sound like a Sartre or Beckett play, that's because it is. [An] exceedingly funny play."

—Albert Williams, *Chicago Reader* October 26, 1990

"For some, this short play will be a wildly escalating cavalcade of sublime silliness. For others, it will be a lot like watching a talking packing crate for an hour."

—Bruce Ingram, *Chicago Sun-Times*
November 16, 1990

SATURDAY NIGHT LIVE

WITH GUEST-HOSTS ERIC IDLE AND MICHAEL PALIN AND A SPECIAL APPEARANCE BY GRAHAM CHAPMAN. NBC-TV, 1976–1984.

 **PYTHON HOSTS AND GUEST APPEARANCES**

Eric Idle (October 2, 1976) Idle's first show includes a clip of the Rutles singing "I Must Be in Love." He also appears in a "Killer Bees" sketch, "Designer Babies," and a "Dragnet" parody (with the police in drag), and is interrupted as he tries to sing his version of "Here Comes the Sun." Musical guest is Joe Cocker. (Also available on Warner Home Video #29030.)

Live from the Mardi Gras, It's Saturday Night Live on Sunday (February 20, 1977) Aired from New Orleans and the Mardi Gras with guest stars Penny Marshall, Buck Henry, Henry Winkler, Randy Newman, and Eric Idle, who is doing a remote broadcast from a location where there is absolutely nothing happening.

Eric Idle (April 23, 1977) Idle hosts the "Save England" Telethon, appears in "The Nixon-Frost Interviews" (with Dan Ackroyd as Richard Nixon), presents the Idle/Weis short film "Body Language," with "The World Heavy Wit Contest" and "Plain Talk," also with Idle and Ackroyd. Musical guest is Neil Innes, who performs a very Lennon-like "Cheese and Onions" from the Rutles, as well as "Shangri-La."

Michael Palin (April 8, 1978) Michael Palin's first appearance on the show features a brief *Ripping Yarns* clip, and he does his monologue as Sid Biggs, his own manager, stuffing fish and live cats down his pants as he sings "White Cliffs of Dover." He also appears as Lisa and Todd's piano teacher in a "Nerds" sketch and is featured in a production of Chekhov's "The Seagull" while performing an escape act. Musical guest is Eugene Record.

Eric Idle (December 9, 1978) Hosting just after he returned from filming *Life of Brian*, Idle does a Tunisian monologue, is part of a madrigal quartet, plays Prince Charles about to marry a thirteen-year-old Mississippi girl in a trailer park in "The Woman He Loved," portrays a game show host in "What Do You," appears in a Candy Slice recording studio, and is a college professor in "Cochise at Oxford." Musical guest is Kate Bush. (Available on Warner Home Video #29036.)

Michael Palin (January 27, 1979) After a monologue in which he discusses his socks, Michael Palin appears in another "Nerds" sketch as Lisa's piano teacher as well as "What If Superman Grew Up in Germany?", "Family Classics" presentation of Chapter 1 of "Miles Cowperthwaite" (reminiscent of the *Ripping Yarns*), and "Name the Bats." .Musical guests are the Doobie Brothers.

Michael Palin (May 12, 1979) Features a Mother's Day monologue, while "Family Classics" presents Chapter 2 of "Miles Cowperthwaite" where Miles is on board the *Raging Queen*. He appears as Margaret Thatcher on Weekend Update, and selling black-market gasoline. Musical guest is James Taylor.

Eric Idle (October 20, 1979) Eric appears despite a heavy fever. (Although they joke about having Buck Henry go on in his place, Henry was actually standing by in case Idle couldn't perform.) Idle does stretcher impersonations for his monologue, plays a salesman in a handmade shoe store, the author of "Prince Charles Tells You How to Pick Up Girls," a female impersonator in "Hardcore II," and guests on "Heavy Sarcasm." Musical guest is Bob Dylan. (Available on Warner Home Video #29036.)

Saturday Night Live 100th Show (March 15, 1980) Michael Palin is a guest and performs in "Talk or Die," a talk show parody that was actually taped in advance for the 100th show.

Graham Chapman (May 22, 1982) Graham makes a brief appearance to promote the film of *The Secret Policeman's Other Ball* during the Weekend Update portion of the show; he wears his colonel's costume from the waist up and a pink tutu below it, to reenact the film's commercial, which NBC refused to air.

Michael Keaton (Host) with an appearance by Michael Palin (October 30, 1982) Palin appears in a dressing room with Keaton and Eddie Murphy in the show's prologue, appears as the storyteller in "A Sense of Fear," and stars as "Topol the Idiot." (Palin was promoting *The Missionary* during this time, accounting for this unusual "guest appearance" role on the show.) Musical guest is Joe Jackson.

Michael Palin (January 21, 1984) Michael's eighty-year-old mother Mary accompanies him (part of her birthday present) on the show and stays on stage, knitting, while he does his monologue. He also appears as the maitre d' of the "House of Mutton." Musical guests are the Motels.

Chevy Chase, Steve Martin, Martin Short (Hosts) with a special appearance by Eric Idle (December 6, 1986) Eric appears in a sketch as a British customs officer, on a show hosted by the "Three Amigos" to promote their film.

NOTES

Saturday Night Live is often compared to *Monty Python's Flying Circus* in spirit, if not in format. Of course, Python preceded *SNL* by several years, but the American cast of *SNL* had become aware of Python fairly early on. Michael Palin says that *Saturday Night Live* seemed to be the American TV show most influenced by Python.

"The approach to the show was loose," Palin states. "I think they'd seen Python, and I know they all liked Python very much. They suddenly realized that a comedy show could be as broad as you wanted, really, and didn't have to fall into one particular type or style.

"All sorts of things you thought were funny could be put together into one particular show and sewn up, which is what *SNL* did. I'm not sure that American shows had done that in quite the same way before. Maybe that was a Python influence, I don't know. And possibly, the emphasis on the surreal and the fantastic was something which people who had seen Python were encouraged to experiment with; they might not have been so encouraged if they hadn't seen Python."

Eric Idle—the first Python to host *SNL*—says producer Lorne Michaels was a fan before the shows were ever seen in America.

"He came and watched us recording a Python show. He came and sat in as we did the dress and then taped it," notes Idle, though he says that they didn't know who Michaels was at the time.

The cast of *SNL* were Python fans even before *Saturday Night Live* had been created. "When we first saw Belushi doing a show and we came backstage, it was really creepy to Gilliam and I, because he practically sat at our feet." Idle laughs, recalling that it was probably around the time they were promoting *Monty Python and the Holy Grail*, in spring of 1975. "He was doing a show with—Bill Murray, I think, and Gilda was in it."

Since the *SNL* crew were fans of Python, it wasn't surprising that they wanted to work with the group members. Cleese had no interest in doing live TV at such a frantic pace, and for Eric Idle and Michael Palin, who each hosted several shows, it was an experience that was alternately rewarding and frustrating.

Idle's first show was at the beginning of the second series of *Saturday Night Live*, though he had actually met the group the previous spring. "I

was a friend of Paul Simon and when we were in New York, he introduced me to all of the *Saturday Night Live* people," he explains. "We were doing the City Center, and they all came along to the opening party that Clive Davis threw somewhere or another. . . . I met Lorne there, and Chevy [Chase], and [John] Belushi, and [Dan] Ackroyd. And then after our show on Saturday night, I think I went and watched [their show] from the floor—I came in on them doing the show live. They still had the Muppets on in those days."

His first show may have been an adjustment for Eric, but he was very well received by the cast and the audience. "Chevy got injured the week before. I said we'd have to visit him once during the show, because he did a [Gerald] Ford fall and injured himself the week before I hosted, and Penny Marshall and I visited him in his apartment, lying in bed. I don't remember how he injured himself—I think he did one of those terrific tumbles off a podium, I think. So, he was lying in bed, and I used to go to visit him."

It didn't take long for Idle to realize the level of priorities of *SNL*, as established by producer Lorne Michaels.

"The show is organized around Lorne's dinner schedule. When I used to do the series, Lorne said `Here's how the show's going to be this week. Monday, we're having dinner with Meryl Streep. Tuesday, we're going to have dinner with—' and it was all names," he laughs.

"It's because he doesn't get up until two, and then they work late at night, after his dinner, so he likes to think he's contributing to the writing by going out to dinner with celebrities," Idle says with a laugh. "The show is actually based on a comfortable life-style for Lorne Michaels—that's the premise of the show."

Eric's second appearance on the show was as one of a number of guests on a special broadcast live from the Mardi Gras in New Orleans, and he says he was one of the few performers who truly enjoyed himself.

"That was fun. I was getting smarter on Lorne Michaels then, realizing that basically, he goes to dinner. We went down to Mardi Gras to try to do a live show, which is a brave thing—insane, but brave. He tried to get me to host the Mardi Gras Ball with all drag—the drag ball—and I thought 'No way am I going to stand here improvising under these circumstances!'

"So, I wrote myself a totally isolated sketch—one of my favorite sketches, one of the best things I ever did. I did it from a deserted street, saying 'Only minutes ago, there were thousands of people here, all dancing and singing and having a great time, only a few moments ago, just before you came here. . . .' It's about a guy desperately trying to fill in on TV. You would cut to the only part of the party that's not happening.

"And it was very strange, because when they did it, they had a live audience in a big building where Randy Newman and the orchestra were, and I had them in my ear. It was a fabulous way to do location filming, because I said the first line, and there was this terrific 'Wahhh' in my ear of the audience laughing, so I slowed the whole thing down. I could pace it, so where I normally would have done it as a sort of film piece, much faster, I could pace it to their laughs, which I could hear in my ear. That was good fun," Idle recalls.

"I was the only person who had a good time. They got Penny Marshall to do the thing I was asked to do. I've got it on video—it was a classic painful moment. She's sitting there—she was supposed to host it with Cindy Williams—and the camera comes up live. She's sitting there reading, and they tell her she's on. She's like 'I'm on? Now?' I mean, they did exactly my nightmare of what would happen, and it happened, and she was left desperate, without Cindy, trying to stumble through a piece—because it was a chaotic show.

"The whole point was, there was this parade, and Buck Henry and Jane Curtin were hosting it, and they always said 'Well, if anything happens, we'll just cut to the parade.' During the entire two hours of the show, the parade *didn't arrive*. The entire parade didn't show up!" he laughs. "So, that was chaos. But it was fun. The only way you could get to any location was by being on the back of police motorbikes, Harleys, so I just remember guys in drag, and these police getting everybody from set to set, all these actors in makeup and costumes. It was really bizarre."

By the time he did his last show in 1979, Idle says the show had become chaos. To make matters worse, he had fallen ill late that week, and by airtime he had a 102-degree fever.

"I'd lost my voice, I had to save my voice all the time. That was chaos. They'd got Dylan on—

Dylan had recently become a Christian, so that freaked people out, ethnically. That show was always more hype than humor, in my opinion," he laughs. "They had Dylan on, and there was this huge attitude—you couldn't focus on writing comedy. I remember realizing I wasn't very well, and then I remember in the afternoon, about three o'clock, realizing that nobody was going to write the monologue—there was not going to be a monologue! So, I just grabbed a couple of people, and we just improvised stretcher impersonations. I had to go on there, and I had nothing—that's when I realized it wasn't as professional a show as one would have enjoyed."

It was a very different show from Python, different from the way they had been used to working in general. Although they were experienced in theater, performing on live television was another matter, particularly on a show that was put together in less than a week. The Pythons were very exacting in their scriptwriting, taking the time to perfect each line, whereas *SNL* was constantly changing sketches up until air time.

"There was a lot of hanging around at *Saturday Night Live*, and then chaos. It was just quite different," Idle relates. "They seemed to be proud of working very late hours, which of course was fun, you didn't have to get into the office [early].

"But Python worked office hours. By and large, it's more efficient to work nine till five, get some stuff done and rewrite it, and then look at it and look at it. They sort of pride themselves on doing a very bad dress and trying to pull together a very average show for air. It seemed like a triumph, but only because you'd just done a terrible dress [rehearsal]!"

Michael Palin shared many of the same frustrations with *Saturday Night Live* but was also delighted at a chance to work with the cast and crew. He likened the experience of doing each weekly show to going into battle.

"Doing *Saturday Night Live* was like being in the trenches a few days before an attack was due. We knew there was going to be a confrontation on Saturday with the viewing public, the critics, the censors, the powers-that-be at NBC, the other performers, our own nerves—everything was finely tuned in a way I never experienced on British television," Palin explains.

"There was this great sense at the time of doing it, of people wanting to see the show and see what we'd done, the audiences all hyped up within the building—it's a very strong sense of being a part of an assault! The plans were hatched all night. People would be working, and people would be sent under the enemy lines all night, and they'd come back at four in the morning with a sketch.

"It was all quite unlike Python working practice. Python was reasonably relaxed, sort of nine-to-five writing time, although we were quite hysterical when we did the show. It all seemed to be much more under control on *SNL*."

Palin says that whenever he did the show, the writers and performers all seemed to loosen up more for him.

"*Saturday Night Live* was always good fun, because the people involved were so nice and friendly, and always liked to see a new face along," according to Palin. "I think that when someone new came along each week, it sort of helped the series go. I was fairly easygoing, they could dip me into most sketches because I could do different kinds of roles.

"It was obvious that when I came along, they did experiment even more with the humor they were using. They did do odd things like the pirate sketch, and suddenly writers were allowed to indulge in more unconventional, odd, or surreal ideas—like Brian McConnachie, especially the `Name the Bats' sketch, and Jim Downey—because I was there, they were allowed more of an outlet than perhaps there would normally have been. The result was a number of fairly strange, off-the-wall, rather silly sketches." He laughs. "Rather than the necessary topical, hard-hitting, solve-the-world sort of sketches.

"But I must say, my satisfaction with it decreased as I did each one. I don't mean that to sound hard on the people involved, but the first time, it's new and original and fresh, and the first one I did with this character of my manager, which I really enjoyed.

"From then on, it just seemed slightly more forced. I found it less exciting and demanding and slightly less satisfying each time, in terms of the performance. I think it actually boils down to the fact that once you've worked with Belushi and Ackroyd and Bill Murray, not to mention all the girls as well, it's quite hard to match that."

Despite the circumstances under which it was created, Idle says that he was able to do some successful writing for the show.

"They never rewrote a word. I never

understood the point in trying to write it late on Tuesday night, because it's not all that topical. I mean, some bits were good. I did a couple of films with Gary Weis. The first one we did was `Drag Racing,' which I wrote. That's the other thing—I wrote tons of their stuff, and I didn't even get a writing credit," Idle laughs.

"`Drag Racing' was me and Dan Ackroyd at Flatbush Airport, racing down in drag. The second one I did with Gary was `Body Language,' which was another little film I wrote for them. So, I worked with him twice. And then Lorne suggested that he co-direct `The Rutles' with me, which was a good move.

"There are some very good bits. There's no question that Ackroyd was brilliant, and Chevy, when he was on, was brilliant. Belushi was a phenomenal performer, and Murray too, and Gilda—I mean, they were great performers. But if you're talking about writing, they went about it in a very bizarre and difficult way. On the other hand, it is qualitatively different from the rest of American television."

Despite disappointments with certain aspects of the show, Idle has some favorite moments. "I liked Nixon/Ford, which I also wrote with Danny. And I thought `Body Language' was a good film. It was very hard to get things very funny. It was always an uphill struggle, and there was always an underlying tension and chaos and the girls were upset because of this and that reason, they didn't have enough material—there was always a whole underlying subtext which I never got, coming from English show business," he laughs. "`This is our show, you know.' And if you ever suggested `Well, maybe we should do some new characters, instead of just sticking to the old ones,' they'd get very shirty. `Well, we do it this way!' `Oh, excuse me.'"

Both Idle and Palin say they aren't interested in doing any more *Saturday Night Lives*, Idle agreeing with Palin's assessment of the show being less fun each time they did it. Still, Michael Palin's last *Saturday Night Live* in 1984 had a special meaning for him in that he co-hosted the show with his mother.

"I think it was quite nice that the last one I did was with my mom. That was really great, to see her coming along, coping with this madness." Palin smiles.

Tim Kazurinski, a writer and performer on the show at the time of Palin's last *SNL*, recalls that everyone considered him a joy to work with.

"He was there the whole week, and all of us were just blown away by how gracious, courteous, sweet, and *normal* he was, because a lot of the hosts that came in every week—people that I had admired and respected my whole life—were nightmares," Kazurinski recalls with a laugh. "Michael seemed like a person, instead of a star or a celebrity."

Kazurinski and Michael McCarthy, another *SNL* writer at the time, agree that Palin's writing background seemed to cause him to care more about the show itself than about the way he looked in it.

"He was more concerned with the overall look of the show, rather than 'How am I gonna look? How's my hair? How's my makeup?'" says Kazurinski. "We wrote this very silly scene called 'The House of Mutton,' in which lamb was in every dish in the restaurant. He loved it and really fought to keep it in, and it probably wouldn't have made it into the show if he hadn't said 'No, I like this one.'"

Palin says that even on his last show, he still enjoyed himself.

"It was always good fun, and a nice way of spending a week in New York. There was always that great high on Saturday night of actually doing it—an unequaled feeling anywhere else," declares Palin. "I've never felt quite like that, before, during, and after doing *Saturday Night Live*—it was quite extraordinary."

The George Harrison Films

CRACKERBOX PALACE

TRUE LOVE

PLUS GING GANG GOOLIE

DIRECTED BY ERIC IDLE, 1976.

George Harrison's association with Monty Python dates back many years. He was a fan of the show almost from the start, and claims Python helped to get him through some rough times around the breakup of the Beatles.

Harrison hadn't actually met any of the Pythons until 1975, however, when Eric Idle and Terry Gilliam flew to Los Angeles to promote *Monty Python and the Holy Grail*.

"I met George backstage at the Directors Guild in L.A., when we screened *Holy Grail*," recalls Idle. "Terry Gilliam and I came over to promote the film. That's when we met, and we became very, very friendly and palled around for months."

Before the days of MTV, many performers used to make short films to promote their singles and albums. Harrison was just finishing up his *33 1/3* album, and asked his new friend to film a couple of the songs.

"This was really long before people did videos. The Beatles always made films, so George said 'Come on, let's make a couple of films,' so I did. I organized and directed each—it was about three days' shooting. They're quite sweet, actually—*Crackerbox* is still a little manic, because we were on a tight budget. We brought all the *Rutland Weekend* people in and used everybody. I quite like *True Love*—it's very sweet," remarks Idle, who brought the films with him when he hosted *Saturday Night Live*.

Although the short films for George Harrison were technically his first directing credits, Idle explains that he essentially served as a director for *Rutland Weekend Television*.

"When I was doing *Rutland,* I directed virtually everything," he reveals. "I mean, I was in charge of everything. I'd say 'Put the camera over here,' and I used to have to edit it all. There were people helping in the studio and all that thing, but the responsibility of what's on was mine, and I had the pressure of all that."

The personal and professional relationship between the Beatle and the Python continued from that point, and Idle contributed Pepperpot voices for some of Harrison's music, most notably the hit single "This Song" (which deals with the lawsuit filed against Harrison over "My Sweet Lord") on the *33 1/3* album; between verses, Eric screeches "Could be 'Sugar Pie Honey Bunch'" "No, sounds like 'Rescue Me!'"

"I did a voice on *Extra Texture* too. That's when I met him, he was mixing *Extra Texture* in L.A. with Tom Scott," he recalls. "I can't remember what I did—some Pepperpot voice. I think I also did the radio ads for *Extra Texture* in England, because it was 'Onothimagain.'"

Harrison even turned up at the City Center in New York for the Python stage show; dressed as a Mountie, he joined the group onstage for "The Lumberjack Song" and was virtually unrecognized by the audience. Harrison appeared on the *Rutland Weekend Television* Christmas special, and in 1977, Idle filmed *The Rutles,* which included an appearance by Harrison.

Their collaboration continued throughout the years, most notably when Harrison helped organize Handmade Films in order to make *Life of Brian.* The first Traveling Wilburys album has liner notes written by Michael Palin, while Eric Idle wrote the notes for their second album (*Volume Three*).

Shortly after *The Rutles,* however, Idle did the last of his short music films. Idle and Rikki Fataar, as "Dirk and Stig" of the Rutles, released a single with "Ging Gang Goolie" and "Mr. Sheene." Although Harrison wasn't directly involved, the promo film was in the spirit of Idle's *33 1/3* films.

"We shot at Ringo's, which used to be Lennon's old house at Tittenhurst. We had everybody dressed up as Boy Scouts, and all the girls were wearing Brownie costumes with suspender belts—garter belts to you. Nowadays that would be sexism. Then it was just sex. It was great. The guys said it was the best day's filming they'd *ever had,*" Idle recalls with a laugh. "So there were three of those little films—that one was for Ringo Records."

RIPPING YARNS

CONCEIVED, WRITTEN, AND PERFORMED BY MICHAEL PALIN AND TERRY JONES. FIRST SERIES OF SIX SHOWS BEGAN AIRING SEPTEMBER 20, 1976, ON BBC-2 ("TOMKINSON'S SCHOOLDAYS" ORIGINALLY AIRED JANUARY 7, 1976). SECOND SERIES OF THREE SHOWS BEGAN AIRING OCTOBER 10, 1979. DIRECTED BY TERRY HUGHES ("TOMKINSON," "MURDER," "ANDES"), JIM FRANKLIN ("ERIC OLTHWAITE," "ESCAPE," "CLAW," "ROGER"), AND ALAN J. W. BELL ("WHINFREY," "GOLDEN").

SHOW 1:

"Tomkinson's Schooldays" Tomkinson, a new student at Graybridge School in 1912, waits in line for his turn at beating the headmaster. Tomkinson runs afoul of Grayson, the prize-winning school bully, and receives a boot in the head. After Tomkinson is accidentally shot by his teacher during French class, he is hopeful that his parents will take him home, but when his mother visits, she says his father is having an affair at the South Pole, while his school fees have been paid for the next four years.

Tomkinson tries to escape from Graybridge during a rugby match, but is caught seventeen miles away by the school leopard. After failing to escape while dressed as a woman, he is forced to join the Model Boat Club, where he is disciplined for constructing a 14,000-ton icebreaker.

Depressed, Tomkinson sees a notice for a school lecture by Rear-Admiral Sir Vincent-Smythe Obleson, the polar explorer. Tomkinson tries to escape in his trunk, but winds up in the headmaster's study when Obleson turns out to be Mr. Ellis, the housemaster.

Tomkinson is brought before the school bully, who allows him to be the first person to test the escape tunnels dug by the chaplain. He is caught and found guilty of smoking, drinking, lying, thieving, breaking the headmaster's writing desk, and escaping without permission, and sentenced to the Thirty Mile Hop against St. Anthony's. During the hop, as other boys are dropping like flies, Grayson gives Tomkinson a strange white powder, which gets him hopping at tremendous speed. Along the way, he stops to visit his mother. As nude men scramble every which way, she tells him he can't drop out of school, and she notices that one of the nude men is her husband.

Back at school, Tomkinson wins the hop, and Grayson has been offered the job as headmaster at Eton. Tomkinson realizes his father was never an Antarctic explorer and resigns himself to life at Graybridge, so when Grayson recommends him for the position, Tomkinson becomes the new school bully.

Featuring:

Tomkinson, Headmaster, Mr. Craffit..........................Michael Palin
Mr. Ellis..Terry Jones
Mummy...Gwen Watford
School Bully..Ian Ogilvie

SHOW 2:

"The Testing of Eric Olthwaite" In 1934, in Denley Moor, Yorkshire, Eric Olthwaite walks home through the rain, after noting the rain gauge outside the Town Hall. Once home, he comments on the blackness of his mother's black pudding and tells the family about Howard Molson's new shovel, which he finds fascinating. His father pretends to be French so he doesn't have to speak to him, while his sister Irene is downright rude.

One morning Eric finds that his parents and Irene have run away from home because he's so boring. He goes to tell his would-be girlfriend Enid, who is supposed to be walking with him, but her mother explains that she has a young man up in her room with her. Enid's father shows Eric his racing vultures, explains that Eric is boring, and recommends that he do something with his life.

The British Ripping Yarns *volume containing the first six scripts.*

Eric applies for a job in a bank but is taken hostage by a robber. They end up escaping in a limousine, accompanied by the mayor and his wife. Eric and the robber, Arthur, escape through the woods. Arthur decides against killing Eric and says that money will make Eric more interesting. They talk together about shovels and precipitation, and decide to form their own gang.

In the weeks to come, the Eric Olthwaite Gang steals shovels and rainfall records, and his reputation grows. Enid runs off to be with him, and they accidentally shoot and wound the mayor. Eric's family proudly holds a press conference before a town hall ceremony, where the mayor happily announces that Eric has agreed to succeed him as mayor. Eric addresses the attentive crowd, as he begins to describe the local rainfall.

Featuring:

Eric Olthwaite, Bank Manager....................................Michael Palin
Mrs. Olthwaite...Barbara New
Mr. Olthwaite..John Barrett
Irene Olthwaite...Anita Carey
Mr. Bag...Reg Lye
Mrs. Bag..Liz Smith

SHOW 3:

"Escape From Stalag Luft 112B" In a German prison camp in 1917, Major Phipps has trouble rousing interest in an escape one evening. Phipps decides to go alone and is immediately captured—he has already attempted over 560 escapes—and so is sent to the notorious Stalag Luft 112B.

The new camp C/O is Colonel Harry Harcourt-Badger-Owen, a suspiciously Alec Guinessian character. Phipps and another prisoner arrive at the camp, and the other prisoners chastise the Germans for not having the guts to get captured. When Phipps attempts to run off, he is shot by Attenborough, a British officer who mocks the Germans for not being able to control the prisoners.

As Phipps recovers from his wound, he confides in the colonel, telling him he's building a glider made entirely out of toilet paper rolls. The colonel explains that all escape plans have to go through several committees for approval, and Phipps grows

contemptuous of his fellow officers' attitudes toward escape, so he makes several more attempts on his own.

One morning after the Germans wake Phipps, he discovers that the barracks is deserted—everyone else has left. Nevertheless, with Phipps as their only remaining prisoner, the Germans step up security. Phipps and the half-dozen guards who accompany him everywhere are run ragged, and they hope that Phipps is planning an escape so that they can go with him. Phipps refuses to cooperate with the Germans, however.

The next morning all forty-five guards have escaped as well, and Herr Vogel is furious. When Vogel shoots the escaping commandant, he is forced to escape himself. Phipps, the lone occupant of the camp, completes his glider, digs an elaborate system of tunnels, and constructs a massive catapult, when peace breaks out. Phipps becomes the only man never to escape from Stalag Luft 112B.

Featuring:

SHOW 4:

"Murder at Moorstones Manor" In 1926 Scotland, Hugo Chiddingfold, eldest son of Sir Clive and Lady Chiddingfold of Moorstones Manor, accompanied by his girlfriend Dora, drives to his parents' estate. Hugo is so in love with his car that he angers Dora, who gets out and walks.

Hugo arrives at Moorstones Manor and greets his mother and father, the latter of whom wants to flog and beat his son—"the family loony"—for letting Dora get out. Their younger

son, Charles, arrives later, accompanied by Ruth. At dinner that evening, Father is telling grisly stories, but when Hugo arrives, talking about camshafts and throttles, they have Manners, the butler, remove him.

As Lady Chiddingfold tucks Hugo in bed, a shot rings out, and Sir Clive and Ruth are found dead in the dining room, with Charles bending over them. When Mother is called to the phone, a shot rings out upstairs, and Charles finds Hugo dead. Lady Chiddingfold accuses Charles of the murders, which he denies, just as Dora finally arrives at the door.

The next morning Lady Chiddingfold tells Charles she has called for Dr. Farson to find out who committed the murders, but Charles is upset and much more anxious to read the wills. As Charles goes upstairs to check on Dora, cleaning his gun at the time, Dr. Farson arrives. He examines the bodies and declares his love for Lady Chiddingfold.

Farson claims he shot Sir Clive so he could marry her, but Manners claims to have shot Sir Clive because of his ill treatment. They suddenly remember Dora has been left alone with Charles, but they discover her holding a smoking gun, claiming she shot Hugo, and the wounded Charles claims it was he. Dora ridicules Manners's claims of murder, saying he isn't capable of it, so Manners shoots Charles. Dora shoots Farson to show she is unimpressed, and everyone begins confession. As a gun battle breaks out, Lady Chiddingfold gets a phone call from a neighbor, with another murder confession.

Featuring:

Charles and Hugo Chiddingfold ....Michael Palin
Lady Chiddingfold ....Isabel Dean
Dora Chiddingfold ....Candace Glendenning
Ruth ....Anne Zelda
Sir Clive Chiddingfold ....Frank Middlemas
Manners ....Harold Innocent
Dr. Farson ....Iain Cuthbertson

SHOW 5:

"Across the Andes by Frog" In a sleepy Peruvian village in 1927, a radio plays a football match to a lone native, as Captain Snetterton and his Royal Sergeant Major lead a small squad of men and native bearers into the village square. They carry boxes marked "Frogs—Keep Moist."

The square is nearly deserted, until Vice Consul Gregory appears, doing up his fly. He tells Snetterton he may have trouble getting him experienced guides because of the cup final. They set off the next morning with an elderly woman as their guide, but she walks too far ahead of them, and doesn't slow down until they mistakenly ask her for schoolgirls.

That night Snetterton and the RSM listen to the frogs, and Snetterton discusses his fascination with the animals. There is a sudden commotion; the natives think the frogs are bringing bad luck on the village and causing El Misti, the volcano, to erupt. They post a guard on the frog boxes.

Later the RSM deserts his guard post for a native girl, whom he says he wants to marry. He resigns and goes off with her, to Snetterton's disgust. Snetterton finds all the guards off with native women, and the frogs have been turned loose. Later that morning Snetterton forces the entire village to comb the area for the missing frogs.

One of the natives turns on the match at Wimbledon, and Snetterton is furious. When he shoots the radio, the natives turn on him. As they charge, he grabs the sole remaining frog and flees. After three weeks of wandering, he eats the frog, and he is never heard from again.

Featuring:

Captain Snetterton..Michael Palin
Mr. Gregory ....Denholm Elliot
RSM Urdoch ....Don Henderson
Peruvian Mountain Guide ....Eileen Way

Native with Radio ....Louis Mansi
Weedy Whining Native ....Charles McKeown

SHOW 6:

"The Curse of the Claw" On a cold, stormy night in 1926 Maidenhead, Sir Kevin Orr tells his butler, Grosvenor, how much he misses his late wife. After the butler leaves, Captain Merson arrives at the door with six Asian bearers on an expedition to India, and Sir Kevin invites them to warm themselves by the fireplace in the library. When the natives become agitated, and Merson explains they are from the Naga Hills in Burma, Kevin thinks they have come to help him with a curse.

In a flashback, Kevin explains about his very strict parents, and Agatha, the girl next door, whom he loved. His childhood hero was Uncle Jack, whose home was falling apart, a man totally unconcerned with contagious diseases.

When young Kevin visits, Uncle Jack points out all of his symptoms and diseases. When he is twenty, Kevin goes to visit ailing Uncle Jack, who presents him with the sacred Claw of the Burmese vulture; it must be returned to Burma before the bearer's sixtieth birthday, so Kevin promises to return it for his uncle. He gets a job on a tramp steamer, where he discovers that most of the crew are women.

The rest of the crew decides they won't go to Burma, and when they won't allow Kevin to return the claw, there is an explosion. Kevin is the only survivor. Kevin returns to tell Uncle Jack the bad news, and Uncle Jack warns him to be ready because the claw will return to their house. Uncle Jack dies, followed shortly by Kevin's parents.

In the present, Sir Kevin presents the claw to the tribesmen. Suddenly the butler reappears to say that Uncle Jack has appeared in his bed, and he and Sir Kevin both start getting younger. Agatha reappears as well, and when they are children again, Kevin's parents arrive to take him home, and the house crumbles to pieces, leaving only the claw behind.

Featuring:

Sir Kevin Orr, Uncle Jack ....Michael Palin
Grosvenor...Aubrey Morris
Captain Merson ....Keith Smith
Kevin's Mother...Hilary Mason
Kevin's Father ....Tenniel Evans
Young Lady Agatha..Diana Hutchinson

SHOW 7:

"Whinfrey's Last Case" A very famous personality stands before a historic building in present-day London, introducing the story as traffic mishaps occur behind him.

Back at the War Office in 1913, General Chapman, Lord Raglan, and Admiral Jefferson fear that the Germans are trying to start the war a year early. They note that they must stop the Germans, or it could jeopardize their chances of ever having a war with the Germans again.

They decide to ask Gerald Whinfrey to intervene, but he refuses, pointing out that he's been saving the country every year since 1898 and needs a holiday. Gerald, fed up with being a hero, gets on the train for the Cornish coast.

Whinfrey, let off at a deserted platform, walks to the local pub. A little old lady behind the bar, too small to be seen, serves him, and later serves as his taxi driver to his cottage called Smuggler's Cottage; she tells him of the violent history of the cottage as she drives.

He is welcomed to the cottage by Mrs. Otway, the housekeeper, and over a dozen assorted domestics in charge of the smallest details. They show him to his bedroom, and after he accidentally sits on the boy in charge of the undermattress area, he goes to sleep.

The next morning he wakes to see seventy or eighty gardeners marching. He overhears the supposed domestics saying that he mustn't leave and suggesting that his kippers be drugged. He fears he is trapped in his room, but remembering it is smuggling country, finds twenty-three different secret passageways leading out of his room alone. He chooses one, emerges on a beach, then heads to town.

Outside the pub, he hears German voices singing Bavarian marching songs, but when he enters, they stop and pretend to be local fishermen. One of them, Carne, the "porter" and "head steward," reveals that he knows who Whinfrey is, and introduces everyone in the pub as a German secret agent. They have taken the place of the locals to help start a war, but as they surround him, Whinfrey realizes they're surrendering to him; they shake his hand and say they're proud to have been caught by the great Whinfrey.

Featuring:

Introducer, Whinfrey ....Michael Palin
Meat Lorry Driver ....Steve Conway
General Chapman ....Jack May
Lord Raglan ....Gerald Sim
Admiral Jefferson ....Antony Carrick
Man in Club ....Anthony Woodruff
Barmaid (Lotte)...Ann Way
Mrs. Otway...Maria Aitken
Mr. Carne ....Richard Hurndall
Mr. Ferris ....Charles McKeown

SHOW 8:

"Golden Gordon" A football match is underway in Barnstoneworth, 1935. At home, Mrs. Eileen Ottershaw listens to the match, and when Barnstoneworth loses, she removes all of the breakable, throwable objects from the room. Her thirteen-year-old son, Barnstoneworth, is learning the names of the 1922 reserve team, but she sends him out to the store. When her husband Gordon arrives home in a foul mood, he smashes the door, a chair, a cabinet, and the curtains, complaining on his team's lousy showing.

Still depressed later, his son recites the team line-ups, but his father notes their dismal records. As he stands to go out, his wife tells him she's going to have a baby. Barely noticing, he goes out to the Barnstoneworth United Social Club. He has a drink and suddenly smashes chairs, bottles, and dishes.

Gordon shows up at the practice on Tuesday night. Several players' mothers won't let them play because of illness, and some players complain about wearing each other's shorts. The manager screams at them, and finally takes off his own shorts and runs through the town,

though he is later arrested, so an emergency meeting is called.

At the meeting, due to their poor record, low finances, and loss of their manager, the chairman announces the club is being sold to the Arthur Foggen Scrap Corporation. Despondent, Gordon decides to see Mr. Foggen. They discuss the championship team of 1922, but Foggen says those days are over.

Mrs. Ottershaw is angry; her son had a history test and got his British prime ministers confused with the Barnstoneworth reserves for 1914. She triesto tell Gordon about the baby yet again, but he rushes off with an idea.

Gordon rounds up all the players from the 1922 team. Foggen and the chairman wait at the grounds, and Gordon arrives just in time with his elderly and middle-age players. They begin play.

At home, Mrs. Ottershaw hears the final whistle and starts to hide their breakables, when Gordon comes home jubilant. The joyous family starts to smash the place in joyous abandon to celebrate their victory.

Featuring:

Mrs. Ottershaw..Gwen Taylor
Barnstoneworth Ottershaw.........................John Berlyne
Gordon Ottershaw.....................................Michael Palin
Barman (Cyril) ....Ken Kitson
Football Manager ....David Leland
Chairman ....Teddy Turner
Arthur Foggen ....Bill Fraser
Mrs. Foggen ....Pat Taylor
Goalkeeper ....Charles McKeown

SHOW 9:

"Roger of the Raj" At Bartlesham Hall in 1914, young Roger breakfasts with his parents, who remain distant and aloof. Roger goes to study Latin with his tutor, Mr. Hopper, who actually teaches him social revolution and the inevitable armed uprising of the proletariat.

Later Mr. Hopper, Roger, and Lord and Lady Bartlesham hunt grouse. His mother accidentally shoots a servant, and Roger gets upset and leaves.

The family is uprooted and sent to India during the war in 1914, where they play croquet and throw dinner parties. When one of the guests, Cooper, passes the port from left to right, he is berated and sent out to shoot himself. When Meredith, another guest, agrees with him, he is sent out, and shoots himself as well. Other officers agree, and there are more suicides.

Roger sneaks off and goes to visit the lovely Miranda in the night. He wants them to marry and open up a chemists' sundries shop, but has to rush off when her father approaches.

After breakfast the next day, Roger secretly meets Miranda, who says she is ready to run away with him that night. That evening Mr. Hopper climbs a ladder into Roger's room, telling him the tsar is dead; he wants Roger's help with the revolution, but Roger explains he's running away with Miranda. Hopper is upset because he wants Roger to lead them, and the regiment won't let Roger leave. When Lord and Lady Bartlesham catch Hopper in Roger's room, he tells them Roger is leading the mutiny.

Outside, Roger addresses the regiment and his parents, and the gunsights on the rifles of the soldiers shift back and forth as he speaks. A debate breaks out, and nobody is sure whom to fire at. Roger spots Miranda and they run away, to begin their life as shopkeepers at Bartlesham Hall.

Featuring:

Roger ....Michael Palin
Lord Bartlesham ....Richard Vernon
Lady Bartlesham ....Joan Sanderson
Miranda ....Jan Francis
Colonel Runciman...............................John le Mesurier
Hopper..Roger Brierley
Major Daintry.....................................Allan Cuthbertson
Captain Meredith ....David Griffin
Captain Morrison................................Charles McKeown
Captain Cooper ....David Warwick

The immediate forerunner to *Ripping Yarns* may have been one of the Python TV shows in the third series. Michael Palin and Terry Jones were, by that time, tending to write longer-form sketches. One day they came into a Python meeting with one long, episodic sketch called "Cycling Tour" that took up the entire half-hour show. Palin played Mr. Pither, who, while on his cycling tour of North Cornwall, has a variety of misadventures; he meets the peculiar Mr. Gullivar, and winds up at the USSR 42nd International Clambake.

Unlike the Python shows that came before, "Cycling Tour" had one linear story from start to finish. (The Python opening credits and music were never even included in the half hour.) The fourth season of Python, without John Cleese to balance the mix, saw Palin and Jones becoming more dominant, and several of those shows have a strong linear story thread throughout, including "The Golden Age of Ballooning," "Michael Ellis," and "Mr. Neutron."

By the time they were offered the chance to create a new TV show, the pair was getting accustomed to working in the half-hour format. Their series is based on the English stiff-upper-lip stories of the early 1900s.

"They're about school life, escaping from German prisoner-of-war camps, plucky stories of chaps doing their best, all with a fine edge of irony. They're all made on film, apart from one, beautifully shot—I'd love to see them in a theater rather than television," admits Palin. "They all have a little hero figure who isn't really a hero—some are seen through the eyes of a child, and I play all kinds of roles. In one I play a boy of about eighteen, which is getting increasingly difficult, and in another I play two men of sixty, which is getting increasingly easier. . . ."

Palin hadn't thought about creating the show until after Monty Python had ended its TV run.

"One of the people who liked my work in Python was a guy called Terry Hughes, who has

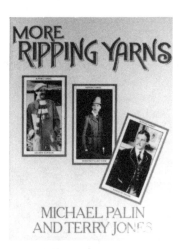

The second British Ripping Yarns *book, with the scripts from the second series.*

now done shows like *Golden Girls* and all that," explains Palin, noting that Hughes also directed the film version of *Monty Python Live at the Hollywood Bowl.*

"He approached me to do a show on my own after Python, a sort of `Michael Palin Variety Show,' and I just really didn't fancy putting on a suit, coming down stairs, singing with the Three Degrees, and introducing Des O'Connor or whatever. So, I talked to Terry about it—we were working on stuff at the time, and we'd just done the Fegg book and all that.

"I just wasn't sure which way to go, when Terry's brother had seen a book on Terry's shelf called *Ripping Tales* or something like that, and he said `Why don't you do something about those sort of stories?' And that was a very good tip. I started something called `Tomkinson's Schooldays,' which I wrote in about ten minutes at one go, and then Terry took over, and together we saw it through," he says.

The result was a very British show; nothing on American TV was comparable to *Ripping Yarns.*

"I've never seen anything in *England* that's comparable to the *Yarns*!" Palin laughs. "It was really trying to put a very, very British literary tradition, the Edwardian era, into the form of a TV comedy half hour. The stories that were around all had to do with the imperial or postimperial stage of Britain's history. They were about winning wars and fighting, pluck and courage, going out to all the far-flung corners of the world.

"That was something that really needed the British approach to work, and I don't quite know what an American equivalent would have been. Then again, in England, I suppose we take our history and our stiff-upper-lip imperialism lightly now, so it's become a bit of a joke. I don't think Americans take their history as a bit of a joke. Not yet, anyway. There's not enough of it!" he says with a laugh.

For someone expecting a "Michael Palin Variety Hour," "Tomkinson's Schooldays" must have been rather unexpected. It was not a variety show, it wasn't sketch comedy; it was nothing like the format of *Monty Python's Flying Circus,* and it certainly wasn't a situation comedy on the order of *Fawlty Towers.* It was a self-contained half-hour story, and Palin hoped to do six such shows. When Hughes saw what they wanted to do with the series, they had to do some convincing.

"Terry Hughes—it's been my misfortune to work with all of these Terrys—was not quite certain about it," relates Palin. "He liked it a lot, but it was a bit different from what was expected. Terry [Jones] and I were insisting that it must be done on film, but he [Hughes] said no, it's got to be an audience show. So, we won some battles, he won others, and what we got in the end was slightly hybrid between something that was shot wonderfully on film, and this studio stuff with an audience, so it was quite difficult.

"Our main difficulty throughout *Ripping Yarns* was to know whether we wanted to have audience reaction or not. But that one ['Tomkinson's Schooldays'] was the only one that was half studio, half film—that was made as a pilot in 1975. As a result, we were given a series, which would all be shot on film, but we still had to show it to an audience to get a reaction."

Ripping Yarns are nine delightfully quirky shows that marked the last work of Michael Palin and Terry Jones as a team, aside from Python collaborations.

Palin and Jones had been writing together for over ten years, and theirs was (and is) probably the closest friendship among the members of Python. After the TV shows ended, the Pythons tended to drift toward their own projects, all the while remaining good friends. Still, the Palin-Jones creative team continued working together.

When the offer came to Palin for his own show, he naturally called Jones. Although they wrote the scripts together, Jones found some friction working with the BBC crews. Throughout the

Python years, Palin was nearly always genial and easy to work with, whereas Jones was more meticulous and determined, and strove for perfection in the editing process. As a result, Jones acted in "Tomkinson's Schooldays" but didn't feel comfortable performing in the series.

"I was in `Tomkinson's Schooldays,' the first one, but I found it a bit awkward," explains Jones. "Generally, I think I had a very bad reputation at the BBC as being an awkward bugger, because I made life hell for poor Ian MacNaughton [who directed nearly all of the *Python* TV shows]! I was always insisting on editing the shows and going all over the locations, and keeping my sticky fingers all over everything, especially during the filming. I found it very uncomfortable doing `Tomkinson's Schooldays,' because Mike had been offered a series of his own, and I think there was a feeling amongst the crew of `Why was I interfering?' and I was saying my usual thing of `I think we could get some shots over there.'

"Finally, I said to Mike `It's either got to be our joint show, or I'll just write it with you.' I think Mike quite liked the idea of doing his own show, anyway," he says, laughing. "I decided `I'll just duck out here.'

"It was quite a difficult time, really. Up until then, Mike and I had been definitely working outright as a team; it was the first time we'd stopped. It was really because Mike wanted to do his own thing."

The first series of six *Ripping Yarns* were successful enough to warrant more. "We picked up an award from the Broadcasting Press Guild, an informal gathering of critics in England, for the best comedy show of the year," reveals Palin. The shows were expensive to produce, however, and so with BBC cutbacks, only three more shows were created for the second series. But the production values remain consistently high for all nine *Ripping Yarns.*

 **CRITICAL COMMENTS**

"The first of six *Ripping Yarns* . . . is a crackbrained spoof of the TV adaptations of books like *Tom Brown's Schooldays,* which depict the horrors of British public-school life in grim detail. Called `Tomkinson's Schooldays,' the half hour is a high-spirited, knock

about farce that's long on eccentric exaggeration and somewhat short on with and invention. . . . Palin's brand of delirium is an acquired taste, but it'll be on display in all six *Ripping Yarns*. . . ."

—Demp, Variety, November 14, 1979

Ripping Yarns: The Books and Videos

 ## THE BOOKS

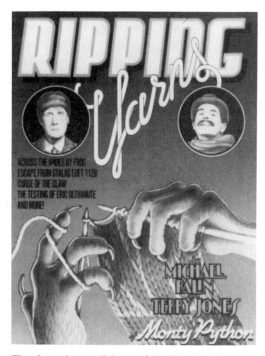 

The American editions of the **Ripping Yarns**

RIPPING YARNS

BY TERRY JONES AND MICHAEL PALIN. PUBLISHED BY METHUEN (U.K.) (1978) PANTHEON BOOKS (U.S.) (1979), ISBN 0-394-73678.

Contains the illustrated scripts of the six shows in the first series.

MORE RIPPING YARNS

BY TERRY JONES AND MICHAEL PALIN. PUBLISHED BY METHUEN (U.K.) (1979), PANTHEON BOOKS (U.S.) (1980), ISBN 0-394-74810-7.

Contains the scripts of the three shows in the second series.

THE COMPLETE RIPPING YARNS

BY TERRY JONES AND MICHAEL PALIN. PUBLISHED BY METHUEN (1990) ISBN 0-413-63820-0 (U.K. HARDBACK) ISBN 0-413-63980-0.

Includes all the scripts.

 ## THE VIDEOS

Ripping Yarns (CBS/Fox Video 3754): "Tomkinson's Schooldays," "Escape From Stalag Luft 112B," and "Golden Gordon."

More Ripping Yarns (CBS/Fox Video 3755): "The Testing of Eric Olthwaite," "Whinfrey's Last Case," and "Curse of the Claw."

Even More Ripping Yarns (CBS/Fox Video 3756): "Roger of the Raj," "Murder at Moorstones Manor," and "Across the Andes by Frog."

Three Piece Suite

"EVERY DAY IN EVERY WAY"

FEATURING DIANA RIGG AND JOHN CLEESE. BROADCAST APRIL 12, 1977, ON BBC-2. WRITTEN BY ALAN COREN. PRODUCED BY MICHAEL MILLS.

Three Piece Suite was a program starring Diana Rigg in three half-hour sketches, and the BBC asked John Cleese to act in one of them.

"I was asked to do one that had been written by Alan Coren, who I knew well. At that time, I think he was the assistant editor of *Punch*, but very much their leading writer. I was delighted to

do it, because I liked him and was particularly an admirer of Diana Rigg. It was a happy experience, the sketch worked pretty well, and I very much enjoyed working with and getting to know her," says Cleese. "She's a very substantial lady—and I speak metaphorically!"

JABBERWOCKY

CO-WRITTEN AND DIRECTED BY TERRY GILLIAM. STARRING MICHAEL PALIN WITH AN APPEARANCE BY TERRY JONES. (1977) 100 MINUTES

Dennis Cooper ....Michael Palin
The Squire..Harry H. Corbett
The Chamberlain...John Le Mesurier
Mr. Fishfinger ....Warren Mitchell
King Bruno the Questionable..Max Wall
Herald ....John Bird
Princess ....Deborah Fallender
Griselda Fishfinger ....Annette Badland
Man with Rock ....Terry Gilliam
2nd Herald...Neil Innes
Poacher..Terry Jones

Screenplay by Charles Alverson and Terry Gilliam. Produced by Sandy Lieberson. Directed by Terry Gilliam. A Michael White Presentation/An Umbrella EntertainmentProduction. RCA-Columbia Pictures Home Video VCF 3116 E.

The Lewis Carroll poem is read as a poacher checks his traps. He suddenly encounters the Jabberwock, which eats his body down to the bones.

It is the middle of the Dark Ages, and the monster has terrified the land. The survivors take refuge behind the city walls, while the residents of other small villages try to avoid the beast.

Mr. Cooper wants his apprentice, his son Dennis, to help him build barrels, but Dennis is more interested in stocktaking. Dennis warmly greets Mr. Fishfinger, father of Griselda, with whom Dennis is in love, and they discuss the monster rumors as Mr. Fishfinger orders barrels.

Dennis rows off to visit the obese, grubby Griselda and woo her, but she is hostile to anything but food. When Dennis returns, his father is dying of heart trouble. He finds the strength to curse his son with his dying breath, however, renouncing him and saying he's taking it all with him. Dennis decides to go off to the city to make his fortune, but when he goes off to tell Griselda, she is different. She throws a rotten potato out, which Dennis catches and treasures.

In the city, King Bruno the Questionable is woken and meets with his subjects, who plead for

him to save them from the beast. Outside the walls of the city, Dennis stands with a long line of peasants trying to get in, including a man with a rock, which he claims is valuable. The guards ask to see Dennis's legs, but when he drops his pants, they reject him.

As the castle crumbles around him, King Bruno meets with his merchants and advisors. He agrees to hold a tournament to find a champion to destroy the monster; the successful knight will also marry his daughter. The princess waits in a tower and is unhappy with the plan, because she wants to marry a prince.

In the rain outside the castle that night, Dennis huddles with the peasants. They agree to give him soup if he goes into the forest and gathers firewood. Dennis encounters the man with the rock, who is suddenly attacked by the Jabberwock, and Dennis runs away.

The next morning, Dennis sneaks inside the city and, wide-eyed, walks the streets until he is caught up in rush hour. He encounters a beggar who has just cut off his foot; he introduces himself as Wat Dabney, a famous cooper. He can't work because the guilds have the town sewn up,

124

Dennis woos his love Griselda, who is more interested in munching on a potato.

but Dennis rejects an invitation to go into the begging business with him. As they talk, three of the king's heralds announce the upcoming tournament.

As the tournament begins, the crowds are enthusiastic, and vendors sell turnips and rats-on-a-stick. Chasing a stray turnip, Dennis accidentally trips a man carrying an armload of armor, and he forces Dennis to carry it all the way to the shop. As Dennis watches the workers, he tries to increase their efficiency and accidentally sets off a chain reaction that destroys the shop. Delighted, one squire buys Dennis a meal, then sneaks upstairs with the innkeeper's wife. The innkeeper starts a fight with Dennis, and both of them are taken to the palace by the king's guards.

The two are brought before King Bruno, but when the innkeeper starts a brawl, Dennis escapes. He runs through the castle and walks in on the princess in her bath. She welcomes him, assuming he is her prince, and helps him escape by dressing him in a nun's habit.

When the tournament continues the next day, the king has the knights play hide-and-seek to keep down fatalities. Dennis finds his friend, the squire, who has him take his place so he can go meet a woman. The squire is accidentally killed that night in a bedroom, so the next day, Dennis is squire to the Black Knight, sent off to slay the beast.

As Dennis and the Black Knight ride through the forest, another knight appears with his squires, and they slay the Black Knight. Just before they can kill Dennis, however, the Jabberwock appears and kills everyone except Dennis. Dennis slays the Jabberwock and returns to the city a hero; even Griselda's family likes him, and wants him to wed their daughter. But the king gives Dennis half of his kingdom and forces him to marry his beautiful daughter, so the princess and the heartbroken Dennis ride off together into the sunset.

 ## NOTES

As Michael Palin recalls, *Jabberwocky* was "six weeks of shit and toothblacking."

Jabberwocky was the first solo feature film created by any of the Pythons. Terry Gilliam had wanted to make a live-action feature based on the Lewis Carroll poem; he planned to direct it himself, and enlisted Charles Alverson to co-write it with him.

Alverson was an old friend who had worked for Harvey Kurtzman on *Help!* magazine; in fact, when Alverson quit, Gilliam replaced him as associate editor.

"*Help!* was going from monthly to quarterly, and I was leaving to take a job. Terry came in from California just out of Occidental College and hit Harv for my job," recalls Alverson. "I had an apartment on East Seventy-sixth Street, and Terry slept on my couch for a while until he got a place in the Village."

The two of them had worked together, but never written until they reconnected at a party at Terry Jones's house in the summer of 1975. After Alverson moved to Cambridge in September of that year, Gilliam asked if he'd be interested in writing *Jabberwocky* with him. The screenplay was completed in early 1976. (Gilliam had originally planned to do the project as a short for the BBC, but producer Sandy Lieberson suggested he film it as a feature.)

The original poem had very little to do with *Jabberwocky*; it served merely as a jumping-off point for their imaginations; Alverson says Gilliam did not have the story plotted out when he suggested they collaborate.

"Terry had the beginning scene, in which Terry Jones gets killed, and he had the end scene, and he had a few points he wanted to make en route, and that's all. We started from the beginning of the story in which Terry Jones gets killed and worked it out. It was a process of saying 'Who's our hero? What's he doing? What does he want to do? Why does he do this?'

"It was worked out scene by scene, arguing and fighting about the socioeconomic premises," Alverson states. "Terry used to come up to Cambridge. I was working in my garage then. I was behind the typewriter and Terry would sit in front of me reading a magazine until I got pissed off at him and made him do some writing.

"See, Terry had never been a writer. He'd written captions for his animation, but he'd never written any continuity, and so we'd say 'What about this? How about that?' And then Terry would go back to London, and I'd work by myself up in Cambridge on three or four more scenes. I'd take them down to London and we'd work on them up in his studio, and he'd rewrite me. Eventually, from just sitting there throwing ideas, he'd sit face to face with the typewriter and we'd hand things back

and forth for rewriting. Terry's a much better rewriter than a writer.

"When Terry gets an idea, once you put that idea down and give it some decent clothes, he can shift it around and make it work—that's his real strong point," Alverson said in a 1978 conversation. "The more he writes, the better he'll write. I'd never written a screenplay before either, and we both learned as we went along. I taught him what I knew about writing—which isn't much—but most of it was me laying down a basic scene and him suggesting or improving it, or saying 'how the hell can we get over this point?' Of course, neither of us knew what we were doing. We didn't have a clue, but we learned a bit."

Gilliam had co-directed *Monty Python and the Holy Grail* with Terry Jones by this point. *Jabberwocky* was his first feature, and he found himself directing actors who had not co-written the script with him.

"I really enjoyed directing *Jabberwocky*," Gilliam recalls with a smile. "It was awful, but I enjoyed it, because it wasn't the same sort of thing as Python. In *Jabberwocky*, the actors added a lot—they changed lines and everything—but they were still willing to let it be the thing that I started. They were helping me get it done, whereas with Python, all of our ideas are in there, and when you start doing a scene, everybody has a different way of doing it."

Gilliam says some of the negative aspects of the film were still lingering more than a decade later.

"I think the smells were the worst thing. I've still got a sweater that smells of burning tires, because that's how we created most of that smoke—it just becomes burnt rubber, which sticks to everything. It gets in your nose, your ears— inside the castle we were using Fuller's earth* all the time, and we'd come out of there with it just stuffed in every orifice! It was pretty foul, and there was oil-based smoke going all the time, so it always smelled like a church," he recalls.

"The thing I remember most, though, was that there was this other film being made at the same time at Elstree, which everybody was pooh-poohing. Everybody thought ours was a wonderful film to be on, and I really knew what I was

The director studies storyboards as he huddles for warmth on location for Jabberwocky.

*a "cleaner" type of dirt scattered around the sets to provide a more authentic "look."

doing, and it was going to be a big success. This other film was being made by somebody who clearly knew nothing about directing and it was just disastrous, until the film came out. The film was *Star Wars*. And the minute the film was a success, they all started wearing their *Star Wars* T-shirts, which they had refused to wear up until that moment!"

Gilliam says that since they were on a budget with *Jabberwocky*, they had to recycle materials.

"We used the old *Oliver!* sets from the film musical. They were still standing, so we just adapted them," he explains. "We had very little money, and to try and do something as ambitious as a medieval film, we were stealing all the time! Anything that wasn't nailed down, our boys went out there and took it! The *Oliver!* set we redressed, and we bought some sets off a German company which had just done the *Marriage of Figaro*—they were five thousand pounds, and we converted them to interiors.

"At the time, Blake Edwards was making one of the *Pink Panther* films, and he had just built a castle out at the back lot of the studio at Shepperton. Amongst other things, he had a wonderful sewer set which I saw, and then wrote a scene for, and he also had a catapult, which we needed for our film.

"Rather than let us have any of these things, or even let us pay for and redress them, he smashed them all up. That was just mean-spiritedness. People were so obsessed by the fact that they thought our film would get out first, and we would have used their things—they didn't realize that there was no intention of that. The whole point was to disguise anything else we got, but he literally burned his catapult and smashed his sewer set. We still managed to scrape through."

Because of the demolition, however, the sewer scene was never shot for the film.

"The scene wasn't in the original script, it was only when I saw this great thing—it was going to be a great way of getting into the castle, it was going to be up through the toilet system, so that Dennis came in completely covered with shit. I think in the end, we probably did the best thing, which is our peeing dawn chorus—the guys on the battlements taking their morning piss on him. Scatology was the order of the day. Anything that was shitty or dirty or anal, we went for!" he laughs.

Despite the lack of the sewer scene, Gilliam says he didn't have to edit any scenes out of the final print.

"I think everything got in there. There was really no fat. The scene that I'm in, playing the guy with the rock, Dudley Moore was originally supposed to do that part, but he went on to bigger things, and I had to stand in for him."

Ever aware of his directorial responsibilities, Gilliam made sure he didn't ask any of his unit to do anything he wouldn't do himself.

"I recall going to an abattoir to get guts from cows to use for the skin of the monster." He laughs. "We took tripe and stomach linings and lungs. I felt I had to do this myself . . ."

Gilliam says that he himself is constantly surprised by *Jabberwocky*.

"One thing that did intrigue me was when we had to show the film to Dutch distributors, and we showed it down at the labs. Someone had forgotten to bring the soundtrack, and we watched the film in complete silence. What impressed me was what a stunningly beautiful film it was! Without the soundtrack, there were no jokes, so it was much less funny, and you could see that it was just a seriously beautiful film!" he relates. "Usually people are distracted because something silly is going on, or people are saying something stupid.

"I watched it on television about a month ago, and found it one of the strangest films I've ever seen," claims Gilliam. "It's all extremes. It's extremely beautiful, it's extremely stupid, it's extremely ugly and dirty, it's extremely funny, it's extremely everything. There's no middle ground in the thing, it's all on the edges, and for that it's most fascinating and possibly deeply flawed!"

Jabberwocky was also Michael Palin's first lead in a feature film; he would later go on to work with his Python teammate in *Time Bandits* and *Brazil*. Although he loved working with Gilliam, he did note what he refers to as the director's natural propensity toward filth in *Jabberwocky*.

"There was dirt . . . mud . . . soil . . . dust everywhere. It was Terry's view of the Middle Ages. No one could see a thing, they all had rotting teeth, and it was all generally falling apart," Palin laughs. "Which is a nice conceit, but it obviously wasn't all like that. It made for a nice theme to the film—whatever you touched crumbled slightly. And it's brilliant—visually it's absolutely stunning—it has a freshness and power that very few other films have. I was very pleased to do it, and it was actually a very happy film, very enjoyable. But dirty. God, it was dirty!"

This cast shot includes Neil Innes (second from left in background) and Max Wall (as king on the throne), in addition to Michael Palin and the rest of the Jabberwocky *cast.*

His first post-Python collaboration with Gilliam cemented a cinematic relationship that would continue through the years.

"I enjoy working with Terry—it's rather bracing. It's not easy, but at the same time, it's not difficult. I find the difficulty is when you find you're doing something you're not enjoying, or you're being asked to do things you may not especially like. It wasn't difficult like that—Terry knew what he was doing. It was just physically hard work, and there was quite a lot of argument and dialectic going on to get the thing done. But that was fine—it just means you worked hard," he explains.

Palin also remembers *Jabberwocky* for another reason, one that involved a scene outside the castle.

"It's the first time I exposed my bottom to the camera," reveals Palin. "Terry Jones, of course, had done that in several Python episodes, and it was my first moment, outside the castle. I presumed they were going to give me some sort of underpants, and they said 'No, no, there were no underpants in the Middle Ages—when you take your trousers down, that's it.' So I just did it in the end.

"The castle was open to the general public at the time. They hadn't been able to get it closed, so there was a whole line of tourists. We did three takes, and they edged closer each take, so by the third take they were practically inches away from my buttocks, old ladies with their cameras clicking away. Somewhere, in yellowing photo albums in the country, are pictures of my bum!"

One of the most pleasurable experiences of *Jabberwocky* for Palin was the opportunity to work with some legends. "I had the chance to work with some wonderful old English actors who are now no longer here—Max Wall, and John Le Mesurier, who is just a wonderful performer who I greatly admired—a marvelous master of the understated. Very funny."

The completed film received mixed reviews, though its reputation has grown since its initial release. Gilliam and Alverson remain justly proud of it, although the year after it came out, Alverson said its flaws stood out for him.

"Some of it is badly written, other bits that were written well enough weren't played right. I think it could have been a lot better, and Terry thinks so too. But it's hard to be objective about your own work, and how it's illustrated and made real. Terry did a good job in a lot of things, he does brilliant images. I don't like the way he handles a camera very much," Alverson noted in 1978, "but he's never done it before, he's learning. I know I couldn't do half as well as he did.

"I thought one of Terry's problems was controlling the cast and making sure he got exactly the performance he wanted, because an awful lot of it's crude. But some things were very good. The best things were the images—the pictures were beautiful."

Alverson says one of the least convincing scenes for him, and one he wished they could have done over, was the climactic fight with the Jabberwock. The monster was actually a man inside a suit; Gilliam had him backward in the costume, so that his leg movement would appear different, walking almost like a chicken. To make the creature appear larger, the filmmaker actually shrank the knight by shooting a child in the armor for a few shots.

"I wasn't really convinced by the fight. I felt Terry went in too much for static shots, where we see the whole of the character, we see what he's doing," said Alverson. "There were three knights, three different sizes, and the kid in the final one was just running at empty air. I would have done it with a bunch of random detail shots and put it together as a composite, rather than show the whole thing—I thought it was a boring fight. I didn't believe he was in danger. I don't know how it looks to somebody who doesn't know the film, but I'd liked to have seen a better film—it should have been a lot better written, because we didn't know what played and what didn't. I think the next one, if there is a next one, will be much better."

There would indeed be a next one—and one after that, and more after that—for Terry Gilliam, even though the release of *Jabberwocky* proved to be a nightmare for the director. Fans of Gilliam are familiar with his battles with Universal over the ending to *Brazil* and the financial fights over *Baron Munchausen,* but not many remember the problems he experienced when his first movie was released.

Against his strict instructions, *Jabberwocky* was identified as a Monty Python film, even though it clearly wasn't, so when ads for *Monty Python's Jabberwocky* began appearing in newspapers across America, Gilliam hit the ceiling.

"It's a sore subject, it really drove me out of my mind," says Gilliam. "It had always been agreed all the way through the thing that it wasn't a Python film. We argued about this, because from their point of view, it was obviously the easiest way of selling this thing. And I said 'Well, whatever it is, you can't sell it this way!' The interesting thing was that in some of the early screenings, the audience understood my point. They gave out brochures to some screenings that gave people the impression that they were seeing the new Python film, and they came out very confused. I said 'If people come to this film thinking it's a Python film, they're going to be disappointed, because it isn't.'

"We actually had meetings, and they agreed 'Yes, the one thing we must not do is sell this as a Python film. It's got to be sold on its own merit.' I thought we'd finally cracked it, I thought 'That's it, fine.' And then it came out: *Monty Python's Jabberwocky.* We sent letters off and stopped it, but our lawyers buggered it up a bit and let them off the hook—I was really angry, I wanted to sue them.

"I was very confused personally on how they should sell the film, but the one thing I knew was that I didn't want it to be sold as a Python film. That was the only thing I knew, and that was the one thing they did. Somebody saw it in California as *Jabberwocky and the Holy Grail!*"

Gilliam actually anticipated the potential Python problem early on, and he says he deliberately edited the film so that people wouldn't anticipate seeing a Python movie.

"Some of the early cuts were quite different from the final ones, and we actually changed them trying to overcome the Python anticipation. Originally, the film started out in a different way—it was much funnier in the beginning. But about a third of the way through, people started to wonder what was happening, because suddenly it wasn't funny. The things they were laughing at in the beginning weren't necessarily meant to be that funny, and yet, because they thought they were supposed to be seeing a Python film, they were laughing twice as much as they ought to. When it became apparent that these things weren't really meant to be that funny, they were going 'What is this? This is awful.' So, we tried to make the beginning slower and less funny, so that people were confronted with the fact that it wasn't going to be that funny a film. I said 'Let's really knock them down at the beginning, so that if they laugh later on, fine.' We never actually solved the problem, because it was another medieval film, and there were three Pythons involved in it, and to sell it as a Python film just really killed it.

"When it's gone out just on its own in countries that haven't seen Python, it's gotten incredible reactions," reveals Gilliam. "It's gotten good reaction in countries that know Python, but in places where they know nothing about Python, it's been terrific, because they have nothing to compare it to. They've gone to it just as a film, and then made up their own minds as it went along.

"Mike and I went to a wonderful showing at a film festival in Spain. It was shown in this small cinema on this back street. They weren't even festival people, it was just guys trying to get out of the sun. It wasn't even subtitled—they were just workers and they couldn't understand English, and they loved it! It was really amazing, it was the best viewing I'd ever seen, and Mike and I just couldn't believe it. Again, those were people coming in with an open mind."

After *Jabberwocky* had been released and Gilliam finally straightened out the misleading publicity, he was to begin work designing *Life of Brian* for director Terry Jones. He had decided not to direct any more Python films, slightly frustrated with the

A poster from the German release of **Jabberwocky**

six-way collaborative split, and he had also tired of doing animation. By 1978 he was making plans for what would become an acclaimed directing career.

"I really want to continue along the way of *Jabberwocky*," he explained, "where I write, design, and direct a film, just do everything, like I did with the animations. It's taking something from an original idea and carrying it all the way through to the final result, and that's what I like doing. That's what I get a lot of pleasure from. Live-action films are just so complicated, and you have to work with so many people, that I just don't think I could get bored with it! With animation, I'm on my own or with one assistant most of the time, and it begins to get boring.

"When I'm working with all these people with different talents and ideas, I can start using them and drawing them in. It's great, it's really exciting. I don't get that enjoyment out of the Python films, because it isn't the same. Unfortunately, I like doing my own thing!" he said.

Gilliam would win acclaim for doing his own thing in the years to come.

 ## CRITICAL COMMENTS

"The film does sag in places and lose its way here and there; but I'm willing to overlook most of this for the gale of laughter it blows around human hypocrisy and humbug. Max Wall's King Bruno is the portrait I'll remember longest—so funny at times that I quite literally laughed till I cried. John LeMesurier's Chamberlain runs him fairly close and Michael Palin's portrait of the idiot apprentice is great fun, too. But taste *Jabberwocky* for yourself."

—Derek Malcolm, *Cosmopolitan,* May 1977

"*Jabberwocky* deserves its Lewis Carroll association; he would have rejoiced in its nincompoop wit and the blue-sky reaches of its nonsense. Not often has the rude been so recklessly funny."

—Penelope Gilliat, *The New Yorker,* May 9, 1977

JABBERWOCKY

BY RALPH HOOVER. PUBLISHED BY PAN BOOKS (U.K.) (1977), ISBN 0-330-25012-4. PAPERBACK ADAPTATION OF THE SCRIPT BY CHARLES ALVERSON AND TERRY GILLIAM.

THE STRANGE CASE OF THE END OF CIVILISATION AS WE KNOW IT

STARRING AND CO-WRITTEN BY JOHN CLEESE. FIRST BROADCAST SEPTEMBER 18, 1977, ON LONDON WEEKEND TELEVISION.

Arthur Sherlock Holmes...John Cleese
William Watson..Arthur Lowe
Mrs. Hudson, Francine Moriarty ....Connie Booth
Dr. Gropinger ....Ron Moody
President...Joss Ackland
Klein..Bill Mitchell
English Delegate ....Denholm Elliott

Screenplay by John Cleese, Jack Hobbs, and Joseph McGrath.
Produced by Humphrey Barclay. Directed by Joseph McGrath.

After international diplomat Henry Gropinger is killed and his diary stolen, the U.S. president gets a threatening note from Moriarty. Following a meeting of international diplomats, the chief commissioner of Scotland Yard decides to contact the grandson of Sherlock Holmes to battle Moriarty's descendant. Holmes accidentally attacks him, and Watson is revealed to have a bionic nose and legs. While the chief commissioner is talking to Holmes and Watson, he is mysteriously stabbed to death.

Holmes and Watson carry the dead commissioner to Scotland Yard on a bus, wrapped in a package. They join the international conference, where the members are killed off in succession. Holmes suggests a convention of the world's greatest detectives, in order to tempt Moriarty into killing them. Hercule Poirot and Columbo arrive, as does Holmes, who is disguised as Kojak. A huge number of TV and movie detectives show up, including a false Watson, and Holmes has to sort everything out and save civilization.

 NOTES

The Strange Case of the End of Civilisation (As We Know It) was a TV movie originally done for London Weekend Television (and later shown on PBS in America), in which John Cleese plays Sherlock Holmes. Curiously enough, fellow Cambridge grad-uate Peter Cook played Sherlock Holmes (to Dudley Moore's Watson) the same year in *Hound of the Baskervilles,* a spoof that he also scripted.

Cleese says he did not originate his own Holmes film, however. "It was an idea of Joe

McGrath's. Joe brought the project to me, and I rewrote it with him. "Connie played Moriarty's granddaughter.

"Some of it, I thought, was terribly funny, particularly Arthur Lowe, who played Watson. He is a wonderful English character actor who had an alarming habit of falling asleep during takes. He couldn't sleep at night, and I think he had some condition similar to narcolepsy, and he twice fell asleep during takes, which was the most amazing thing I had ever seen. The first time, he was off camera, but the second time, he was on camera!"

The film was poorly received in Britain, and Cleese admits the final result was a disappointment and takes his share of the responsibility.

"That was something that I completely misjudged. Oooo, one of my cock-ups!" he laughs. "I thought it was very good when we were doing it. The audience mostly didn't like it, in England it was pretty much of a flop. In America, oddly enough, people liked it much better. I still think, in retrospect, there were some very funny things in it, but by and large, I got it wrong.

"But it was a bit of a mess-up. Consequently, I tend to not go back and look at my old stuff with much interest. I think I'll do that in my retirement, when I have the time. So, I haven't seen it recently and I can't judge it, but it wasn't a success."

THE STRANGE CASE OF THE END OF CIVILISATION AS WE KNOW IT

BY JOHN CLEESE, JACK HOBBS, AND JOSEPH MCGRATH. PUBLISHED BY STAR BOOKS (U.K.) (1977), ISBN 0-351-30109-0.

Contains the script and stills from the LWT production of the film. Two editions were published; one was a TV tie-in with a photo cover, the other a "Humour" edition with a painted cover. The contents are identical.

THE MUPPET SHOW

SPECIAL GUEST JOHN CLEESE. FIRST BROADCAST OCTOBER 1977 (U.K.), MAY/JUNE 1978 (U.S. SYNDICATION).

John Cleese agreed to guest star on Jim Henson's *The Muppet Show* (and later, in *The Great Muppet Caper*) due to his friendship with Muppeteer Frank Oz, who has since grown into directing features (including *Little Shop of Horrors*).

Cleese was the human guest in the variety show, participating in the sketches and interacting with the Muppets. In one of the most memorable, he plays a pirate with a parrot on his shoulder (at one point he asks "Do you want to be an ex-parrot?"); in other sketches he declines to sing "The Impossible Dream," and takes charge of the Swinetrek.

"I was always enormously fond of Frank Oz, and we've remained vaguely in contact. I saw a great deal of him when he was in London shooting all the television shows for the Muppets," explains Cleese. "I never knew dear Jim Henson anything like as well—it was more of an acquaintanceship. He was simply a man I liked and admired, and his calm was legendary.

"Frankie and I have got similar kinds of interests, and we've remained great buddies. Oddly enough, yesterday I was working on a script with someone, and Frank doesn't know this, but I'll probably ask him to direct it. I'm very fond of the man, and a great admirer of his work.

"With him there as a kind of bridge, I felt enormously at home on that project. If I had to offer one criticism, they were always *so* perfectionist on the technique, and I always wanted them to take that amount of care on the script."

Still, Cleese himself says he is surprised at how quickly he came to accept the world of the Muppets.

"I had a little scene with Kermit on the TV show. We did it two or three times, and it wasn't quite right—we were rehearsing our way toward a good take. We did the shot and the director shouted `Cut!' I knew it was a good one, and without thinking, I *patted Kermit on the head!*" he laughs. "One gets sucked into it so easily. . . ."

***Cleese and friend during his appearance on* The Muppet Show.**

The Post-Python Commercials

☞ ## PARTIAL LISTING OF ADVERTISEMENTS FEATURING JOHN CLEESE

Sony (1977–80): Cleese wrote and performed dozens of radio and TV ads in Britain over the years. A typical ad would show him in tropical splendor, promising to tell viewers how they could get a brand-new Sony product and a tropical holiday—the answer, of course, is to work very, very hard and save up lots of money.

General Accident Insurance Company (1978): A series of British ads for the insurance firm; typically, Cleese would get in an accident, but remain calm and collected because he is insured by General Accident.

Callard & Bowser (1982): Half a dozen radio commercials for the British candy company produced by an American ad agency; these marked Cleese's first major ad campaign for the American market.

American Express (1983): Cleese began appearing in several American TV commercials for this company, portraying an upper-class gent whose butler is eligible for the American Express card, though he is not. (This role won Cleese a Clio Award in 1984.)

Kronenbourg (1984): Another series of four American radio spots, in which he mangles their "better, not bitter" slogan.

Compaq Computers (1984): A series of American TV ads in which Cleese portrays a foolish executive who wastes money on more expensive, less effective computers.

Schweppes (1989): On the videocassette of *A Fish Called Wanda*, Cleese performs in a commercial for the beverage company, posing as his own twin brother and delivering a message on subliminal advertising.

The Talking Yellow Pages (1989): A British TV ad series that shows him using the Talking Yellow Pages for a variety of reasons, such as searching for a ring to win a princess.

American Express (1991): Cleese is featured in a series of print ads, here showing him dressed up in grossly elegant drag, as he strives to look like "a Nancy Reagan socialite."

Panasonic (1991 and 1992): American TV ads showing Cleese demonstrating a variety of Panasonic products within other products (a shot of Cleese with a stereo system is revealed to be an image in a video camera, which is revealed to be an image on a TV, etc.), using Panasonic's "Smart. Very Smart" slogan.

Schweppes (1991 and 1992): A series of American TV ads similar to the commercial at the beginning of the *Wanda* videocassette.

PARTIAL LISTING OF COMMERCIALS FEATURING ERIC IDLE, MICHAEL PALIN, AND TERRY GILLIAM

British Gas Board (1972): A carnival atmosphere dominates this animated ad for "The Great Gas Gala." Produced by Terry Gilliam during the Monty Python TV series, the commercial, set in a fairground, is very much like his *Flying Circus* animation.

The Nudge Bar (1972): When a candy manufacturer introduced a new product called the Nudge Bar, who better to promote it than the original "Nudge, Nudge" man, Eric Idle?

WXRT Radio (1984): Michael Palin stars in ads for Chicago rock station WXRT in a series of appeals delivered in front of a blue curtain. The most successful of these shows Palin holding up

a pizza, comparing other stations' records to it, while another has him in a Beatle wig for the station's "Rampant Beatlemania."

Metro Motors (1989): Eric Idle stars in this TV ad as a race car driver, his first non–candy bar commercial.

Orangina (1989): This elaborate, expensive commercial for the orange drink was directed by Terry Gilliam on the condition that it be shown only in France. The plot involves passengers on a corporate jet who find an inventive way to shake their bottles of Orangina.

NOTES

Most of the Pythons have done some TV commercials, if only for their own films, but only John Cleese turned commercials into a gold mine.

John Cleese began making commercials around 1973, and discovered an extremely lucrative new career for himself in Britain, America, and around the world, including Australia, Denmark, Norway, Sweden, and Holland. He writes most, though not all, of them. He explains that he applies the same general principles to his ads as he does

his training films, emphasizing the key points, whether the commercial is British, American, or Norwegian.

"If the people briefing me are quite clear on what they want to get across, then I will think and come back to them with certain questions. If they clarify those questions, I will then usually do some rough recordings, and hand the tapes over to them. They will then come back and say what they think works," explains Cleese.

"Then we have a stage of cutting, changing, reshaping, and then another stage of fine-polishing. So, it goes through a few backwards and forwards, but basically, I'm writing them.

"In America, though, I don't pretend to know the sensitivities, so I listen very carefully to what the people say. If somebody says `You can't say that' in England, I would say `Don't be so bloody silly, of course it's all right.' But if somebody says that in America, I don't feel I'm in any position to argue."

Several of his American commercials make fun of the relationship of Britain and the U.S., including the Callard & Bowser radio ads. One of the commercials is as follows:

Look, all you American persons, it's been suggested that I urge you to go out and buy Callard & Bowser's extremely fine, rather sophisticated British candy ... a sort of call to action. Well, frankly, the last thing you Americans need is a call to action. I've never seen such an active bunch in my life, if you're not making millions or defending the free world or putting men on the moon, you're out jogging. I mean, if ever there was a nation of get-up-and-go, let's-get-this-show-on-the-road, it's you U.S. persons, isn't it? You don't need a call to action. You need a call to keep still for a couple of minutes. Put your feet up, open a packet of Callard & Bowser's superior candy, and wallow in the sensual pleasure of a bit of toffee or butterscotch or even juicy jellies. Trouble is, two minutes of that sort of pleasure you'd all feel guilty and have to rush back to work and start slaving away again—the old American work ethic. So to help you, we've made Callard & Bowser candy jolly tricky for you to find. You may have to comb the streets to find a shop that stocks it. And then it may be jolly tough discovering where it's hidden. But when you do find it, you'll have experienced enough blood, sweat and toil to be able to really enjoy it. . . . clever bit of marketing, really, isn't it?

(Co-written by John Cleese and Lynn Stiles)

Although a few big stars in America still shun U.S. commercials, Cleese says negative aspects of commercials were never a consideration for him.

"First of all, I didn't want to come to America and be a big star, because it just isn't what my life is about. It's never occurred to me to do that. It's suited Dudley [Moore] fine, for example, he's done marvelously well, but it's never occurred to me as being a possibility, and it would never happen. It's just not what I want to do with my life. I've been enormously happy working in England because of the freedom I've got."

Of all the commercials he's ever written, the one he may be the proudest of was actually performed by his mother. When *Life of Brian* was opening, each of the Pythons had their mothers record a radio ad for the film. John's eighty-year-old mother Muriel read an appeal to the radio audience, stating that she is 102 years old and kept in a retirement home by her son; unless enough people see his new film and make him richer, he will throw her into the streets, where she will die. As a result, Mrs. Cleese actually won an award for best radio entertainment commercial of 1979.

"Commercials have been all-important, because they've given me a real financial base, which you just don't get from working in English television. I could do a series every year for English television for the rest of my life, and I'd never be able to stop working. Something like the television commercials for Sony in England enabled me to commission six different friends to write scripts—not for me, just friends who wanted or needed to write. I was able to commission them to do it. You can only do that if you've got a considerable source of funds, and that's where the commercials come in," explains Cleese.

"*Families and How to Survive Them* cost me something over twenty thousand pounds from the time I paid for Robin Skynner's time, paid for one or two flights—but that's fine. That meant I was able to make sure that book happened. In fact, I was able to provide the circumstances under which it could happen from the money from commercials. It's the way the world's constructed. You earn these ridiculous sums of money from commercials, and you can spread it around and make all these other things happen!"

John Cleese even filled in for Eric Idle on one of his commercials; Cleese has easily done more commercials himself than the rest of the Pythons put together.

"I have done very little commercial work, but I did one in the early seventies for a chocolate bar, where I did `Nudge, Nudge,'" reveals Idle. "I then went over to Australia and did one for a product called the `Nudge Bar,' which I advertised as `Nudge, Nudge.' They asked me to come back again, and I didn't want to go all the way to Australia, so Cleese went. He went on as my brother, and he said he wasn't the Nudge Man, he was his brother. He took that commercial over!"

Idle says, "I did one a few years ago with Nigel Mansel, who's a racing car driver, for Metro Motors. That was quite fun, jolly good. But with two commercials in eighteen years, I'm not going to give John Cleese a run for his money. He does eighteen commercials in two years—he knows where the easy money is!

"I'd like to do hundreds more, I'd love to—it's new money for old rope, really," Idle says with a laugh.

Terry Gilliam has done three commercials; his early, animated film for the British Gas Board; one elaborate, high-budget commercial when he was between films—an Orangina ad that was shown only in France—and a third one that Gilliam has completely forgotten about.

"There actually was a commercial I was involved in and I barely remember it. There was animation, and I can't remember. It's a weird one, it's like I block it out, but there's another commercial in there somewhere. It takes place at an art gallery and Rodin's *Thinker* is involved. . . .

"I had always said I wouldn't do commercials, but when I was asked by the British Gas Board, I thought `everybody has to have gas, I'm not selling anything—it's like coals to Newcastle.' People have it whether they want it or not," Gilliam says, laughing. "So, they gave me a completely free hand to do anything I wanted, which was great. I did two based all around a big animated fairground."

After *Brazil* was completed but before it was released, Gilliam was approached about doing another commercial, this one for the orange drink Orangina.

"I agreed to do it at a point where it looked like *Brazil* was not going to be released in the States and I was really depressed," Gilliam explains. "They came to me with a really nice idea, and I just

thought `I've got to do something to keep myself busy,' and I agreed to do it.

"It takes place on a strange executive jet (which goes through strange turbulence to shake the Orangina). Charles McKeown and Terry Baylor [both of *Life of Brian*] were in it, and it was a chance for me to try some blue-screen work, which I hadn't done before, but then used in *Munchausen*.

"They caught me at a really low moment, and it taught me not to do commercials again, because everything became more complicated. But it worked out—it was an interesting one. It's actually a good commercial. In the end, what made me angry was that there's a forty-five-second version and a thirty-second version, but the best one, the really perfect version, is a minute long. They wouldn't do a minute one, though, so we had a forty-five-second one which wasn't shown in very many places, and the thirty-second one. Then they did stupid things like change the music, and they basically just ruined a whole element of the thing. It's still a good commercial.

"The deal I made was that it could only be shown in France, not in England, so that nobody would ever know what a sellout I was," he laughs. "I leave that to John and Eric!"

By and large, Gilliam tries to stay away from commercials, and doesn't plan to do any more.

"I do avoid them, because it's a lot of seemingly second-rate people who are desperate to get into the movies who are having their chance to play around," Gilliam relates. "They complicate what should be simple, they're so neurotic, and you waste time in pathetically stupid meetings. The money is far too good for what it's about. Somehow, I felt I didn't want to contribute too much to the conquest of the world by advertising. I'd rather make films, I'd rather concentrate my energy on that."

Director Gilliam doesn't plan to dive into commercials any further. Photo from the Collection of Terry Gilliam, used by permission

Michael Palin says he is rather reluctant to do commercials, and has done very few. His Chicago-area radio ads were unusual for him. "I thought it was a good station, and they just wanted me to do some funny commercials. I rather liked the idea of going to Chicago for a day or two. In the end, it was done in an amazing rush, one day on the way back from Australia or somewhere like that, the end of some mad journey. We didn't make them in quite the comfort we'd hoped!

"That was done because I'd liked the music the station played, and they'd written to me and made a nice request, and I thought `Yeah, these guys know what they're doing, and if I can help, I will.'

"I don't much like doing commercials, they take up a lot of time for a lot of frustration," declares Palin, who says his most famous commercials were in Britain with John Cleese during the Python years.

"We did a Hunky-Chunks dog food commercial in 1970 or '71. No bones about it, we needed the money! You'd put up with all sorts of humiliation, provided you could earn some money, and the money for commercials was quite substantial. So, John and I did this ad for Hunky-Chunks dog food that was to be tested in one particular consumer area of Britain, I think it was the southern area. As far as I know, the product never, ever appeared outside that region, so I can only think that the commercials must have been fairly disastrous."

Graham Chapman apparently didn't do commercials, although he was keen to promote his own films. The most famous instance of this was when he appeared in the colonel's jacket and a tutu as a member of the Oral Majority to promote *The Secret Policeman's Other Ball*. The commercial was banned by NBC-TV, and so Chapman went on *Saturday Night Live* and performed the ad live during the show.

If John Cleese and Eric Idle are the keenest of the Pythons to do commercials, Terry Jones is the most reluctant, and has refused all offers.

"I've never done any, I've always said no to them," notes Jones. "I don't really approve of the commercial world, and as long as I can avoid doing them, I will. They're very pernicious, I think, and TV commercials undermine a lot of values. I'd rather stay out of it!"

The Pythons themselves did some short films in the early days of the team (including a political short); however, they were actually more similar to industrial training films of the type later produced by Cleese's Video Arts.

Perhaps one of the most significant aspects of the films is that they allowed Terry Jones his first directing experience, long before *Holy Grail*, though the movies themselves were relatively minor.

"They were things that would be shown in sales conferences," explains Terry Jones, "explaining what the new product was."

"We did one or two films in the early days of Python for commercial companies, usually training films," notes Palin. "We did one for Guinness and we did one for Gibbs Hair Shampoo. Gibbs Hair Shampoo was quite a good one. We all played sort of Biggles flying aces in World War One. It was for Harmony Hair Spray—I don't quite remember how the hair spray got into it, though."

"And we also did one for Bird's Eye Peas. These were all in-house videos, attempts to motivate their salesmen to sell rounder peas or more heavy-duty hair spray, whatever," Palin says, laughing. "We didn't feel quite so compromised doing those, because we could make the films ourselves and direct them ourselves, so in a sense, I suppose those little films are forerunners of things like *Grail* and *Brian* and all the rest."

THE RUTLES: ALL YOU NEED IS CASH

CONCEIVED, WRITTEN, AND PERFORMED BY ERIC IDLE WITH NEIL INNES AND AN APPEARANCE BY MICHAEL PALIN. FIRST BROADCAST MARCH 22, 1978 (U.S.), MARCH 27, 1978 (U.K.). 71 MINUTES.

Dirk McQuickly, Presenter, Etc ....Eric Idle
Ron Nasty ....Neil Innes
Stig O'Hara ....Rikki Fataar

Barry Wom ....John Halsey
Leggy Mountbatten ....Terrence Baylor
Iris Mountbatten, Chastity ....Gwen Taylor
Mick Jagger ....Himself
Bill Murray the "K" ....Bill Murray
Paul Simon...Himself
Brian Thigh...Dan Ackroyd
Eric Manchester ....Michael Palin
Interviewer ....George Harrison
Hell's Angel ....Ron Wood
Martini ....Bianca Jagger
Ron Decline..John Belushi
Woman on the Street..Gilda Radner

Written by Eric Idle. Produced by Gary Weis and Craig Kellem.
Directed by Eric Idle and Gary Weis. Songs by Neil Innes.
Produced by Pacific Arts, Inc./Broadway Video PAVR 540.

The film opens with a *Hard Day's Night*–style montage of the Rutles running from crowds of screaming girls, as we hear "Get Up and Go." A presenter tries to give a capsule history of their career, walking down the street, but the camera truck begins driving off. After another musical montage, the presenter starts out showing a rare film of the group at the Cavern, where they meet Leggy Mountbatten in 1961. His mother reveals that Leggy's chief fascination was in their trousers.

At the Rat Keller, the presenter discusses Leppo, the fifth Rutle, and shows some of the original rats. He interviews the record producer who signed them, and their initial success is seen, as they play "Between Us" in concert.

The presenter asks Mick Jagger about the Rutles, and he describes the early days. A Pathetique News newsreel describes Rutlemania in London and shows the Rutles' command performance before the queen, where they sing "A Girl Like You." Arriving in America, they greet the press and hear Bill Murray the "K," as the newsreel ends.

Paul Simon is interviewed and discusses their appearance in Ed Sullivan in February 1964, and we see them play "Hold My Hand." Two music historians are interviewed on their music, and the presenter goes to New Orleans to unsuccessfully interview Blind Lemon Pie, to find where their music originated.

Clips from *A Hard Day's Rut* are shown, and the group plays "I Must Be in Love." Brian Thigh, the man who turned down the Rutles, is interviewed, as their worldwide success is shown. The group goes off to film their second movie, *Ouch!* and we see clips from the film as the title track plays. After that is the concert at Che Stadium in 1965, where they play "It's Looking Good."

In 1966 Nasty (the John Lennon character) is misquoted in an interview as saying the Rutles were bigger than God, whereas he actually only said they were bigger than Rod Stewart. Bob Dylan introduces the Rutles to tea, and they produce the *Sgt. Rutter* album under its influence. They also participate in a live TV broadcast of "Love Life," the high-water mark of their career. The interviewer, wading through the surf, describes Leggy's difficulties with bullfighters, while Stig (the George Harrison figure) becomes involved with Surrey mystic Arthur Sultan and his Ouija board, and the group travels with him to Bognor. While there, they learned Leggy had accepted a teaching post in Australia.

Tragical History Tour, their first flop, follows the story of four Oxford history professors on a walking tour of English Tea Shops, and there is a clip of "Piggy in the Middle" from the film. Rutle Corps is formed, and the company began losing money even faster than the British government. Rutles' Press Officer Eric Manchester is interviewed on the pilfering; Stig is injured when he asks one of the Hell's Angels living in the basement to leave.

Yellow Submarine Sandwich, a full-length animated film, proves to be almost the only success for Rutle Corps; a clip from the film is shown, accompanied by "Cheese and Onions." With the group in turmoil, Dirk and Nasty both marry; Nasty finds love with a Nazi artist called Chastity and they hold a press conference in a shower. One of their art films, *A Thousand Feet of Film,* is shown, which features dozens of feet. Rumors that Stig is dead are not true, and the various clues are revealed. He actually had fallen in love with Gertrude Strange, a large-breasted American girl.

Meanwhile, Nasty meets with Ron Decline, the most feared promoter in the world, to settle Rutle Corps' problems, while each of the others was accepting financial advice from other groups. The final meeting included 134 lawyers and accountants,

and *Let It Rot* was released as an album, a film, and a lawsuit. The group performs "Get Up and Go" on the rooftop in their final concert.

They are shown today, and the presenter forces a woman on the street to tell what she knows about the Rutles, and she eventually takes over the interview. The presenter finally meets up with the camera truck, and Mick Jagger has the final words.

From left, Ron Nasty, Stig O'Hara, Dirk McQuickly, and Barry Wom, as the Rutles, strike a classic pose from the early sixties. Copyright Python Productions

 ## NOTES

All You Need Is Cash, better known as "The Rutles," was a parody both of the Beatles' careers and the documentary form in general. Its beginnings were rather humble—it started out as a short film for *Rutland Weekend Television.*

"I remember writing a terrific joke of a guy basically talking to a camera, and the camera car just gradually pulling further and further away, and him having to suddenly chase after it," explains Idle. "That was the gag. I thought that was really very funny. Very, very infrequently something you write makes you laugh out loud. That gag was one.

"And I thought 'Why doesn't he talk about the Rutles?' Neil had a sort of song that was very Beatle-y. [Sings] 'I feel good, I feel bad, I feel happy, I feel sad. Am I in love? Ahh, oohh, I must be in love.' I thought 'Well, that's nice,' so I put those two together, and it just naturally led to a lit-

tle bit of documentary. And that's all it was, really, was this joke about the Rutles, and the walking away from the camera gag, and then the black-and-white version of *A Hard Day's Rut*—which wasn't called that then—it was a parody of the Dick Lester movie. It was just the gag about the Rutles 'from these streets' speech, the gag of him pulling away, and the song."

That was the film that originally aired on *Rutland Weekend Television.* When Eric was asked to host *Saturday Night Live* for the first time on October 2, 1976, "The Rutles" was one of the pieces he brought with him.

"There were a couple of pieces—there was 'The Rutles,' and there was something else which didn't get selected," he explains. "I think it was a sendup of *Tommy* called *Pommy,* and I was playing Roger Daltry on a beach. It was about a deaf, dumb, and blind man trying to get out of a cinema during a Ken Russell film. There was another Neil song sending up *Tommy*. . . ."

"And that's what aired on *Saturday Night Live*. They put that on and the response was amazing, the letters that were written in to the Rutles. I had the idea to do it as a show for TV in England, and Lorne Michaels said `Hang on, I've got a larger budget at NBC—why don't you do it for NBC, and you'll get more money to spend?' It seemed like a wise thing at the time, so that's what I did. NBC bought it as a prime-time special, and then repeated it later [as a late-night movie], which was how they got their money back—they had two runs of it."

With Lorne Michaels as executive producer, Idle took advantage of the talent pool in the original *Saturday Night Live*, as well as his rock-and-roll friends. With John Belushi, Dan Ackroyd, Bill Murray, and Gilda Radner from SNL, he added interview segments with Mick Jagger and Paul Simon, along with a cameo by Rolling Stone Ron Wood, and George Harrison playing the man who interviews Eric Manchester. Although Palin would later meet Lorne Michaels and host *Saturday Night Live*, his role as Manchester was entirely due to Idle.

"George [Harrison], of course, was desperately keen to meet any Pythons, and we, at that time, were desperately keen to meet any Beatles, so it was one of those things where nobody knew how to make the first move," reveals Palin. "Eric was rather a veteran of this sort of thing, and, having much more cheek in just approaching anyone he wanted to, had made friends with George. He just asked me to go along and do it. There I was, one Sunday morning, down in the West End, being interviewed by George Harrison, playing somebody else. Very bizarre."

Rutlemania

The Rutles were successful enough to inspire a fan club and some records, and even some bootlegs. The album released at the time also included a souvenir booklet, and its subsequent release on CD included complete bonus tracks heard in part in the film but not included on the original LP. The music was entirely the creation of Neil Innes, who didn't even listen to any Beatle music when he was creating the songs. He says the songwriting was difficult, especially when he had to capture the innocence of the early era, but he had a terrific time doing it. After the songs were finished, he assembled a group of musicians that he turned into a real group. They worked together and lived together for two weeks, and at the end of that time, they had finished the album.

 ## CRITICAL COMMENTS

". . . A takeoff on the Beatle legend that, wondrously enough, is almost as fun as the original. . . . *All You Need Is Cash* will appeal primarily to those who have acquired the taste for a peculiarly British brand of zaniness. . . . As a send-up of the entire TV documentary form, and that's really its primary target, the special should tickle just about everyone."

—Harry F. Waters, *Newsweek*, March 27, 1978

The Rutles on video.

"*All You Need Is Cash,* a frantic spoof of Beatlemania, is 90 minutes long and has about three genuine laughs. . . . The few laughs that can be found in *All You Need Is Cash* are visual. Idle and Weis have reshot sequences from Richard Lester's mod Beatle films to poke wicked fun at their most faddish excesses; similar pranks have been pulled on the psychedelic animation of *Yellow Submarine.* . . ."

—Frank Rich, *Time,* March 27, 1978

THE RUTLES

BY NEIL INNES FOR THE ERIC IDLE FILM. (1978) WARNER BROS. HS 3151 (U.S.), WARNERS K 56459 (U.K.). CD RELEASED (1990) ON RHINO RECORDS R2 75760.

SIDE ONE (1962-67)

Hold My Hand

Number One

With a Girl Like You

I Must Be in Love

Ouch!

Living in Hope

Love Life

Nevertheless

SIDE TWO (1967-70)

Good Times Roll

Doubleback Alley

Cheese and Onions

Another Day

Piggy in the Middle

Let's Be Natural

The original LP included a twenty-page booklet with plenty of material from the film. The CD release includes six bonus tracks: "Goose-Step Mama," "Baby Let Me Be," "Blue Suede Schubert," "Between Us," "It's Looking Good," and "Get Up and Go."

A five-song EP titled *The Rutles* (Warner Bros. Pro. E723) was also released on yellow vinyl in 1978; it includes "I Must Be in Love," "Doubleback Alley," "With a Girl Like You," "Another Day," and "Let's Be Natural."

"Ging Gang Goolie/Mr. Sheene" (EMI 2852), a single by "Dirk and Stig" (Idle and Fataar), was released in the U.K. only.

ANIMATIONS OF MORTALITY

BY TERRY GILLIAM WITH LUCINDA COWELL. PUBLISHED BY METHUEN (1978), ISBN 0-458-93810-6 (U.S. PAPERBACK), ISBN 0-413-39370-4 (U.K. HARDBACK), ISBN 0-413-39380-1 (U.K. PAPERBACK).

The "aging animator" reveals the twisted and sordid little secrets of the Wonderful World of Animation in a book made up of Gilliam's animation artwork. Ostensibly a guide to animation presented by Brian the Badger, it includes Gilliam's work from Python as well as his pre- and post-Python animation. Of special interest is the title sequence for *The Marty Feldman Comedy Machine* and his 1972 commercial (his first) for the British Gas Board. The lessons are as follows:

Lesson 1: Creating Nothing Out of Somethings

Lesson 2: How to Ruin the Pleasure of a Painting Forever

Lesson 3: Discovering the Secret of Cut-Out Animation

Lesson 4: Where Ideas Come From

Lesson 5: Looking the Part

Lesson 6: Meaningless Political Statements

Also included are Animators of the World, some pages from Gilliam's sketchbook, Escape From World Domination, and a Moral Lesson.

 ## NOTES

Terry Gilliam apparently hadn't attached much importance to his original animation artwork during the Python years, and so when the rest of the group wanted to include some of his animation in *Monty Python's Big Red Book,* Eric Idle reportedly had to ransack Gilliam's garage to dig it out.

A few years later Gilliam had apparently changed his mind, and decided his animation was worth whatever immortality a book would bring it. "The reason I did the book was because, basically, I thought it would be quite easy to just get my old artwork out to put in the book. In fact, we had to redo most of the artwork—it works in the animation because it's moving and everything, and you can get away with it looking less good. When it's still, you can see all the flaws in it."

"So, I had to redo all the artwork, and it turned out to be a lot more work than we had planned on," Gilliam relates. "Then I did a lot of original stuff because I'd get bored with the old stuff. We're also using a lot of the old stuff in different ways. There are a lot of things in there on how to be an animator and how to do animation—or how to avoid doing animation. *Animations of Mortality* is a slightly pretentious title. . . ."

Like so much of Gilliam's work, it isn't easy to attach a short, convenient description to his book. "I told the publisher to advertise it differently to each market. They could advertise it in proper serious art review books as a serious art book, then they could advertise it in lighter fiction books as a light comedy book. They could advertise it in finan-

cial sort of magazines as a serious study of business methods in animation."It's a lie, totally, because it's a bit of all those things. It's a rather silly book, but it's what I wanted to do, rather than a collection of artwork, which is a bit dull," notes Gilliam. "I decided to do a book with a shape to it, with a character. Brian the Badger comes in and tries to explain how animation is done, and he's totally obsessed with good business practices. He's a terrible, greedy, money-hungry little creep, and he actually gets killed in the book by the Black Spot. It's very hard to do a fiction book that you actually have to read from beginning to end to actually get the sense of it, because there's a flow to it like a novel. But basically, it's all pictures."

 ## CRITICAL COMMENTS

"If you're a fan of Terry Gilliam, this book will enable you to study his work in detail. It does give some small glimpses into the nuts and bolts of animation, but enough people have already tried to imitate Gilliam unsuccessfully to prove that he's unique. . . . parts of the text let the book down. It's difficult to compete verbally with the apparent simplicity and fluency of Gilliam's visual style. But that is really what the book is about."

—Adam Sweeting, *Television and Home Video*, November 1979

THE ODD JOB

CO-WRITTEN, CO-PRODUCED BY, AND STARRING GRAHAM CHAPMAN. (1978) 86 MINUTES

Arthur Harris..Graham Chapman
The Odd Job Man...David Jason
Fiona Harris..Diana Quick
Tony Sloane..Simon Williams
Inspector Black ....Edward Hardwicke
Sergeant Mull...Bill Paterson
Raymonde..Michael Elphick
Bernard ....Stewart Harwood
Angie ....Carolyn Seymour

Screenplay by Bernard McKenna and Graham Chapman.
Produced by Mark Forstater and Graham Chapman. Directed by
Peter Medak. Released by Columbia Pictures/Presented by
Atlantic Television Inc./Charisma Films.

Arthur Harris brings home a bonsai tree for his wife Fiona on their anniversary, but she leaves him just as he arrives home, admitting she's been having an affair for the last two years.

Fiona runs off to Arthur's best friend Tony, and admits she made up a story about having an affair. Tony tries to seduce her. A drunken Arthur calls Tony, who brushes him off, but Fiona rebuffs him. Arthur goes to see his neighbor Angie, but he runs off before she can seduce him.

Drunk and depressed, Arthur is about to slash his wrists when Fiona calls. He tells her he's going to kill himself. Before he can carry out his threat, the doorbell rings.

A man seeking odd jobs is at the door, so Arthur asks him to turn on an electrified chair. When the man sees what the job is, he refuses to do it for ten quid. Arthur tries to barter with him for the job, and they strike a deal in which the Odd Job Man agrees to kill him when Arthur isn't expecting it. After a brief struggle, Arthur agrees to go for a walk in the park the next day, where the job will be done.

In the park, everyone else but Arthur falls into the Odd Job Man's traps. Afterward, Fiona returns to Arthur, telling him how much she loves him. They decide to go out and celebrate, but Arthur is afraid the Odd Job Man is stalking him. They go out in the car, and the Odd Job Man follows on his motorcycle. Arthur checks out their restaurant to make sure it's free from any danger posed by the Odd Job Man, while the Odd Job Man sabotages their car. Shortly after, the police drive off all the illegally parked cars on the street, and the officer in Arthur's car loses control and lands in the Thames. The Odd Job Man sees it pulled out of the river and is upset that he has failed.

Arthur gets angry with a policeman outside the restaurant, and the policeman and his partner

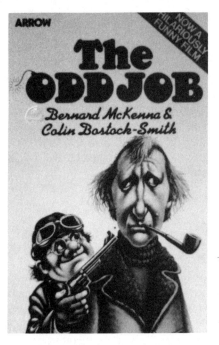

ask him to come to the station. There the police explain that one of their officers was driving Arthur's car, and the brakes and steering had been tampered with. Arthur denies that anybody wants to kill him, and he and Fiona leave. At home, he hides, trying to be careful, and even attacks the guard in the lobby of their building.

The next morning the Odd Job Man sneaks in and poisons Arthur's milk bottles, but the attempt fails when the caretaker steals a bottle, drinks it, and dies.

Arthur tells Fiona the whole story, and the police arrive to question them about the caretaker. They later decide to watch Arthur closely. Tony arrives, and Fiona leaves with him. Arthur visits Angie and ducks onto her balcony so he can slip away without being seen by the Odd Job Man. He meets up with Tony and Fiona, and they visit Tony's mobster friends for help. The Odd Job Man makes it into their nightclub, but blows up the wrong man.

At Arthur and Fiona's home, the Odd Job Man is sabotaging their balcony when Tony and Fiona arrive. She throws Tony out, and the Odd Job Man hides in the back of Tony's car, killing Tony by mistake. The gangsters bring Arthur home, when the Odd Job Man phones and tells Arthur to meet him in Regent's Park. Seeing it as a good opportunity to get the Odd Job Man, the gangsters accompany Arthur and Fiona. When they spot some policemen, however, the gangsters run off, and the police follow.

The Odd Job Man chases Arthur through the zoo and beyond. After they struggle at Arthur's apartment building, he tells the Odd Job Man that the job is canceled. As he leaves, Arthur and Fiona try to return his gun, but have an accident.

The Odd Job deserves better than to be forgotten by many Python fans, but it was a star-crossed production from the beginning. Based on a TV script written by McKenna, Graham Chapman, having given up alcohol early that year, decided to expand it and act as co-producer on his most ambitious post-Python project. Unfortunately, his first choice for director had to drop out of the project when he was injured.

Graham was also very hopeful of using his good friend Keith Moon in the role of the Odd Job Man, but the Who's drummer's reputation had preceded him, and the film executives didn't want the reputed wild man to play the part. (Chapman always greatly regretted this. He felt if Moon, who was trying to quit drinking anyway, had been allowed the role, he might have turned himself around soon enough to avoid dying only a few months later. Moon was set to play a member of the repertory company in *Life of Brian*, but died just before the production got underway. We are left with only tantalizingly brief glimpses of his acting talents.) "The executive producers weren't too sure. Anyway, it was finally cinched in the end when Keith couldn't make it because of his commitments with the Who, which is a pity," revealed Chapman.

"I'd rather have postponed the film, but by then there was too much money involved. So, we had to go ahead with David Jason, who did a very good job."

The Odd Job also marked the first time Graham Chapman had produced his own project, which he was surprised to find he enjoyed.

"It was a very interesting experience, actually, and quite fun. I didn't really expect it to be so much fun," he noted shortly after its completion. "I've enjoyed being involved with every stage of the film, right from the choice of script to performers, except I wasn't involved with my own choices! Originally, I wasn't going to be in it, I was going to be producer. That was my idea—I just wanted to have the script developed and written, and then produce it. But if we had someone like me [perform in it]—who was prepared to do it for practically nothing—we could make it on a low budget. So that's the way it turned out in the end, with me in it.

"After the writing period and after performing the thing, I still had a lot of decisions to make as a producer that I wouldn't normally have as a writer or performer—except, of course, with the Python group, which is rather different. We have much more influence, because we act corporately as producers as well.

"Normally, as soon as the thing's finished, an actual writer has very little influence on whatever the company that produced it decides to do with it. And so, this not being a Python venture, the interesting thing to do was produce it. I quite enjoyed all the politics, the silly games that people play in order to try and get their way. It's kind of fun if you nearly win, anyway—I didn't exactly win, because I really wanted Keith Moon to play the Odd Job Man, and I still think that would have been right.

"There's always compromise, and nothing is ever as you'd quite intended. It's about the same for a producer as a writer and a performer. It's never quite exactly what you wanted and hoped for, but it's near enough. And I think we've produced a good film, so I'm quite happy."

Odd Job received a royal premiere in October 1978 while Chapman and McKenna were both in Tunisia filming *Life of Brian*, so neither could attend. The film was not released theatrically in America,

 **CRITICAL COMMENTS**

"Nicely crazy, murder-by-mistake movie. . . . Carolyn Seymour is spectacularly sexy."

—Hinxman, *London Daily Mail*, October 6, 1978

"... This has its amusing moments and lines but comes over as ... dated."

—Marjorie Bilbow, *Screen International*, October 7, 1978

THE ODD JOB

BY BERNARD MCKENNA AND COLIN BOSTOCK-SMITH. BASED ON THE GRAHAM CHAPMAN FILM. PUBLISHED BY ARROW BOOKS (U.K.) 1978, ISBN 0-09-918950-X.

The novelization of the Graham Chapman film.

TO NORWAY, HOME OF GIANTS

FEATURING JOHN CLEESE. PRODUCED BY THE NORWEGIAN BROADCASTING COMPANY (1979) AS THEIR ENTRY FOR THE MONTREUX TELEVISION AWARDS.

A short film hosted by John Cleese (as Norman Fearless) spoofing travelogues, which examines some of the more peculiar aspects of life in Norway, along with a look at the inedible native cuisine.

"In 1979 I got a call out of the blue from Norwegian television. Would I be their front man in a program they were making to enter in the Montreux Light Entertainment Festival that year? I said yes, and I jumped on a plane, and I did about two and a half days' filming in and around Oslo with a delightful crew. I'd been to Norway two or three times round about that time, so it was all fairly familiar, they're extremely nice people. Temperamentally, they're very like the British, and they all speak wonderfully good English," explains Cleese.

"Interestingly, a Swedish guy was directing it, but I didn't add much—I just did what was on the page, and we produced a spoof travelogue of Norway. I got about three hundred pounds and a suit that was made for the program, and I returned to England. I got messages that they were very happy with it, and it was going to be the Montreux entry."

Cleese soon found he was going to be running against himself, in entries from two different countries, at the Montreux competition.

"To my amusement, the BBC rang me up and said 'The program which we were intending to enter, which was actually a *Goodies* program, hasn't turned out as we'd expected, and we would like to enter *Fawlty Towers* instead. How would you feel about it? I said to them 'I'm already appearing at Montreux.' They said 'What are you talking about?' and I said 'I'm representing Norway.' There was this damned silence. But, in the end, they said they'd still like to use *Fawlty Towers*, so I appeared that year representing both Britain and Norway. The irony is, I got two prizes for the Norwegian show, and absolutely nix, bupkiss for the U.K.!

"This may have been to do with the fact that with typical European thoroughness, they showed *Fawlty Towers* as the very first of all the program's shows, which happened to be transmitted on a Sunday morning at nine o'clock, and they hadn't quite gotten the sound system sorted out. But *Home of Giants* got two little awards. It's okay, but not up to full British or American standards."

AWAY FROM IT ALL

CONCEIVED, WRITTEN, AND NARRATED BY JOHN CLEESE. (1979) 13 MINUTES. PRODUCED BY TAYLOR-HYDE INTERNATIONAL AND PYTHON PICTURES.

A travelogue parody narrated by Cleese as Nigel Farquar-Bennet; the film was shown as a short subject in Britain prior to showings of *Life of Brian*.

"It was a delightful program, and I'm really rather proud of it. It gets about an eight and a half out of ten—I didn't get the commentary quite right, but the rest is terrific," says Cleese. "I co-wrote it with the lady I was walking out with at that time, who was a recently qualified barrister called Clare Taylor, so she is credited, with somebody with a silly name at the end, who is me."

The whole project came about because feature films in Britain were so often sent out with short subjects.

"Python wanted a short to go out with *Life of Brian*, and I said I'd always wanted to do a spoof travelogue. So, I watched about five or six terrible, rank travelogues from the fifties and early sixties called `Look at Life.' We bought the footage from about four of them, edited the footage together, and then I wrote an insane commentary, which just sent up the whole convention of travelogues, but quite subtly, so at the beginning a lot of the audience just thought it was another one of these terrible travelogues.

"That delusion continued for most of them until a particular moment when we cut back to Venice for a third time. My voice incidentally was disguised by one of those modulators that breaks the voice up and puts it together again in a slightly different shape so that people don't recognize it— my voice said `Back to Venice again, and more of those fucking gondolas!' at which point, the house exploded. Nothing's ever happened to it since, but I'm particularly fond of it."

HOLLYWOOD SQUARES

GUEST-STARRING GRAHAM CHAPMAN. NOVEMBER 5-9, 1979

Graham Chapman appeared all week long with host Peter Marshall and the celebrity players on the game show, in which contestants try to play tic-tac-toe with the squares of the guests. The celebrities either bluff or tell the truth about a variety of questions. Among the questions and Graham's responses throughout the week:

- What does the Queen always carry in her purse? (Graham answered "Cheese." The correct answer is a crossword puzzle.)

- True or false: Research indicates that freak shows are becoming a thing of the past because they are running out of freaks. (True, due to advances in medicine.)

- Is there a Brian actually mentioned in the Bible? (Graham answered "Yes, in Exodus." The contestant agreed, but the answer was false; Graham explained "Well, he went early.")

- Which of these is not an authentic recognized medical ailment: nun's knee, tailor's bottom, or jockey's crotch? ("I assume that jockey's crotch is the same as jeep-driver's bottom," he joked, before answering "Nun's knee." The correct answer was jockey's crotch.)

- What's the best thing to do when you can't remember a person's name for the second time? ("You go `ni!' and that distracts everyone," he joked. He suggested causing a distraction. The correct answer is to tell them you've forgotten.)

- Are there any one-hundred-year-old doctors still examining patients in America today? (Graham noted one, but said he shouldn't be examining patients because he's absolutely mad! Graham said no. The correct answer was yes.)

- Did Shakespeare have any children? (Graham said "He had nine that he didn't talk about, one that his wife talked about, and the official answer is no." The correct answer was yes—three that we know of.)

- Cary Grant stated that he only had one vice left—what was it? (Graham described his family and answered "Gambling." The correct answer was sex.)

- True or false: The original Lassie wasn't house-broken until she was five years of age. ("I'd like to answer this question in the same way Lassie would have done, which would be 'Woof!' for true, or 'Woof! Woof!' for false, or 'Grrr!' for 'I didn't like the question.' In this case, 'Woof!' and 'Grr!'" The correct answer was false.)

- How does Prince Charles sign his name? ("Tim," joked Graham, changing that to Edward Charles. The correct answer is Charles.)

- According to the column "Bowling Along," can a nun bowl in her habit? (Graham has Peter Marshall repeat the question in a higher voice, then answers "Grr!" His real answer was yes, which is correct.)

- When asked to identify the historical figure with a long, foreign name, he answered "Johann Gambolputty de von Ausfern ..." completing the entire name for an impatient Peter Marshall. The correct answer was Stalin.

 NOTES

After completing *Life of Brian*, Graham Chapman rented a house in Hollywood, where he decided to live for a time. While there, partly to promote *Brian*, he appeared for a week on the perennial game show *Hollywood Squares*, with eight other celebrities, including George Gobel, Gordon Jump, Dottie West, Valerie Bertinelli, and Vincent Price. Although he enjoyed the experience, the format was obviously limiting, and Graham didn't have much of an opportunity to display his own creativity; it marks the last appearance of any Python on a (nonparody) game show.

CHAUCER'S KNIGHT: THE PORTRAIT OF A MEDIEVAL MERCENARY

BY TERRY JONES. PUBLISHED BY WEIDENFELD AND NICOLSON (U.K.), ROUTLEDGE CHAPMAN & HALL (U.S.) (1985), ISBN 0-413-57510-1.

This lengthy, scholarly work examines a few dozen lines of Chaucer's *Canterbury Tales,* reinterpreting the conception of Chaucer's knight as a chivalrous, heroic figure.

Jones examines the battles and other references made to the knight, pointing out the historical records. He concludes that Chaucer was actually using satire, and his knight was actually a vicious, cold-blooded mercenary. As Jones puts it, he is actually "explaining a lot of 600-year-old jokes."

Heavily annotated with footnotes and other materials.

Terry Jones has long had an interest in things medieval, and *Chaucer's Knight* had long been a pet project for him. Although he knew the book would not be particularly commercial, he felt the need to correct what he saw as the misinterpretations of this part of Chaucer's work, even though it involved only about thirty lines from the general prologue. The book points out that the battles Chaucer attributes to his "veray, parfit gentil knight" were not the triumphs most literary interpreters assume them to be, and Jones provides a preponderance of evidence in its 300-plus pages.

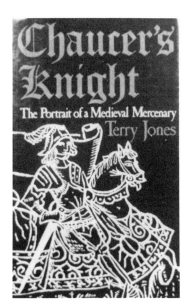

The original hardback edition of Chaucer's Knight.

"I really decided to do it because I'd gotten this feeling that there were these thirty lines of Chaucer that I just didn't understand. I started work on it when I was in university," explains Jones. "I wrote an essay on what it meant when Chaucer said the knight was at Alexandria, but all I turned up with there was when I read the literary critics, they said it was a great victory, and when I read the historians, they said it was a terrible massacre. I felt 'Well, there's some difference here.'

"To begin with, I went off on the wrong track, but it gradually became an obsession. All the time we were doing Python, for a period of about ten years, I spent time moonlighting at the British Museum, just reading everything I could that would illuminate what Chaucer meant in these particular lines about the knight," he relates.

"Eventually it took quite a while to realize that the history of the fourteenth century was quite different from what we'd been taught, and this movement from the old feudal hosts to the mercenary army, a paid standing army, was very significant in Chaucer's day. The idea that Chaucer could have written this description of a knight without actually mentioning that movement was just ridiculous."

Both the theory and the fact that it was being proposed by a Python drew a great deal of attention among scholars.

"It had quite an impact on the academic world. I think it took a lot of people by surprise, especially the line where Chaucer says he'd been on raids into Russia. Russia was a Christian country, and no English had ever pointed out that it was a Christian country. For Chaucer's knight to have gone on raids as this great Christian militarist fighting evil for Christianity was sort of negated by the fact that he was going on raids into Russia, which was Christian—it was Greek Orthodox, but it was still Christian."

Jones says he still isn't completely satisfied with his work, though it is convincing others of his theory.

"Eventually I think the academic world will come around to realizing that a lot of my thesis is right. I keep thinking that I'd really like to rewrite it. I can still find it very unreadable, because there are aspects of my first ideas and attitudes that are in the book and shouldn't be there.

"I'd revise quite a bit of it if I rewrote it now. I did rewrite when the paperback came out, especially the chapters on Prussia, because new material came up and I included that. The paperback is more accurate than the original!"

CRITICAL COMMENTS

"This lively and readable book belongs to a type for which in the crowded field of Chaucer criticism there is still a place. It presents a single, clearly defined hypothesis, supported with every argument and every scrap of evidence that diligence and ingenuity can discover."

—J. A. Burrows, *Times Literary Supplement,* February 15, 1980

"Leaving Monty Python far behind him, Terry Jones shows himself to be an historian of impressive competence . . . a masterly and exciting book."

THE BIG SHOW

FEATURING GRAHAM CHAPMAN. FIRST SHOW BROADCAST MARCH 4, 1980, ON NBC-TV. OTHER REGULARS INCLUDED MIMI KENNEDY, JOE BAKER, PAUL GRIMM, CHARLIE HILL, EDIE MCCLURG, AND SHABBA-DOO. DIRECTED BY STEVE BINDER, TONY CHARMOLI, WALTER C. MILLER. PRODUCED BY NICK VANOFF.

March 4, 1980 Featuring Steve Allen and Gary Coleman. Graham appears in sketches about an aggression clinic, as an airline pilot, and as a general in an end-of-the-world movie.

March 11, 1980 Featuring Gavin McLeod and Marie Osmond. Graham is featured in a theater critic sketch.

March 18, 1980 Featuring Dean Martin and Mariette Hartley. Graham appears in the Bookshop Sketch (from the *1948 Show*).

March 25, 1980 Featuring Tony Randall and Herve Villechaize. Graham is featured in a genetics lecture and a drugstore sketch.

April 8, 1980 Featuring Steve Lawrence and Don Rickles. Graham appears in the Beekeeper sketch (from the *1948 Show*).

April 29, 1980 Featuring Barbara Eden and Dennis Weaver. Graham portrays a temperamental English star appearing in a one-line blackout directed by Weaver, as well as a dentist who falls in a patient's mouth.

May 6, 1980 Featuring Gene Kelly and Nancy Walker. Graham appears in a sketch with the two guests, as an aircraft designer, and tries to check out of a hotel.

May 13, 1980 Featuring Steve Allen and Shirley Jones. Graham appears with Steve Allen, and as another airline pilot.

 ## NOTES

While living in Hollywood late in 1979, Graham Chapman became involved in an attempt by NBC-TV to revive the variety show. The idea was to feature a different pair of hosts each week, who would perform in sketches with a regular repertory company, which included Graham.

Graham recycled a few sketches from *At Last the 1948 Show* during the series, including the bookshop sketch also performed on *Monty Python's Contractual Obligation Album. The Big Show* had its moments, but this lavish attempt to revive the varietyshow format never caught on with viewers, and the series lasted less than three months.

Graham said afterward that he found working in American television somewhat constricting.

150

"There were quite a few writers involved in that program. I don't want to denigrate them, but it was very difficult trying to get reasonable material in—almost impossible! But it was quite a pleasant experience for me," said Chapman, who noted that it was one of the first times he had actually done television while sober.

"I did quite enjoy it, but it was bizarre, all those ice skaters and swimmers and things—I felt weird! I was the only one doing sketches—it was odd."

THE TOM MACHINE

VOICE-OVER BY JOHN CLEESE (1980) 47 MINUTES. WRITTEN BY PAUL BAMBOROUGH. PRODUCED BY THE BRITISH NATIONAL FILM SCHOOL. DIRECTED BY PAUL BAMBOROUGH.

A short science-fiction film about a robot maid, voiced by John Cleese, that dominates its human master.

PETER COOK AND CO.

GUEST-STARRING JOHN CLEESE AND TERRY JONES. FIRST BROADCAST ON ITV SEPTEMBER 14, 1980. STARRING PETER COOK, ROWAN ATKINSON, JOHN CLEESE, TERRY JONES, ROBERT LONGDEN, BERYL REID, AND PAULA WILCOX. WRITTEN BY PETER COOK. PRODUCED BY PAUL SMITH. DIRECTED BY PAUL SMITH.

John Cleese and Terry Jones appeared in several sketches during this one-shot TV special created by old cohort Peter Cook. Cleese appears as Neville Chamberlain, who is filmed by Cook as director Eric Miller; Cleese also gives Cook fishing lessons in another scene.

Besides appearing as E. L. Whisty, Cook appears as New York taxi driver Herb Natky, cowboy Lee Van Wrangler, and Professor Henrick Globnick, an expert on ants.

A LIAR'S AUTOBIOGRAPHY, VOL. VI

BY GRAHAM CHAPMAN

PUBLISHED BY EYRE METHUEN (U.K. HARDCOVER) (1980), ISBN 0-413-47570-0, MAGNUM BOOKS (U.K. PAPERBACK) ISBN 0-417-07200-7. RELEASED IN THE U.S. BY METHUEN (HARDCOVER) ISBN 0-416-00901-8. PORTIONS WRITTEN WITH DAVID SHERLOCK, ALEX MARTIN, DAVID YALLOP, AND DOUGLAS ADAMS.

After a wild preface and Chapter Nought, which deals with his struggle to quit drinking, the book begins with Chapman's childhood and a stream-of-consciousness approach that includes the "Oscar Wilde Sketch" and Biggles. His Cambridge days include his admissions interview, his exam inorganic chemistry, his anatomy classes, and joining the Footlights club.

Medical school includes the beginning of his drinking days, performing in *Cambridge Circus*, and his first sexual experiences. Anecdotes about the *Cambridge Circus* tour of New Zealand and New York follow, along with work on *The "Frost Report*, and Graham describes his awakening homosexuality and coming-out party. *At Last the 1948 Show* and *Monty Python's Flying Circus* are dealt with in a chapter and a half, followed by the story of Brendan and Jimmy, and the tale of how he became the guardian of John Tomiczek.

After a chapter of violence, Graham describes an incident at the Hard Rock Cafe where he was supposed to emcee the U.K. debut of Paul McCartney and Wings, and he tells of Python experiences in Tunisia, Germany, and on tour. Graham concludes with stories about Keith Moon and a chapter of name-dropping.

 ## NOTES

One would not expect an autobiography by any of the members of Monty Python to be an ordinary, conventional book, and with *A Liar's Autobiography, Volume VI*, one would not be disappointed.

The first autobiography by any of the Pythons is a fairly straightforward narrative, interspersed with wild flights of fantasy.

"I was originally thinking of writing something like 50,000 to 60,000 words, but it seems to be getting very, very much longer than that," Chapman noted when he was over halfway through the writing process. "It is developing more into an entity of its own than a quick book, as it were. An interesting process—I'd never thought of writing a book before that's not just a mixture of sketches. This is, to some extent, but it very much has an autobiographical theme, with a hell of a lot of lies and fantasy—not hairy-fairy fantasy, but fantasy with guts and filth. Actually, most of the filth isn't fantasy. There was a little bit of exaggeration sometimes, mostly to keep things cleaner than they actually were."

Graham began to consider writing an autobiography during one of the low points in his drinking days, when he was afraid he might not live much longer, and *A Liar's Autobiography* ended up being mostly truthful.

"Nearly all of it's true, except for the imaginative sequences which are obviously not true. Biggles doesn't actually live in this house, and my father was never actually a group captain in the air force, as he frequently becomes in the early stages of the book," he noted. "Nevertheless, it really all becomes a part of the convention and so it has a kind of truth about it. But if you get a little bit bored with a character, he suddenly becomes something else.

"It's a difficult book to describe, really, because I don't think there's been one quite like it. Certainly there have been books along the same lines, but I think it's got an oddness all its own. I hope so, anyway—otherwise I've been wasting my time living these thirty-seven years. I'm lucky that someone's actually paying me to write it all down."

Douglas Adams was the first to collaborate with Graham on the book, but soon dropped out; he felt that they weren't getting anywhere because it wasn't the sort of book that could be done as a pair. Adams was pleased with the final result, however, but says the only very bad section was the part that the two of them co-wrote.

Graham had written a large portion of the sequel to *Volume VI* on his word processor, but before he could complete it, the machine was stolen in a burglary at his home, and the computer discs along with it. So, with Graham gone, we won't be seeing *A Liar's Autobiography, Volume II*.

 ## CRITICAL COMMENTS

". . . This is a very funny book. . . . Definitely not a present for your Aunty, this is, to choose a line at random, `an intercoursingly good book.'"

—Robert Hewison, *London Evening Standard*, October 1980

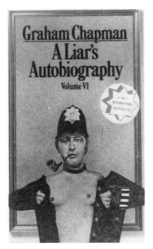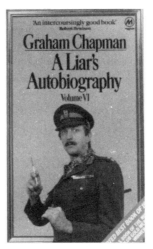

The British hardcover edition of Liar's Autobiography **and the paperback version**

"Required reading for 'Monty Python' fans.... Chapters Two through Seventeen prove: a man who claims to be a liar will sometimes, in spite of himself, tell the truth."

—*The New Yorker*, May 1981

"Graham Chapman, in this wild Monty Pythonish account of his life, fantasies and neuroses to date, marches firmly to the front ranks of British humorists."

—The *News* (Adelaide)

THE TAMING OF THE SHREW

STARRING JOHN CLEESE AS PETRUCHIO. FIRST BROADCAST OCTOBER 23, 1980, ON BBC-2 (U.K.). FIRST U.S. BROADCAST JANUARY 26, 1981, ON PBS. PRODUCED AND DIRECTED BY JONATHAN MILLER AS THE OPENING PRODUCTION OF THE THIRD SEASON OF THE SHAKESPEARE PLAYS.

Kate	Sarah Badel
Petruchio	John Cleese
Bianca	Susan Penhaligon
Baptista	John Franklyn-Robbins
Gremio	Frank Thornton
Hortensio	Jonathan Cecil
Lucentio	Simon Chandler
Tranio	Anthony Pedley

A rich merchant of Padua, Baptista Minola, has two daughters. Kate, the older, is considered a shrew and avoided by men, while her younger sister, Bianca, is very ladylike and has a number of suitors.

Baptista insists that Kate must be married first, so two of Bianca's suitors team up to find a husband for Kate.

Meanwhile Lucentio, a language tutor who is new in town, sees Bianca and immediately falls in love with her, and schemes to be hired as her tutor.

Petruchio arrives in town. Hortensio, one of Bianca's suitors, introduces him to Baptista, and Petruchio asks Baptista for Kate's hand in marriage. They set a wedding date, and Baptista promises Bianca to the man who can provide the largest dowry. Lucentio hires an older man to impersonate his rich father.

After Petruchio and Kate are wed, he proceeds to "tame" her, and she becomes a dutiful wife; Lucentio survives the unexpected appearance of his real father, and marries Bianca.

 ## NOTES

The classic Shakespearean comedy involves Petruchio and his attempts to conquer and wed the shrewish Kate. The series, a joint production of the BBC and PBS, was designed to provide a filmed record of all of Shakespeare's plays, and each production is as faithful as possible to the original text.

Jonathan Miller, one of the original *Beyond the Fringe* crew, asked John Cleese to play the lead in his first Shakespearean production. Although Cleese didn't consider himself a major fan of the playwright, he accepted Miller's offer. Miller and Robin Skynner, his one-time therapist (with whom he wrote his *Families* book), helped shape Cleese's more dashing, debonair Petruchio.

"That was the first time in my life that I have ever spent six weeks rehearsing something. I have either had to make it up on the floor, or else have a five-day turnaround in a television studio— no, I mean a weekly turnaround, it's five days rehearsal," explains Cleese.

"It was extraordinary to be able to explore something and, with the help of Jonathan Miller and Robin Skynner, discover insights in that play which made it, I think, a really interesting play psychologically. Normally, it's played as horseplay and a romp, and rather nasty. But played the way we did, I think it says an incredible amount about male-female relations in a very constructive, slightly old-fashioned way."

 ## CRITICAL COMMENTS

"Miller has directed a very straightforward, highly realistic and beautifully performed version of the comedy that is all the funnier because it is utterly devoid of the sort of slapstick that is usually its fate. Cleese is an admirable Petruchio—intelligent, practical, and thoughtful."

—Cecil Smith, *Los Angeles Times*, January 25, 1981

"Mr. Cleese eschews the hand-on-hip, dashing-cavalier approach to Petruchio for a portrait of a clever man whose outrageous behavior is quite obviously an act designed to woo a woman he admires. Mr. Cleese speaks the lines less trippingly on the tongue than conversationally on the ear. At times the language balance is lost. . . . But in the end the interpretation works marvelously well. What is lost in mellifluous cadences is gained in textual comprehension. I don't think I have ever heard the puns and witticisms, many of them rather racy, delivered with such clarity."

—John J. O'Connor, *The New York Times*, January 26, 1981

GREAT RAILWAY JOURNEYS OF THE WORLD: CONFESSIONS OF A TRAIN-SPOTTER

WRITTEN BY AND FEATURING MICHAEL PALIN. FIRST BROADCAST NOVEMBER 27, 1980 (BBC-2), FIRST U.S. BROADCAST NOVEMBER 22, 1982 (PBS). WRITTEN BY MICHAEL PALIN. PRODUCED BY KEN STEPHINSON. SERIES PRODUCED BY ROGER LAUGHTON.

Palin goes from Euston Station in London north to Kyle of Lochalsh in Scotland, traveling on trains ranging from an old steam locomotive to an Intercity Express, and stopping at several railroading points of interest along the way. He takes the "Flying Scotsman," a steam locomotive, part of the way, stops at the National Railway Museum and sees one of the first locomotives, and rides the most modern trains in present-day Britain.

 NOTES

Conceived as one of the *Great Railway Journeys of the World* for the BBC, a seven-part series that included trips by various travelers literally around the globe, Palin's journey across Great Britain was the fourth show of the series. Although he had loved trains and travel since he was a boy, the opportunity to do the program came from nowhere.

"A lot of things came from out of the blue," explains Palin. "I had been talking on the radio about my favorite form of transport, which happened to be the train. The next morning, a guy rang me up and said 'I'm a director, I'm based in Manchester for the BBC, we've got one more in a series of *Great Railway Journeys* to do, a train journey around Britain. Would you be prepared to be our traveler?' Thank you, Ken Stephinson! I did that with him, and I think probably as a result of that, along came *80 Days* years later."

Confessions of a Train-Spotter established Palin as an amiable, friendly, entertaining traveler, and when the BBC decided to do a real-life *Around the World in 80 Days,* it was no wonder Michael Palin was their guide. His reputation was established even more firmly two years later when he went around the world again, this time from North Pole to South Pole.

The decision to do the initial, less grueling train trip was somewhat of a career change for Palin, but it was obviously an enjoyable experience.

"It was a different direction for me, because at that time, I was still just writing and performing for film or television. To be asked to do something like that was a nice change of direction," he states. "I remember Denis O'Brien of Handmade Films, who was sort of our Python manager for a while and doing my financial management, could not believe that I wanted to do a thing on railroads when I could have had any film I wanted! But I said 'I love railways,' and he said 'Don't worry, I'm going to get you a really big fee.' He was totally defeated by a lady called Barbara who worked in the basement at BBC-Manchester in a sort of soundproof box. He couldn't budge her. There's a man who can rock Hollywood, but he couldn't move this lady in Manchester.

"So, I got paid very, very little, but of course it's paid off enormously in the long run, which I knew it would. It's typical of the BBC. They don't pay you much the first time around, but they do tend to make the sort of programs that sustain, and keep getting repeated, so I can't complain."

One of the endearing traits of Michael Palin—and indeed, all of the Pythons—is that they have been less concerned with making huge sums of money and more concerned with doing a project that interests them. And railroads have always interested Michael.

"I thought a railway journey through England and Scotland not only will be beautiful, lovely scenery and all, but I get to ride on one of the old steam engines and all that—things I'd always wanted to do, things I'd have given my right arm to do twenty years before. So I said, why not now?" he says. "I didn't think about whether I should be doing it for career reasons, or money reasons or any other reasons, I just thought it would be a good thing to do, and a great experience, which is rather the way I approached *80 Days* in the end. And of course, I'm glad I did both!"

DR. WHO: THE CITY OF DEATH

CAMEO APPEARANCE BY JOHN CLEESE. FINAL EPISODE OF THE "CITY OF DEATH" SERIAL BROADCAST BY THE BBC (1980-81 SEASON).

Dr. Who	Tom Baker
Romana	Lalla Ward
Count	Julian Glover
Kerensky	David Graham
Art Gallery Visitor	Eleanor Bron
Art Gallery Visitor	John Cleese

When the truth of Scaroth's cataclysmic plans is finally revealed, it sends the Doctor on one of the strangest journeys of his career. The TARDIS materializes in an art gallery at one point, and two patrons speculate and comment on it.

 NOTES

"It was lovely to do," says Cleese of his appointment with the Doctor. "It just took an hour and a half, so I enjoyed it. Douglas Adams, who was scripting *Dr. Who*, suggested to the director that we should do it. It was very painless and quick—I only live six minutes from the BBC television center!"

When rumors surfaced that Cleese was to play the lead role in a *Doctor Who* feature film, he merely laughed it off.

"I heard that rumor, but I never got an approach, as far as I remember," he explains.

Cleese admits he's never even seen a complete episode of the TV show. "I'm afraid that's one of the programs that I've only ever caught five or ten minutes of—I don't think I've ever watched one from beginning to end—like many shows. I'm the only person in the world who has never seen a complete *Kojak*, because I'm not a great television watcher."

LAVERNE AND SHIRLEY

GUEST-STARRING ERIC IDLE. FIRST BROADCAST FEBRUARY 24, 1981, ON ABC-TV. FEATURING PENNY MARSHALL, CINDY WILLIAMS, MICHAEL MCKEAN, DAVID L. LANDER, AND GUEST-STARRING PETER NOONE AND STEPHEN BISHOP.

Laverne and Shirley help out in the DeFazzios' restaurant. The girls are excited when two British pop stars, Eric and London, come in, and they take their order.

Eric and London lament their tax problems. When the girls bring their orders, they are invited to a party kicking off the tour.

They perform "Love, Love, Love" ("Your love, love, love, Fits me like a glove, glove, glove . . ." a song co-written by Idle and Stephen Bishop) at the party that night, promising to perform the flip side, "Fits Me Like a Sock," later. Laverne and Shirley talk with them, and London tells them the brownies are blowing him away. They mistake Lenny and Squiggy for Simon and Garfunkel, who are there because they've heard they're passing around Mary Jane in the Jolly Room. London tempts them with Acapulco

Gold, but they decide to eat brownies instead, not realizing they're laced with pot.

London tells Eric they should marry American girls and save themselves a bundle in taxes, and decide Laverne and Shirley are daft enough to marry them that quickly. They propose to the girls, saying they love them, and ply them with brownies.

The four of them fly to Vegas. At Ernie's Discount Wedding Chapel and Bingo Parlor, the girls are still giggling, but when they find out they've been eating marijuana brownies, they get angry. The girls are unable to complete the ceremony, and the boys leave them money for their bus fare home.

 NOTES

The first guest appearance by a Python on an American sitcom was the result of a favor Idle did for his friend Penny Marshall (who plays Laverne), he explains.

"I first met Penny Marshall when Terry Gilliam and I went to L.A. to promote *Grail*. We were invited to dinner by Carl Reiner, and she was then married to Rob [Reiner]. So Penny's been a friend of mine for a long time. She called up and said 'I want you to be on *Laverne and Shirley*.' I said 'What? . . . Oh, get out of here. . . .' But I went on," relates Idle.

"It was fun doing the show, because one of everything is very interesting, because you're learning. And it was interesting to me because it was totally unlike English TV, because it was three-camera film. It's quite different to have three-camera film, filming film rather than taping tape. It was just interesting to learn about the

whole experience of American sitcoms—like every day's a new script!" he recalls with a laugh.

The controversey that often surrounded Monty Python even followed Idle to the seemingly innocuous sitcom; for a time, his *Laverne and Shirley* episode was under fire for its drug references.

"It was the only one that got banned, I'm glad to say—I believe it got banned in syndication, though no longer," he laughs. "We got banned, because it was about taking drugs. On the show, I was playing a pop singer, and we took some hash cookies, and we were seen to enjoy them. It became very controversial—in fact, we married them! We got married to them, or were about to— we went to Vegas and had a wedding ceremony. It was a very interesting experience, and I enjoyed it. It's always interesting to learn another area of your trade—it may become useful. . . ."

AN EVENING WITH GRAHAM CHAPMAN

FIRST LECTURE MARCH 2, 1981, AT FACETS MULTIMEDIA, CHICAGO

For many years the quietest and shyest of the Pythons, Graham Chapman seemed the least likely of the group to forge out on his own and perform what was essentially a stand-up lecture before hundreds of audiences.

But that is exactly what he did, speaking on

college campuses and in comedy clubs across North America and Australia throughout the 1980s, keeping the Python name alive while the other group members were involved in their own projects. The original idea to do such a lecture series came about almost by accident, however.

While touring America and promoting *A Liar's Autobiography* in early 1981, his schedule for Chicago included an evening stop at a local film society. When he read the schedule more closely, he was rather surprised to see that he was to deliver a few remarks prior to a Python film screening. Although he was slightly concerned, he decided to go through with it and answer questions from the audience.

Graham arrived at the film society with his son John Tomiczek. An overflowing crowd was packed into the small screening room, with nearly as many people waiting outside. Overcoming his initial nervousness as he began answering questions, he easily won over the already enthusiastic crowd with witty ad libs, one-liners, and stories about the Pythons. "I had a wonderful time, they had to drag me off the stage," he observed later.

Returning to England, he reflected on his triumphant experience in Chicago, and after listening to a tape of that evening's performance, he planned the first of his official lecture tours, a twenty-three-city swing through American college campuses. In addition to the financial and travel opportunities it opened up, it did wonders for his confidence and allowed him to bask in the attention that he could previously enjoy only under the influence of alcohol.

Graham continued his lecture tours throughout the 1980s, usually doing at least one or two tours a year unless other performing or writing commitments interfered. Most of his bookings were on college campuses, though the first tours sometimes included comedy clubs. The club dates were not always as successful as the college lectures, however, as many of the club audiences expected Graham to do a stand-up routine, which he had no interest in doing. Nevertheless, to appease some club audiences, he did try performing "One Man Wrestling," an old, very physical sketch in which he wrestled himself. At other points during the tour, he performed "Medical Love Song" (from the *Contractual Obligation Album*), and for one charity appearance, he even performed the "Elephantoplasty" sketch on stage for the first time ever. (It was originally recorded for the *Matching Tie and Handkerchief* album, but never performed on stage or screen.)

For the most part, the audiences were wildly enthusiastic at a chance to see a member of Monty Python live on stage, and Graham usually drew capacity, even record-setting crowds. The lecture changed in format through the years, as he became more comfortable performing it, and knew what the audiences wanted to ask. He was comfortable in discussing his alcohol abuse and homosexuality in ways that never failed to get laughs. (He always made it a point to bring up the latter unapologetically, even when he wasn't asked.)

Early performances were usually question-and-answer affairs. On two or three occasions he showed a pair of favorite Python sketches to the audiences, allowing himself to take a short break. (He usually included "Sam Peckinpah's Salad Days," "The Lifeboat/Undertakers," and "Irving C. Saltzberg.")

Later performances turned into more traditional addresses to the audience. As he became more seasoned, he realized that most of the crowds tended to ask the same questions anyway, so he simply delivered the stories and answered questions without going to the audience. There was usually a question-and-answer period toward the end of each speech, but that became increasingly brief, and eventually was done away with entirely.

By the late 1980s, Graham had become involved with the Dangerous Sports Club, a college group that pioneered bungee-jumping, and he eventually replaced one of the Python film segments with film of the club's activities. (He had planned to make a documentary film about the British club, which he called "adrenaline junkies" who got their kicks hang-gliding over active volcanoes and skiing down dangerous slopes in bathtubs, bicycles, and pianos, as well as their early bungee-jumping. In May 1986, as part of a benefit show for Bob Geldof's Sports Aid, he was launched from a catapult in London's Hyde Park; he also tobogganed down a steep slope in St. Moritz while in a large wooden gondola with the club.)

The shows started with a tried-and-true bit Graham had developed when he had to emcee a concert by the Who. After trying and failing to entertain the rock-and-roll audience at the first show, before the next concert he appeared and asked the audience for two minutes of abuse. The crowd responded enthusiastically with vigorous shouting, profanity, and even a few thrown objects. Keith Moon was delighted at the result, and Graham revived it for his lecture tours.

Beginning each show with a call for abuse, the audiences were happy to comply, and Graham would get into the spirit of things, berating a section of the crowd that was too quiet and praising some of the more rowdy participants. At the end of the time, the spent crowd was happy to sit back and listen, as Graham would note "Thank you. That should save a bit of time later on."

Although no two shows were the same, many of the stories were used in most of his performances. He always discussed the other Pythons and their current activities, his friendship with Keith Moon and the time Moon burgled an adjacent hotel room (through an outside window) to get Graham a bottle of gin, censorship of the Python TV shows, his activities with the Dangerous Sports Club (in later tours), and the results of a talk show in which he discussed his homosexuality.

He also demonstrated a game called "Shitties," which he had learned from Moon. It involved depositing coins into a glass on the floor using cheek muscles. This was also a crowd pleaser.

Graham became quite expert at working the crowds and loved the performances. Not only did he delight his audiences, the shows also helped to instill him with a self-confidence he had lacked for too long.

When Terry Jones, who had been accustomed to the painfully shy Graham during the Python years, saw one of his lectures in America, he almost couldn't believe the man who always sat back, quietly puffing on his pipe, during their Python meetings was the confident performer he was seeing live on stage.

 ## CRITICAL COMMENTS

"The humor rooted in Britain made an audience in Springfield, Missouri laugh, applaud, and laugh again. . . . Graham Chapman and . . . some Monty Python film clips and an assortment of quick, often irreverent observations entertained by just being there. . . . More than 200 people packed into standing room-only space. . . ."

—Pam Maples, *The Springfield Daily News*, November 12, 1981

PAPERBACKS

HOSTED BY TERRY JONES. FIRST SHOW (OF A SERIES OF SEVEN) BROADCAST JUNE 3, 1981 (BBC-1). PRODUCED BY ROSEMARY BOWEN-JONES AND JULIAN JEBB. DIRECTED BY NICK BRENTON.

June 3, 1981 Guests include Fidelis Morgan, J. L. Carr, and Paul Theroux.

June 10, 1981 Guests include fantasy author Michael Moorcock, and Joe Keeton, who helps Jones undergo hypnotic regression.

June 17, 1981 Guests include Angela Carter, Reay Tannahill, and Jill Tweedie on erotica.

June 24, 1981 Guests include Charles Levinson, Robert Neild, and E.P. Thompson discussing the nuclear threat.

July 1, 1981 Guests include Rupert Bear artist Alfred Bestall and Jan Pienkowski discussing children's books.

July 8, 1981 Guests include Iris Murdoch and Paul Theroux, with a discussion of travel books.

July 15, 1981 Guests include Robert Blythe, Peter Porter, and Quentin Skinner.

NOTES

Terry Jones was offered the opportunity to host *Paperbacks* (a book review show) when prior host Robert Kee dropped out. Each show was dedicated to a particular theme.

"Somebody offered me the chance to introduce six shows, and I did it because it was an opportunity to do some reading!" notes Jones. "I thought `I never do any reading, apart from my Chaucer work.' I read stuff about the late fourteenth century, but I never do any modern reading, so here was a good excuse to do a bit of reading and meet a few authors."

One of Jones's favorite shows, however, featured Alfred Bestall, longtime artist on Rupert Bear. Bestall, who was in his nineties, agreed to appear on the show, which led to Jones writing and presenting a documentary on Rupert the following year.

"It was out of that series that I did the documentary on Rupert. One of the *Paperbacks* shows

was about children's books, and I suddenly realized I could invite Alfred Bestall, who wrote *Rupert* for forty years. I'd grown up with his stuff. He was always this name to me, and I suddenly realized I could actually meet him. He was about ninety, and he came on the show, and it was a great thing. Having met him, I then decided to make the documentary about *Rupert.*"

Although the show with Bestall was one of Jones's favorites, he says several of them were very good.

"We had a lot of interesting people on," he explains. "After about three shows, they decided I was being too political. There was this great upheaval at the BBC—I did one show on nuclear weapons, and it was a very strong, political show. They got the heebee-jeebees about it at the BBC!

"Then I had Iris Murdoch on, and they said `Stick to literary topics.' I had interviewed Iris Murdoch on her philosophy," he laughs.

 ## CRITICAL COMMENTS

". . . The new linkman is Terry Jones, who is in my experience one of the pleasantest people in theatrical makeup today but whose performance in this context is difficult to distinguish as yet from one of his own `Monty Python' spooves."

—Russell Davies, *Sunday Times*, June 7, 1981

THE GREAT MUPPET CAPER

APPEARANCE BY JOHN CLEESE. (1981) 95 MINUTES. FEATURING KERMIT, MISS PIGGY AND ALL THE MUPPET REGULARS, WITH CHARLES GRODIN, DIANA RIGG, ROBERT MORLEY, JOAN SANDERSON, PETER USTINOV, AND JACK WARDEN.

WRITTEN BY TOM PATCHETT & JAY TARSES AND JERRY JUHL & JACK ROSE. PRODUCED BY DAVID LAZER AND FRANK OZ. DIRECTED BY JIM HENSON. PRODUCED BY UNIVERSAL PICTURES.

The Muppets find themselves in London, investigating a jewel heist. Miss Piggy is hoping to use the home of an aristocratic British couple (Cleese and

Sanderson) to impress Kermit, unbeknownst to the couple. Miss Piggy sneaks into their house while they dine, discussing the weather, and when Kermit arrives, Miss Piggy impatiently answers the door. Kermit insists on seeing the inside of the house, while the husband, Neville, hunts them down.

When he finds them, they ask him to recommend a good restaurant. Determined to maintain his reserve, he complies.

 ## NOTES

Like most of the other celebrity guests in *The Great Muppet Caper,* Cleese's scene is rather brief, and he agreed to the role, again, as a favor to friend Frank Oz. His six-and-a-half minute appearance allows him to play the upper-class, pompous, ever-so-proper British stuffed shirt that he does so well, though he interacts with Kermit and Miss Piggy only briefly. After his stint hosting an episode of *The Muppet Show* on TV, Cleese says he had no problems working with the Muppets, even though their human operators were usually lying below camera range at his feet. "Those little creatures are

so realistic that it doesn't seem to require *any* jump of imagination," he explains.

"The trouble about doing a day-and-a-half on a big movie is that I'm in and out before I know the cameraman's name. It's very funny, because when I first arrive, there's a tremendous greeting. When I've finished, everybody's already thinking about the next scene, so I have a strange sense of not having quite said good-bye. I can never quite realize that I've finished with the part," notes Cleese, who has apparently left his Muppet days behind him.

TIME BANDITS

DIRECTED AND CO-WRITTEN BY TERRY GILLIAM. FEATURING AND CO-WRITTEN BY MICHAEL PALIN. ALSO FEATURING JOHN CLEESE. (1981) 110 MINUTES

Robin Hood	John Cleese
King Agamemnon	Sean Connery
Pansy	Shelley Duvall
Mrs. Ogre	Katherine Helmond
Napoleon	Ian Holm
Vincent	Michael Palin
Supreme Being	Ralph Richardson
Ogre	Peter Vaughan
The Evil One	David Warner
Kevin	Craig Warnock
Randall	David Rappaport
Fidgit	Kenny Baker
Strutter	Malcolm Dixon
Og	Mike Edmonds
Wally	Jack Purvis
Vermin	Tiny Ross

Screenplay by Terry Gilliam and Michael Palin. Produced by Terry Gilliam. Directed by Terry Gilliam and songs by George Harrison. Produced by Handmade Films (executive producers George Harrison and Denis O'Brien). Thorn EMI-Paramount Video VHS 2310.

Terry Gilliam (right) directs Katherine Helmond and Peter Vaughan, playing Mr. Mrs. and Ogre in **Time Bandits.** *Photo copyright handmade Films/Time Bandits*

When young Kevin is sent to bed by his boorish parents, a knight on horseback bursts out of his closet and rides off. The next night Kevin is eager to go to bed, and brings a Polaroid camera to gather evidence of any more strange events.

As he drifts to sleep, six dwarves emerge from the closet, explaining that they have stolen the Map of Holes in Time and Space from the Supreme Being. They run off through a Time Hole as the Supreme Being chases them, and Kevin follows through the hole.

The six bandits and Kevin emerge in wartorn Italy. They encounter Napoleon, who is enjoying a puppet show. He likes "little things hitting each other" and is delighted when the gang entertains him. He entertains them at a banquet, but they manage to burgle his mansion and escape through another Time Hole. They wind up in Sherwood Forest and meet Robin Hood's gang. The oversolic- itous Robin thanks them for the treasure they've carried with them and appropriates it for the poor. They pass by a pair of lovers, who have been robbed and tied to a tree. The Evil One watches from the Fortress of Ultimate Darkness and plots to regain the Map.

After leaping through a Time Hole, Kevin emerges in ancient Greece, where he is adopted by King Agamemnon. Just as he settles into life there, the gang returns and forces him to accompany them through another Time Hole.

They arrive on the *Titanic* and disrupt another pair of star-crossed lovers. After the ship sinks, the Evil One sends them to the Time of Legends, where they are captured by an Ogre and his wife. Kevin fixes the Ogre's bad back and the gang throws the Ogre and his wife overboard. The gang gets a lift from a giant, and they discover the Fortress of Ultimate Darkness, where they are captured. They escape, but Evil captures the Map from Kevin. The rest of the gang arrives with help from the past, including a tank, cowboys, medieval knights, and Roman soldiers, who lead the attack on Evil. The Evil One conquers them easily, but the Supreme Being arrives in time to defeat Evil.

 ## NOTES

Terry Gilliam had been planning to shoot a film called *The Ministry* (which would later be known as *Brazil*) but was having trouble stirring up inter- est. "I finished a first draft, but nobody seemed very interested in financing it. I was desperate to keep something underway, so I wrote another story based on *The Minotaur.* That didn't get any interest either," explains Gilliam.

"Finally I thought—Let's go commercial, write a film for kids. Let's do something that *might* get made. Out of desperation, one week- end I just sat down, and *Time Bandits* poured out of me very quickly.

"The project got interest right away from Denis O'Brien, who, with George Harrison, put up the money for *Brian.* He just said `Go ahead.' Michael Palin started writing dialogue with me, and we finished the script in February. By May [1980], we were filming in Morocco with Sean Connery."

His first day of filming on the big-budget project saw him jumping in headfirst.

"We began by not doing the easy stuff first but the most difficult," Gilliam explains. "Which meant flying off to Morocco and doing the fight with the Greek warrior and the bull-headed warrior. I hadn't directed a film in four years, so I was a bit rusty. We were up on this hill in 130-degree heat, and everything was going wrong on Day One. I've got twenty-five setups on my storyboards to do, and they're all elaborate, and it's a fight, and we've got these cumbersome costumes.

"Craig Warnock, the boy, was so nervous dealing with Sean Connery that he completely froze up. Everything was going as badly as it could go, and we started sliding behind very quickly," he reveals.

Gilliam claims that Sean Connery came to their rescue on that crucial first day.

"Connery was just great. He sensed immediately that we had overreached ourselves and said 'Listen, all you've got to do is shoot my stuff first, get it out of the way, I'll do it in one take and we can be out of it. Then you can spend time afterwards with the boy.' And that's exactly what we did. Sean, in a strange way, got me through that film on the first day—he said 'Just cut out all this fancy stuff, just do the basics and get it on film!'

"It was nice too, because I think he could see immediately that I'd bitten off more than I could chew, and I was doggedly pursuing my own little storyboard. Sean is incredibly efficient, and he's had a lot of experience. He wouldn't allow me to film him getting on his horse, because he said 'I'm not going to be good at this, I'm getting too old for this.' Some stars trust the director, other stars won't give the director anything that could make them look bad. Sean is a bit like that, he creates situations that you've got to get around—they're all do-able, they just take a little bit of fiddling. But we were sitting in these dusty hovels, and he's got his box lunch like everybody else, because we had no trailers, nothing. I think he really enjoyed it—it was like going back to basics for him."

Although they were minuscule compared to the difficulties he would have on his subsequent movies, Gilliam had some other troubles filming *Time Bandits*.

"The real problem was we were rushed, and didn't have enough time for preproduction. We could only get Sean Connery for two weeks before he began *Outland*. We had to start in May, which didn't give us enough time. Halfway through shoot-ing, we really ran into trouble. That was when we realized we hadn't planned an *ending* for the film," Gilliam revealed.

"So, we did a big battle scene—a Sherman tank, Greek archers, American cowboys, medieval knights, laser guns, and giant toys, all fighting in the Land of Legends. It was supposed to take five days to film; it took *weeks,* because we were in such a state of confusion.

"The weather was consistently against us. I've never seen anything so appalling. Every time we went outside, it pissed down. Every time we went inside, closed the studio doors and started pumping smoke and Fuller's earth into the air to create a dust storm, it would be blistering hot outside and suffocating inside. It was awful. We were filming in Morocco on a mountain; we were sweeping up all the dust on this mountaintop and putting it into plastic bags, which we then threw into the air. The locals thought we were quite mad!"

It was a mostly successful shoot, and Gilliam was able to bring the movie in on a surprisingly small budget, the final product looking as if it had cost much more than it actually had. Gilliam noted that some of the simplest-looking shots, such as the gang jumping through a Time Hole, were the toughest to shoot, while others that looked difficult, including sequences of the Giant walking, were actually accomplished very easily by placing the camera on the ground and shooting almost straight up. He also kept his camera lower to the ground for another reason: "To emphasize the dwarves' viewpoint, we filmed with cameras four feet off the ground, instead of the normal six."

Not everything shot for *Time Bandits* made it into the final cut, however, to Gilliam's regret.

"There's one really good scene, a wonderful scene with the Spider Women, which takes place after they escape from the Giant. It's two ancient, old ladies, Edwardian ladies sitting in their parlor with lace everywhere. The lace is part of what they're weaving, and they're weaving webs. Each of the Spider Ladies has eight legs under these great broad skirts—you look down and see all these tiny little feet.

"And they're basically these lonely women looking for knights in shining armor, beautiful young men, and they trap Og in one of their web-snares and drag him into their cave, and hanging in the webs above them are these knights in shining armor.

"It's a nice, spooky, funny scene. The problem was, we had run out of money, and it required a scene on either side of it to connect with everything that was happening, and we just ran out of money and time. We couldn't afford to shoot the scenes that we had written for either side," he explains.

"A couple of months after we had finished shooting, out of desperation, I came up with the idea that if we lost that scene, we'd have to get from the Giant to the Fortress of Ultimate Darkness, and we had to do it as quickly and economically as possible. I came up with the idea of having an invisible barrier—they were actually there already, but they just couldn't see it. So that's what we shot to replace the three scenes that would have been required instead."

The cast of *Time Bandits* included a variety of major international stars, actors who weren't always known for their work in comedy; Gilliam said this was an attempt to expand the appeal of the movie beyond just Python fans.

"It's an insurance policy to make sure the audience didn't consider it another Python flick. Frankly, we didn't expect to get the actors we wanted. In the script, we had King Agamemnon pulling off his helmet to reveal himself as none other than Sean Connery, or someone of equal but cheaper stature. Our little joke, it was. Denis said 'Well, let's find out if Sean Connery wants to do it.' We were stunned when he said 'Yes.' Everybody we showed the script to wanted to do it!"

For the still-unseasoned director, it was an incredible way to do a film. "It was an amazing experience. We had these expensive, big-name stars turning up every week or two, and only a few days to work with each of them. We had to develop a relationship to convince them—unless they could convince me—of a way of doing a scene. But we did it, and then they were gone. There's not much margin for error, and that makes it very difficult. The pressures are awful; it's hard to enjoy anything, because you're so worried all the time," Gilliam explained shortly after wrapping the production.

Although he had to work with very experienced stars like Sean Connery and Ralph Richardson, Gilliam also cast some more familiar faces, like Palin and Cleese.

"*Time Bandits* was a slightly different kettle of fish [than *Jabberwocky*], because he asked me to write it," explains Palin. "I wasn't a writer on *Jabberwocky,* but he [Gilliam] asked me to be co-writer on *Time Bandits*. He had the vision and the idea and I fleshed it out."

According to Palin, he was very pleased with the final result.

"The effects are wonderful, things like the giant with the boat on his head and the horse coming out of the wall. That's magically wonderfully done. It felt like a children's book brought to the screen as very few other people could do it. I liked the things like the family that never unwrapped anything, and they sat and watched television."

Still another of the guest roles was filled by another Python, at the request of the executive producer.

"Apparently, the role of Robin Hood had originally been written for Michael Palin," reveals John Cleese. "[Executive producer] Denis O'Brien was keen for me to be in the film, though Terry didn't want me—I only learned that eighteen months later—but Denis felt I would help sell the film in America, so he insisted that I be in it.

"I was sent the script, pointed at Robin Hood, and read the stage directions—'to be played like the Duke of Kent'—I thought it was very funny, and said I would love to do it," he notes. "I enjoyed doing *Time Bandits* enormously, despite the fact that Terry made me shave my beard off—I did it the morning of the shooting, seven A.M. in the forest!"

Aside from the loss of beard, there were not too many mishaps on the production, although one of the most interesting was actually caused by the director.

"The gang tends to plummet out of the sky a lot, since the Time Holes' exit points are usually up in the sky. They tend to land on Michael Palin and Shelley Duvall most of the time. Mike and Shelley play two young lovers in various historical periods. Each time they're about to get it together at last, bang, they're interrupted by the gang.

"I was on top of a ladder, trying to convince them that it's perfectly safe to jump onto this couch where Mike and Shelley are sitting, showing them how to do it; I fell directly onto Shelley and nearly broke her neck. There was a terrible note from the doctor—he had to report each day's injuries, like 'Someone got scratched—right hand,' or 'Someone got punched in the eye.' This day it said `Miss Duvall treated for neck injuries because director fell on her."

The neck incident failed to ruin the director's career.

Time Bandits proved to be a huge international success, and Terry Gilliam established a reputation in Hollywood as a director who could bring in an expensive-looking movie on a modest budget. This would change.

 ## CRITICAL COMMENTS

"Gilliam has a great off-centre sense of things here, knowing the reality contained in a child's bedroom late at night is not the same reality that exists at any other time. It is slightly more funny, violent, and bizarre. Gilliam has held onto the value of wonky dreams and put them in the best place that ever could be found outside of the mind—on film."

—Ron Base, *Toronto Star*, November 6, 1981

"The sheer technical accomplishment—sets, costumes, special effects—is dazzling. . . . A teeming and original stew that stirs in many genres and moods. . . . the sheer bric-a-brac inventiveness of the endeavor is a delight. . . ."

—David Ansen, *Newsweek,* November 9, 1981

"Murk swirls through every setting with Bruegelesque squalor and Boschian doom; as a traveler on this time flight, the viewer is less welcome than ignored."

—Richard Corliss, *Time,* November 9, 1981

Gilliam (left), Palin (right) and unidentified friend (center) promote the Time Bandits *book at a London bookstore. Photo copyright Tara Heinemann*

165

TIME BANDITS

SCREENPLAY BY MICHAEL PALIN AND TERRY GILLIAM. PUBLISHED BY HUTCHINSON BOOKS (U.K.), DOUBLEDAY (U.S.) (1981), ISBN 0-385-17732-1.

The complete screenplay, illustrated with photos and containing material removed from the final cut of the film.

TIME BANDITS

NOVELIZATION OF THE TERRY GILLIAM FILM BY CHARLES ALVERSON. PUBLISHED BY ARROW BOOKS (U.K. ONLY) (1981), ISBN 0-09-926020-4.

The novelization of the movie, written by Alverson, who collaborated with Gilliam on the screenplay of his *Jabberwocky*.

TIME BANDITS

COMIC-BOOK ADAPTATION OF THE TERRY GILLIAM FILM. PUBLISHED BY MARVEL COMICS (1981). ADAPTED BY S. J. PARKHOUSE. ART BY DAVID LLOYD AND JOHN STOKES.

THE INNES BOOK OF RECORDS

GUEST-STARRING MICHAEL PALIN. FIRST BROADCAST SEPTEMBER 28, 1981, ON BBC-2

Longtime Python cohort and Bonzo Dog (Doo-Dah) Band member Neil Innes finally got his own comedy and music series from the BBC, and Michael Palin guested on the first of the weekly shows.

For Palin, the show reminded him of some of the old Python filming; he had to lie below an underpass on a modern estate outside Bristol, waiting to be prodded by the famous BBC pointed stick and told to act. In another sketch, he was dressed as a police constable, a role familiar from his Python days.

The program features several of Innes's songs, performed almost as music videos, but with Innes playing an astonishing variety of roles, from a Scottish Highlander and Stoop Solo to a World War II soldier and Charlie Chaplin. His first song, "Don't

Make Me Use My Imagination," features Innes as an artist painting by numbers, as various famous paintings come to life, including Rembrandt's *Woman Bathing* and *Whistler's Mother,* who is revealed to be half Rastafarian. Other highlights of the first program include Stoop Solo performing "I Give Myself to You" and an appearance by the Urban Spaceman.

According to Palin, Innes is the closest anybody's ever come to being a seventh Python. In addition to working with them on their films, Innes was an essential part of the Python stage shows presented across Canada, on Broadway, and at the Hollywood Bowl. In addition, as part of the legendary Bonzo Dog (Doo Dah) Band, he performed with Palin, Terry Jones, Eric Idle, and Terry

Gilliam on *Do Not Adjust Your Set* in the days before Python.

Palin also appeared briefly on an Innes single called "Recycled Vinyl Blues" during the introduction: "Excuse me, I'd like to make a hit record." "Certainly, sir, have you got any old records with you?" "No, why?" "We've got to have the old records to melt them down and make the new ones." The song begins, and there are bursts of other, older songs that leak through during various moments in the record; the label had to include the titles, authors, and publishers of eight other songs.

THE INNES BOOK OF RECORDS

(1979) POLYDOR RECORDS (POLYDOR SUPER 2383 556)

SIDE ONE	SIDE TWO
Here We Go Again	Theme
Montana Cafe	Human Race
All in the Name of Love	Spontaneous
Kenny and Liza	Love Is Getting Deeper
Amoeba Boogie	Etcetera

The soundtrack album from the TV series features highlights from the shows, though Palin doesn't appear anywhere on the record.

Terry Jones's Children's Books

FAIRY TALES

BY TERRY JONES. PUBLISHED BY PAVILION BOOKS (1981). U.K. HARDCOVER ISBN 0-9075-16-03-3; PENGUIN BOOKS U.K. PAPERBACK ISBN 0-14-032262-0; PUBLISHED BY SCHOCKEN BOOKS IN U.S. (1982). ILLUSTRATED BY MICHAEL FOREMAN.

A collection of thirty short stories Jones wrote for his daughter Sally in the summer of 1978. Titles include "The Corn Dolly," "The Silly King," "The Wonderful Cake-Horse," "The Fly-By-Night," "Three Raindrops," "The Butterfly Who Sang," "Jack One-Step," "The Glass Cupboard," The Wooden City," "Simple Peter's Mirror," "The Sea Tiger," "The Witch and the Rainbow Cat," "The Snuff-Box," "The Man Who Owned the Earth," "The Wine of Li-Po," "The Beast with a Thousand Teeth," "Dr. Bonocolus's Devil," and "The Boat That Went Nowhere."

The stories were later adapted for radio, television, and a record album. Several episodes of the TV series, called *East of the Moon*, are available on video in Britain.

THE SAGA OF ERIK THE VIKING

**BY TERRY JONES. PUBLISHED BY PAVILION BOOKS (1983). U.K. HARDCOVER
ISBN 0-14-031713-9; PENGUIN BOOKS U.K. PAPERBACK
ISBN 0-14-032261-2; PUBLISHED BY SCHOCKEN BOOKS IN U.S. (1983).
ILLUSTRATED BY MICHAEL FOREMAN.**

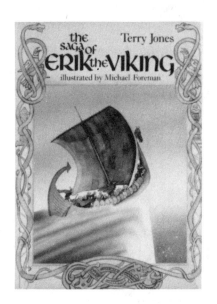

A story written for his son Bill, *The Saga of Erik the Viking* tells of Erik and his fellow Viking warriors who set sail to find the land where the sun goes at night. Along the way, they encounter a storm, the Enchantress of the Fjord, a Sea Dragon, the Old Man of the Sea, an Enchanter and his daughter Freya, Dogfighters, the Starsword, three wonderful gifts, Wolf Mountain, the Great Bird, the Spell-hound, plus adventures at the Edge of the World and the Secret Lake. Each of the twenty-seven chapters is a complete story in itself; the book won the 1984 British Children's Book Award.

Jones wrote his original screenplay for *Erik the Viking* based loosely on this book, but after going through numerous changes, the film has almost nothing to do with the story in the book.

NICOBOBINUS

**BY TERRY JONES. PUBLISHED BY PAVILION BOOKS (1985). U.K. HARDCOVER;
PENGUIN BOOKS U.K. PAPERBACK ISBN 0-14-032091-1; PUBLISHED BY PETER
BEDRICK BOOKS IN U.S. HARDCOVER, ISBN 0-87226-065-8. ILLUSTRATED BY
MICHAEL FOREMAN.**

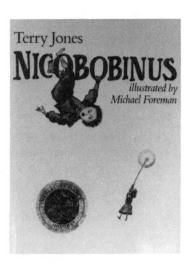

The story of Nicobobinus and his friend Rosie, who set off to discover the Land of Dragons. The Golden Man turns his hand, neck, and feet to gold, and when Nicobobinus is kidnapped, Rosie rescues him from a ship. They are captured by a ship of evil pirate monks, and they make Nicobobinus one of their order. When he tries to escape, they hang him over a cliff in a cage, which lands on Rosie's ship. They pass through the Ocean of Mountains and the City of Cries, discovering the dragon that heats the palace of King Pactolus. They are brought before the Great Dragon and do battle with the Dragon-slayers, before returning home at the conclusion of the book's thirty-one chapters.

CURSE OF THE VAMPIRE SOCKS

BY TERRY JONES. PUBLISHED BY PAVILION BOOKS (U.K.), (1988) ISBN 1-85145-233-8. ILLUSTRATED BY MICHAEL FOREMAN.

An original collection of children's poetry.

FANTASTIC STORIES

BY TERRY JONES, WITH ILLUSTRATIONS BY MICHAEL FOREMAN. PUBLISHED BY PAVILION BOOKS (1992).

A collection of short stories similar in tone to Jones's original volume of *Fairy Tales,* though consisting of somewhat longer stories.

 # NOTES

Terry Jones became a successful author of children's books with the publication of *Fairy Tales,* stories he wrote to tell his daughter Sally at bedtime, a sideline he says he came to love.

"I think in some ways, my children's books are my favorite things. They're the most me. They don't do much over in the States, but over here, they're used in schools a lot. They've devoted assemblies to them, and I don't quite know why." Jones laughs. "That's terribly rewarding. It's lovely when people say `Our kids just love them,' or `We're reading *Erik the Viking* at the moment.'"

Writing a children's book is not that difficult, he says.

"Just write what you'd like to hear yourself, basically. That's also what I remember Chaucer saying—you don't write in a style, you just write as you talk. That's what I try and do. I don't know what the trick is, but I just try and write how I talk. I think it does help to actually read things out, because it's amazing—you can kid yourself until you read something out, but when you actually read something

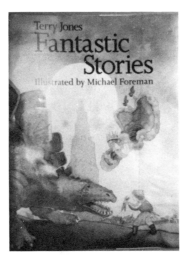

terrible to someone, you know. It's the same as performing—you know if you're embarrassed by it or not, and if you like it or not. At that moment of doing the lines, you can tell whether it's working or not."

His *Fantastic Stories* actually started out as another book of fairy tales, but his imagination took hold and stretched him even farther.

"Originally this was going to be another book of fairy tales, and a lot of them *are* fairy tales," Jones reveals.

"But even though most of them are really fairy tales, there are some bizarre elements in them, and they're a bit longer than the original tales. It's like a companion book to Fairy Tales, but it's just a bit different."

Fantastic Stories actually was written due to continued requests—from his publisher.

"I don't suppose [my children's books] are seen much in the States, but I get an awful lot of correspondence on them actually, and the first two have been published in three different forms and reprinted endlessly. They just keep going, really, so my publisher had been nagging me to do another book of them. Hence, *Fantastic Stories*!"

CRITICAL COMMENTS

"Here is an author setting out to rival the classic fairy tales and making an exciting job of it."

—Rachel Billington, the London *Economist,* on *Fairy Tales*

"Jones, with his exuberant command of the genre, ingeniously weaves contemporary values into the imagery of his tales. . . . a volume of highly original fairy tales that is beautiful to look at and great fun to read aloud."

—Carol Van Strum, *New York Times Book Review,* on *Fairy Tales,* January 16, 1983

"As in *Fairy Tales,* their first collaboration, Mr. Jones and Mr. Foreman fashion from traditional materials a tale of high deeds and adventure that is startlingly fresh."

—Carol Van Strum, *New York Times Book Review,* on *The Saga of Erik the Viking,* October 30, 1983

"Jones blends his wacky humor with his zeal for medieval history into an adventure so rowdy and preposterous, children will surely love it."

—Kristiana Gregory, *Los Angeles Times,* on *Nicobobinus*

"An irreverent, parodic, often witty romp. . . . It reads rather like a Monty Python script, minus the onstage gore."

—Beverly Lyon Clark, *New York Times Book Review,* on *Nicobobinus,* August 24, 1986

Terry Jones's Children's Videos

EAST OF THE MOON

BASED ON STORIES BY TERRY JONES. (VIRGIN VIDEO VVC 533)

The Island of the Purple Fruit (animated)   Boodle-Dum-Dee (Song)

Some Day (Song)   The Fly-By-Night (story)

EAST OF THE MOON

BASED ON STORIES BY TERRY JONES. (VIRGIN VIDEO VVC 534)

An Old Fashioned Day in the Country (song)

Think Before You Speak (song)

The Witch and the Rainbow Cat (story featuring Innes)

The Sea Tiger (animation)

 ## NOTES

Based on the Terry Jones *Fairy Tales*, these ran as part of the children's TV series based on his stories. They were scripted, with words and music, by Neil Innes.

STEVE MARTIN'S BEST SHOW EVER

GUEST-STARRING ERIC IDLE. FIRST BROADCAST NOVEMBER 25, 1981, ON NBC-TV

A variety of comedy sketches written and performed by an assortment of talents, including a short piece by Eric Idle, "Did the Dinosaurs Build Stonehenge?"

 ## NOTES

"That was a *Saturday Night Live* sort of spinoff," explains Idle. "I didn't want to go over and hang around with celebrities waiting to get on camera, which is what Lorne likes to do. So, I said `I'll be in it, but you have to give me a budget, and I'll go and shoot a sketch.' So I directed it, and went down to Stonehenge and did `Did Dinosaurs Build Stonehenge?' and did a very silly academic thing, took a crew down, did it on video, edited it, and sent it over."

WHOOPS APOCALYPSE

FEATURING JOHN CLEESE. FIRST SHOW OF SIX BROADCAST DECEMBER 1981 ON LONDON WEEKEND TELEVISION. U.S. VIDEO RELEASE (1981). 137 MINUTES

President Johnny Cyclops..Barry Morse
The Deacon ....John Barron
Premier Dubienkin ....Richard Griffiths
Commissar Solzhenitsyn..Alexei Sayle
Jay Garrick ....Ed Bishop
Shah Mashiq Rassim ....Bruce Montague
Abdad ....David Kelly

French Foreign Minister..Charles Kay
Kevin Pork...Peter Jones
Foreign Secretary ....Geoffrey Palmer
Lacrobat ....John Cleese

Written by Andrew Marshall and David Renwick. Produced by Humphrey Barclay. Directed by John Reardon. Released by London Weekend Television/Pacific Arts Video Records.

One of the most expensive programs ever produced by London Weekend Television, *Whoops Apocalypse* consists of numerous sketches involving the events just prior to World War III. The actors satirize British, U.S., and Russian politicians.

"The First Week" sees a revolt in Saudi Arabia, and U.S. forces are on full alert. American president Johnny Cyclops, advised by the deacon, gets a report by an Arabian agent whose tongue was ripped out that they're going to cut off oil to America. The Russian commissar interrogates an American couple he suspects are spies, and the American ambassador meets with the Soviet premier.

In "The Second Week," the president and the deacon decide to back the shah of Iran, who is given asylum by the Conservative Party in Britain. The shah is brought to France, but as his ship crosses the English Channel, it explodes. The deacon tells the president he is actually being kept safe by the government, and he is on a ferry to Britain.

"The Third Week" finds the president working on his reelection campaign. The left wing Labour Party has won a decisive election victory, and Kevin Pork discusses his program of radical reform at a cabinet meeting. Pork tells them he's actually Superman. His X-ray vision has revealed that the shah is actually on a cross-Channel ferry bound for Dover, and a British assault team captures him.

John Cleese as one of half-a-dozen characters he portrayed in Whoops Apocalypse **(London Weekend television Photo from the Collection of John Cleese)**

In "The Fourth Week," the newspapers report that the Saudis are cutting off U.S. oil. The president calls Pork, but Pork hangs up on him. Two American soldiers find that one of the terrifying Quark Bombs is missing.

In "The Fifth Week" the Cubans recover the bomb and show a videotape of testimonials from terrorists attesting to the effectiveness of Lacrobat, who can apparently get the bomb to the Middle East. Pork demonstrates his heat vision, and the president reads a message to the shah's parrot in hopes of getting it to the shah.

In "The Sixth Week," Lacrobat drives the missing Quark Bomb through America in a pickup truck, where he is stopped by the police because it looks too phallic. The American ambassador meets with the Russian premier, who had discovered that the shah is still alive. The president directs his aides to free the American tourists, the Hoppers, who are being interrogated. The couple escapes their guards, but their rescue helicopter lands on them.

"The Seventh Week" finds the shah and his servant still captive on the cross-Channel ferry, and they decide to contact the CIA themselves by radio. Lacrobat smuggles his truck, complete with sea lion, onto a ship at Dover, while the shah tries to radio for help. The Russians, who are interrogating the shah's parrot, intercept the radio message. The president goes on live TV as a guest on the *Celebrity Knees* game show, where he is slightly wounded by the CIA to get sympathy from the public. The French police seek the bomb inside the sea lion, but when Lacrobat flees, he is knocked out by the shah, who assumes his disguise. In his disguise, the shah is captured while Lacrobat gets away with the bomb, and the Russians invade Iran.

In "The Final Week," a psychiatrist examines the president, and a live pink elephant is brought in; it is decided that the president needs brain surgery. The Russian leader visits Iran, and Britain joins the Warsaw Pact, which pleases Pork. After receiving a lobotomy, the president traces

Lacrobat, who is in Greece transporting the bomb, along with a casket. The casket has slid out the back of Lacrobat's hearse and is recovered by the U.S. military, which cremates it in Israel. The president fires a warning bomb over uninhabited Russia to get them to pull out of the Middle East, while the shah and his assistant end up on a space shuttle. Pork's two assistants turn out to be Green Lantern and Hawkman inside their Russian cell. A mishap on the space shuttle makes the Russians think it is a nuclear missile heading for Moscow, and they vote to retaliate, perhaps triggering World War III.

 NOTES

Whoops Apocalypse gave John Cleese the chance to play a variety of characters in a single project, which was one of the things that attracted him to it.

"I enjoyed that a great deal because my old pal Humphrey Barclay was in charge of that. I did it because I liked Humphrey a great deal—I've been a pal of his since Cambridge days, and I always know that anything he asks me to be in is going to be well organized and well thought out," notes Cleese.

"It was also great fun for me, because I'm not thought of as a great character actor, to be able to play six completely different characters. I played a Swede, an Indian, a Frenchman, somebody from the West Country, a South American terrorist in which I'm absolutely unrecognizable—it's the best disguise I ever did. It involved putting in false teeth.

If I change my mouth, people don't recognize me. It's funny—the characteristic part of my face is the lower half. I just loved the opportunity to play these wild, different characters. I shot one a day, on film, which took the pressure off."

Cleese says if the series wasn't as successful as it might have been, it may have been due to the script.

"I very much liked the two guys who had me do it, David Renwick and Andrew Marshall, who were brilliant comics, but despite their great talent and their high intelligence, they tended to sacrifice the story for jokes, and that's why the movie they made of it didn't work."

The *Whoops Apocalypse* film, released a few years later, starred Peter Cook and did not involve John Cleese.

PASS THE BUTLER

A PLAY BY ERIC IDLE.

FIRST PRESENTED NOVEMBER 3, 1981, BY THE CAMBRIDGE THEATRE COMPANY, UNIVERSITY OF WARWICK, COVENTRY. FIRST LONDON PRODUCTION JANUARY 26, 1982, AT THE GLOBE THEATRE. ORIGINAL PRODUCTION DIRECTED BY JONATHAN LYNN.

In an English country house, Sir Robert Charles, minister of defense, lies unseen inside a life support system. His children, twins Hugo and

Annabelle and their younger brother Nigel, sit counting deaths in the newspaper, along with the sixtyish Kitty, a nanny.

Butler, the butler, brings Sir Robert a birthday present, and Lady Charles arrives to prepare for the afternoon's ceremony in which they are going to switch off Sir Robert's life support, as they can no longer afford the electricity and Sir Robert always wanted to die in office. Sir Robert's friend Ronnie arrives for the switching-off ceremony, and Harris, a journalist who arrives that morning, is horrified to discover their scheme. Before they can switch Sir Robert off, however, Harris reports that the prime minister has been killed, and Sir Robert is now the new British prime minister.

When Police Inspector Slater arrives, they bind and gag Harris before he can give them away. As they talk to Slater, they notice the machine has been switched off. When they discover Slater is actually a journalist, they bind and gag him too and place him next to Harris. They free Harris when he turns out to be a police inspector masquerading as a journalist. Harris tries to discover who has murdered Sir Robert, the prime minister. The entire household acts suspiciously, and Sir Robert is found to have been a transvestite. The family secrets are all revealed, as is the real killer.

 NOTES

Eric Idle says although he had always wanted to write a play, *Pass the Butler* wasn't necessarily intended for that form; he says he came up with the story and wrote it in France in 1979 after determining that it worked best as a play.

"All I attempt to do is have ideas, and then I try to slot them into what is the best format for the idea. Some things are film ideas, some things are play ideas, and this was clearly a play idea," he explains.

"I wrote it when I was in a little tin shack in the woods. We were just going away for two weeks, and my wife said 'Well, why don't you read me the play, as far as you've gotten?' So I brought it down and I read it to her. The tin shack burned down three days later, there was a tremendous fire that totally destroyed everything," he laughs. "So, she saved it!"

He says he loved the whole experience, even though he wasn't as closely involved with the production as he would have liked to be when it ran in London.

"Well, I was not involved very much in the West End production, because we were in the

The script of Eric Idle's **Pass the Butler.**

West Indies writing *Meaning of Life* at that stage, but I certainly was on the [initial] tour. We started in Warwick, and went into Cambridge, and each place I went I would tape it, and come back and study it and listen to what the audiences were doing, and cut things and move them around. It played very well with an audience.

"I came back in time for the first night [of the West End production], and it was a very strange first night. I mean, they tensed up for the first time, and it shows how artificial the first night is. You take what is really going well in front of an audience, and then you take half the seats and stalls out and give them to critics and their dates. You've got all the tension, and put all of the friends and relatives and aunts and uncles in the dress circle, and you have a really strange experience. They tensed up.

"Funny play. It goes on all over the time, I get royalties from all over the world. It's the longest-running play in Sweden, and Oslo had two productions of it on in three years, or something strange like that. It's very big in Scandinavia."

CRITICAL COMMENTS

"Eric Idle of Monty Python notoriety has written a rollicking, knock-about, semi-farcical comedy-mystery whose production, while not entirely satisfying, has enough hilarity and wit to generate the enormous electricity that the plot requires. . . . Idle aims typically British barbed arrows at class distinction, marriage, government, America, sex, and politics. . . . *Pass the Butler* is fast and funny, and you have to be sharp to catch such lines as `Time and tide wait for Onan.'"

—Terry Fisher, *Drama-Logue*, February 9-15, 1984
(reviewing a production in Van Nuys, California)

FAERIE TALE THEATRE: THE TALE OF THE FROG PRINCE

WRITTEN, DIRECTED, AND NARRATED BY ERIC IDLE. (1982) 53 MINUTES.

STARRING ROBIN WILLIAMS AS THE FROG/PRINCE ROBIN AND TERI GARR AS THE PRINCESS, WITH RENE AUBERJONOIS, CANDY CLARK, ROBERTA MAXWELL, MICHAEL RICHARDS, AND DONOVAN SCOTT. WRITTEN BY ERIC IDLE. PRODUCED BY JONATHAN TAPLIN (EXECUTIVE PRODUCER SHELLEY DUVALL). DIRECTED BY ERIC IDLE. PRESENTED BY SHOWTIME. A PLATYPUS PRODUCTION WITH MERCURY PICTURES IN ASSOCIATION WITH LION'S GATE FILMS. RELEASED BY CBS/FOX—PLAYHOUSE VIDEO 6372.

When a very beautiful, very vain princess loses her golden ball in a well, a frog who is actually a prince retrieves it in exchange for a promise to be invited to dinner and to sleep on the princess's pillow. She reneges on the promise but he turns up anyway and, after a narrow brush with the chef, entertains everyone at dinner. While spending the night on the princess's pillow, he saves her from a scorpion. She is so grateful that she kisses him, breaking the spell.

FAERIE TALE THEATRE: THE PIED PIPER OF HAMELIN

STARRING ERIC IDLE. (1985) 47 MINUTES.

STARRING ERIC IDLE AS THE PIED PIPER AND ROBERT BROWNING, WITH TONY VAN BRIDGE, KERAM MALICKI-SANCHEZ, PETER BLAIS, PETER BORETSKI, JAMES EDMOND, TOM HARVEY, KENNETH WICKES, AND CHRIS WIGGINS. WRITTEN BY NICHOLAS MEYER. PRODUCED BY BRIDGET TERRY AND FREDRIC S. FUCHS. DIRECTED BY NICHOLAS MEYER. PRESENTED BY SHOWTIME. A PLATYPUS PRODUCTION WITH GAYLORD TELEVISION ENTERTAINMENT IN ASSOCIATION WITH LION'S GATE FILMS. RELEASED BY CBS/FOX—PLAYHOUSE VIDEO 6792.

Robert Browning explains the phrase "pay the Piper" by relating the story of the Pied Piper, presented entirely in verse. In Hamelin in 1376, citizens at a town meeting discuss solutions to their problem: rats. The mayor and Town Corporation, facing irate, fruit-throwing citizens, agree to hire the Pied Piper to lead the rats out of town for 1,000 guilders. The Piper succeeds and leads all the rats into the river, but when the mayor refuses to pay him, the Piper leads the children out of the town and into the mountainside.

 NOTES

When Shelley Duvall was organizing her *Faerie Tale Theatre*, she phoned her friend Eric Idle to write and direct the very first program, *The Frog Prince.*

"Well, Shelley came to me and said `I'm doing *Faerie Tale Theatre*'—it was the very first one," notes Idle. "She said `Would you write it and direct it?' The cast was Robin Williams and Teri Garr, and that was such a lovely cast that I wrote it quite effortlessly. It was quite easy to write. Then I went over and directed it.

"And it was fun, really, putting Robin in a mask and making him use body language. I think he often has problems with what to do with his face—men who are very verbal and physical often have trouble with the face. We put Robin in a mask and he was wonderful as the Frog, he was really great. And Teri Garr was just very funny.

"It was one of those things I just had to roll up my sleeves and get on with—it was a bit like doing *Rutland Weekend Television*, you know—suddenly everything's at a standstill, and I'm watching, trying to get this thing together, and I went [clap!] `Come on, let's go!' and I got cameras and grabbed people—it's television, and I know about television from about fifteen or twenty years. It was fun. And really, I ought to be receiving royalties ever since, because *I did the pilot.*" He laughs. "*The Frog Prince* won an Ace Award for me and the first of a million for Shelley Duvall."

Despite the Ace Award, Idle didn't appear on-camera in a *Faerie Tale Theatre* production until three years later, in *The Pied Piper.* David Bowie was slated to star in the title role for Duvall, when fate stepped in.

"Shelley called me up—it was very funny, an odd experience. I was having dinner with Bowie, and I said `So you're about to go and do *The Pied Piper* with Shelley,' and he said `No, I'm not going to do it, I've got some songs to write.' I got home that night, and there was a weepy message on the answering machine from Shelley saying `Can you come over? There's been a disaster! David's canceled! Can you please come and be the Pied Piper?' I always used to be a sucker for show business, help 'em out in a crisis—I've learned better now. So, I flew, almost within twenty-four hours, because it was all set in Toronto—they'd set it all up there for David's tax purposes," explains Idle.

"I remember the dressers being terribly disappointed, because they'd designed this special jock strap for David that they were hoping to lace him into. I said [deep voice] `I'll put that on, thank you very much,'" he laughs. "Anyway, it was fun. It was directed by Nicholas Meyer, we became good friends. In performances, I thought it my Richard IVth!"

SMALL HARRY AND THE TOOTHACHE PILLS

BY MICHAEL PALIN, ILLUSTRATIONS BY CAROLINE HOLDEN. PUBLISHED BY METHUEN/MAGNET BOOKS (1982), ISBN 0-416-27160-5.

Small Harry lived with his friend Big Alf in a caravan alongside the highway, but when Big Alf dies, Small Harry is left without a home, a job, or money. A man tells him that Big Alf was wealthy because he invented the Big A Toothache Pill, and he has left Small Harry a huge house in Scotland. Small Harry doesn't believe him, but eventually decides to find out for himself.

THE LIMERICK BOOK

BY MICHAEL PALIN. PUBLISHED BY HUTCHINSON BOOKS (1985).

An original collection of limericks written by Palin for children.

THE MIRRORSTONE

BY MICHAEL PALIN, ILLUSTRATIONS BY ALAN LEE, AND CONCEIVED AND DESIGNED BY RICHARD SEYMOUR. PUBLISHED BY JONATHAN CAPE BOOKS (U.K.) (1986), ISBN 0-224-02408-6. U.S. EDITION PUBLISHED BY ALFRED A. KNOPF.

The story of Paul, a young boy who is a very good swimmer; he starts to see strange reflections in mirrors. He is brought to another world by Salaman, a mysterious wizard who invented the Mirrorstone, the most perfect mirror in the world. Salaman wants to send him to another world, but when Paul runs away, he falls in a puddle in the street and ends up in an underwater castle, where Salaman sends him on a quest for the powerful, magical Mirrorstone, from which he barely escapes. The book is illustrated with a number of holograms.

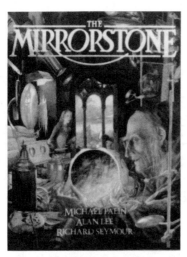

The Mirrorstone *cover, with hologram on the cover.*

CYRIL AND THE DINNER PARTY

BY MICHAEL PALIN, ILLUSTRATIONS BY CAROLINE HOLDEN. PUBLISHED BY PAVILION BOOKS (1986), ISBN 1-85145-069-6.

When he is three years old, Cyril discovers he has the power to turn people into other things. He livens up a dinner party by turning his aunt into an ornamental clock, his grandfather into a seal, and his Uncle Frank into a parrot. He turns other guests into a terrible smell, Long John Silver, a hot tap, and an ostrich to relieve his boredom.

CYRIL AND THE HOUSE OF COMMONS

BY MICHAEL PALIN, ILLUSTRATIONS BY CAROLINE HOLDEN. PUBLISHED BY PAVILION BOOKS (1986), ISBN 0-85145-078-5.

The parents of Cyril, an ordinary boy who has the power to turn people into other things just by looking at them, take him to the House of Commons. He turns a Conservative member into a sheepdog, and the speaker and other Liberals are inflated and become airborne. Their proceedings are completely disrupted, members are turned into wood, and a swimming pool appears. Cyril finally turns everything back to normal so he can hear a boring man talk about reflating the economy.

 NOTES

Like writing partner Terry Jones, Michael Palin decided to try his hand at writing children's books. (Even though their *Dr. Fegg* book was actually aimed at older children, it was marketed for older readers and Python fans.) Palin got off to a later start than Jones, but proved to be relatively prolific.

As he explains, even though he had children of his own that he read to, he actually got started writing books for kids because he was asked.

"I'm probably a lazy old sod, and wouldn't have done anything if I hadn't been pushed. I had three children growing up at that time, and I spent a lot of time reading them stories. I felt I knew what was a good story to read and what was a bad story to read," he declares.

"So, I felt `I want to have a go at that,' because there's nothing better than the attention of a child, and they're really gripped by a story—it's wonderful, they're a great audience. So, I think I wanted to have a go at that and see if I could do that, and make it something that a parent would enjoy reading, and the children would also be involved with," notes Palin.

"It's a tough audience to write for, but I've found that it's very gratifying when it works."

PRIVATES ON PARADE

STARRING JOHN CLEESE. (1982) 93 MINUTES

Major Giles Flack	John Cleese
Acting Captain Terri Dennis	Denis Quilley
Sergeant Major Reg Drummond	Michael Elphick
Corporal Len Bonny	Joe Melia
Acting Lieutenant Sylvia Morgan	Nicola Pagett
Captain Sholto Savory	John Standing
Leading Aircraftman Eric Young-Love	Simon Jones
Private Steven Flowers	Patrick Pearson

Screenplay by Peter Nichols (based on his own play). Produced by Simon Relph. Directed by Michael Blakemore. Presented by Handmade Films/Videocassette release by HBO Video TVF 1628.

Set in a British army garrison in Singapore during the unstable period following World War II, young Private Flowers is assigned to SADUSEA (Song and Dance Unit, Southeast Asia), which is run by Major Flack, who is very uncomfortable running a unit. Captain Dennis, a more effeminate officer, makes him a part of his "Jungle Jamboree." He rehearses the men as Major Flack bursts in and warns them against blasphemy, telling them that World War III is on the way. Sylvia Morgan helps Flowers get through rehearsal.

That night Flowers learns Sylvia is Sergeant Drummond's girl. The major bursts into the barracks and tells Young-Love that his car was stolen by Chinese Communists the previous night, while he was on duty. On his way out, he smells women's perfume on some of the men.

Drummond encourages Flowers to see Sylvia. Later Drummond hits her, afraid she's told Flowers some of his secret affairs. Flowers falls for her and they make love.

Inside information is allowing guns and ammunition to be diverted to the enemy; the major is convinced his unit is being used on a secret mission to stop the thefts.

After the opening night of "Jungle Jamboree," Flack orders all of the unit to undergo military training before they go on tour into the jungle. When the major learns that Flowers and Sylvia are engaged, he tries to talk Flowers out of it. Drummond takes Savory into the jungle, where they expect their payoff, but are killed.

The major decides to accompany the unit as it leaves on its jungle tour, as they are smuggling ammunition. Captain Dennis tells Flowers to stop avoiding Sylvia, despite what the major told him, as she is pregnant. The major is happy to get into the remote jungle; at a desolate outpost, a terrorist attack occurs during the show. Several in the unit are shot, and Len is killed. The SADUSEA unit is going to be sent home; Sylvia tells Captain Dennis that the baby was actually Drummond's, and he marries her so she can go to Britain.

 ## NOTES

Although it was based on the successful play of the same name, *Privates on Parade* was not nearly as successful as a film. Co-executive producer Denis O'Brien bought the play's film rights when he took over management of Monty Python, and reportedly wanted all of the Pythons to star in the film, strictly as actors.

When the group rejected this idea, he signed John Cleese to star as Flack. This marked the first time Cleese would star in a non-Python feature film and portray the same character throughout. Despite his best efforts, though, Cleese's talents were not shown to their best advantage in the role, and he regards the film as a learning experience at best.

"I thought *Privates on Parade*, being sort of antiwar not so many years after Vietnam, might have a chance in America, and it shows how wildly unrealistic it was. I don't think it was very good. I think I learned a great deal about why scripts work and don't work from that—that didn't even work well in Australia, the only thing I've ever done that didn't really work in Australia," notes Cleese.

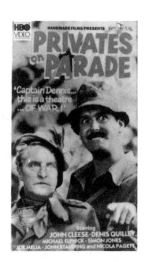

After some early screenings, O'Brien reportedly suggested some additional scenes to make the movie more commercial, and more footage was added in which Cleese—as Major Flack—does a silly walk on the parade grounds. The extraneous material was tacked onto the end of the film and is seen as the credits roll. It was used in the trailers for the film, which misled some audiences into thinking they were going to see a movie in which John Cleese does silly walks. This didn't help matters, but Cleese thinks the root of the problem was more basic.

"I think the trouble was that every single person working on it didn't really know anything about film," Cleese observes. "We're talking about Peter Nichols, Michael Blakemore, who is a great director and writer, and myself—I don't think any one of the three of us really knew what we were doing vis-á-vis film. An important learning experience—a shame, because it was a great stage play."

 ## CRITICAL COMMENTS

"... It hasn't the broad appeal of Monty Python at its best, but it has some good people and some funny moments. You may be surprised at the end to find that you've come to care about some of its people as much as you have, but it's hard to imagine the film having more than a limited appeal. . . . The cast is often quite scintillating, with Cleese and Quilley frequently hilarious in their virtuoso turns. . . . "

—Kevin Thomas, *Los Angeles Times*, June 20, 1984

THE MISSIONARY

CONCEIVED, WRITTEN BY, AND STARRING MICHAEL PALIN. (1982) 93 MINUTES

Reverend Charles Fortescue ....Michael Palin
Lady Ames ....Maggie Smith
Lord Ames...Trevor Howard
The Bishop...Denholm Elliot
Slatterthwaite...Michael Hordern
Reverend Fitzbanks ....Graham Crowden
Corbett...David Suchet
Deborah..Phoebe Nicholls
Ada ....Tricia George
Emmeline ....Valerie Whittington
Singer in Gin Palace ....Neil Innes
Arthur Pimp ....David Leland

Screenplay by Michael Palin. Produced by Neville C. Thompson and Michael Palin. Directed by Richard Loncraine. Released by Handmade Films/Columbia Pictures.

The Reverend Charles Fortescue, a missionary, returns to London in 1906 after ten years in Africa. As the ship docks, he accidentally bumps another passenger, Lady Ames, with a fertility object.

He arrives in Oxfordshire with the Reverend Fitzbanks; Fortescue is engaged to his daughter Deborah, and the three of them have lunch together. Later Deborah tells Charles about the filing system she invented for his hundreds of letters.

The bishop of London assigns Charles to start a mission to the fallen women in the East End of London. Fortescue tries to raise money, and Deborah makes him an appointment with Lord Ames, the richest man in London. Lady Ames invites him back the next day, and Slatterthwaite, their butler, eventually shows Charles to Lady Ames. Fortescue has missed the last train back to London, and so that evening Lady Ames joins him in bed, promising him a sizable donation to his mission.

Fortescue finds and services his first fallen woman. In three weeks his mission is a huge success due to his moral leadership and personal availability, as he allows his charges to climb into his bed. Lady Ames catches him with three naked women and withdraws her funds, so the girls decide to hit the streets to raise money for the mission.

The bishop stops by and says other churches are complaining because he's stolen all the business from their missions. Fortescue learns from the bishop that Lady Ames has attempted suicide because of him. The next day, the morning of his wedding to Deborah, Fortescue tracks down Lady Ames in Scotland, where a grouse hunt is going on. He tries to talk her out of killing Lord Ames, missing his own wedding in the process.

Michael Palin's first original film on his own, *The Missionary* is a beautifully shot, underrated comedy filled with unique Palin characters and gentle humor. When Denis O'Brien and George Harrison of Handmade Films approached Palin, they essentially gave him a blank check to make whatever type of film he wanted.

"*The Missionary* was the first time I'd been given carte blanche to make a film of my own," Palin relates. "Denis and George said 'Come up with a script and have a go, come up with an idea and do it.' I think I needed, then, to try something on my own. You always feel yes, there's something you really want to say, but when you actually start thinking about it, of course, it's like being asked, given all the ice creams in the world, which flavor do you want? It's really difficult, you can't decide what to go for.

"I came up with the idea of a missionary who comes back a changed man, and what he was particularly good at in Africa makes him particularly susceptible to the hypocrisy back in this country. He suddenly finds himself the object of quite a lot of people's affections. He's really only trying to do his best, and he has to do that quite regularly!" he explains.

"The idea of *The Missionary* formed in my mind about March of 1981, after doing *Time Bandits*, and I put the script into Denis O'Brien and George Harrison's hands, knowing that George had always been quite keen on the *Ripping Yarns*," notes Palin, but he says *The Missionary* is quite different.

"I suppose it's a bit similar to a *Ripping Yarn* in that it's a period tale and a comedy, but it's really quite a long advance on from *Ripping Yarns*, with the sort of casting we can do, and the quality, and the extent to which we can get locations and spend a bit more money on it.

"So, it was really about this area that I explored a little with Terry in *Ripping Yarns*, which was British hypocrisy and the different levels on which the British operate. I thought this would be good ground. Richard Loncraine wanted to direct it and loved the script, and we suddenly started getting good actors, like Denholm Elliot and Maggie Smith.

"Throughout, I had the say on casting, but Maggie was actually Richard Loncraine's selection.

Rev. Charles Fortescue helps out Ada (Tricia George), a fallen woman who decides to pay him back in other ways. Photo copyright Handmade Films/The Missionary

I think she was marvelous. I wasn't quite sure who to suggest for that part, and she's absolutely perfect. Trevor Howard, we thought of together for the crusty old English reactionary, which he did very well. He liked Python, and that helped.

"A lot of these straight actors are bored stiff doing the straight roles all the time, playing Shakespeare and classical Greek tragedy, and they really want to play a bit of comedy. The difficulty was, I wanted them to play themselves straight, and the comedy would come out of that—it's not a film for silly walks and people wearing goose costumes. It's a comedy that comes out of the look of the period, from realistic and authentic characters," he explains.

Some of the most interesting filming that took place involved the establishing shots at the beginning of the movie, where his title character is in Kenya.

"When we were filming in Africa, I had to do some scenes of me passing by wild animals. The ranger who was guarding us as we were doing the filming actually had to cover me with a gun as I walked past the elephants. I thought elephants in the zoo were really rather nice things, without guns and all that, but apparently in the wild they become the fiercest animals of them all! So, there I was, doing my jaunty comedy walk, being covered by a man with a gun behind a bush. I never discovered whether he was going to shoot me or the elephant. . . ."

Palin says that although it isn't perfect, he is happy he had the opportunity to make *The Missionary.*

"Although I think it had faults, especially toward the end, I was able to break out of the slightly restrictive world of Python, playing all the parts ourselves, into getting the best people around to do them—there's no doubt Maggie Smith introduces an enormous extra element to the work she does. The same with Denholm, and of course, Michael Hordern, who played the butler—I can't imagine anyone doing that as well," notes Palin.

"I was pleased that it was a departure from Python. It was more conventional, but a lot of the humor worked very well. Unfortunately, I don't think the drama worked quite as well as it should have done, but it's still a nice film, a beauty to watch."

 ## CRITICAL COMMENTS

". . . Such a breath of fresh air in today's movie scheme, the word-of-mouth could easily turn the film into a sleeper. The film aims to succeed and, for the most part, succeeds handsomely."

—Robert Osborne, *The Hollywood Reporter,* November 3, 1982

THE MISSIONARY

BOOK BY MICHAEL PALIN.

PUBLISHED BY METHUEN (1983) ISBN 0-413-51010-7 (U.K. HARDBACK), ISBN 0-413-51390-4 (U.K. PAPERBACK).

Contains the screenplay of the film illustrated with numerous photos from the movie, with an original prologue and "After the Story" follow-ups on the principal characters by Palin.

THE RUPERT BEAR STORY

PRESENTED AND DIRECTED BY TERRY JONES.

FIRST BROADCAST DECEMBER 9, 1982 ON CHANNEL FOUR (U.K.).

A tribute to Alfred Bestall, the nonagenarian responsible for drawing the adventures of the cartoon bear nearly from its inception. The documentary includes Jones's thoughts on Bestall and Rupert as well as an interview with the author of the series.

 **NOTES**

Terry Jones originally met Alfred Bestall when he was a guest on the *Paperbacks* show hosted by Jones.

"It was a one-hour documentary on *Rupert Bear* and what it meant to me," explains Jones.

"The first half hour was me praising *Rupert Bear* and just saying why I liked it so much, why I liked the books. The second half was `in search of Alfred Bestall,' I tracked him down to his little cottage and interviewed him."

THE NEWS IS THE NEWS

GUEST-STARRING MICHAEL PALIN.

BROADCAST JUNE 15, 1983, ON NBC-TV.

Michael Palin appeared on the first episode of this short-run, live show that satirized current news events. He files a report from 10 Downing Street on the British election, citing the issues of the campaign, and includes a report on Shirley MacLaine. The series featured Palin's friend Simon Jones as a regular.

YELLOWBEARD

WRITTEN BY AND STARRING GRAHAM CHAPMAN.

ALSO FEATURING JOHN CLEESE AND ERIC IDLE. (1983) 97 MINUTES

Yellowbeard	Graham Chapman
Moon	Peter Boyle
El Segundo	Richard "Cheech" Marin
El Nebuloso	Tommy Chong
Lord Lambourn	Peter Cook
Gilbert	Marty Feldman
Dan	Martin Hewitt
Dr. Gilpin	Michael Hordern
Commander Clement	Eric Idle
Betty	Madeline Kahn
Captain Hughes	James Mason
Blind Pew	John Cleese
Mr. Crisp and Verdugo	Kenneth Mars
Flunkle	Spike Milligan
Triola.	Stacy Nelkin
Mansell	Nigel Planer
Lady Churchill	Susannah York
Lady Lambourn	Beryl Reid
Queen Anne	Peter Bull
Mr. Prostitute	Greta Blackburn

Written by Graham Chapman, Peter Cook, and Bernard McKenna. Produced by Carter DeHaven. Directed by Mel Damski. A Hemdale Film released by Orion Pictures/ Videocassette release by Video Treasures SV 9138.

Graham Chapman in the title role as Yellowbeard.
Photo copyright Orion Pictures

After seizing the treasure of El Nebuloso, the vicious pirate Yellowbeard serves twenty years in prison after being betrayed by his right-hand man, Mr. Moon. Everyone tries to discover the location of his buried treasure, which Yellowbeard determines to recover upon his release. His wife Betty tells him he has a son, Dan, who is a gardener, which enrages Yellowbeard.

At Lambourn Hall, Com-mander Clement of the Secret Service is ordered by the Queen to follow Yellowbeard and capture his treasure. When Yellowbeard escapes from prison, Gilbert is freed by Moon and they determine to follow him. When Yellowbeard arrives at his wife's inn, she tells him the only copy of his treasure map was tattooed to his son's head. Blind Pew gives Clement directions to find Yellowbeard and kills the rest of the men in the inn.

Dan talks Yellowbeard into taking him along on the treasure hunt and convinces him to take along Lord Lambourn and Dr. Gilpin as well. Blind Pew hears their plans and reports to Clement, after which Moon and Gilbert blow up the blind man. At the docks, Moon and Gilbert's men press-gang Dan, Lambourn, and Gilpin aboard a ship captained by Hughes. Yellowbeard has snuck on board the *Lady Edith*, while Clement follows in a Royal Navy frigate.

Captain Hughes is overthrown in a mutiny led by Moon and Gilbert, who make Dan the new ship's captain in hopes that he'll lead them to the treasure. That night Yellowbeard secretly changes course toward the island where his treasure is buried. When they arrive, Yellowbeard secretly swims ashore, where El Nebuloso and his daughter Triola see the new torture device designed by Verdugo, their servant. El Segundo's men capture Dan and torture him, but Triola falls in love with him.

Yellowbeard forces his way into the castle, followed by Lambourn and Gilpin, and they free Dan and kill Nebuloso and battle Moon's men. Dan helps his father find the treasure and makes Yellowbeard proud of him.

 NOTES

Graham Chapman had long wanted to film his pirate movie. He finally got the budget and the big-name cast he had hoped for but was forced to give up the control he desired over the final product, and the results are uneven.

Shot on location in England and in Mexico, the shipboard sequences were filmed on board MGM's *Bounty*, which doubled as both ships. The production was unfortunately the last for Marty Feldman, who died of a heart attack in Mexico

City just after completing his role; James Mason also died not long after his work in *Yellowbeard*.

Chapman rounded up several old friends for the production, including Feldman, Peter Cook, John Cleese, and Eric Idle. *Yellowbeard* was his most ambitious solo project, so they were all happy to participate.

After the filming had been completed but about three months before the movie opened, Graham sat down and conducted a lengthy interview over three sessions, during which he discussed his thoughts on *Yellowbeard* and related subjects. Many of the following highlights see print here for the very first time.

When asked to describe *Yellowbeard*, Graham turned to his friend and co-star, Feldman.

"Marty summed it up as `a rollicking comic yarn for the young in head.' It is quite a fair summary. Don't go expecting anything too deep, but you do need to think a little bit," he explained.

Many members of his cast were people he'd originally hoped for, he noted. "I was kind of amazed in the end that we'd finally got a lot of them. I'd always thought of John, Eric, and Marty, though I didn't actually think of Marty for the part he played. Nevertheless, I very much wanted to use Marty, at first in one of the mad Spaniard parts, but after reading it himself, he chose to be Peter Boyle's henchman. He is actually much more suited to that, really, and Cheech and Chong were more suited to playing the mad Spaniards, so that worked out very well. I didn't think of Cheech and Chong originally, they were suggested by Orion. I didn't know their work very well at that time, but after I'd seen more of it, I thought `Yes, that's a good idea too.'

"Very early on I wanted Peter Boyle to play the evil pirate, the ex-henchman of Yellowbeard. Madeline Kahn was a suggestion from quite early on too, as Betty. Initially we were thinking of English character actresses for that part, but when Madeline Kahn was suggested and I went back and saw *Young Frankenstein* and *Blazing Saddles*, I thought she was just superb, and was a very happy choice," noted Chapman.

During preproduction, a wide variety of names were considered for and wanted to be in the film, including Robin Williams, Olivia Newton-John, Adam Ant, and Oliver Reed; it gave Graham even more confidence in the project to know he could choose carefully from such a talent pool.

"It was a very nice feeling, because when it comes to actually making decisions, you've got all sorts of considerations. We were thinking of Adam Ant for the part of Dan, Yellowbeard's potential son, and also Sting, who wanted to play the part [which went to Martin Hewitt]. However, we felt that from the point of view of the audiences being able to identify with the character, it would be useful—in an odd way—to have an American playing that part—with an English accent, mind you, but an American, so at least we could be sure that the younger people are going to understand him. Also, with Sting, although he looks much younger than he is, perhaps he's just a touch too old for the part."

One of Graham's oldest friends, singer-songwriter Harry Nilsson, came down during the shoot, though he ultimately didn't have a song in *Yellowbeard*.

"Harry made it down for the filming. I'm hoping Harry is still doing a song for the film. There's not really a great deal of room for a song interlude—it's a big film. At one stage we had a rather longish montage sequence of life at sea, which would have been suitable for a song, but in order to keep that in, we'd have had to cut a lot of comedy," explained Chapman. Although Nilsson did write a song for the film, "Black Sails in the Sunset," Graham felt it wasn't quite right for the movie, and different music accompanied the closing credits instead.

Another friend, Keith Moon, actually provided the initial inspiration for *Yellowbeard*, according to Chapman.

"Keith approached me with the idea of an adventure-comedy, combining the two elements of comedy and adventure—an interesting sort of topic. I suppose with *Holy Grail*, we'd been in that area, and I liked that—it was fun to do the swordfighting, with a lot of stunts and physical acting, and so that attracted me to it. Also, the escapist element attracted me to it. Especially in times of depression throughout the world, one really owes it to people to try and cheer them up a bit, to transcend all the gray times.

"Thinking of adventure-comedy and knowing Keith Moon, Keith was, in every sense of the word, a modern pirate—a person that did what he wanted to at the spur of the moment, was beholden to no one, and didn't give a damn what anyone thought. A wonderful sort of buccaneering spirit, he had, and sad to say, died young, as did pirates—they didn't last long with their sort of life. They lived on the edge all the time, they were living in danger and loving it, and Keith was much the same. At that stage, of course, I was thinking of Keith being in the movie—he would have made a very good Yellowbeard, a very good outrageous pirate, with his staring eyes and his presence.

"After that suggestion of Keith's, and the elaboration on it—Keith's concept was more of a collection of adventure yarns strung together—I took it firmly in the direction of pirates, along with Bernard McKenna at that point. We wrote a little synopsis which was more firmly rooted in *Treasure Island* at that stage, which we were quite pleased with. When we read it to Keith, he was unfortunately in hospital with the DTs at the time, so he was in no receptive state. Not long after that was his death, of course, so as soon as we finished *Life of Brian*, I thought `What the hell, we'd might as well finish it, for Keith if nothing else,' and Bernard and I started writing in earnest," he declared.

Graham noted that during early stages, *Yellowbeard* was more like a parody of *Treasure Island*. "As a very rough starting out point, from the point of view of period and certain similarities in character," he stated. "I'm sending up the period and the genre, really. We do follow a group of people. There is a young man, and a doctor, and a lord that the adventures happen to, and of course there is an island involved. Those are the similarities, but that's where the similarities stop.

"Bernard and I spent a long time working on it in L.A., possibly *because* we were in L.A. and found the life-style rather distracting—great fun, but it really didn't suit two lads from England in terms of actually getting down to work. We did spend a long time trying to get the thing finished, and we did. At that stage, there were some good elements to it, but we really didn't have the character of Yellowbeard in it. . . .He was kind of a historical fact, and this was an adventure which happened twenty years later, after he'd roamed the seas. It was about his son, who was just twenty years old. With Peter [Cook], we did a rewrite, and Yellowbeard was really brought back into it, which we felt might really be the clue to it, because the fleeting glimpse we had of him in the earliest script was exciting.

"Bernard liked it less, so I was thinking of the person I would most like to write with in the entire world. I thought, well, Peter Cook, because in my view he's one of the funniest people in the world. So, I said `Please,' and he said `Yes,' and we

spent a month, writing six days a week, and totally rewrote it, including the new character, really, of Yellowbeard. The rest after that was a matter of straightening it out, removing the absolute pinnacles of lunacy which were just too far out, and editing it and carving it into shape, which I did with David Sherlock."

Despite Chapman's presence and writing, as well as John Cleese and Eric Idle being along, Chapman pointed out that much of the humor in *Yellowbeard* was different from Monty Python humor.

"Obviously, it's inevitable that there are quirky little sections that could be slightly reminiscent of Python, but if any of it is comparable to Python, then I suppose you need to think of *Holy Grail*, really. It's not in the Python style—there's more of a story to it," he explained.

Even though he was kept busy with his behind-the-camera workload, Chapman enjoyed many of his acting scenes.

"Although they terrified me before I did them, I liked the fight scenes a lot," he revealed. "They were a challenge and an enjoyable experience when you'd actually finished them, but terrible to wait around for, not being experienced in that direction. I found it quite exhilarating.

"I really did enjoy doing my scenes with Madeline. I found that playing a scene with her, I got so much from her, that it was a joy to push it back at her," he recalls, laughing.

The different comedic styles of the actors—the group that had worked with Mel Brooks, the Pythons, and Cheech and Chong—seemed to be very disparate, but Chapman said they meshed together very well.

"Just to talk of one of them, for example, Kenneth Mars is a wonderfully loopy man who was the rather strange German writer in *The Producers*, and was also excellent in *Young Frankenstein* as the mad burgomeister. He plays a couple of parts in *Yellowbeard* and is really superb, totally mad.

"There are people blending in from different comedy schools, really—Cheech and Chong on one hand, people from Mel Brooks, like Marty, Madeline, Peter Boyle, and Kenneth Mars, and then three Pythons in it as well—three quite different schools—but there are similarities among these schools, and that's what I was hoping to use. There's also quite a lot of mutual admiration among the three schools, as well as envy," he joked.

"I was very pleased with the atmosphere that we had going during the shooting. It was an optimistic movie to shoot, despite the fact that we were in a constant battle with finance in terms of not really having enough money to give ourselves anything resembling a comfortable time, or enough in the way of facilities, such as toilets near the set. That had to fall along the wayside—and so did we—particularly in Mexico. But that led to a group spirit, it was almost as though we were all fighting a war and we were determined to win," explained Chapman.

There was almost a revolving door for the cast throughout the shooting, as different actors would come and go while shooting continued.

"We had a sort of constant cast running throughout, with myself, Peter Cook, Martin Hewitt, Michael Hordern, and Marty and Peter Boyle, and other people coming in at various stages to do their sections. The first part of the movie, it was John Cleese and Eric, but Eric overlapped—he then came out and did his part at sea, and for the last part of the movie, there was a whole section with Eric, and James Mason to blend in as well. Then the next big surprise that I had waited for was to find out what Cheech and Chong were really going to be like.

"There were really sort of three major stages, I suppose—Cleese, Mason, Cheech and Chong. I was wondering how they would fit in, because they're really the most disparate, in a way. Eric just blended in splendidly, I think he had a good time and enjoyed playing his part, and had a tremendously good sidekick played by Nigel Planer, who was quite a find. He made a convincing foil for Eric—it was in danger of becoming the Clement and Mansell show at one stage, they were being so funny. John had a great time, largely because Blind Pew is such an outrageous, way over-the-top character—he had a wonderful time, and threw in a couple of little extra jokes for us, which was rather nice, one of which he didn't tell me about, and I didn't see it until they did it, and I about fell out of my chair at it!" he laughed, referring to the scene where Clement pays Blind Pew with a coin on a string.

"James Mason was absolutely splendid as the English sea captain, and Cheech and Chong blended in too without leaving any noticeable scars—I enjoyed having them around. And then, because of different people coming in all the time, it also helped to keep us fresh."

Doing a period film like *Yellowbeard* wasn't as difficult as he had expected. "I was anticipating, without ever having worn them, that the costumes would be a bit awkward to wear and move in, but they're not. You feel very free in them—I was quite surprised about that!"

The biggest problem with filming in Mexico, however, was the heat.

"Because a lot of the film takes place on boats, we wanted to make sure we had good weather if possible," explained Chapman. "Inevitably that meant sunshine, which meant it was very hot. It was up around a hundred degrees most of the time in the middle of the day. Particularly from my own point of view, I found that because I was wearing all that facial hair, and having to look bedraggled in it, I was dampened down occasionally—which sounds kind of refreshing until you try it! You get straggly hair flapping into your eyes, which isn't too nice, blowing around on the beach, the false eyebrows and the largest beard I've ever seen, and the frizziest, most fly-away wig I've ever worn too. So, it didn't make for a lot of comfort."

One of the more annoying problems on the set in Mexico involved the lack of toilets.

"That was a problem when we were shooting some of the jungle sequences, and a lot of the stuff early on in Zihuatanejo. We had no trailers at that point, and so no toilets—just tents in jungles, and that was it. We had a few tents with fans in them, but that was all.

"We did the captain's cabin in—well, it's hard to call it a sound stage. It was a corrugated iron warehouse, although 'warehouse' makes it sound a bit luxurious. It was a shack, and the cabin was built in that. Just to make it slightly more bearable, so at least some kind of an attempt had been made at air conditioning, we had fans blowing over blocks of ice trying to keep it cool. That was appalling." He laughed. "It was kind of a closed-off set too, with lights inside it and a temperature outside of a hundred degrees or so. It was really unpleasant!"

Graham classified the shooting schedule as "very tight."

"*Yellowbeard*'s quite a big film, in that there are a lot of sights in it, and a big cast, and most of all, it involves ships. They were notoriously difficult to shoot on, but I don't think we lost a day due to the ship—it was absolutely splendid. That boat must have liked us, for some reason—we certainly liked it. That was one of the greatest experiences, just working on that boat. The only person who was really seasick was the Spanish doctor.

"Most of the film was shot two or three miles offshore, far enough out so that we had a good sweep of the sea to be able to use. We would go out about seven in the morning and come back when it got dark, so we were out there most of the day. It was a rather strange experience to find that, after a while, the hotel rocked as much as it did. Very odd to have that sensation, it didn't seem right—the boat was perfectly all right, but the land was rocking a lot!

"The captain and the crew were tremendous, just great at getting it heading just the right way for sunlight and wind as well as swells, so that we had some measure of continuity. That's one problem we had, to try to keep the sun in the same direction at the same time, the sails flapping the same way, those kind of complicated things—plus, it's all going up and down at the same time. It's a *miracle* we got it done, really."

Yellowbeard involved its share of swashbuckling stunts, according to Chapman, though some were more dangerous than others.

"This is the first time I've ever worked with real, pro stuntmen, and that was an enjoyable experience. We used them a lot for the fights, obviously, and shipboard, of course—people had to fall from riggings," revealed Chapman. "There was one very difficult stunt, which was Marty Feldman's on-screen death. He was supposedly tripped by a chair and had to fall into a vat of acid about twenty-five or thirty feet down. The vat of acid really wasn't that big, because there was a little island in the middle of the vat of acid where we had the torture chair, so he didn't have a great deal of width to fall into from that height. I shouldn't think it was more than six feet from the edge of the pool to the island in the middle, which isn't very much from that height. It was no distance at all. So, he really had to run up to the edge of the parapet blind and fall into the six-foot width of water—which was only about four

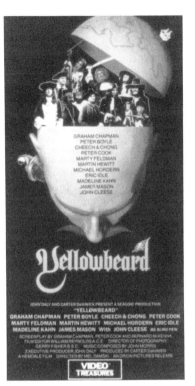

feet deep. He had to run off the edge and then fall vertically while doing a turn in midair. It was tricky, but it was a splendid stunt."

Graham said he had a few tricky moments during the shooting himself.

"The nastiest moment I had, the only point where I thought I might have a big problem, was swimming toward the boat at the beginning, because I had to appear to climb up a rope to climb onto the ship at the end of it. I had to swim fully clothed, and with piratical boots on. They were huge, thigh-length boots, and when you're moving in the water with those, they just fill up, like swimming with huge pools on your legs, and it drags you back. That was really very energetic. Partway toward the boat, I really thought I was going to go under," he said, noting that they were actually out in the sea. "If it hadn't been for our stunt coordinator yelling instructions at me from behind—he was swimming, dressed as a pirate too—telling me how to breathe properly in that kind of situation of terror, I don't think I would have made it! It was a very nasty moment, and I'm not a particularly strong swimmer, so that obviously didn't help me psychologically at all.

"It was quite a good experience just to be able to mess around in a childhood dream, that was the great thing about it," he said, noting it was his most ambitious personal project. "I think it is, obviously, just from the scale of it and the sort of people involved."

The low point of the entire production actually occurred at the end, with the death of Marty Feldman in Mexico City.

"I was on the set at the studios in Mexico City. I didn't actually hear about it then, I'd just heard that he'd been taken to hospital. As I'd finished that scene, I asked what was the matter. I'd gotten the impression that he was certainly very ill, which was a great surprise.

"He generally seemed to be in pretty good condition at the beginning of filming. During a stunt, he'd dislocated his coccyx; it was just a little painful for him from time to time, but that was all, and it happened four weeks before. I myself thought he was a little bit tense and on edge, and what certainly hurt was that he was smoking a great deal—he smoked about eighty cigarettes a day at that point. But there was nothing sufficiently extraordinary about him, no `Goodness me, he's on the way out.' I mean, he was very much good old Marty, he was right back on the form and having a very happy time performing and acting. He was only ever anxious when he was not acting, which was typical of Marty, and he was in very good form. So, it was completely out of the blue.

"I'd seen him the evening before, and he was looking slightly better than he had been throughout the entire schedule up to that point. But I gather even up to an hour before he died, or before the attack happened—he'd been out shopping, and he'd been seen in the lobby and was joking around. Suddenly, an hour later, he had these terrible chest pains, couldn't move, and went downhill from there. But during the shooting, he was very much the old Marty I remembered, which was great."

Shooting *Yellowbeard* was very similar to shooting a Python film, Chapman noted. "I suppose because John and Eric were around, it was extremely similar. I think it was more comfortable for me than *Brian* on location, obviously much more tropical and luxurious in a way than a barren, harsh Tunisia."

One change he said he would have liked would have been to have more time. "It would have been nice to have had a lot more time to shoot it, because we were really on quite a low budget for that size a movie and cast—it didn't leave us much for luxuries, hence the lack of toilet facilities. It was very, very tight, a lot of work, and I think it did give us a group unity, because we all did feel we were fighting some kind of battle to get the film made."

The movie pirates were actually held hostage for a time by customs agents, something real-life pirates would never have put up with. "There were awkward things that happened, like making the move from England to Mexico. We should really have had a week's gap there, but we didn't. We just had a day's gap. It was made doubly awkward, because the costumes hadn't arrived—or, they had arrived, but had been impounded somewhere by Customs, and some of them were hanging around there for two or three weeks. So, it meant a lot of improvisation from the wardrobe department, especially when they had to

match what had already been filmed. That was absolutely infuriating, because that sort of delay was for no reason. I suppose someone in Customs was waiting for the odd tip," he laughed. "The costumes were there, although some of them did go to Paris instead of Mexico City, another little problem that mainly involved Air France. There were an enormous number of costumes."

Another bit of costume difficulty actually involved the extras in Mexico.

"They were very good. We only had one problem in Acapulco, when some of the extras went off keeping their costumes and didn't come back the next day, which wasn't too helpful. But other than that, there was no problem with the extras.

"We did travel around a bit, although the main center for us was Zihuatanejo, and we did also have a couple of days in Acapulco, which was passing as Portsmouth, plus two weeks in Mexico City. I think all of us found that Mexico City section the most unpleasant, and I'm sure it was for Marty, because he had the air to cope with. Understanding what happened now, he had to cope with 7,500-feet elevation, less oxygen, and an enormous pollution problem up there. It really is the worst, most polluted town I've ever been in. I mean, I haven't been to all of them, but it makes Los Angeles at its worst look incredibly clean. The air is kind of yellow, really not pleasant, and there's not a lot of oxygen knocking around."

One of the brighter aspects for the cast and crew involved the cooperative sun.

"The thing that really sticks out in my mind is the incredible luck with the weather—it rained most of the time we were in England, which is just what we wanted, really, to make England look slightly drab. The sun was continuous in Mexico, except for a couple of days—one of those was while we were doing interiors, and the other was a day off. We were incredibly lucky—the rest of the time, it was clear skies!"

Other aspects of the filming were more meticulously planned, even though they proved unpleasant for the actors. Studying history books revealed some devices that Chapman and partner David Sherlock decided to incorporate into the script. Their research showed that historical pirates used to burn fuses in their hair and beards.

"The most famous pirate to do that was Blackbeard. He used to cut lengths of gunners' matches—they were called gunners' matches, but what they were effectively were fuses—lengths of rope dipped in a saltpeter solution and allowed to dry. Then, if you lit them, they glowed sufficiently for you to be able to light a trail of gunpowder or a cannon, but also billowed out smoke, which, if tied into a beard, does look rather effective and unusual," explained Chapman.

"It was all very well. The ones in the hair were fine, except one had to have someone standing by with a bucket of water or spray to put me out after each take. I hadn't really taken into account the ones in the beard, because that means you have smoke coming up your nose all the time, which is rather unpleasant. But I suppose it did look rather fierce-ish."

He said he did watch a number of pirate films before going to work on *Yellowbeard*.

"I had a look at every one we could think of. Two of the most impressive to me, the ones that stick out in my mind, were the Errol Flynn *Captain Blood,* a wonderful effort and really the archetypal pirate movie for me, and also a wonderful one with Charles Laughton playing Captain Kidd—he played a wonderfully evil character in that. What I was really looking for, though, thinking of Yellowbeard in a way, was all the atrocities that pirates may have committed in the past. I was particularly interested in those. I was more interested in writing an original pirate adventure-comedy rather than a spoof, so I didn't really watch them with an idea of sending up things. In fact, I was watching a film I greatly admired at the time I was about seven, *The Crimson Pirate*, when I thought it was the best film *ever made*. I quite enjoyed it, but it was a slight disappointment compared with the version many years ago when I was seven, because it was just too over-the-top wonderful, but over-the-top.

"I focused on the unpleasant side of piracy rather than the romantic side. In reading matter, they certainly weren't romantic. They lived for a very short time, really—twenty-one was quite old for a pirate. They were only pirates for about three or four years, and then they were dead. But during those years they did live life to the fullest, because there were no rules for them—they did what they wanted. They set up their own rules on their boats and that was it, so consequently, their lives were very short," he revealed.

Chapman said he tried to focus on the over-the-top aspect of Yellowbeard when creating the character. "That was one facet of him that really attracted me, and also made me slightly afraid of playing him to begin with, because he was such an outrageous character, throwing everything into it all the time, with no time to relax—he was always running around the place doing something. So for me, that made him the other end of the spectrum from Brian, really. Brian was someone who was good and running away from things, and Yellowbeard was bad and running straight at them. It was quite the reverse!

"He was a weird one, I don't quite know where he came from. I think he's an amalgam of lots of pirates, bits of Newton, and *lots* of Keith Moon's spirit."

Chapman said he was never initially interested in directing, though *Yellowbeard* started him thinking about it.

"I've become more interested in it, and I suppose that's really because no matter how marvelous a director one has, you never quite get the interpretation you intend as a writer. I mean, you're so close that no one else would notice but yourself—perhaps it's slightly irrelevant, but it does cause a certain amount of anxiety sometimes. So, I have thought of it, but of course the problem in this one is that acting and writing and taking a sort of artistic producer's role is enough, I think. But I would consider some other combination of doing maybe two or three of the four possible jobs. I certainly wouldn't want to attempt all four at once, because then there's no one to say 'I don't like that bit.' I think the other input is important."

Before *Yellowbeard* was released, Graham indicated he wasn't especially enthusiastic at the thought of a sequel. "I've been asked about it, and while I love all the characters, I don't know at the moment that I would like to—it'd be going over old ground. One's done a lot of pirate jokes and looked at areas that haven't been used in pirate films before, so we might be a little short of those as well, although the characters are certainly strong enough." He laughed. "There might well be a Clement and Mansell film—I think Eric and Nigel Planer come out very strongly."

The participation of both Idle and John Cleese was apparently instrumental to *Yellowbeard* at one point.

"Graham was very keen that I should be in it," says Cleese. "He'd asked me a couple of times before, and I'd said no. It didn't really fit in with what I was trying to do. Then he asked me again and pressed me quite strongly to do it—very nicely, of course—and I discovered there was this one part that could be shot entirely in England, and wouldn't take very long, and that I thought was amusing. So, I did a quick rewrite on those scenes, and it was something like four days' work."

Idle says he was happy to do the project, especially since his participation was apparently crucial.

"At one stage, it was like, if John and I agreed to be in it, then Orion would put the money up. Well, okay, I'm not going to stand in the way . . ." explains Idle.

Eight years later, Idle looked back on the experience with some mixed feelings, although he says he had a great time during the filming.

"I always thought the script needed a lot more work, but I watched it again the other day and it seemed to me it was very funny up to about two-thirds of the way through. It's really quite enjoyable on video," Idle states.

Idle noted that *Yellowbeard* satirized pirate movies, but was also concerned with historical piracy, as opposed to the Pythons' *Life of Brian*.

"If you're going to be funny, you have to parody the film's faults. *Brian* worked a lot more because we looked at all the biblical movies and then we parodied the film look and the version of that, so there's a grammar for us to reference ourselves when we look at it. So, *Yellowbeard* didn't quite conform to that, and suffered thereby."

One of the reasons Idle says he enjoyed the filming so much was the contractual arrangement he had with the filmmakers.

"I made a very smart deal with that. I agreed to be in it if I could play all of my scenes first." He laughs. "So, I had a week or ten days in Rye, which was fun because Marty was there, and Peter Cook, and John Cleese and everybody, and Peter Boyle.... It was fun with Graham, Marty, and John, because it was just like the mid-sixties again, when we all worked together back then.

"And then we went to Mexico, and we were there for three weeks, and that was fun too, because I had insisted that they do my scenes. So, all these guys had to wait at the hotel while I did my scenes," Idle recalls, laughing. "I had three wonderful weeks there filming and then bugged off, and then it all went a bit—then they'd fly in the next two comedians from L.A., and the next two were in, you know what I mean? It was all like `Cheech and Chong fly in for their bit—' Nobody met anybody. And you can't really create a style for a movie like that—everybody's got to see what everybody else is doing. There was no real rehearsal."

Chapman was himself disappointed with the final result and unhappy with the cut turned in by the director, who was primarily known for his work in television; he noted that the completed film didn't have the sweep and majesty it was capable of having and tended to look more like a TV movie. Graham was also not allowed in on the editing process, which didn't help the final result. Despite its problems and drawbacks, *Yellowbeard* still has a great many highlights, chief of which may be Graham's rousing, over-the-top portrayal of the lead character.

 ## CRITICAL COMMENTS

"A raunchy, energetic and glossy swashbuckler spoof. . . . The movie has a zealous pace and good production values. And even those of us who find Monty Python–style humor really silly have to admit there are many moments of hilarity here."

—Linda Gross, *Los Angeles Times*, June 23, 1983

"This spoof of pirate movies is dedicated to Marty Feldman, who died after completing it. And a fitting tribute to his British vaudevillian spirit is *Yellowbeard*'s non-stop foolishness, broad and bawdy humor, pell-mell pacing and marvelous cast."

—Stephen Schaeffer, *US*, August 15, 1983

FAMILIES AND HOW TO SURVIVE THEM

BY ROBIN SKYNNER AND JOHN CLEESE. PUBLISHED BY METHUEN (1983), HARDCOVER ISBN 0-413-52640-2; PAPERBACK ISBN 0-413-56520-3. U.S. EDITION PUBLISHED BY OXFORD UNIVERSITY PRESS.

The book is made up of dialogues between therapist Skynner and his former patient Cleese dealing with the complexities of human relationships and how they work. They approach serious topics in a slightly lighter, more accessible format, using ordinary language in ways that ordinary people can grasp.

Chapters include "Why Did I Have to Marry You?" which deals with love and marriage; "I'm God, and Let's Leave It Like That," which involves the arrival of a baby and its effect on a family; and "The Astonishing Stuffed Rabbit," involving a baby's first realization of its own identity and the beginning of the separation from its mother. "Who's in Charge Here?" sees the child making choices, developing attitudes, and dealing with guilt, self-control, sexual identity, authority, aggression, and parental boundaries. Finally, "What Are You Two *Doing* in There?" deals with sex.

 ## NOTES

John Cleese reluctantly began group therapy with Robin Skynner as a result of problems in his first marriage and to treat a probable psychosomatic illness. After his experiences in therapy, Cleese was so impressed that he wanted to share his knowledge with others. Since their therapist-patient relationship had concluded, they decided to collaborate on a book designed for laypeople who would probably never participate in group therapy on their own.

"Professionally, it was a huge departure for me," notes Cleese. "It wasn't a departure from what I was interested in. When I was fifteen, what I

really wanted to do was study biology, and go into the psychology department somewhere in a university, and do all those tests that B.F. Skinner used to do on pigeons and rats.

"It's not surprising that twenty years later, I got back to it—my principal readings over the years being psychiatry or psychology. When I'd had this experience in the group which Robin Skynner ran, with his wife as co-therapist back in 1974, '75, '76,

and '77—three and a half years I was into it—I was going back. Apart from the fact that I needed therapy at the time to get me through a difficult time in my life when my first marriage broke up, I was also going back to what fascinated me. What did Samuel Johnson say? The proper study of man is man."

Cleese says that at first, he found it difficult to open up in his first sessions with the group.

"I was more apprehensive at the beginning," he admits. "For a number of years, I had a fear of the press, not least because there are sections of the British press which are so dishonest and so untrustworthy and so treacherous that one is completely vulnerable. There is nothing that you can say to someone that cannot be distorted.

"At one stage, that worried me a lot. Now, it doesn't really worry me very much, and I don't quite know what the difference is, but something in me's changed. And I think it is well known in England how awful most of the press are, and therefore there's a great deal of skepticism about almost everything they print."

Families is presented in a very user-friendly format, which Cleese says was intentional.

"It's light, hopefully, with a certain amount of humor with a serious purpose. It's not just to keep people amused or to keep people reading, although that's obviously a function of something that's light and amusing and entertaining—it's easy for people to keep reading. The real purpose of a lot of the humor is to relax people. Things that might make them slightly anxious if they were handed forward in a very solid and confrontative way can be absorbed and chewed over because they're put across in a relaxed, playful way."

His work with Robin Skynner was even helpful in his comedy, he says. "When you begin to see a little bit more of what's the healthy way, it's easier to see what is unhealthy and make fun of that."

Families and How to Survive Them established a new reputation for Cleese and turned into a best-seller that has sold consistently in Britain.

The pair decided to do a follow-up book called *Life and How to Survive It*. Although it was originally targeted to have a psychological approach to relationships in the world of business, its focus changed during the writing.

"It's a study, first of all, of the research that's been done on people who are exceptionally mentally healthy, by which I mean they don't have any of the ordinary neuroses or the ordinary slight psychosomatic problems," explains Cleese.

"They're happy, energetic, and fulfilled. A study has been done on these people to see how the families function, and how they're different from ordinary midrange families that you and I come from—ones that are fine but have problems. We, then, look at those ways of functioning, and then see how they apply to larger groups, seeing whether corporations that are really successful function in similar ways, whether they function like a very healthy family or like an ordinary midrange family," he reveals. "And then we go wider. We go to political parties, and into nations, and then value systems, and even into religions."

 ## CRITICAL COMMENTS

"It achieves what it sets out to do—explaining in ordinary language to ordinary people just how relationships work."

—*The Sun*, London

THE YOUNG ONES

GUEST-STARRING TERRY JONES. BROADCAST MAY 29, 1984, ON BBC-2. FEATURING ADRIAN EDMONDSON, RIK MAYALL, NIGEL PLANER, CHRISTOPHER RYAN, AND ALEXEI SAYLE.

Terry Jones is featured as a vicar in the "Nasty" episode, where the trio rents nasty videos.

 ## NOTES

The Young Ones, a comedy series with Python and rock-and-roll influences, was a hit on British TV in the early 1980s, and Terry Jones says he was asked by the group to do one morning's filming for the show.

"Rik Mayall and Alexei Sayle were there, and they were fans of Python," reveals Jones.

"I was asked to be a drunken vicar that throws up on the graves, and I went along and did it. To tell the truth, I've actually never seen it!"

THE GOLDEN SKITS OF WING COMMANDER MURIEL VOLESTRANGLER FRHS AND BAR

BY JOHN CLEESE (WRITING AS MURIEL VOLESTRANGLER). PUBLISHED BY METHUEN (1984), ISBN 0-413-41560-0.

A selection of sketches written or co-written by John Cleese; many are from *Monty Python's Flying Circus* but others are much more obscure. In addition to the Python sketches, the contents include sketches from the *Double Take* (the 1962 Cambridge Review); *Cambridge Circus*; *I'm Sorry, I'll Read That Again*; *The Frost Report*; and *At Last the 1948 Show*; as well as several Amnesty International Benefits. Co-authors include Graham Chapman, Tim Brooke-Taylor, Marty Feldman, David Hatch, and Michael Palin.

Non-Python sketches include "Shirt Shop Skit" (by John Cleese, Tim Brooke-Taylor, and Marty Feldman; *1948 Show*); "Goat Skit" (by John Cleese and Graham Chapman; *Frost Report*); "Bookshop Skit" (by John Cleese and Graham Chapman; *1948 Show*); "Cricket Commentators Skit" (by John Cleese and David Hatch; *ISIRTA*); "Regella Skit" (by John Cleese; *Double Take*); "Hearing Aid Skit" (by John Cleese and Graham Chapman; *1948 Show*); "The Good Old Days Skit" (by John Cleese, Marty Feldman, Graham Chapman, and Tim Brooke-Taylor; *1948 Show*); "Lucky Gypsy Skit" (by John Cleese and Marty Feldman; *1948 Show*); "Railway Carriage Skit" (by John Cleese, Graham Chapman, and Marty Feldman; *1948 Show*); "String Skit" (by John Cleese and Graham Chapman; *Frost Report*); "Slightly Less Silly Than the Other Court Skit Court Skit" (by John Cleese; *Cambridge Circus*); and "The Courier Skit" (by John Cleese and Graham Chapman; *Frost*).

 NOTES

Cleese compiled this collection of his favorite sketches when he realized that, in the past, he had been just giving away his material.

"Each year Graham and I got a request from Frank Muir for two or three sketches for the *Frank Muir Christmas Sketch Book*. I suddenly realized one year that I must have given him half a book's worth of material." He laughs. "I thought `Why don't I do one myself?' I'd rather like to have a little collection of my favorite sketches, and I thought it probably wouldn't make much money, but it'd be fun to do anyway. I quite enjoyed it, going back, choosing my favorite sketches. A lot of them are with

Graham, a few are on my own, and one or two are with other people.

"The book came out and sold a reasonable number of copies. I don't think it ever made much money, but the royalties were duly split among the various writers in proportion, and I'm quite pleased to have it around. I send it to charity signings sometimes."

Cleese says he chose the unusual title for the volume in order to make it more interesting.

"I decided it was not going to be *The John Cleese Sketch Book*, or even *The John Cleese and Graham Chapman Sketch Book*. I just thought that was kind of boring. So, I used my pseudonym, which went back to a character that I did in the *1948 Show*. I had it once printed on the cover of some matchbooks that I used to leave at people's parties, so they used to wonder who on earth this lady was, and why they hadn't noticed her!"

THE COURAGE TO CHANGE

BY DENNIS WHOLEY, ONE CHAPTER DEVOTED TO GRAHAM CHAPMAN. PUBLISHED BY HOUGHTON MIFFLIN (1984), ISBN 0-395-35977-5.

Wholey profiles a variety of well-known alcoholics and relatives of alcoholics, including Pete Townshend, Jason Robards, Grace Slick, Shecky Green, Sid Caesar, and Doc Severinsen. In the chapter on Graham Chapman, he discusses how society seems to accept drunken behavior from comedians and also explains how, as a medical doctor, Chapman was able to monitor his symptoms, confident that he would be able to quit drinking before his body deteriorated too badly.

THE DRESS

STARRING MICHAEL PALIN. (1984)

FEATURING MICHAEL PALIN, PHYLLIS LOGAN, DERRICK BRANCHE, DAVE HILL, AND RACHEL PALIN. SCREENPLAY BY ROBERT SMITH. PRODUCED BY FOREVER FILMS/NATIONAL FILM FINANCE CORP. DIRECTED BY EVA SERENY. RELEASED BY PARAMOUNT BRITISH PICTURES AND CHANNEL FOUR.

This short film involves Palin as a man who buys a dress for his mistress but suddenly becomes attracted to his wife when she puts it on.

 ## NOTES

Michael Palin became involved with *The Dress* as a favor to its director, who asked him to play one of the two leads.

"I was approached by a lady called Eva Sereny, who is a stills photographer—she's worked for Spielberg and all that," notes Palin. "She wanted to get into film directing. It's very hard just to go in first time, especially a female director, so she got some money working with somebody else, and then made a short film. I was asked to play one of the two main roles. It was partly because I liked Eva very much, and also Phyllis Logan, who had taken the other part, a very, very good actress. I was really happy to have the chance to work with her. I had just finished yet another rewrite of *American Friends*, and this was going to take two weeks, so I said `Sure,' it would be good to get the acting experience. Apart from *Brazil*, it was the only totally straight, slightly unpleasant sort of character, that I've played."

A PRIVATE FUNCTION

STARRING MICHAEL PALIN. (1985) 93 MINUTES

Gilbert Chilvers ....Michael Palin
Joyce Chilvers ....Maggie Smith
Dr. Swaby ....Denholm Elliot
Allardyce..Richard Griffiths
Sutcliff..Tony Haygarth
Lockwood ....John Normington
Wermold. ....Bill Paterson
Mother ....Liz Smith
Mrs. Allardyce...Alison Steadman

Written by Alan Bennett. Produced by Mark Shivas. Directed by Malcolm Mowbray. Released by Island Alive/Handmade Films. Videocassette release by Thorn EMI HBO Video TVA 3010.

During the preparation for the Royal Wedding in 1947, rationing is still affecting everyone, including chiropodist Gilbert Chilvers and his wife Joyce. As Gilbert attends to Mrs. Allardyce, her husband and the rest of the snobbish town leaders select the invitees to the town celebration; their daughter, who studies piano with Mrs. Childers, practices. Gilbert services the feet of the butcher's wife, and witnesses a raid by the police to find illegal meat.

At home, Gilbert discusses his patients' feet, but his wife is more interested in being invited to the dinner. The butcher is arrested for selling horsemeat just before she can buy her ration.

Meanwhile, at a local farm, Allardyce and his associates go to feed Betty, a pig they're hiding for the town's wedding celebration. Dr. Swaby is upset because Gilbert is opening up a competing office downtown. Gilbert arrives at the farm and is asked to treat Betty's foot. While he treats Mrs. Sutcliff, the inspector arrives at their farm and looks around.

Joyce and her mother sit in their car, which is on blocks, lamenting their lack of gasoline rations. When she goes shopping, the butcher runs out again before Joyce can receive her allotment. Gilbert arrives at the farm with table scraps for the pigs, just as Allardyce is leaving. Gilbert sees where Betty is being hidden. Back in town, Dr. Swaby has Gilbert thrown out of his office and runs over his bicycle; Gilbert becomes fed up enough to suggest that he and Joyce steal the pig from Sutcliff's farm.

Allardyce, Swaby, and the others find the pig is ill with diarrhea, and they decide to kill it early. That night Gilbert and Joyce lure the sick, illegal pig into their car and bring it home. She wants Gilbert to kill the pig with his tiny chiropodist tools, but he can't do it. They try to gas it in the oven, and her mother is afraid they're trying to get Dr. Swaby to put her away. The pig survives the gas, and they try to warn her mother not to mention the pig, but she fears they're trying to send her to an old-age home.

While the town fathers fret about the missing pig, the inspector barely misses seeing it when he has his feet examined. Joyce finally insists that Gilbert kill the pig with a large knife, but he succeeds only in cutting his finger; Joyce tries to kill it herself.

Allardyce's daughter tells her father she saw a pig at the Chilvers' house, and some of the town leaders approach him at a local pub as he drinks and try to negotiate. They all arrive at the house and find the pig, and Joyce insists they all have a drink. Gilbert and Allardyce want to free the pig somehow, while the inspector sits outside. The butcher finally kills the pig, and Allardyce and Gilbert are inconsolable. But the Chilverses finally attain the social status they have been hoping for.

 ## NOTES

Michael Palin recalls that he was hired onto *A Private Function* simply as an actor by one of the *Beyond the Fringe* creators, and given the opportunity to team again with his *Missionary* co-star.

"The phone call came from Alan Bennett, who is a very well-respected writer who I like very much indeed, a marvelous eye for detail. To be asked by him to be in a film is something you just sort of accept," explains Palin. "I worked with a tremendous cast—I got to work with Maggie again."

He says he didn't realize until later that one of the reasons they were asked to do the film was so that it could be made! "I was so pleased to have a chance to do it, and I suddenly realized that actually, they asked me and Maggie in the hope that we'd get Handmade Films to put money into it! I remember going to the first meeting with Alan and the producers, and I thought they were going to tell me when they were doing it, and the locations, and how big the caravan would be and all of this sort of stuff, when in fact they were asking me about where they might get the money. I said `Hang on!'" he recalls, laughing.

"But we did give the script to Denis [O'Brien] and George [Harrison], and they have been wonderful supporters throughout the last ten years, and they supported this! I don't think Denis understood it at all, really. I don't think he knew quite why he was doing it, he just felt that if I wanted to do it, it was good enough for him! And I'm very grateful to him for that. I think that turned out into a pretty idiosyncratic and interesting movie, very different from anything else I've done, and will stand the test of time. It keeps getting repeated, and is noted with interest."

The film was well received by critics, and Palin notes he had agreed to star in it before there was even a script.

"I hadn't actually seen the script first, it was just Alan Bennett's reputation. He's a very fastidious writer, very careful and thorough, so he'd know the area he'd been involved in with intense personal detail, and he has a very good ear for dialogue. So, I was pretty well converted before he even began doing it. Then I read the script, and it had a lot of the qualities that I like to put in my own scripts. It's a slightly self-regarding way of talking about it, but I think I saw in Alan things I liked, and that was fine. . . ."

 ## CRITICAL COMMENTS

"A classic comedy of class struggle . . . expertly performed. . . . Here's hoping that *A Private Function* scores at the box office and triggers a renaissance of British film comedy. * * * 1/2"

—Gene Siskel, *Chicago Tribune*, April 12, 1985.

"*A Private Function* is in the great tradition of eccentric British comedy. . . . There is something intrinsically funny about characters who are proper in their impropriety, and Palin and Smith know all the nuances."

—Roger Ebert, *Chicago Sun-Times*, April 12, 1985

A PRIVATE FUNCTION

BY ALAN BENNETT. PUBLISHED BY FABER AND FABER (1984), ISBN 0-571-13571-4 (U.K. PAPERBACK).

The book of the film starring Michael Palin.

SILVERADO

CO-STARRING JOHN CLEESE. (1985) 132 MINUTES

Paden.	Kevin Kline
Emmett	Scott Glenn
Jake	Kevin Costner
Mal	Danny Glover
Sheriff Langston	John Cleese
Hannah	Rosanna Arquette
Cobb	Brian Dennehy
Stella	Linda Hunt
Slick	Jeff Goldblum

Screenplay by Mark and Lawrence Kasdan. Produced by Lawrence Kasdan. Directed by Lawrence Kasdan. Released by Columbia Pictures/RCA-Columbia Home Video 60567.

In the old West, Paden and Emmett ride off for the town of Turley. They stop in a saloon, where Mal, a black man, is refused service, and starts a fight. Sheriff Langston arrives to break up the fight and orders Mal out of town and out of his jurisdiction. When he leaves, Paden and Emmett tell the sheriff whom they are looking for, and the sheriff leads them to the jail, where they find Jake—Emmett's brother—about to be hanged. Afterward, Paden and Emmett decide to bust him out of jail.

The next morning the sheriff plays chess with himself, awaiting the hanging, when he is suddenly called away. Paden, Emmett, and Jake trick the deputy and escape. The sheriff finds the gallows have been set on fire, and Paden, Emmett, and Jake flee town. The sheriff and his deputies give chase, but when the gunfire gets too heavy, he decides they've reached the end of his jurisdiction. Mal's shooting has saved them, and the four of them travel on to Silverado, where they join forces to battle Cobb and his bad guys.

 NOTES

John Cleese proved to be a curious yet effective addition to Lawrence Kasdan's epic Western. He was clearly excited about this role, as he explained that he had never dreamed of doing a Western.

"It's so ridiculous, such an absurd notion, that it has to be attractive," he explained shortly before he left for New Mexico to begin filming. "It's very nice to have the chance of doing one or

Cleese played it straight in Silverado, **but proved to be a rather silly sheriff between takes. Photo from the Collection of John Cleese, used by permission**

two things that are slightly straight, because I'm best at comedy and I expect to get paid well at comedy. I don't expect to get paid well for straight parts because it's not a skill of mine. It may turn out I have the skill, but everybody who does it is taking a slight risk. I have a couple of funny lines in it, but it's not a comedy at all, but a straight, exciting Western, beautifully constructed, as you would expect from Mr. Kasdan. To my delight, he's written a small part about a tall, English sheriff. It's very short, but it's wonderful, so I go to Sante Fe and have riding lessons in a Western saddle."

After the film's release, Cleese noted that although he appears only in the first half hour of the film, the whole experience was wonderful.

"Silverado was a joy, to suddenly disappear to New Mexico at the invitation of dear Larry Kasdan for the two and a half weeks of riding lessons, and some of the finest scenery I've ever seen, and the chance to get to know a delightful, lovely group of people," Cleese relates.

"It was very interesting to be on a film as big as that—three times as big as the biggest Python film. I think Silverado's budget was more than $20 million. I came to realize that the amount of planning and logistics that went into every single day of shooting—the amount of food that had to be provided, the number of tents that had to be put up so that people could stay warm—was most impressive. It was like being part of an army!

"Filming was very enjoyable. My single complaint was that as New Mexico is at seven thousand feet, it was a damn sight colder than I had guessed. The hours of daylight were quite restricting because it was winter, so we were all

getting up at five-fifteen A.M. so as to be available to be shot at first light. Apart from the temperature and the hour at which we had to get up, it was ideal.

"I have the most considerable respect for Larry Kasdan, and I found it very interesting trying to see why he is so good. I realized it was because he visualized so precisely—more than anyone I've ever worked with before—exactly what was going up on the screen at the moment he was writing it on the paper."

One of the added benefits to Silverado was that Cleese learned how to ride a horse. He was particularly proud of this ability because he wanted to impress his daughter Cynthia, and was rather annoyed that most of his horseback riding was in long shots. There were other problems as well.

"Every time I got really comfortable on a horse, they gave me a bigger one. I was too tall! They didn't want me to look silly, so the one I finished up on was pretty big, but I adored the riding. Altogether, I went through four or five horses—I don't think they all had to be destroyed after I had ridden them, but every time I got one that I *really* liked, there was another, *bigger* one waiting for me the next day," Cleese recalls with a laugh.

"It was strange, and I got a little lonely. I went out and quite consciously bought a couple of novels by P. G. Wodehouse and Somerset Maugham at one point, because I needed an injection of Englishness. It was nothing to do with unfriendliness, I just felt a little strange after I'd been there a couple of months. A wonderful experience, though, and I was very sad to leave them all."

Director Lawrence Kasdan stays warm between takes with Kevin Kline and John Cleese during Silverado **shooting in New Mexico. Photo taken from the Collection of John Cleese, used by permission**

CRITICAL COMMENTS

"This movie is more sophisticated and complicated than the Westerns of my childhood, and it is certainly better looking and better acted. But it has the same spirit; it awards itself the carefree freedom of the Western myth itself. * * * 1/2"

—Roger Ebert, *Chicago Sun-Times*, July 10, 1985

NATIONAL LAMPOON'S EUROPEAN VACATION

WITH AN APPEARANCE BY ERIC IDLE. (1985) 94 MINUTES. STARRING CHEVY CHASE, BEVERLY D'ANGELO, DANA HILL, JASON LIVELY, VICTOR LANOUX, JOHN ASTIN, PAUL BARTEL, MEL SMITH, AND ERIC IDLE. SCREENPLAY BY JOHN HUGHES AND ROBERT KLANE. PRODUCED BY MATTY SIMMONS. DIRECTED BY AMY HECKERLING. RELEASED BY WARNER BROTHERS/WARNER HOME VIDEO 11521.

Clark Griswald and his family win a trip to Europe on a game show, *A Pig in a Poke*. In London, Clark is trying to drive, and hits a very polite bicycle rider, played by Eric Idle. The biker insists he isn't hurt, though he is bleeding profusely, and Clark asks him for directions. Later, in Rome, Clark accidentally smashes into the man from London, complete with broken leg, in a revolving door. The man remains polite as he flees Clark. Finally, after a chase in which Clark's car ends up in a fountain, he discovers he has knocked the polite Londoner into the same fountain.

 ## NOTES

Although the sequel to *National Lampoon's Vacation* was generally considered disappointing, Eric Idle has a few nice moments with his role. The filming itself proved to be even more memorable, however, and directly contributed to his lack of dialogue during his final scene.

"I'd met Chevy when he'd injured himself way back. I did a day in London right at the beginning of the film and it went quite well, and then I went to Rome for a two- or three-day shoot, and we actually did a whole fountain scene in Frascati. Actually, Frascati doesn't have a fountain in the main square—the film built one," explains Idle.

"I eventually ended up living in that town during *Munchausen*. I just remember one memorable party with Keith Richard in Rome. I was trying to be very good, because I was filming the next day, and he said `Come on, sing, Eric, come and sing.' I sang *all night*, 'cause I had finished my talking part. Chevy comes to me the next day—I think it was the day after, actually, because I'd lost my voice totally, because we'd sang all night," he laughs. "A real good ding-dong! And then Chevy comes up and says `All right, I've rewritten the scene, and this is what you say—' And I went `[raspy, inaudible sound]' So, I don't speak in the last scene there, I just flounder about in the water."

After *European Vacation*, Idle did some work on another possible sequel to be set in Australia, though it was never filmed. "It's a little-known fact that I wrote a *Vacation* for Chevy—*Vacation Down Under*," reveals Idle. "We spent some time working together on it. It had some nice shark gags, but I can't pretend it was in any way finished. . . ."

SPIES LIKE US

CAMEO APPEARANCE BY TERRY GILLIAM. (1985) 109 MINUTES. STARRING CHEVY CHASE, DAN ACKROYD, STEVE FORREST, DONNA DIXON, BRUCE DAVISON, BERNIE CASEY, FRANK OZ AND CHARLES MCKEOWN, WITH TERRY GILLIAM. SCREENPLAY BY DAN ACKROYD, LOWELL GANZ, AND BABALOO MANDEL. PRODUCED BY BRIAN GRAZER AND GEORGE FOLSEY, JR. DIRECTED BY JOHN LANDIS. RELEASED BY WARNER BROTHERS/WARNER HOME VIDEO 11533.

Two men who want to be government spies are set up as decoys and sent on a counterespionage mission in a comedy patterned after the Hope-Crosby *Road* movies. (Hope even makes a brief cameo here.) A number of prominent directors appear in cameo parts, including Michael Apted, Martin Brest, Constantin Costa-Gavras, Joel Coen, Ray Harryhausen, Seva Novgorodtsev, Frank Oz, and Terry Gilliam as a German doctor.

Chase and Ackroyd are captured by Afghani freedom fighters, but freed to join a United Nations medical team in the desert, a medical team that includes Gilliam as Dr. Imhaus. Later, when the pair is forced to perform an appendectomy before the other doctors, Imhaus is critical and, in his best German accent, pronounces the patient dead.

 ## NOTES

"John Landis asked me to do it," Terry Gilliam explains of his appearance in *Spies Like Us*.

"He had asked me a couple of times before to appear in his films, because he's got this thing about directors appearing in his films. I think he takes directors who are better than him, and then humiliates them publicly by making them appear as bad actors!" he laughs. "That's my secret to thinking about this one. He got me down there for a couple of days' filming."

BRAZIL

CO-WRITTEN AND DIRECTED BY TERRY GILLIAM.

FEATURING MICHAEL PALIN. (1985) 131 MINUTES

Sam Lowry	Jonathan Pryce
Jill Layton	Kim Greist
Harry Tuttle	Robert DeNiro
Mrs. Ida Lowry	Katherine Helmond
Mr. Kurtzmann	Ian Holm
Spoor	Bob Hoskins
Jack Lint	Michael Palin
Mr. Warren	Ian Richardson
Mr. Helpmann	Peter Vaughan

Screenplay by Terry Gilliam, Tom Stoppard, and Charles McKeown. Produced by Arnon Milchan. Directed by Terry Gilliam. Released by Universal Pictures/MCA Home Video 80171.

Terrorist activity increases in Gilliam's "post-Orwellian view of a pre-Orwellian world." A literal bug in the system at the Ministry of Information Retrieval causes a government assault squad to arrest the wrong man (Mr. Buttle instead of Mr. Tuttle), as his terrified family and their neighbor Jill watch him being taken away.

Sam Lowry, a lowly clerk in the Ministry of Inform-ation, dreams of a fantasy world. On his way to the office, he runs into his old friend Jack, whose career is moving upward fast. Sam notices Jill, who tries to retrieve Mr. Buttle, but is a victim of the bureaucracy.

In the office of his boss Mr. Kurtzmann, Sam learns that his mother has arranged his promotion to Infor-mation Retrieval, which he doesn't want. They have lunch with his mother's friend Alma and daughter Shirley, but the restaurant is rocked by a terrorist explosion.

As Sam dreams of flying and a beautiful woman who looks like Jill, he wakes up sweating, but can't get his air-conditioning repaired. Harry Tuttle, an outlaw heating engineer, breaks into his apartment and repairs his air-conditioning but is interrupted by the arrival of two official repairmen from Central Services; Sam gets rid of them by insisting on seeing the proper government paperwork. Tuttle finishes and makes his escape into the night.

The next day Sam discovers Mr. Buttle is dead, and Mr. Kurtzmann has him deliver a refund check to Buttle's wife. When Jill looks in to comfort the distraught widow, Sam sees her and tries to follow, but she escapes in her truck. Learning her name, he allows himself to be promoted so that he can gain access to her files at the ministry. When he arrives home that night, he discovers the Central Services repairmen have torn apart his apartment. Sam decides to attend a party that night at his mother's in order to meet Mr. Helpmann and arrange his promotion.

After arriving at his new job and tiny office, Sam tries to find out about Jill, while in his fantasy world he does battle with a stone creature. He goes to another department to learn more and discovers Jack in a blood-splattered white apron. He learns that Jack actually killed Buttle due to a mix-up, and they are looking for Jill because she's causing trouble. Sam gets her file and tells Jack he'll track her down. Jill is in the lobby of his building, and he leads her away. She almost escapes in her truck, but Sam catches up to her and tells her he loves her. She doesn't believe him and tries to lose him; she explains that there are no actual terrorists, and he makes her run a roadblock.

Walking through a store, Sam is diverted by his mother's friends, and when a bomb goes off, he suspects Jill. She is furious and shows him he was wrong, and as they pitch in to help the wounded, Jill is arrested by a government trooper. In his fantasy world, Sam battles an armored warrior that turns out to be himself, and he wakes up in a government van where prisoners are being taken in, but can't find Jill. When he tries to uncover more information, Jack tells him to stay away.

At his apartment, the two repairmen have completely torn his place apart and had him evicted, so Tuttle helps him sabotage their plans and they meet with a very messy end. Sam finds Jill and they flee to his mother's empty house, but before they can get romantic, Sam rushes out with an idea for saving Jill. He slips into Mr. Helpmann's office and changes the records to indicate that she is dead. When Sam returns, just before his fantasies can come true, government troops burst in and capture him. Jack plans to interrogate him. Sam is freed by the "terrorists" and runs off with Jill, but it is only another fantasy.

 ## NOTES

The checkered history of *Brazil* is well known to Gilliam fans and has even been the subject of a book, *The Battle of Brazil,* by Jack Mathews.

Brazil was actually going to be filmed by Gilliam as a follow-up project to *Life of Brian* in 1978, but its gestation period grew to several years. It started out as a film he was going to write with *Jabberwocky* collaborator Charles Alverson; although he had developed the story himself, he wanted Alverson to assist with the dialogue. At one point he was simply calling it *The Ministry*, and although the title and his collaborators changed, the 1985 film is not vastly different from his original concept, although he had apparently anticipated more extensive fantasy sequences for Sam.

"It's certainly the same in spirit," noted Gilliam shortly after its completion. "Details have changed, but the same muse is at work. Whoever's making this film is still making the same one he was trying to do back then. I'm still waiting to meet the force behind it all—I only know it's not me.

"This film is a strange organic thing. The people who are hired to work on it change all sorts of details, but *Brazil* remains the same film in spirit. I've become totally mystical about film-making. It's *the movie that wouldn't die*—despite trying to kill almost every one of us involved, it's still alive and well."

The inspiration for the movie actually occurred while scouting locations for *Jabberwocky*. "We were at this steelmaking town in Wales, on the beach at sunset," Gilliam relates. "There were these great bays where the ships come in bringing the coal, and the coal is transported by conveyor belts over the beach to the steel plant. The beach was covered with coal dust, so it's a pitch-black beach. The sun was going down out there on the sea, and I had the image of someone sitting with a portable radio picking up strange Latin American music in this desolate world—that's where the movie started. None of that is in the film, but that's how it began—and we went from there."

Raising the money for the film proved more difficult than he had anticipated. *Brazil* had to be put on hold for several years, and it was not until *Time Bandits* proved to be a success and Gilliam could not be interested in any other project that studios finally took him seriously about his pet project.

"The problem was that I did *Meaning of Life* right after *Time Bandits*, so as far as Hollywood was concerned, I was out of circulation. By the time I was back to trying to get the money, I had gone cold. It was hard to get any interest until I turned down another project they were very excited about. They decided if I was turning it down, I

must have a really good reason—and that was *Brazil*. They started looking at it more seriously."

Although Alverson wasn't credited with the final screenplay, Gilliam did bring in playwright Tom Stoppard and actor-writer Charles McKeown to collaborate on the script. "It seemed a good idea to get somebody who's as clever verbally as the pictures were going to be—that's really why [Stoppard] was involved. It was a tidying-up opera-tion—Tom was trying to make sense out of many jumbled thoughts, which he did. We tightened up much of it," Gilliam reveals.

"After Tom had done a few drafts, I started working with Charles McKeown to finish it off in its present form. Even the screenplay that the three of us ended up with isn't what's actually in the film—that has all changed during the filming and editing. In that sense, it's very organic.

"Little things were added all the time. Jonathan Pryce was always coming up with new and interesting ways of doing things. When we got on the set with all these objects, things began changing, and we really had to use them. I have a preconceived idea that I'm working toward, and I still storyboard it all, but things can change on the set, and I must go with it. It's a process where I know where I'm going, and I'll go off on tangents. In the editing stages, I try to bring it back to where I was originally going—but it has altered in the process."

The final result is a dazzling, depressing, completely original film that has been described as "Walter Mitty Meets Franz Kafka," a label Gilliam agrees is accurate.

"We've got another catchphrase which is rather boring—'a post-Orwellian view of a pre-Orwellian world'—it's really tedious-sounding, and I think Mitty and Kafka are the truth of the matter. It's really about someone who doesn't take reality seriously enough, and spends too much time day-dreaming. It can be a dangerous thing—one has to keep one's eyes peeled. It creeps up from behind when one isn't looking," Gilliam noted shortly after completing the production.

"I spend a lot of time trying to avoid being categorized. This film is probably all categories—and none. It's a comedy—it's very funny, and also very tragic. It's exciting, like an adventure, and it's terrify-ing, like a horror film—it's a bit of everything. We're very greedy about what we're trying to do. We want to put people through their paces. Hopefully, we run the gamut of experiences in *Brazil*.

"People have compared it to *Citizen Kane, One Flew Over the Cuckoo's Nest, A Clockwork Orange, Dr. Strangelove*. The audience will come away from it saying 'It reminded me a bit of that,' but it has elements of them all.

"The film takes place everywhere in the twentieth century—that was the original idea. We're surrounded by things from another technology, items out of date from another era, and we always seem to accept it as normal—so, we tried to push that idea almost to the cartoon level," explains the former Python animator.

Shooting the picture involved its own nightmares, he notes. "We had some terrible troubles. We were out at this British offshore petroleum refinery which had been shut down. We were filming in the middle of winter and the cold was unbearable. We had to fill the place with black smoke and huge explosions. Physically, that was the worst day we ever experienced—by day's end, everybody was pitch black. One couldn't see anything but the whites of eyes. There were these terrible underworld terrorist figures all creeping around, trying to stay warm and alive," relates Gilliam.

"We shot for nine months, and it was *extremely* painful. Each film gets harder and harder. I don't know how to judge them anymore—they all become nightmarish, and *Brazil* puts all the others to shame. *Everything* at every stage was difficult.

"Even though it doesn't look like a special effects film, it is. George Gibbs, the guy who's doing the main SFX, did the physical effects on *Indiana Jones and the Temple of Doom,* and said this one was far more complicated. There's something happening in every scene—there are little machines working away, things are exploding—they're very small explosions, but they are exploding! We have people flying, fifteen-foot-high samurai warriors—some very involved SFX.

"Unfortunately, much of the model work was supposed to be shooting concurrently with the main filming, and it didn't work out that way. We ended up doing it afterward, as we did in *Time Bandits*. It took forever. It was much more complicated, more things needed to be made, and the way they worked was more complex—it was like multiplying the problems of *Time Bandits* by ten!

"There are some FX which are done with live-action and are full size, but the rest is all models—there's a truck chase, ministry buildings slowing up—all standard model work. They were just more complicated because to have a man in a silver suit of armor, flying with an eighteen-foot pair of wings, is tricky. Most people don't even realize it's a model, they just assume we've somehow flown him. It really works."

Gilliam says he was very pleased with his cast as well, starting with Jonathan Pryce. "Jonathan is brilliant, he's the best I've ever worked with—even more than the Pythons. He's not only extremely funny and inventive, he's a great serious actor as well, and the combination is extraordinary."

Fellow Python Michael Palin appeared in his third film for Gilliam with *Brazil*. "Michael plays Jonathan's best friend. Who would you rather have for your torturer than your best friend? Mike is ambitious, he's the image of success and does everything right."

Working with Robert DeNiro in such a small role was very interesting, according to Gilliam. He says DeNiro originally wanted to play the role of Jack, but it had already been promised to Palin.

"I met Robert DeNiro through our producer [Arnon Milchan]. He said Bobby was interested in the things we were doing and got us together, which eventually led to him doing the movie. It's the first time he has ever done a bit part in a film. In many ways, his character does the same job that Sean Connery's did in *Time Bandits*—he's there for a brief time and then gone, but his character is absolutely crucial. It was a new experience for him to come and do a week-and-a-half's worth of shooting and then leave. Normally, he's in the center of it all from the word 'Go!'

"DeNiro works in a slightly different way than we do. We tend to get things done in one or two takes, where he works in a much more American way, rehearsing on film. But he's very intelligent and intense. Once he gets involved with something, he thinks about it nonstop—he just won't let it go, even if he's only on screen for five minutes. I'm sure he spent as much time thinking about it as he does for a lead role in a film."

Although he had plenty of offers to do a sequel to *Time Bandits*, Gilliam says there was no question about it when he got the chance to make *Brazil*. "Actually, I think *Brazil* is the sequel. It's a strange thing, but I think the character Jonathan Pryce plays in *Brazil* is like the boy in *Time Bandits* fifteen years later. He has the same problems, he still dreams, but he's a bit older and things have changed. If I were making a trilogy, this would be part of it. Actually, I think I'm going to call this the fourth part of my trilogy." He laughs.

"*Brazil* looks quite extraordinary. It doesn't look like other films, that's what's nice about it. Very quickly, one realizes that *Brazil* is part of another world."

The world of *Brazil* unfortunately included the same types of people who tried to interfere with his Monty Python work. "The people are different, but the arguments are the same—they believe it's only a cult film, and the public isn't sophisticated enough to understand it. We've been hearing this for fifteen years now and it gets very tiresome, because the experts are invariably wrong in underestimating the project," Gilliam explained in 1985, when the fate of the film was still unknown.

Twentieth Century–Fox had the rights to *Brazil* everywhere but in the U.S., and released Gilliam's version. But Universal refused to release the director's cut in the States when he turned it in, even though American critics—who had to be flown out of the country to see it—lavishly praised the picture.

There was originally talk of releasing Brazil for Christmas 1984, and an Easter 1985 release was finally agreed upon. The release was then pushed back to fall, and it was only after a massive effort by Gilliam and Milchan, assisted by many of the nation's top critics, that it was released for a week on December 18, 1985, in New York (and a week later in L.A.) to make it eligible for the Oscars. Prior to that, the L.A. Film Critics voted it Best Picture—even though it still hadn't been released!

Brazil's troubles began in January of 1985, when Gilliam turned in his cut to Universal, which insisted it was seventeen minutes longer than they had contractually agreed upon. They compromised, and Gilliam agreed to cut seventeen minutes from the film. He delivered his 131-minute version on time a month later.

"It took me more than a month to recut it," says Gilliam. "Normally, when people reedit a film for the States, they just chop out scenes to save time. To shorten it without actually losing anything, I did cuts within scenes—we redubbed the film, put in some new opticals, and made the ending appear less pessimistic. It makes my viewpoint very clear, but still has the same impact as the original ending, with one more element—it almost becomes religious!

"We turned in the shorter version that didn't change the film's content or shock in any way, and Universal told me 'Oh, yeah, terrific, works a lot better, it's wonderful. We think actually, though, it needs a major rethink.' Universal insisted they wanted to *keep* cutting it—their whole argument was over the length, not the content, but I think they felt the ending was too strong for the American public. The 'up' happy ending that they wanted would be a complete and utter travesty of the film. Everybody agrees that the ending really emblazons *Brazil* into one's brain. Universal wanted to try a happy ending at some preview showings to convince me, but there's no way we could change the ending, it's the one thing that's totally nonnegotiable. It's the essence of the film, as far as I'm concerned. There are no surprises in what I did—it's exactly what was scripted, so if they didn't like the ending, they should have told us and not given us the money."

Gilliam's shocking, downbeat ending of the film upset studio executives and actually caused most of the problems with its release.

"There are several endings to *Brazil*, and the penultimate ending is a happy, fairy-tale ending, and the audience cheers. *Then* comes the *real* ending, and the audience goes out quietly thinking. The studio executives hear the cheering three minutes before the film ends, and would *love* to end the movie that way and have the audience go out dancing in the street. Unfortunately, that's not the ending we set out to have—it has always been very crucial to the whole idea of *Brazil*," says Gilliam.

Frustrated, Gilliam and Milchan began doing interviews of their own, and in October 1985 they placed a full-page ad in *Daily Variety* reading "Dear Sid Sheinberg: When are you going to release my film, *Brazil*? Terry Gilliam." They flew journalists out of the country so that they could legally see the movie.

"We tried to warn Universal that we were very serious," says Gilliam. "*Brazil* is a very special film—it's not infinitely malleable. They just kept plodding on, using the 'scientifically proven' process of previews to determine the best film to release, which really forced our hands."

The movie was shown at the Deauville Film Festival in France, to an enthusiastic response. "It's such an obvious, simple story—struggling artist against huge established filmmaking machinery. Judith Crist, Joel Siegel, and others were raving about *Brazil*, and it isn't often that people get so excited about a film that they're willing to go public and commit themselves," he says.

Universal eventually took his reedited film away from him. "Universal started fiddling with it—I had no involvement. In one cut, I heard they were trying to end it by turning it into a revenge film like *Rambo*! They don't think the American public is ready for an antiauthoritarian film like *Brazil*. Anybody with any intelligence who has seen the movie understands what it's about, and either likes or dislikes it on that basis."

Gilliam likes to use a culinary analogy.

"The difference is between McDonald's hamburgers and Cordon Bleu cooking. McDonald's hamburgers are a safe, neither good nor bad, meal. It's quick, it's easy, it's almost predigested. A Cordon Bleu meal is a spectacular affair, with lots of ideas, changes, and surprises. That's what *Brazil* is about—it's constantly surprising. One minute we're zipping along in a sort of Steven Spielberg truck chase, and the next, there are several disturbing images that make one think `Wait a minute! That wasn't all just fun.' It really jerks the audience around. Sometimes the story is in the background instead of the foreground.

"It switches between very comic things and very tragic things, and people aren't used to that—it's bled out of the cinematic experience. Cinema today can either be fun, frolicky escape, or serious artistic statement—the two are seldom blended together in one film. I hate great successful films like *Gremlins* and *Ghostbusters*, because most of them are only on one level—they're McDonald's hamburgers. I miss the chance to see movies that give you those same sort of spills and thrills, but also let your brain come along for the ride."

Universal, finally forced to relent under the pressure, released *Brazil* nationally in early 1986; not surprisingly, the studio failed to promote it adequately and it proved to be a box-office disappointment. Nominated for Academy Awards for Best Original Screenplay and Best Art Direction, it didn't win any.

And Universal still didn't give up—when *Brazil* was shown on broadcast TV, it was so severely edited (the studio restored the happy ending it so loved) that Gilliam threatened a lawsuit.

Perhaps the greatest irony of *Brazil,* however, was the way Gilliam's battle with the huge corporation was reflected in his movie.

 ## CRITICAL COMMENTS

"Gilliam's jokes are black and gory, but his plot is intricately coiled with spectacular adventures and wild fantasies. It's so astonishing to watch. . . ."

—Philip Strick, *The Times* London, February 22, 1985

"There is not a more daft, more original or haunting vision to be seen on American movie screens this year. . . . A terrific movie has escaped the asylum without a lobotomy. The good guys, the few directors itching to make films away from the assembly line, won one for a change."

—Richard Corliss, *Time,* December 30, 1985

"What Gilliam presents is a vision of the future as the decayed past, and this vision is an organic thing on the screen—which is a considerable accomplishment."

—Pauline Kael, *The New Yorker*, February 10, 1986

"After the promises of *Jabberwocky* and *Time Bandits*, Terry Gilliam delivers with this ferociously creative black comedy, filled with wild tonal contrasts, swarming details, and unfettered visual invention—every shot carries a charge of surprise and delight."

—Dave Kehr, "Critic's Choice," *Chicago Reader,* January 17, 1986

THE BATTLE OF BRAZIL

BY JACK MATHEWS. PUBLISHED BY CROWN BOOKS (1987), ISBN 0-517-56538-2 (HARDBACK).

The story of Terry Gilliam's battle with Sid Sheinberg and Universal Pictures to release his own, original version of Brazil, rather than the severely edited, shorter, more commercial version preferred by the studio. The book includes the annotated screenplay by Gilliam, Stoppard, and McKeown.

LABYRINTH

SCREENPLAY BY TERRY JONES. (1986) 101 MINUTES

Sarah ....Jennifer Connelly
Jareth...David Bowie

Screenplay by Terry Jones (story by Jim Henson and Dennis Lee). Produced by Eric Rattray. Directed by Jim Henson. Released by Tri-Star Pictures, Henson Associates, and Lucasfilm Ltd./Embassy Home Entertainment 7666.

Sarah, a fifteen-year-old-girl, has to baby-sit her little brother Toby when her father and stepmother go out. When she wishes the Goblins would come and take him away, they appear, grab Toby, and run off with him. Jareth, the Goblin King, appears to her, and she tells him she wants her brother back. He tries to tempt her with a magic crystal, but she still wants her brother returned.

Jareth shows her the castle beyond the Goblin City where her brother is being held, but it is beyond the huge Labyrinth; he gives her thirteen hours to solve the Labyrinth before her brother becomes a Goblin forever. She encounters Hoggle,

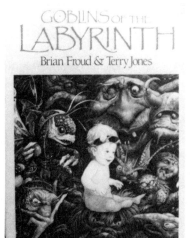

who is spraying fairies, and he shows her the entrance to the Labyrinth. After getting directions from a worm, she discovers the marks she's been making to keep from getting lost have been wiped out.

After going through a door, she falls into the Pit of Hands and is lowered to the floor. She sees Hoggle in with her, and she gives him a plastic bracelet to show her a shortcut out. They pass through a tunnel of false alarms, and when they see Jareth, he sends the Cleaners after them. After they escape, Hoggle leads her outside, and they get directions from an old man with a duck for a hat. Sarah saves a huge, grim-looking creature from some

Goblins, and they encounter a couple of talking door knockers.

Hoggle, who has become separated from her, runs into Jareth, who orders him to give Sarah a magic apple. Meanwhile, Sarah has encountered the wild Fireys, who want to cut her head off Hoggle comes back to save her, but they almost fall into the Bog of Eternal Stench. They try to cross the bridge, which is defended by Sir Didymus, and it crumbles under their feet; Sarah is saved when Ludo calls up the rocks for them to walk on. Jareth again appears to Hoggle, and so

Hoggle offers Sarah the apple. She eats it and dreams she is inside the castle dancing with the Goblin King, and back in her room at home.

Ludo and Didymus rescue her outside the gates of Goblin City, and Hoggle saves them from a giant robotic warrior. They are attacked by Goblins in the city, but Ludo calls on the rocks to save them. Sarah faces Jareth alone and she realizes he has no power over her that she hasn't given him. He is defeated, and Sarah returns home with Toby, where her friends say good-bye.

 ## NOTES

Although Terry Jones isn't sure how much of the completed film is actually his, he did receive credit for writing the screenplay. Having made a name for himself as a children's book author, in addition to his Monty Python work, he seemed a logical choice to pen the Jim Henson movie.

Actually it was his second children's book that led to his collaboration with the Muppet creator, he says. "I had been thinking about turning *Erik the Viking* into a film, and I thought it was something Jim Henson might be interested in," explains Jones. "I rang up his office, and they said `That's funny—he was trying to reach you yesterday.' So, Jim and I met up—he was setting up *Labyrinth* at that stage—and he wanted to know if I would like to write the screenplay.

"Jim's daughter Lisa had just read *Erik the Viking* and suggested that he try me as screenwriter—and that's how it came about. I hadn't really known Jim before our *Labyrinth* meeting. We had bumped into each other when the Pythons were first in the States. We were in the street, getting out of cars, when he called out `Hi, I'm Jim Henson!' That was about 1975, but we hadn't met since then."

Although it was Jones's screenplay, the original idea belonged to Henson. "Jim had the basic story for *Labyrinth*," explains Jones, "but I really agreed to do it in the basis of the characters. I wanted to have a fairly free hand at the episodes. I just started fresh, using the same characters. I'd undertaken the thing in a rather cavalier fashion. I'd read their synopsis, and they'd had a novella of the film-to-be. It was about ninety pages of story,

and I thought it didn't work at all, so originally I said I wasn't really interested. Then after a couple of bottles of wine with Jim, I said `All right, maybe I'll spend three weeks writing and see if something comes up.'

"That's what I did, and it was great. I had all of Brian Froud's drawings in a stack—he does the conceptual designs and drawings on which the models are based," he reveals. "I had this pile of drawings, so I sat there with this basic story outline and had all these characters. When I came to a new scene, I just picked out a character I liked and wrote a scene around it, like the old man with the hat with the duck's head, and the hat talks back—it just seemed obvious. It was there in the drawing.

"In some ways, *Labyrinth* was Brian Froud's project. I think he came up with the idea of doing something about a labyrinth. Whenever I got to a situation where I wanted to invent a character, I would flip through his creations until I came to one that I liked, and give it words—I was collaborating in a funny way with Brian Froud, because I was springing off his drawings."

The film was much like a fairy tale. Because there were only two human stars in *Labyrinth*, played by Jennifer Connelly as Sarah and David Bowie as Jareth, Jones was able to concentrate much of his attention on the creatures.

"I thought the first draft I wrote was pretty good, really. I thought it was fun, and everyone was excited about it. Then it disappeared for a month, and Jim came back and said `We've got some problems.' The main problem was this labyrinth—the original idea was to do this thing about the labyrinth. They wrote this magical character, Jareth, who is all-powerful and does magic. I thought there was no contest. This girl goes into the labyrinth, and you've got this magic character, so she can't win.

"So, in my version, she goes into the labyrinth, and eventually she finds out there is no solution. She keeps thinking she's solved it, and then it keeps cheating on her. The idea in the end is that she finds out there's no solution, you've got to enjoy it. When she gets to the center, she finds out that the character who seemed all-powerful to begin with *isn't* all-powerful. In fact, he's someone who uses the labyrinth—which is basically the world—to keep people from getting to his heart. She gets there and annihilates him in the end. So, it's about the world, and about people who are more interested in manipulating the world than actually baring themselves at all, having any kind of emotional honesty. Jim couldn't understand the story at all.

"The other thing I thought was, you mustn't get to the center of the labyrinth before the girl does, because that's your hook for the audience—what is at the center of the labyrinth? Jim had two problems. One was that Jim wanted Michael Jackson or David Bowie to play Jareth, so he wanted him to appear all the way through, and he wanted him to sing. That was a real shock. Then he also wanted to go to the center of the labyrinth before the girl does. Both were things I felt were wrong.

"But I wrote a second version which had Jareth singing. He went for David Bowie, and it all went away for about a year. When the script came back, I didn't recognize any of it. Jim said `Can you do a bit more to it? David Bowie doesn't want to do it anymore because it isn't funny anymore.'

"It was more or less mine up until the part where Sarah goes down the Pit of Hands, which was mine. It's sort of mine up to the point where she eats this apple, which is something Jim wanted to put in and I didn't like at all—that's when I thought it was no longer mine, it was nothing I had much to do with."

Because of Henson's story and the changes made to his script, Jones says he doesn't feel very close to the movie.

"I didn't really feel that it was very much mine. I always felt it fell between the two stories. Jim wanted it to be about one thing, and I wanted it to be about something else. But Jim was great, really smashing to work with—he was the kind of person one wanted to do things for because he was so nice and so straight—even when we disagreed about things. He was always open to other ideas.

"The things I like most about *Labyrinth* are not necessarily things I contributed," notes Jones. "I had an idea to do this Shaft of Hands—she falls down this dark shaft with these hands sticking out, hands all talking to each other—and it actually works! They realized it much better than I imagined it when I wrote it down as an idea. In a way, my best contribution was just starting off something that the puppet makers have made much better and improved. I just started the ball rolling, but I think it's the sequence that works best."

In addition to *Labyrinth*, Terry Jones also worked on another fantasy film, although his contributions weren't utilized in the final version of *Gremlins II*. "I hadn't meant to get involved with it, but I talked to Steven Spielberg and Joe Dante. I told them I didn't think I was the right person to do it, but I suddenly got an idea. My outline involved many of the same characters [as the first film] and a forgotten rule, but it all took place in America, so I didn't think I was necessarily the best person to actually write it down."

THE GOBLINS OF THE LABYRINTH

BY BRIAN FROUD AND TERRY JONES. PUBLISHED BY PAVILION BOOKS (1986), ISBN 0-85145-058-0 (HARDCOVER).

Terry Jones used Brian Froud's drawings of the characters he created for *Labyrinth* and wrote a variety of funny descriptions and stories about them, much in the same way he developed Froud's character sketches to write scenes for his screenplay.

THE TRANSFORMERS: THE MOVIE

WITH THE VOICE OF ERIC IDLE. (1986) 86 MINUTES. FEATURING THE VOICES OF ORSON WELLES, ROBERT STACK, LEONARD NIMOY, ERIC IDLE, AND JUDD NELSON. PRODUCED BY JOE BACAL AND TOM GRIFFIN. DIRECTED BY NELSON SHIN. RELEASED BY DE LAURENTIIS ENTERTAINMENT GROUP.

This animated feature, based on the Transformer toys and the cartoon series, sees the giant transforming robots battle to save the universe from an evil, living planet (with the voice of Orson Welles). Eric Idle provides the voice for robot Wreck Gar.

 NOTES

"They just called me up and then flew me to New York to record it," explains Idle. "I think it's the only film I was ever in with Orson Welles.

"I am a Transformer. I always forget about that, it's not even on my c.v.! I was a couple of days recording it in New York. Recording animation is like doing radio, and then they put the visual bit on."

He notes that he was usually the only one in the studio when he recorded his character's voice.

"It was mainly my character that was done that day," he reveals. "It's like a twenty-four-track. They have the other characters there and I did my bit, and then they mix them in. We're not talking Shakespeare here.

"This was one of the hardest jobs I did, it was so stupid!" he says with a laugh. "It's hard to put real meaning into such strange lines that are essentially meaningless."

Idle notes that he never saw the final film, but "Ten-year-old kids were quite big on it! Dhani Harrison [George's son] was very big on it at one stage, and was very impressed that I was in the *Transformer* movie."

THE MIKADO

STARRING ERIC IDLE. FIRST ENGLISH NATIONAL OPERA PRODUCTION SEPTEMBER 18, 1986.

The Mikado ....Richard Angas
Nanki-Poo..Bonaventura Bottone
Ko-Ko, Lord High Executioner ....Eric Idle
Pooh-Bah ....Richard Van Allan
Pish-Tush...Mark Richardson
Yum-Yum ....Lesley Garrett
Pitti-Sing ....Jean Rigby
Peep-Bo..Susan Bullock
Katishka ....Felicity Palmer

Written by Gilbert and Sullivan. Produced and directed by Jonathan Miller. The English National Opera production was first staged at the London Coliseum. Additional lyrics to "I've Got a Little List" written by Eric Idle.

Gilbert and Sullivan's classic Japanese opera is here set at a 1920s Grand Hotel, an English seaside resort. Nanki-Poo has come in search of Yum-Yum, his love, who is the ward of Ko-Ko. Now the Lord High Executioner, Ko-Ko will not allow Yum-Yum to marry anyone but himself, and Pooh-Bah advises Nanki-Poo to give up. Yum-Yum and her two sisters can see no way to prevent her wedding to Ko-Ko, but when the Mikado orders an immediate execution, Ko-Ko agrees to allow Nanki-Poo to marry Yum-Yum if he will be his execution victim in one month's time. All is well, until the elderly Katishka arrives. She reveals Nanki-

Poo is the crown prince and her husband-to-be, and is furious.

As Yum-Yum prepares for her wedding the next day, the Mikado arrives. Ko-Ko realizes that since he hasn't yet performed an execution, he will be beheaded himself, and so bribes Pooh-Bah to sign a statement swearing that Nanki-Poo has already been executed. He then has Yum-Yum marry Nanki-Poo to keep him quiet. When the Mikado sees his son's name on the death warrant, Ko-Ko, Pooh-Bah, and Pitti-Sing are all condemned. Ko-Ko then decides to marry Katishka, and so his life is spared.

 NOTES

Jonathan Miller, of *Beyond the Fringe* fame, transferred his acclaimed, highly successful production of *The Mikado* from Japan to 1920s England. After a successful run in the fall, it was revived again the following spring in London, and the production was also presented in Los Angeles (with Dudley Moore and Ko-Ko) and in Houston (with Idle as Ko-Ko again).

Eric Idle says his involvement began when he got a phone call from Miller. "He called me up in France and said `I want you to be in *The Mikado*.' I said `What are you going to do?' and he said `I'm going to get rid of all that Japanese nonsense, for a start.' I said `I've got to see this, I want to be a part of this.'

"I love Jonathan. When I first went to London in 1962, I went to see *Beyond the Fringe*. I rolled around and nearly died. I had never seen anything so funny. Still really haven't laughed as much in the theater. Jonathan Miller, Alan Bennett, Peter Cook, and Dudley Moore—I decided that I wanted to do comedy after that. I bought the record and learned all their routines. They were GREAT," enthuses Idle.

The Mikado was not the first time he had worked with Miller, however.

"I was in Jonathan's *Alice in Wonderland* in 1966—it was like the second gig I did. The first was a Ken Russell film called *Isadora*, where I played the part of Death's chauffeur and drowned the children in the Seine, accidentally. A true story—that was the Ken Russell film. Then I was in *Alice*. Peter Sellers was in it, every theatrical knight in the world was in it, that was the BBC's classic little black-and-white piece. So, I always wanted to

work with Jonathan, I always loved him, and the experience was great. I mean, he's such fun, and he's so interesting and entertaining."

One of Idle's biggest worries was the singing involved with the part. "Jonathan said `Would you mind coming and singing, so you can prove to us you can sing, because we were a little bit nervous offering you a part in this opera . . .' So I flew in and stood on the stage of the Coliseum, which is the largest theater in London, I think a two-thousand seater, and they ran me through a few of the songs. Of course, it was a doddle," he laughs.

"It was really fun, because I clearly wasn't an opera singer. I had to rehearse the whole show with the opera company, but they were very supportive. It was interesting, because I was always a bit scared of singing publicly, or at least apprehensive, but I realized quite early on that they were far more apprehensive about speaking, because they would `Tend To Speak Like This [loud, overenunciated], If You're Not Careful, Singers!' So, when I realized that, it was fun. Then it just got more and more fun, and progressively sillier, and it was a terrific production. It looked great."

Before getting involved with the production, Idle says he was "sort of" a Gilbert and Sullivan fan, and had even tried to film his own Gilbert and Sullivan operetta in the early 1980s. "I like a lot of what they do. I like a lot of Gilbert's writing, he's very clever, and I love Sullivan's tunes, like everybody else. I tried to do a film of *The Pirates of Penzance*. I did a screenplay at one stage, after *The Rutles*, and I wanted to do it very much live action. I went down to Penzance—there's a beautiful castle there that he'd obviously written it for, and I wanted to make a sort of Victorian film of it. I tried to get that going and nobody wanted to do that.

"Of course, suddenly there was the Joe Papp production [on Broadway], suddenly I had the screen-play. [Producer] Ed Pressman bought it. He loved it and wanted to make it, and then he decided he wanted Papp. He was in a terrible, silly bind because he couldn't shoot anything on location, because I'd gotten all the locations. He shot the stage version on a sound stage, which is the worst of all possible worlds. He made a big mistake, it was a big error.

"He should have done my screenplay and their cast, because I loved Kevin Kline playing the Pirate King, he's terrific—I'd wanted Albert Finney or Michael Caine to play this part; in my version, Bette Midler was to be the Pirate Queen. I went to the very Victorian, because Victorian paintings are Cinemascope—they take that shape, all big and wide, and I wanted to do that, like it was done by the pre-Raphaelites and various Victorian painters, and the beginnings of photography. So, I'd gone into it quite in depth, and I think Pressman made a mistake—he admitted to me afterward that he did, anyway. It was very nice of him to say. Well, you never know—mine might have been a flop, too."

 ## CRITICAL COMMENTS

"The famous list was one of Idle's own devise and included a money-grubbing Ronald Reagan among those to be punished. In addition to Idle's wit and the marvelously comic performances by the rest of the cast, what made this *Mikado* memorable was the lovely Edwardian English country house setting, the turn-of-the-century English costumes and the nimble choreography. . . . The Gilbert and Sullivan original is still witty but a trifle dated. The HGO transformation is comical, topical, and endearing."

—Michael Killian, *Chicago Tribune*, November 16, 1989
(on the Houston Grand Opera's British Opera Festival)

THE MIKADO

STARRING ERIC IDLE.

PRODUCED FOR THAMES TV AND FIRST AIRED DECEMBER 30, 1987. PRESENTED ON AMERICAN TV AS PART OF THE PBS GREAT PERFORMANCES SERIES OCTOBER 28, 1988. TELEVISION DIRECTION BY JOHN MICHAEL PHILLIPS.

The 1986 English National Opera production, featuring Eric Idle as Ko-Ko.

THE MIKADO

STARRING ERIC IDLE. SOUNDTRACK RELEASED BY MCA RECORDS MCAD-6215.

The soundtrack of the production, recorded at Abbey Road Studios, London on October 11 and 12, 1986; featuring Eric Idle as Ko-Ko.

CLOCKWISE

STARRING JOHN CLEESE. (1986) 96 MINUTES

Brian Stimpson...John Cleese
Pat ....Penelope Wilton
Gwenda Stimpson ....Alison Steadman
Mr. Jolly ....Stephen Moore
Laura ....Sharon Maiden

Screenplay by Michael Frayn. Produced by Michael Codron. Directed by Christopher Morahan. Released by Universal Pictures/Cannon—Thorn EMI Screen Entertainment TVA 9962.

Brian Stimpson, a headmaster at a middle school, is obsessed with time and efficiency, so when he is named chairman of the Headmasters Conference, he practices his speech in his office, calling out to reprimand students with a loudspeaker from his vantage point. He announces to the student body that he is going to Norwich for the honor, and as they prepare to sing the hymn, the piano player, Mr. Jolly, is late.

Later Stimpson reprimands Jolly, saying he used to be late himself but has reformed. His wife is less than pleased to drive Stimpson to the train station, and he gets on the wrong train while he practices his speech. He gets off the train in time but leaves his speech on the train to Plymouth. Stimpson takes a taxi home so that his wife can drive him to Norwich, but she and the car are missing. While trying to catch another taxi, he runs into Laura, a student driving during a free period, and has her drive him to where his wife works, so he can find his wife.

His wife has just left with some patients, so he asks Laura to drive him to Norwich. She agrees. As he pumps gasoline for her, his wife spots him with the young lady, and Stimpson forgetfully drives off without paying. As they drive, Laura says she didn't call her mother but rather her boyfriend, to tell him she's going to Norwich with another man.

Meanwhile, Mrs. Stimpson tells Laura's mother that her daughter has run off with her husband, and determines to drive to Norwich. Laura's mother and father head for Norwich on their motorcycle as well.

Stimpson insists on driving because Laura doesn't have her license, but before he can pull back on the road, he hits a police car. Not only is the car damaged, the police ask him about driving away from the gas station. He decides to call the conference to let them know he'll be late, but none of the pay phones work. One of the locals reports him for vandalizing the phone; she turns out to be Pat, an old girlfriend. He asks her to drive them to the conference, and Pat's mother thinks her daughter is being kidnapped. Stimpson gives Pat the wrong directions, and they end up in a field filled with cows, driving through grass.

Time is running out for headmaster Brian Stimpson (John Cleese) in Clockwise.(Universal-Cannon-Thorn-EMI Screen Entertainment Photo from the Collection of John Cleese)

The car becomes mired deep in mud, and Stimpson is splattered as he tries to push them out. He kicks the car in frustration and falls in the mud. A farmer pulls them out with his tractor, while Stimpson has gone off on his own to find a tractor. He ends up in a monastery and has a bath, when Laura and Pat show up with their car. An irate Pat drives away, while Laura and Stimpson, in a monk's robe, chase her.

Later, the police have recovered Pat and the car, and they drive off just as Stimpson and Laura approach. The pair sit dejected by the side of the road, while at the conference, Laura's parents ask the headmasters where Stimpson has taken Laura. Mrs. Stimpson and Mr. Jolly have both arrived, and the headmasters have them all wait upstairs. The police also show up, looking for Stimpson.

In the country, Laura thumbs them a ride, and a middle-age man picks them up. Laura insists they all stop for a walk in the woods, and she gets the man to take his clothes off so that Stimpson can make off with his suit, but the sleeve is torn in the struggle. Laura and Stimpson leave in the man's car and arrive exactly on time for his speech, though he wears a very ill-fitting suit.

Stimpson starts to struggle through the speech when Laura's mother bursts in and sees her, along with her father, and they point out Stimpson to the police. His wife enters, and Stimpson continues to go mad; when he asks them to sing the hymn, he walks out into the arms of the police.

 ## NOTES

In the autumn of 1984, John Cleese was enthusiastic about making *Clockwise*, calling it "The only really funny script I've ever received through my letterbox—it was written by Michael Frayn of *Noises Off* fame. He's a top-class playwright who's written two or three of the best plays that I've seen in the past ten years; he's written a wonderfully funny script about a headmaster, so I'm going to do that next summer."

He emphasized that he hadn't planned to do any film at that time until he read the *Clockwise* screenplay.

"If Michael Frayn's screenplay had not been so funny, I wouldn't be running around looking for a movie next year," he explained. "It's just that when you see something that's just so joyfully funny that it actually causes your wife to shout in and say `Are you all right?' because you're emitting these strange, whimpering animal noises, because you've gotten past the point where you can laugh loudly at a thing. When you see a script like that, you just always want to do it. It simply gets the adrenaline going because it's so wonderful."

Originally titled *Man of the Moment*, *Clockwise* did very well in the U.K. and very poorly in the U.S. Although part of the reason was the lack of promotion, Cleese maintains that it failed to make concessions to an American audience. Some jokes, such as the lack of a working pay phone,

were very familiar to British audiences, but Americans didn't have the same sort of experiences and so the scene wouldn't get the laughs of recognition in the U.S.

Despite its drawbacks and lukewarm reviews in America, *Clockwise* has many wonderful moments and plenty to entertain Cleese fans; it marked his last major film role prior to *A Fish Called Wanda*. In fact, Cleese says much of the success of *Wanda* is the result of the failure of *Clockwise*.

"*Clockwise* was a huge learning experience," reflects Cleese. "I look back to it in amazement at the thought that I really believed at the time that *Clockwise* might be successful in America.

"I just wish that other British filmmakers could see how completely unrealistic their illusions are about their films working in the States. The fact that *Clockwise* never even opened in Chicago is still something that astounds me, but I think I needed to be thrown in the deep end, to be shocked by the coldness of the water, to snap me out of the vague, wildly overoptimistic feeling that certain films made in England might work in America. You've got me right up against the reality of it, as a result of which I was able to make *Wanda*.

"*Wanda* wouldn't have worked anything like it did if I hadn't failed with *Clockwise*."

CRITICAL COMMENTS

"A delightfully jaunty farce. . . . With Cleese in top form,
Clockwise is 96 minutes and four seconds of fun."

—Ira Hellman, *People Weekly*, November 10, 1986

"Top farce, high comedy and Cleese make this movie not only
witty and wise but also touching and very, very funny."

—Judith Crist, *TV Guide*, October 10–16, 1987

EAST OF IPSWICH

*WRITTEN BY MICHAEL PALIN. FIRST BROADCAST ON BBC-2 ON FEBRUARY 1, 1987.
70 MINUTES. FEATURING EDWARD RAWLE-HICKS, JOHN NETTLETON,
PAT HEYWOOD, DONA KIRSCH, PIPPA HINCHLEY, JOAN SANDERSON.
SCREENPLAY BY MICHAEL PALIN. PRODUCED BY INNES LLOYD. DIRECTED BY
TRISTRAM POWELL. PRESENTED IN AMERICA ON THE ARTS AND ENTERTAINMENT
CHANNEL/LIONHEART TELEVISION.*

On a family vacation to Suffolk in 1957, Richard Burrill complains to his parents because they aren't going to Torquay again this year.

Arriving at the resort, the woman who runs the resort, Miss Wilbraham, lays down the rules, and their meal is less than enjoyable. Afterward, another guest discusses his intestinal surgery, and Richard decides to go upstairs and unpack.

The next day the family goes to the beach, and while Richard walks with his father to the toilet, he spots a couple of girls. Another boy, Edwin, invites him along to meet the girls, and as they start talking, they learn the girls' father runs the local Bible Club.

Later Richard goes for a walk and starts talking to Julia, who lends him money for ice cream. His mother and father insist on taking him for a day trip the next day to see churches, though he would rather stay and see Julia. When the family returns, Richard stops by Julia's cottage to return the money, but her father deflects him. Edwin drags him out to a coffeeshop and introduces him to Julia and Anna. Edwin leaves with Julia and sticks

Richard with Anna, an exchange student from Holland. He excuses himself and his parents lecture him when he returns to the hotel.

The next day Edwin reports that Anna and Julia are going home on Saturday because Anna ran off the previous night, and the girls aren't allowed to go out any more. When Richard and Edwin help out after the Bible Club meeting, the vicar takes them out to the coffee bar with twin girls. He leaves them, and the girls take Richard and Edwin into the alley for twenty minutes of kissing. After talking with Edwin, Richard steals a condom from his father's wallet.

Richard sees his parents talking with Julia's parents, and they agree to let Julia and Anna go with him and Edwin to the Bible Club's Sausage Sizzle that night. The four of them decide to go to a jazz club first. Anna leaves with some motorcycle types, and Richard goes with her. When they fall off the motorcycles, he pulls out his handkerchief. The condom falls out, and Anna suggests they use it. Their parents are shocked to find Richard and Anna in the field, and the Burrills leave the next day.

 ## NOTES

East of Ipswich came about when Michael Palin got the opportunity to write a TV movie.

"I've really got David Puttnam to thank for that," he explains. "David was putting together a series called *First Love*, which was going to be stories about first experiences with love, first love affairs, and with different writers and a different cast each time, shot on film. It was sold to television in this country, but with a theatrical option elsewhere. A very good idea, just what everyone was thinking was a good idea at the time—unfortunately, the theatrical option never really worked-out. You make something for telly, it ends up on telly, and that's that. So, it never really got theatrical airing. By the time it came to my chance to do one, they'd given up on theater, it was just being made for television. But that's what it was."

Palin decided to write a fictionalized version of his first meeting with his wife.

"He said `Do you have an idea?' and I said `Yes, I have got one,' and roughly based it on how I met Helen. In fact, it was shot at exactly the same seaside resort where we met in 1959. If you like, it was a precursor of *American Friends*, in that it was sort of a family biography or family memoir, as it were."

CHEERS
"SIMON SAYS"

GUEST-STARRING JOHN CLEESE. FIRST BROADCAST MARCH 5, 1987, ON NBC-TV. FEATURING TED DANSON, SHELLEY LONG, RHEA PERLMAN, JOHN RATZENBERGER, WOODY HARRELSON, KELSEY GRAMMER, GEORGE WENDT, AND GUEST-STARRING JOHN CLEESE AS DR. SIMON FINCH-ROYCE. WRITTEN BY PETER CASEY AND DAVID LEE. PRODUCED BY DAVID ANGELL. DIRECTED BY JAMES BURROWS.

Frasier announces he's meeting an old school friend, Dr. Simon Finch-Royce, for a drink. Diane is excited, as Simon is a noted marriage counselor. After singing a song from their old school musical with Frasier, Simon says he is over to accept an honorary degree, and Diane asks him to have a session with her and Sam before they marry. Sam objects, but Simon says he'll be delighted. Frasier insists on paying for the session as his wedding gift.

Sam, Diane, and Simon go into Sam's office for their session. Diane's story of her life nearly puts them all to sleep, and Sam interests Simon with his stories of womanizing. After asking them hypothetical questions, Simon decides the two of them shouldn't marry, and should never even see each other again.

Diane is furious, then decides Simon was only testing them, and takes Sam back to the hotel where Simon is staying. Simon tells them that it wasn't a test, and Diane fails to convince him that she and Sam are a perfect couple, and they leave. Back at Cheers, they admit they lied in their answers to Simon, and Diane insists they go back to his hotel. Simon is sitting down to dinner as Sam and Diane return, but she can't change his mind, and they leave. A few minutes later Sam and Diane get Simon out of the shower, but he insists they aren't compatible, and kicks them out. They finally get him out of bed later, and he goes wild, claiming they are perfect for each other, shouting it from his window, and promising to kill himself if they aren't. Diane is finally satisfied.

 NOTES

John Cleese's first experience on an American sitcom is a winner all the way. In fact, he even won an Emmy Award for his guest appearance on *Cheers* as noted marriage counselor Simon Finch-Royce. Cleese had long been a fan of the show, and was more than happy to appear when he was invited. He still looks back on his experiences with the executives and cast members with pleasure.

"That was an absolutely delightful experience. I'm very fond of the Charles brothers, and Jimmy Burrows is probably the best director of that kind I've ever worked with. He's phenomenal, and he has a memory that is breathtaking. He knows everything that is happening, even the lines that have just been changed at that morning's readout. He's just got it all in his mind. And he's a great director anyway. A particularly nice bunch of people to work with," Cleese enthuses. "They're all absolutely lovely—in particular, I like Ratzenberger and Wendt and Rhea Perlman—these people made me feel *so* welcome in those five days. Of course, I was terrified, because the first thing that I had to do when I came on was sing, and this has always been my Achilles' heel. Apart from that, it was a lovely experience."

According to series regular George Wendt, everyone at *Cheers* was as delighted as Cleese during that week.

"It was great fun to be working with such a legend. I can't think of anything to say about him that isn't stupid or cliché, but we were all thrilled to be working with him. Please don't print anything I've said because it sounds like stupid fawning bullshit," Wendt says, laughing. "But that's basically the way it was. We were thrilled."

Wendt, who plays lovable barfly Norm Peterson, says that everyone who works on *Cheers* is a huge fan. "Everybody in the world is a fan of Python and all their subsequent work," he declares.

For Wendt, the happiest moment of the week occurred off-camera, when he witnessed one of Cleese's rare real-life silly walks.

"The best part was walking to lunch with him through the parking lot. He was telling some anecdote, and there was this hedge, and a little pathway through the hedge in the parking lot. I walked through the pathway, and John, all six foot five of him, stepped right over the hedge in a very silly walk, and never missed a beat in the story!" he smiles.

Cleese was supposed to do a second appearance on the show on April 13, 1989, reprising his role of Simon Finch-Royce, in which he would return to collect the money due him from Frasier, but scheduling conflicts could not be worked out.

Still, there is a rather cyclical aspect to his appearance on *Cheers* in the first place—Cleese says his own *Fawlty Towers* had an influence on the creation of the American show.

"Jimmy Burrows told me that *Fawlty Towers* was in the front of their minds when they created *Cheers*," notes Cleese. "But instead of confining the action to a hotel, they decided to focus the show down even further, to the equivalent of a hotel's bar!"

STILL CRAZY LIKE A FOX

GUEST-STARRING GRAHAM CHAPMAN.
FIRST BROADCAST APRIL 5, 1987, ON CBS-TV. 93 MINUTES

Harry Fox	Jack Warden
Harrison Fox	John Rubinstein
Cindy Fox	Penny Peyser
Josh	Robby Kiger
Detective Inspector Palmer	Graham Chapman
Nancy	Catherine Oxenberg
Elinor Trundle	Rosemary Leach

Written by George Schenck and Frank Cardea. Produced by William Hill. Directed by Paul Krasny. A Schenck Cardea Production in association with Columbia Pictures Television.

Lawyer Harrison Fox takes his family to London, including his father, Harry, who is a detective. Harry discovers and chases a man ransacking his room, but when he tackles him, the police arrest Harry. When he is taken to Scotland Yard, Detective Inspector Palmer tells him he attacked the Duke of Trent. The duke drops the charges, so Palmer lets him off with a warning.

The duke arrives home, greeting his wife Nancy, and calls his contact, explaining he broke into the room to find out the man's name. Harry finds out about Mr. Hanratty, the man who had the room before him, and the Fox family decides to go sightseeing in Bath, where there is a ceremony honoring the Duke of Trent. Harry tells the duke he's going to find out why he was in his room.

Nancy tells Harry she believes him and thinks her husband is involved in some kind of trouble; he promises to tell her if he finds out anything. Back in his room, a man disguised as a bellboy delivers Mr. Hanratty's suit to Harry. While Harrison and his family go out for a business dinner with his associates, Harry looks around the duke's boat. When he finds the duke stabbed in the back, the police rush in, and Harry is charged with his murder.

Palmer interrogates Harry, and he is denied bail, with the trial to come in six or seven months. Handcuffed to some flimsy scaffolding, he makes his escape disguised in judge's wig and robe. Harry phones Nancy, who agrees to help him. Harry calls

his son, who meets him at a train station; they duck in a train to talk, and the train pulls out. After arriving in the country later, Harrison calls his wife. Palmer, in the room questioning her, overhears the conversation. Nancy meets up with father and son in a country chapel and gives them some clues.

The next morning Harry takes Harrison along to find a witness, and an old man captures Harry, the murder suspect, for the reward. To make sure they don't get away, he has them take off their clothes; they escape and steal the clothes and car from some American tourists. They talk to a friend of the duke's at Beachy Head, and find that the duke was murdered by Soviet agents to conceal the fact that the minister of foreign affairs is a spy. They discover Palmer, who holds a gun on them, and reveals a surprising new development; there is a chase, and Harry is exonerated.

 NOTES

In this made-for-TV movie that attempted to revive the CBS series, Graham Chapman is very effective in a semiserious role as a British detective with a surprising secret.

PERSONAL SERVICES

DIRECTED BY TERRY JONES. (1987) 103 MINUTES

Christine Painter	Julie Walters
Wing Commander Morten	Alec McCowen
Shirley	Shirley Stelfox
Dolly	Danny Schiller
Rose	Victoria Hardcastle
Timms	Tim Woodward

Written by David Leland. Produced by Tim Bevan. Directed by Terry Jones. Released by Vestron Pictures—Zenith Productions/Vestron Video #5221.

Christine is a café waitress who is having trouble paying her rent; when her landlord indicates he would accept sex in lieu of money, she agrees. In the café she talks with her friends and fellow tenants, Shirley and Dolly, who work as hookers. When Shirley leaves for the weekend, Christine quits her job at the café and answers phones and arranges appointments for the hookers. She turns down a marriage proposal from Sydney, her rich,

middle-age boyfriend, and when one girl quits, she decides to go into business for herself.

When Shirley returns, Christine tells her about her new occupation, and they both service ex–Wing Commander Morten, who claims to have flown 207 missions over occupied territory in bra and panties. Two customers, Timms and Bevan, interrupt them, revealing themselves to be police, and arrest them. Christine gets off in court, and

Christine, Shirley, and Dolly decide to go into business for themselves, specializing in kinky older men, usually retired military or government officials. They all attend the wedding of Christine's sister Elizabeth, who is marrying a policeman. In the bathroom, Christine accidentally discovers that Dolly is a man, then has a huge fight with her father, who refuses to accept her illegitimate son David.

Their business continues successfully, and when Christine has tax problems, one of her clients who works for the Inland Revenue helps her out. They decide to buy a house with WC Morten, and use "slaves" to help them clean it up. Christine throws a sex party; afterward, at David's sixteenth birthday party, she offers him one of her girls. Her father shows up later to apologize; he wants a girl as well.

Christine throws an elaborate Christmas party, but the police raid it and arrest as many people as they can (except for those with diplomatic immunity). Morten gives reporters a complete tour of the house. As her trial begins, Christine sees the familiar face of one of her clients, who is serving as the judge.

 NOTES

Personal Services is the thinly disguised real-life story of English madam Cynthia Payne (here called Christine Painter), who ran the best little whorehouse in London, which catered to the rather kinky tastes of older government officials and military men. Jones says many aspects of the story appealed to him.

"I read the script and thought it was really good. It was just so honest, so raw, and I thought it was very funny and touching as well. One of the things that appealed to me most was the character of the major, who was somebody who was anarchic. He was seventy-four years old, and he felt 'I'm going to die in a few years, and so I don't give a shit what I do—I'm going to do what I like. If I sound like a silly old fart, I don't care,'" Jones says with a laugh.

"There's a deep anarchy in old age which I thought was really interesting, so that was one reason I wanted to do it. Also, it was the only script I've ever picked up and thought 'I wouldn't change a word'—it's all there."

Although the film received good reviews, it wasn't promoted or distributed well enough in America for it to succeed.

"It's a film that I'm sure will be rediscovered in the States. It never had any life in the States. It was Vestron, and their entire personnel changed after they bought it, and the new lot didn't like it, and had a vested interest in it not working. I remember David [Leland] was over there, and he said 'What's happened to it? There's not a single advert for it,'" he recalls.

Still, Jones feels the film was worth the struggle; he notes that the main reason he decided to direct *Personal Services* was because of the screenplay written by Leland, an old friend.

"It was a terrific script. David and I co-directed it, really. David worked all the time with Julie, and we kind of did it together. I would hope it's as near to what David wrote as he wanted."

 CRITICAL COMMENTS

"*Personal Services* is not a sensational movie, nor does it want to be. It is a study of banality, with flashes of genuine comedy. . . . * * * 1/2"

—Roger Ebert, *Chicago Sun-Times*, May 29, 1987

"Julie Walters offers a fascinating performance as Christine, a woman who is tough, flamboyant and practical one moment and naive, uncertain and romantic the next. . . . Director Terry Jones wrings more from this tale than most filmmakers get out of three times as much footage. Blessed with a finely constructed script that captures the spirited vulgarity and the underlying seriousness of the business at hand, Jones is ever on the lookout for opportunities to barb the hypocrisy surrounding prostitution. . . ."

—Johanna Steinmetz, *Chicago Tribune*, May 29, 1987

PERSONAL SERVICES

BY DAVID LELAND. PUBLISHED BY PAVILION BOOKS (1987), ISBN 1-85145-146-3.

The screenplay of the film directed by Terry Jones, illustrated profusely with photos, and including an introduction by Terry Jones.

THE GRAND KNOCKOUT TOURNAMENT

WITH JOHN CLEESE AND MICHAEL PALIN.

BENEFIT EVENT FILMED JUNE 1987. FIRST U.K. BROADCAST JUNE 19, 1987 (BBC). FIRST U.S. BROADCAST AUGUST 12, 1987 (USA CABLE NETWORK). PRODUCED BY ALAN WALSH. DIRECTED BY GEOFFREY CD WILSON AND MARTIN HUGHES. A BBC PRODUCTION IN ASSOCIATION WITH KNOCKOUT LTD.

A series of silly games for charity, involving four teams led by members of the royal family.

"Call Out the Guard" sees each team trying to pull its cannon to safety by pulling a large capstan while in complicated costumes (won by the Red Team).

"The ASDA Marathon" involves using a slippery pole to cross a pool, while members of another team throw food at the contestants in an attempt to knock them into the water. Cleese throws food in this game, while Palin tries unsuccessfully to cross.

"The Joust" sees the knights on "horseback" knocking down targets as they are pulled by their teammates.

In addition, Hal Linden interviews Cleese and Palin between events.

 NOTES

This charity event, organized by Prince Edward and held at Alton Towers, an amusement park in North Staffordshire, England, is based on the popular British television show *It's a Knockout*. This mock-feudal sports event involved four dozen celebrities, playing on four teams led by Prince Edward, Princess Anne, and the Duke and Duchess of York.

The U.S. broadcast was hosted by Hal Linden, Jennifer O'Neill, and Helen Shaver. Featured on Prince Andrew's Green Team were Margot Kidder, John Travolta, and Michael Palin; the Blue

Team of the Duchess of York (Fergie, to most Americans) included Meat Loaf and Jane Seymour; Prince Edward's Yellow Team included Christopher Reeve and John Cleese; while Princess Anne's Red Team was led by Walter Payton, Kevin Kline, Tom Jones, Sheena Easton, and Jackie Stewart. Rowan Atkinson moderates the games as Lord Knock.

At the time, Cleese, Kline, and Palin were getting ready to shoot *A Fish Called Wanda*, and though Cleese says he was happy to participate, he was a little leery about his cast and himself.

"I was delighted to do it, but I was extremely nervous at that time that I might do something that would give me an injury that I'd have to carry throughout *Wanda*," he recalls, laughing.

"So, I said to them, `Look, I'm very chicken, I don't want to pull some muscle or dress up as a carrot and fall over and rip my back, and not be able to act properly. So, Kevin [Kline] and I didn't do much—we hung around and smiled and tried to be friendly. I was on Prince Edward's team, and he was extremely nice, and wrote me an extremely nice and funny little thank-you note later."

On the air, John Cleese joked with Hal Linden that it was started as part of the Magna Carta, "the second paragraph, that the British were allowed to enjoy themselves once a year. As you know, they don't find that particularly easy, but on a Sunday in early June, they are allowed to do this and have a good time, and then they go back to their depressed and rather disorganized way of life the rest of the year. It's rather sad, really."

THE DANGEROUS FILM CLUB

HOSTED BY GRAHAM CHAPMAN.

FIRST OF FIVE MONTHLY SHOWS BROADCAST AUGUST 1987 ON CINEMAX. PRODUCED BY MARY FRANCIS SHEA AND ANDREA CVIRKO. DIRECTED BY PAUL FUENTES.

Show 1: (August 1987) Highlights include part one of "A Trip Through the Brooks Home," "Service," "The Trouble with Fred," "Dog Baseball," "Jean-Jean and the Evil Cat," and "School Safety Patrol."

Show 2: (September 1987) Includes "Snack of the Dead" and "Hold the Mayo."

Show 3: (October 1987) Includes "Spontaneous Combustion" and "Doggie Doo Check."

Show 4: (November 1987) Includes "Brides" and "Croutons and You."

Show 5: (December 1987) Includes Julie Brown's "The Homecoming Queen's Got a Gun" and "Pervasive Percussion."

The first show begins with Graham slipping surreptitiously past police lines, to find a movie projector.

First is a segment on how to recognize dangerous film, followed by a mattress-walker and part one of "A Trip Through the Brooks Home." Graham then portrays Police Sergeant Willie Dawkins (ret.), who presents the abridged version of *That's Not How It Seems,* showing two minutes of the original thirteen-hour epic, with several interruptions by Dawkins. Following "Service" is an introduction by Graham and Dangerous Career Advisory. Graham then interacts with a teenager from a 1950s film (*Leisure Time*) and his father, who is selling aircraft secrets. "The Trouble with Fred" follows, and Graham, in a pith helmet, then introduces "Dog Baseball" and the animated "Jean-Jean and the Evil Cat." Graham winds up the show as a French painter, in bed with curlers, behind a desk, and in other situations as he encourages viewers to send in their own films; the credits roll over a "School Safety Patrol" film.

 NOTES

The title inspired by Graham Chapman's increasing involvement with the Dangerous Sports Club, *The*

Dangerous Film Club featured Graham presenting a variety of home movies, videos, animation, and other strange films. The opening sequence shows Graham slipping past police lines into a building, to find a movie projector and film. His linking sequences were shot in a variety of locations and costumes; in the first show alone, he portrayed Police Sergeant Willie Dawkins, a French painter, a hard-hitting announcer (in a black-and-white segment), a man in a pith helmet, a spokesman for "Dangerous Careers Advisory," and as himself in hair curlers.

THE SCREWTAPE LETTERS

BY C. S. LEWIS
READ FOR AUDIOTAPE BY JOHN CLEESE. (1988) 3 HOURS. RELEASED BY AUDIO LITERATURE, INC. (ISBN 0-944993-15-X) ON TWO CASSETTES.

John Cleese reads from the 1941 book, which is made up of letters from Screwtape, the devil, to Wormwood, a lesser demon; Uncle Screwtape gives advice on the best ways for Wormwood to tempt his human patient and win his soul in this classic of Christian literature.

"*The Screwtape Letters* was the suggestion of a friend of mine in San Francisco, a professor of philosophy at San Francisco State. He knows that I have a trivial and superficial interest in certain religious matters. He asked me to read the book, and I was very impressed. During the *Wanda* publicity tour, I took the weekend off and spent about six or seven hours those days in a recording studio in San Francisco," explains Cleese.

"Some of it I thought was pretty good. The book has a weakness. It tends to peak about 40 percent of the way through and then become slightly repetitive. But the first two-fifths of it were really rather good. I enjoyed doing it.

"The religious ideas behind it are very good and very interesting. I did it not just because I liked the book, but also because I wanted to help his company, which records books of this kind with people like Peter Coyote and Alan Arkin."

CONSUMING PASSIONS

BASED ON THE PLAY SECRETS BY MICHAEL PALIN AND TERRY JONES. (1988) 98 MINUTES

Mr. Farris	Jonathan Pryce
Mrs. Garza	Vanessa Redgrave
Ian Littleton	Tyler Butterworth
Graham Chumley	Freddie Jones
Felicity	Sammi Davis
Ethel	Prunella Scales
Mrs. Gordon	Thora Hird
Jason	Andrew Sachs
Dr. Forrester	John Wells
Dr. Rees	Timothy West

Screenplay by Paul D. Zimmerman and Andrew Davies. Produced by William P. Cartlidge. Directed by Giles Foster. Produced by the Samuel Goldwyn Company. Videocassette release by Virgin Vision (70070).

Old Graham Chumley is seen in a commercial for Chumley's Chocolate Factory, while employee Ian Littleton gets ready for work by listening to motivational tapes.

Mr. Farris arrives at work, where Felicity in Research and Quality Control informs him that their newest chocolate contains no nutritional value at all, but he doesn't seem to mind. Chumley doesn't care for the new continental chocolate commercials, but his old-fashioned company has been taken over by Farris's conglomerate, so he doesn't have any authority.

When Littleton, a junior management trainee, arrives at the factory, he inadvertently causes three workers to fall into a vat of chocolate. By the time he gets Farris, Chumley, and their secretary Ethel to help, the men are part of the new batch of chocolates and have been shipped out. Chumley and Littleton travel to Pottersea to try to intercept the "Passionelles" but are unsuccessful. "You have turned the population of Pottersea into cannibals," Chumley tells him. After returning to the factory, Littleton meets Felicity, and he asks her out.

Littleton is fired, but Farris insists he be rehired because he knows too much. Littleton is made head of special projects ("Three men dead, and I just promoted the man who killed them," says Chumley). His first job is to make sure the families of the victims won't be filing claims against the chocolate company. In the course of his duties, he is seduced by Mrs. Garza; the chocolate widow says she won't file any complaints as long as Mr. Littleton "looks after her." She insists he use his company

credit card to buy her furniture and a new bed.

The company's research shows that the only chocolates the customers like were the batch shipped to Pottersea. Farris says they need to find a regular supply of the "secret ingredient." Littleton is recruited to obtain corpses from a medical school, and Farris strikes a deal with Dr. Forrester after haggling over the price; Littleton is assigned to add the bodies to the vats. Littleton is interrupting dates with Felicity to service Mrs. Garza. He tries to resign, but he is blackmailed into staying and becoming executive director of requisitions. He begins making his midnight pickups, and the Passionelles become a national sensation.

The supply of secret ingredients begins to run low, and after a "corpse" rises and steps into the vat, Felicity discovers human tissue in the special chocolate. Littleton has a breakdown in the executive offices and has to rush off to see Mrs. Garza. Felicity discovers him at Mrs. Garza's, but the widow squares things with Felicity. As Littleton and Felicity drive away, he confesses to her about the chocolate, but she isn't too upset; Farris takes Littleton's place in Mrs. Garza's affections.

Littleton is to receive the "Chocolate Man of the Year" award at the company banquet, where Farris escorts Mrs. Garza. During the party, Littleton confronts Farris in the factory and finally receives the award.

☞ **NOTES**

The TV play *Secrets*, written by Michael Palin and Terry Jones and broadcast in 1973, had been floating around for many years, with sporadic interest being shown in the concept from several quarters.

"It was rewritten by various people," Palin recalls. "We did, for a while, work on a screenplay treatment for Sam Goldwyn, Jr. We got up to a certain point where he and ourselves could not

agree on the way it develops, so we said someone else should do it. We suggested Paul Zimmerman, who had written *King of Comedy* and was a friend of ours.

"Paul came in and made his changes, which made it a different sort of thing again. By this time, we were all thoroughly confused, and Sam Goldwyn brought in yet another writer or two! So, what was eventually *Consuming Passions* was a really strange mishmash of different sources, and was not particularly what we wanted in the end."

The final version had changed a great deal from their *Secrets* script, says Palin.

"It was quite a long way different from our original," he reveals. "The idea was there, but some new characters had been brought in, and a lot of the dialogue had been changed. We always felt it was difficult to resolve the end without it becoming absurd. We wanted it to have some sort of satirical significance; we were never able to do it, and certainly no one else who did it after us was. It was just a mess at the end, I'm afraid."

 ## CRITICAL COMMENTS

"Deliciously dizzy, [from] Michael Palin and Terry Jones, those wild and crazy guys from Monty Python."

—Kathleen Carroll, *New York Daily News*

"Hilarious. * * * 1/2 *"

—Jack Garner, *Gannett News Service*

JAKE'S JOURNEY

WRITTEN BY AND FEATURING GRAHAM CHAPMAN.
UNAIRED PILOT FILMED FOR CBS-TV 1988. WRITTEN BY GRAHAM CHAPMAN AND DAVID SHERLOCK. PRODUCED BY MARC MERSON AND ALLEN MCKEOWN. DIRECTED BY HAL ASHBY.

Jake is a young teenager who reluctantly moves to England with his parents; he discovers a bizarre parallel land beyond time, where he encounters an ancient, mystical, cantankerous old knight called Sir George.

 ## NOTES

Jake's Journey was to be the first TV series created by any of the Pythons for American television. CBS-TV was initially interested in the time-traveling comedy, and the pilot was written, shot, and filmed. Due to the vagaries of television networks, however, CBS changed its mind several times, and the pilot remains the only completed episode of what would have been a London-based sitcom.

Graham received a telephone call in late 1987 from Wits End Productions, which started him thinking about the project.

"They wondered if I was interested in writing something to be shot in England for American television, based on Mark Twain's *A Connecticut Yankee in King Arthur's Court*. At the time, I wasn't really sure—I knew a little bit about the book, but not enough, so I thought I'd read it and see," Chapman revealed.

"I read through quite a bit and skimmed through more, and thought 'That's a nice area there—how clever of him to have done that,' but couldn't see how that was going to shape into a series without being too much in one vein. I wanted more flexibility, and therefore introduced the element of time travel. I grafted onto it the Mark Twain stuff, and a few notions from *The Once and Future King*, where Merlin the Wizard was a tutor to Arthur.

"That relationship had always fascinated me in the book, because Merlin took him into all kinds of worlds which were impossible for human beings to go into—Arthur finds out what it's like to be a fish, for example. That was attractive as a possibility, quite apart from just being able to go into other worlds populated by humans. It seemed fitting with those times, because of the elements of mysticism," Chapman explained.

"That was the genesis of it, plus a bit of *Alice in Wonderland*. Everything is not necessarily in order when one looks at it, but it has its own internal logic, everything behaving as though it has every right to be that way. In the end, it's a blend of all that—but unfortunately, written by David Sherlock and myself," he laughed. "So, it turns into something that's a slightly different animal than any of them. I suppose it's best described as a fantasy-comedy, or a comedy-fantasy . . . a fantacom. . . ."

Chapman had never planned to write an American TV pilot, let alone a series, but they made him an offer he couldn't refuse.

"I had gone as far as expressing very mild interest—and didn't think about it any more. People then went away and mentioned things like 'money' to my agent. They reported back to me that there was actual money to be earned from writing what would effectively be only about twenty-three minutes' worth of material. The money looked quite good, and I thought that this was a script for a pilot, and on the whole, scripts for pilots don't get made. I assumed that this one would have a similar fate—I would simply end up being the richer, and not much more agony about it," he chuckled.

"But they liked what we had written. At the end of a tour of college dates last November, I had a week in Los Angeles at which I thought I was going to a meeting to talk about this pilot. When I got there, I found they were actually expecting words written down on paper with which to go and impress the network," he explained in a 1988 interview.

"Of course, I hadn't done a thing, so David and I spent three days stuck in a hotel room, getting something down on paper. That was the challenge, because it obviously couldn't be done. We were supposed to go in there and impress them—not likely! But it seemed like a bit of a challenge, so we thought 'Why not?'

"We finished up with eight or nine minutes' worth of material, which we then read to the head of comedy—who *laughed*! That was a good start. So, after bickering about whether this bit or that would be understood by the American masses—which had nothing to do with the main story at all—we really had no more great problems," Chapman notes.

Cut from the final version was a very brief sequence set in 1939 Europe, which Chapman says was inserted mainly to indicate to audiences that Jake could actually travel through time, rather than just go to one strange medieval era. Curiously left intact for the "American masses" was a brief moment where they encounter a giant lobster on a cycling tour. Another Pythonesque moment that remains, though heavily edited for time in the pilot, is a verbal encounter with a witch. ("Come in!" "I am in!" "Then I must be out. . . .") Another battle, won by Chapman and Sherlock, was over the network's desire for a time machine—instead, the traveling is accomplished but not explained.

The pilot—with an unusually high budget (for 1988) of $1.2 million—was shot in Britain with Hal Ashby directing. The cast included Chris (*Max Headroom*) Young as Jake and Peter (*Princess Bride*) Cook as the king. Chapman wrote for himself a small role as the queen who never spoke, because she was so stingy she didn't want to give away her words—but he ended up becoming more involved than he had planned.

"I had only been interested in writing it and maybe taking a character role here and there, and I didn't want to give up the character role in the pilot even when I did take the bigger part.

"That came about when they had gotten two weeks into the shooting, and still hadn't come to a decision about casting George. They did want the person in the pilot to do the series, so at that late date—and I must say that since writing this stuff, I secretly cherished the notion of playing that role, but didn't want to because of several other considerations.

"But at this point, I did actually say that I wouldn't mind. They seemed to like that thought, and so did I! I quite enjoyed it, despite the fact it meant going back into armor, albeit even worse, because it was a full set of armor, and rusting," Chapman said, and explained that the figure of George actually is similar to that of Merlin.

"He's a tutor figure, but is also a retired knight—or should have been, with a scraggly gray beard and rusty armor, but in reality, he could be looked on as a tutor figure, but one wouldn't necessarily know that from the first episode. This tutor-pupil relationship is not actually teaching him anything one could put one's finger on, but George is stopping Jake from learning things wrongly, and stopping Jake from getting fixed ideas about things, keeping him open-minded—probably one of the best lessons we could learn."

According to his original conception, Chapman said that Jake would be drawn to George in whatever time period he happens to be occupying, though their relationship and purpose would not necessarily be apparent.

"Jake—who has no control over it at all—is rather inconveniently brought back to wherever George happens to be. George pulls Jake into his world to help him out, really, to do jobs and errands for him, things that he can't be bothered to do, or is too lazy or too old to do. It can be quite inconvenient for Jake, though it often does happen when Jake himself is at personal moments of crisis—so it can also be convenient. It loses Jake no time at all—he goes away in a bubble, I suppose, and comes back to the same spot precisely, and carries on as usual. And he may or may not have learned something in the process, which may or may not help him in current life."

Chapman said that he had some ideas on the ultimate purpose of George, although he never divulged it.

"I might know what it is, but I'm not letting on until very much later—I'm not sure that even I do. It's an archetypical tutor-pupil relationship, which has been seen many times before in literature. He might be training him for something, he might not—or the other way around."

Chapman had high praise for his co-star as well. "Chris is very good indeed, a very good choice in terms of his looks and his acting. And, he was literally only sixteen when we shot the pilot."

The first few shows were to have been centered around the medieval times, but Chapman said he and Sherlock had planned their time-hopping future shows.

"Other episodes will be taking place in prewar Austria, after quite a bit of medievalism in the first few. I can see that we would want to get to the Elizabethan period at some point, and we would get to the Roman period at some point, all of which are quite rich," he noted.

"But we may be able to extend ourselves a little bit and make ancient Greece and Egypt, by virtue of nipping over to Spain to shoot, which has been suggested. I certainly looked interested when they mentioned that!" he laughed.

"And we'd also like to go into the future as well. There's one episode that we have thought about quite a lot which does involve another planet."

Sadly, Graham never had the chance to film those episodes of *Jake's Journey*, but the show was coming together when he became ill in late 1988. CBS initially passed on the series, but ordered several episodes written during the U.S. Writers Guild strike, and planned to go into production with it. Apparently every CBS executive was very excited about the series, except for one person—network president Lawrence Tisch. When he ultimately rejected it, the Disney Channel decided to pick it up, but time ran out. Graham never gave up hope, but *Jake's Journey* was one project he was not able to see to its fruition.

A FISH CALLED WANDA

CONCEIVED, WRITTEN BY AND STARRING JOHN CLEESE. ALSO STARRING MICHAEL PALIN. (1988) 108 MINUTES

Archibald Leach	John Cleese
Wanda Gershwitz	Jamie Lee Curtis
Otto West	Kevin Kline
Ken Pile	Michael Palin
Wendy Leach	Maria Aitken
George Thomason	Tom Georgeson
Eileen Coady	Patricia Hayes
Judge Knott	Geoffrey Palmer
Portia Leach	Cynthia Caylor

Screenplay by John Cleese. Produced by Michael Shamberg. Directed by Charles Crichton. Released by MGM/UA. Produced by Prominent Features. Videocassette release on CBS/Fox Video 4752.

American jewel thieves Wanda and Otto arrive at George's apartment, where animal-loving Ken is feeding the fish. Otto makes fun of Ken's stutter. When George enters, Wanda introduces Otto as her brother, and they make plans for their jewel heist.

Barrister Archie announces that he has just won a case, to his wife and daughter at home, but they are unimpressed.

The gang plans their robbery, and Otto is quietly incensed whenever George kisses Wanda. They pull off the jewel theft with precision, but when they drive away, they are spotted by Mrs. Coady, an elderly lady walking her three dogs. George hides the diamonds, and just before Otto and Wanda become passionate, Otto makes an anonymous phone call and turns George in to the police. Otto and Wanda discover George has moved the diamonds just before Wanda can do in Otto, and so they go to visit George in jail. George suspects Otto may have turned him in and threatens to turn in the jewels if he's convicted.

Wanda sees Archie, George's barrister, and flatters him, figuring George will tell his barrister whatever he decides to do. George gives the key to Ken to hide and tells him to keep an eye on Otto.

At George's apartment, Otto and Wanda are about to jump in bed when Ken returns, and they see him hide the key in the aquarium with Wanda, his fish. Ken suspects the truth about the couple, so Otto makes a pass at the terrified Ken,

while Wanda hides the key in her locket. Ken tells Wanda that George moved the jewels, though he doesn't know where. Wanda later learns the key is to a safe-deposit box.

Mrs. Coady picks George out of a police lineup, and Wanda, posing as a student, goes to interview the flattered Archie. He is horrified to find out that she is George's alibi and says it would be unethical to talk to her; Wanda says she's really there because she wants to make love to Archie.

That evening, the scenes cut between Otto and Wanda making passionate love and Archie's wife and daughter complaining as he clips his toenails.

The next day George pleads not guilty. Otto finds out that George has ordered Ken to kill the elderly witness, and Wanda arranges to get together with Archie the night his wife and daughter are going to the opera.

Wanda surprises Archie at home that evening, and as they kiss, she sees the jealous Otto spying on them. She hides when Wendy and Portia arrive home unexpectedly, losing her locket, which Wendy finds, thinking it's for her. Otto and Wanda escape unseen.

Meanwhile, Ken tries to kill Mrs. Coady with an attack dog, but the animal turns on him and finally makes off with one of her tiny dogs, which upsets Ken terribly.

Otto finds out about a secret meeting Wanda has planned with Archie, but Archie can't get the locket back from his wife. Archie and Wanda meet at a friend's apartment and she makes him promise to get the locket. When they laugh at Otto's stupidity, he suddenly appears and makes Archie apologize by hanging him out the window.

Elsewhere, Ken, dressed as a rasta, tries to run down Mrs. Coady. He succeeds only in killing a second dog, which traumatizes Ken.

Wanda is furious with Otto, and insists he apologize to Archie at his home. When Otto arrives, Archie, disguised, is in the process of staging a burglary in order to get the necklace back. Otto beats him up, thinking he is doing Archie a favor.

Archie and Wanda get together at another apartment for sex, and Archie gives her the necklace. Wanda goes upstairs to change, and when Archie has stripped, a nice family walks in the

JOHN CLEESE   JAMIE LEE CURTIS   KEVIN KLINE   MICHAEL PALIN

A tale of murder, greed, lust, revenge and seafood.

METRO-GOLDWYN-MAYER
MICHAEL SHAMBERG/PROMINENT FEATURES "A FISH CALLED WANDA"
JOHN CLEESE · JAMIE LEE CURTIS · KEVIN KLINE · MICHAEL PALIN
STEVE ABBOTT · JOHN CLEESE "JOHN CLEESE · CHARLES CRICHTON
JOHN CLEESE "MICHAEL SHAMBERG "CHARLES CRICHTON

Lobby cards from A Fish Called Wanda.

door. Archie finally decides he has to end their affair, and when he returns home, Otto is there to apologize. Archie is frightened, but Wendy hears him shouting that his affair with Wanda is fine.

Ken finally succeeds in killing Mrs. Coady, along with the third dog, and George tells him the location of the jewels. At George's apartment, Otto tortures Ken to find the location of the loot by eating his pet fish in front of him. Ken finally tells him, but the key is no longer in the aquarium. In court, Wanda incriminates George, and after Archie lets a few things slip, he sees Wendy watching in the gallery. George goes berserk and attacks Wanda, and Wendy slaps Archie. In the confusion, Archie tries to convince George to tell him where the jewels are, and Archie and Wanda rush off to George's apartment together. Archie frees Ken, and they rush off to the hotel at the airport where the jewels are; Otto has taken Wanda there as well.

They all buy tickets for Rio, and Wanda locks Otto in a broom closet. Otto escapes and forces Archie into a barrel of tar, but before he can kill Archie, Otto finds he is stuck in wet cement, and Ken runs him down with a steamroller. Archie and Wanda make their escape on the plane to Rio with the jewels.

 ## NOTES

A Fish Called Wanda turned out to be the most successful non-Python project John Cleese had done since *Fawlty Towers* many years before. The project literally took years for him to put together, from constructing the story with veteran director Charles Crichton to the eventual promotion of the movie. As early as 1984, Cleese explained that he and Crichton had begun their collaboration, even though they hadn't determined a title at that point.

"Dear Charlie Crichton is working on it, referring to it with a gleam in his eyes as *Corruption*. I think he likes that [title], and I quite like that," explains Cleese. "I always wanted to call a movie *The Last Prawn*. I don't know why. I don't think it would quite work for this one—I may have to write another one."

Over the years, the prawn became a fish, and after its release, Cleese says it was worth it all.

"I couldn't have been more pleased, because it was the first time I've really done a film of my own," he reveals. "Well, I couldn't say it was of my own, because the number of people that contributed to it was huge, but nevertheless, as Charlie Crichton said, it was basically my project. It was my impetus that got it going, I chose the team, and that's what I really take the credit for, and I basically did the dialogue. Everything else was tremendously a team effort. And because of that, because I put more of myself and more time into it than any other project, I was very touched indeed by how well liked it was."

The plot of *A Fish Called Wanda* is as elaborate and complicated as those of the old Ealing comedies that Charles Crichton used to direct.

Cleese had long been an admirer of Crichton and his films, including *The Lavender Hill Mob,* and even worked with him on some of his Video Arts films. When he began *Wanda,* Cleese developed the story alongside Crichton, and at various points in the production, Cleese and Crichton were sharing directing and writing credits as they pieced together their story.

"It is intricate, and I believe it works," says Cleese. "I believe it's almost watertight. I think what anyone does at any time is totally justified— even things like what people are doing when they're off the screen is either implied or is there. It was just a question of working on it a very, very long time, and going through the story again and again and again, and being prepared to rewrite the story every time you had a new idea that you wanted to fit into the movie that would require more rewrites.

"We were juggling scenes, so that the nude scene went from me and Jamie being in the state of undress, to just me being undressed, on a suggestion of Jamie's, which was quite correct because it was funnier. The farce scene, when Wendy arrives home early and catches them all in the house, originally had Wendy's father in it as well as Michael Palin.

"I went through at least three completely different plots before we got anywhere *near* what we finished up with, which probably then took another six or eight drafts, plus a lot of rehearsal. Almost every scene in there was reshaped and done in different ways. In the courtroom, I was originally going to blow George's alibi, to get rid of him so that I could be with Wanda; that was in the script for some time. Then it became obvious that it was much funnier if Wanda blew it for her purposes, because my astonishment would play off her mercenary and manipulative behavior better," explains Cleese.

"So, almost everything there took a lot of shaping before it all fitted. There were odd moments when you get an inspiration—the scene in which Michael Palin tried to kill the old lady and got the dogs instead— it was a week before I felt that was right, because I thought 'Will the idea of him trying to kill someone be bought by the audience, or is it just outside the limits of this movie?' And it was really only when I told Charlie about it, and he sat with the idea for two or three days and came back and said he thought it was fine, that I thought 'Yeah, I think it is fine.' So, even what might look like a moment of inspiration took a week before I decided whether it was right or not. It's a very slow process."

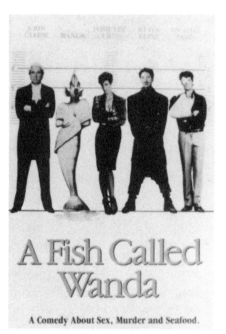

A Fish Called Wanda

A Comedy About Sex, Murder and Seafood.

The best-selling Wanda *videocassette*

Even after he thought he had finished the film, Cleese says they screened it for audiences and did a brief bit of reshooting. He says the original ending merely involved Archie and Wanda flying off on the jet, and didn't end the movie with the desired laugh.

"We changed the ending so that Otto survived and gave us a good joke by coming to the airplane window. We went out on Otto falling off the plane, which was much better than the original ending, which lacked a good laugh," he reveals.

"And then we made Jamie's character a little more sympathetic—I hadn't written it right, and it was a little cold at the end of the movie. We put in a different scene in the car, when I jump into the car with her outside the court, in which there's that little row, and suddenly the ice is broken.

"We put in a little bit of protest, which we shot inside the car, when Kevin jumps into the car to drive off with Jamie, after I've gone into the flat

to see Ken. There's four seconds of argument—'Wait, wait, Otto!' 'Come on, baby, let's go!' That made a big difference. We also put in a shot of Jamie calling me from the airport, going 'Come on, Archie, pick up the phone' to indicate that, having got rid of Otto, she immediately tried to get back in touch with Archie.

"And at the end of the naked scene, Jamie had originally come down the stairs and said 'Oh, bad luck, Archie, third time lucky,' and left. She was dumping him too much, she was too unsympathetic, so we just cut that. It made a huge difference! And I think that was it, I don't think we shot anything else. There was about seventy-five seconds, but it changed it radically by warming up Jamie's character."

Cleese says the hardest filming for director Crichton involved the dog-killing scenes and the steamroller sequence, although he nearly had a problem breaking up on one take.

"I think it's when she says to me 'I want you,' and I say 'What?' [during the scene in Archie's office]—I said it so perfectly on that take that I just begin to break up. We shaved it as fine as possible. I can still see me just beginning to go—nobody else sees me—then we cut to a wider shot when we go to the phone," he says.

He also had to work with special effects supervisor George Gibbs in order to be hung out the window upside-down by Otto, he explains.

"I had a wire up each trouser leg, attached to a harness which I had on underneath my body, a full body harness made of canvas, which took the hooks and wires. But I was never dangled backwards and downwards outside the window, because they had a trolley thing on rails on the window underneath. So, I lay on that, facing outwards. They pushed that out horizontally so it stuck out, and then they fed the wires down from the window above.

"When they wanted to get me up, they just lifted me, very gently, so eventually my shoulders and head were just hanging on the trolley. Then they'd lift me up, move the trolley back in, and I'd be hanging there. When they wanted to get me back down again, they brought the trolley out, lowered me down from the window above onto the trolley, and I could get lying straight out again and take a break before I went up," he explains.

Cleese says compared to his Monty Python filming, he found *Wanda* much more interesting.

"There was a greater feeling of teamwork, in a funny kind of way. It was particularly more exciting at the rehearsal stage. With Python, once we'd done the writing, the real work was done—rehearsing was just completing the process. I felt with *Wanda*, we were contributing more with the acting," he relates.

"Also, of course, it was a much more interesting thing for me to play than another Python sketch character, because I was going into areas I'd never gone into before. I also learned far more from working with Kevin and Jamie, American styles of acting, than I would have learned working with these guys I've worked with for so long. Which isn't to say it isn't a pleasure to work with Michael, but as a learning experience, it's more intriguing to work with people from different backgrounds."

His fellow Python agrees that *Wanda* was a learning experience for them both.

"It was the first major film that John had really written on his own, post-Graham. In a sense, for both of us, it was a post-Python experience," notes Michael Palin. "He'd been very interested in having a character who stammered—this was ages ago, since 1985. He'd asked me about that character, knowing that my father had had a stammer, or a stutter, as they say in America. We discussed how the character would speak, and that's how it led to me doing the part, and he always had the part of Ken Pile there ready for me.

"John is very generous once he's decided he wants to use somebody, he's very generous with the time he spends with you, the chance he'll give you to rewrite the script if you want to. He also wanted to work with Jamie very much. Who wouldn't? And Kevin, he'd become friends with in the States, and that was our little team. John very single-mindedly and rather efficiently got it together."

Palin's character became the target of controversy after the movie was released, and some stutterers' groups claimed to take offense at the character of Ken. Despite protests from the film-makers, ABC-TV edited out portions of Kevin Kline's insults that were directed at Ken when it was broadcast in 1991. Despite such small-minded attacks, the film became phenomenally popular. Palin says the huge success of *Wanda* surprised them all, just as the success of Monty Python surprised the group many years before.

"I never had any idea it was going to be big. You really just don't know. We regarded Python as something that essentially worked amongst the group of us. We had *no idea* how it would work beyond that, just *no idea* how people would react to the silly things we were doing. Python's success came very slowly, really, in fact, as each year goes by, more people begin to regard it as a more of a sort of distinguished show. So, we were brought up on surprises," explains Palin.

"*Wanda* felt good when we were doing it, but again, you never know who your audience is going to be. I think the degree of its success took all of us completely by surprise—in fact, it was a global, international success in every country except for Japan, massively popular."

Still, for John Cleese, the realization of *Wanda*'s success came very gradually.

"It was a process of, first of all, showing it in New York and realizing that it was gonna be okay if I fixed certain things. And then, in L.A., having wonderfully expert criticism from Rob Reiner and Steve Martin and Harold Ramis, among others. Then coming back and reshooting the ending, and suddenly realizing that it was working, and doing all that publicity in the States for six weeks.

"And I remember, the crucial moment was getting the two thumbs up [from Siskel and Ebert]—that was when I *really* felt `Now we've made it.' It was like we'd moved it up into a different league, when we got that," reveals Cleese. "My only criticism is that it's not about anything important.

"It went on for week after week, with good figures coming in. It isn't the money, it's an indication of how much people like it—it's measured by the number of people coming in, and that's measured by box office. Then there were great thrills, and I was very, very pleased when we ran it in Edinburgh to see that the Scottish audience loved it, and the biggest thrill of all in some ways was watching it at the Venice Film Festival, and seeing an Italian audience laughing in exactly the same places as the British and American audiences. So, that was an exciting moment, very rewarding!"

CRITICAL COMMENTS

"One of the year's funniest, most offbeat films.... it's all quite original, adult, and funny. . . ."

—Gene Siskel, *Chicago Tribune*, July 29, 1988

"*A Fish Called Wanda* is the funniest movie I have seen in a long time. . . . The film has one hilarious sequence after another. For classic farce, nothing tops the scene in Cleese's study. . . . The timing in this scene is as good as anything since the Marx Brothers."

—Roger Ebert, *Chicago Sun-Times*, July 29, 1988

"The movie blithely places live actors in situations usually the preserve of drawn characters. . . . *Wanda* defines gravity, in both senses of the word, and redefines a great comic tradition."

—Richard Schickel, *Time*, July 18, 1988

A FISH CALLED WANDA: A SCREENPLAY

BY JOHN CLEESE. PUBLISHED BY METHUEN BOOKS, 1988. U.K. PAPERBACK, ISBN 0-413-19550-3; U.S. PAPERBACK BY APPLAUSE THEATRE BOOK PUBLISHERS, ISBN 1-55783-033-9.

Contains the finished screenplay, with a photo insert of the eight lead actors.

The Wanda *script book.*

NUMBER 27

***WRITTEN BY MICHAEL PALIN. FIRST BROADCAST OCTOBER 23, 1988, ON BBC-1.
STARRING NIGEL PLANER, JOYCE CAREY, HELENA MICHEL, ALUN ARMSTRONG.
PRODUCED BY INNES LLOYD. DIRECTED BY TRISTRAM POWELL.***

An evil property developer runs up against a ninety-year-old lady
who tries to get him to change his ways.

 ## NOTES

Michael Palin's second teleplay was the result of the success of his first one.

"Having gained a bit of confidence from doing *East of Ipswich,* which was a seventy-five-minute teleplay, which sustained pretty well, I read the newspaper," explains Palin. "There was this story about property owned by Eton College, the country's premier public school, which was being left to wrack and ruin quite near where I used to live in London. Terrible pressure was being put on tenants to sort of get them out—houses weren't repaired, and all that. So, I was very indignant about this, and that set me to writing one of my few contemporary stories. It was set in the present day, and it was about the 1980s Yuppie era of money washing about, and young guys going around buying up property here and there.

"I wrote that not knowing where it was going to go, and who was going to take it. In the end, Tristram Powell, the director of *East of Ipswich,* decided that he'd like to do it, and the same producer said he would produce it, so we got it together for the Beeb again, and I was very, very happy to do it. It was a very happy experience. I just wrote the script, which was fine, I was happy about that, and I consulted on the casting," says Palin.

ATTACKS OF OPINION

***BY TERRY JONES. PUBLISHED BY PENGUIN BOOKS, 1988; U.K. PAPERBACK
ISBN 0-14-032895-5. ILLUSTRATED BY GERALD SCARFE.***

Twenty-nine topical, sometimes controversial articles written by Jones for the London *Guardian* newspaper on subjects that include the Obscene Publications Bill, nuclear power, *The Sun,* Margaret Thatcher, the Contras, the Zeebrugge disaster, the trade unions, terrorists, the ozone layer, the *Spycatcher* affair, the INF agreement, democracy, the poll tax, education, gay rights, the national health service, pollution, and much more.

 ## NOTES

In 1987 Terry Jones was invited to contribute four pieces to the London *Guardian'*s "Input" column, which was published every Wednesday in the *Young Guardian* supplement. He began April 8, 1987, and didn't stop until May 13, 1988. The columns are 550 to 600 words each, and deal with Jones's opinions on a wide variety of newsworthy topics.

"They had occasional people writing columns, and when I started writing them, they asked me if I'd carry on writing them. They were usually sort of political," explains Jones.

"In fact, one of the nicest I did was the `Ro-Ro-Ro' thing—roll-on, roll-off, roll-over ferries. It was after the Zeebrugge disaster," he says of the dangerous ships used to cross the English Channel; the aforementioned disaster was one of the worst sea accidents of the 1980s.

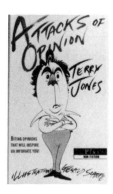

Jones writes that the ferries ". . . can achieve in a matter of 180 seconds what it takes a conventional ship half an hour to do, i.e., capsize. It's a bit like crossing the Channel on a greasy log."

"I got very good reaction to the columns, but I don't think I ever had any reaction to the book itself!" he notes. "I liked doing the columns, because it was amazing how people would react to them. I still write occasional stuff for the *Guardian.*"

THE ADVENTURES OF BARON MUNCHAUSEN

CO-WRITTEN AND DIRECTED BY TERRY GILLIAM. STARRING ERIC IDLE. (1989) 126 MINUTES

Baron Munchausen ....John Neville
Berthold...Eric Idle
Sally Salt ....Sarah Polley
Vulcan..Oliver Reed
Adolphus ....Charles McKeown
Albrecht...Winston Dennis
Gustavus ....Jack Purvis
Queen of the Moon ....Valentina Cortese
Mr. Jackson ....Jonathan Pryce
Mr. Salt...Bill Paterson
Sultan ....Peter Jeffrey
Venus ....Uma Thurman
Heroic Officer ....Sting
King of the Moon ....Ray D. Tutto (Robin Williams)

Screenplay by Terry Gilliam and Charles McKeown. Produced by Thomas Schuhly. Directed by Terry Gilliam. Released by Columbia Pictures. Videocassette release by RCA-Columbia Home Video 50153. (Criterion video disc contains commentary by Gilliam and additional footage.)

In the late eighteenth century, a walled city is under siege by the Turkish army, though a local theatrical group within performs the story of Baron Munchausen. Their performance is interrupted by the real Baron Munchausen, who calls their show lies; he claims he can end the war with the Turkish sultan because he started it.

The baron gets on stage and tells the audience about his visit with the sultan. With the help of

Albrecht, the strongest man on earth, Berthold, the fastest man alive, Adolphus, who has super-powerful vision, and Gustavus, who can blow harder than a hurricane, the baron retrieves a bottle of wine and wins a wager with the sultan, and they carry away all of his treasure. The sultan is furious and sends troops after them, but they escape.

As the cannons fire, the baron explains to the audience in the theater that the sultan is still after him, but everyone flees due to the bombardment. Sally saves the baron from the winged figure of Death; the baron is upset because there's no place in the world for the fantastic any more. He chases Sally to the wall of the city and ends up riding a cannonball over the Turkish troops, which convinces Sally he's really the baron (though everyone else thinks she's lying). The baron plans to find his servants and save the city, and makes a huge hot-air balloon out of the ladies' knickers.

The baron and Sally, who stows away, fly off ahead of the firing local troops. They land on the moon, where the baron claims to be a close friend of the king. The King of the Moon, whose head is traveling without his body, proves his power to the baron and Sally, while his headless body tries to molest the queen. The king imprisons the baron and Sally in a cage, where they discover the elderly Berthold. The queen helps them all escape as the baron flirts with her, although the king chases them riding on a three-headed gryphon, throwing giant asparagus spears at him.

The three of them fall back to earth and land in the volcano at Mt. Etna, where Vulcan is settling a labor dispute with his giant employees. They see his prototype nuclear missile, and he invites them to tea, where Albrecht is serving. Vulcan's wife Venus arises from the sea, but when she dances with the baron, Vulcan becomes jealous, and he throws them all into the volcano.

After landing in the ocean, the four of them are swallowed by a huge sea monster. In its belly, among the wrecked ships, they find the decrepit Adolphus and Gustavus, who are convinced they are dead. Sally won't let them give up and saves them all from Death, and the baron applies snuff so that the sea monster blows their ship out to sea. They find they've arrived home, and the sultan's army attacks them. The baron's men make their way to shore and use their newly regained abilities to defeat their army.

 ## NOTES

Terry Gilliam may have thought his battle to release *Brazil* would be his worst experience in film, but shooting *The Adventures of Baron Munchausen* turned out to be a nightmare. There were problems with the different crews and scheduling, and when the budget continued to rise, Gilliam nearly had the movie taken away from him; he had to make massive cuts in the script to keep control.

With all of the problems of the production behind him, Gilliam looks back with pride and relief on the star-crossed movie.

The Adventures of Baron Munchausen is a wild, spectacular fantasy, based loosely on the legendary teller of tall tales. Bringing to life the stories and flights of fantasy seemed well suited to the director of *Brazil* and *Time Bandits*.

"This is really the same old rubbish I'm always doing." Gilliam laughs. "Fantasy and reality, or truth and reality—whatever form it takes—that which the world perceives as truth, and that which really is truth. I like the idea that a good lie is probably better than what appears to be the truth—and maybe even more truthful than truth."

Originally, Gilliam claims he had no intention of filming *Baron Munchausen*, however.

"I never meant to make it—it was one of those things that crept up on me. The whole thing really started when we were making *Brazil*," Gilliam reveals.

"The idea of *Munchausen* had been around for some time, because I liked the (1962) Czechoslovakian film, in particular. I liked the stories. When we were doing *Brazil*, and I was convinced *Brazil* would be the biggest disaster of all time, Arnon Milchan and I were saying `Look, we'd better have something planned for next.' When he asked what I wanted to do, I told him I'd been thinking about Baron Munchausen, and he turned out to be a big fan.

"So, we went to Twentieth Century–Fox and he said `Terry and I want to do *Baron Munchausen*.' And he said `Wow! We're all Munchausen people here!' And they did a deal. We actually had a deal to make the film with Twentieth Century–Fox.

"After *Brazil*, Arnon and I went separate ways, and Fox ultimately turned it down, because the people who had made the deal were no longer there—there were new people at Fox. But I had nothing else happening, and momentum on the *Baron* just kept going. Occasionally, art overtakes life." He laughs.

"At one point, I was being pretentious, and pretending I was making a trilogy with *Time Bandits, Brazil,* and *Munchausen*—the young boy as fantasist, the man as fantasist, and the old man as fantasist—there are connections for this.

"The book is really just a series of tales that don't have any narrative connection, so Charles McKeown and I invented a tale about a town under siege, the group of actors trapped in it, trying to perform *The Adventures of Baron Munchausen,* when the real baron turns up and starts doing all the things that only happen in fantasy."

The most difficult character for the director to cast was the title character, as the baron is also the most important role of the film. "I did a lot of screen tests with a lot of different people in mind, it went on and on and on. But the extraordinary thing was that one name kept popping up—John Neville. It kept popping up every month or so—somebody would pop in and say `I've got just the guy for you—his name is John Neville,' and I'd say `I *know* that, but . . .'

"John Neville was the director of the Stratford Ontario Shakespeare Festival, he did fifteen productions a season. We had approached his agent and been told he had no time for films. So, I kept looking for somebody else.

Terry Gilliam at his desk working on another screen-play. Photo copyright Kim "Howard" Johnson

"Then one day when we were in Rome working, I was telling the lady doing the makeup about the problems in casting the baron, and I said the person I kept thinking about is John Neville. She said `Well, I know him, I grew up with his daughter. I have his phone number, I'll call him.' She called him in Canada and said `Terry Gilliam's making a film, and he'd like to meet you.' He turned out to be a Python fan! I met him and said `Bingo! Baron Munchausen!'

"What I had been looking for was a star, a great actor who had faded or disappeared, and that's what John was. In the sixties in England, he, Burton, O'Toole, they were all just the top—he was equal to all those guys. Then he left the West End stage and went into provincial theater, then emigrated to Canada. In effect, he disappeared from the world as most of us know it! He was doing incredible work all through Canada, setting up theaters and all. So, he fitted the bill," Gilliam smiles.

Munchausen was actually based on a real German cavalry officer who liked to exaggerate his exploits. A book written by Rudolph Erich Raspe was released in 1785; the baron was a popular radio character in America for many years, while two dozen screen versions have been shot in Europe. The films include a Georges Méliès silent short, a 1948 German version, and a 1962 effort from Czechoslovakia. Although the man with the rights to the German version threatened a lawsuit, Gilliam wasn't worried.

"After all, Rudolph Erich Raspe is dead! However, the man with the rights to remake the German film—which he's been trying to do for years, apparently—has been running around making lots of noise, claiming that we're violating his rights, which is all nonsense, because it's public domain. What we've done has no relationship to the German film at all. As far as I'm concerned, he's wasted a lot of lawyers' time."

Gilliam is no stranger to controversy, both in his Monty Python years and in film, particularly his previous movie, *Brazil.* And *Baron Munchausen* faced problems that would have broken most directors. Forced to begin production before he was ready, the project soon ran into budget problems that caused the studio to threaten to replace him. Still, Gilliam retained his sense of humor through it all.

"I just grow thicker and thicker skin. I'm a walking callus," he says with a laugh. "This film was terrifyingly difficult, even before those other pressures from the studio began. The fact that the film was falling apart at the seams was bad enough—the organization was terrible. It was a very foolhardy thing to go to a foreign country—in this case, Italy—that isn't particularly equipped to do SFX films, mixing English and Italian crews. At one point, the crew was English, Italian, German, and Spanish. They were speaking in four different languages, which in this kind of film was a very silly thing to do.

"On the other hand, this film was about the impossible and going-on impossible adventures—and that's what the making of the film is also about," Gilliam laughs, "Life imitates art again!"

Fortunately, Gilliam had the strong support of his cast—including fellow Monty Python member and old friend Eric Idle—even though the director required him to make sacrifices.

"Eric was great, because I think he enjoyed the process. He was constantly supportive, and once he shaved his head, he was a good person—it just took a little while to get him to shave his head. That altered his personality to no end, and improved him as a human being," Gilliam jokes. "Now that his hair's growing back, I'm frankly less fond of him!

"But it's good to have friends around when doing this sort of thing, because everybody's relaxed. Ideas come more easily. When everyone is more relaxed and confident in their work during a film, they try things and suggest ideas more often. I've just got to stay open to all of those ideas and suggestions, use the good ones, and hopefully reject the bad ones.

"At one point, we were out in Spain, and things were at their very, very worst. I was ready to quit. I knew there was no way we'd get through the film. Eric really came in there, saying `You've *got* to, if for no other reason, you must make this film *to spite John Cleese.*" he laughs. "That got me going!"

And that's why Eric Idle says he made the comment. "I had to motivate Terry to keep going. I didn't want the film to go under, because I'd already gotten my head shaved, and I wanted to be sure I got paid!" he recalls with a chuckle.

Idle agrees that an ordeal like *Munchausen* was easier to face with a friend; he says that Gilliam was under tremendous pressure during the shoot but managed to handle it all wonderfully.

"Terry's very good at dealing with pressure, which is why he's a very good director," Idle explains. "What he does, basically, is take a pure artistic line, saying `This is not my responsibility. Here I am this morning, I want to shoot this shot. Money is a producer's job.' I think that's absolutely the only possible way to deal with a situation like that. The moment I would think about taking on vast responsibilities, I wouldn't be able to do anything—I would just stay in bed and have a nervous breakdown."

Following Michael Palin's roles in *Time Bandits* and *Brazil*, Idle says he's happy to take over the Python role here.

"It's important and very useful to have old friends around. Michael always played the role of the old chap you used to do comedy with, who you can talk to—because filming is madness. It's good to have an old colleague like that, so he can't pull any `I'm the director' shit. Still, when there's a crisis, I'll take him off and have a coffee and say `Don't worry.' I really enjoyed playing that role. It's tough directing. One needs supporters and pals, and it's best if they're on the set too, because they're up to their necks in water when you're asking."

Despite the decades, Idle says his old colleague hasn't changed much in the past decades.

"I still see the same guy who came along in *Do Not Adjust Your Set* in 1967. He's just an old, old friend. One changes when making a film—the project is running out of control with the budget, and it's really tough to keep going. Every day he had to get up, and there were forces that he had no control over whatsoever, enormous forces. People doing bad deals, ripping off, trying to get him fired—all of that can come between the tremendously difficult mosaic of putting a film together," explains Idle.

Making *Munchausen* was completely different from making a Python movie, however.

"Oh, it was much more demanding," Idle maintains. "A Python project is so well prepared in every way—we know what we're going to do as actors, because we've written the script. It's very closely budgeted; I don't think we ever went over budget. Gilliam probably went over budget with the `Crimson Permanent Assurance' sequence in *Meaning of Life*, but that was about it. With the *Baron,* we're dealing with a huge, epic film where there are so many things that can go wrong, and we're doing it with people who are not Python. Python people will actually jump in water and ultimately do all of these strange scenes for you. When we're dealing with proper actors, they won't, because they're big stars—why should they? It's a different approach totally," reveals Idle.

"It was a good experience, but a tough film. It was really horrible and unpleasant in many stages—I had flu in the middle of the night while we were shooting in Spain. It was freezing, and they were exploding everything, just blowing everything up. I was called to the set, then at about four in the morning, they came and dug me out of a caravan where I was shivering, trying to keep warm, to go and do the acting. This is about as low as one can get in show business. There's not much lower than that!" he says, laughing.

He says he was happy to work with Gilliam here, despite such unpleasant moments.

"I felt it was unlikely that I'd work with Gilliam again, and I've always respected him—he's a wonderful director," Idle notes. "I was thinking that I'd be too old to work with Gilliam next time around—he'd kill me in another few years, so I'd better go do my stint now.

"I had my head shaved for six months. That bastard Gilliam," he laughs. "Pure sexual jealousy. . . . I also had false teeth made, horrible ugly false teeth. I look a real wreck in that film. Didn't get laid from that one, that's for sure!"

When a casting crisis arose due to the script rewrites, Idle called his friend Robin Williams in to play the King of the Moon. Although he appeared in the same scenes as Williams, they actually never filmed any scenes together, except through the illusion of SFX shots.

"We never had any scenes together directly—it appears so in the film, but we never acted together. Robin's character attacks us, riding a three-headed gryphon, throwing asparagus spears at us—it's a pretty hysterical scene," Idle explains. "It's pretty interesting, really weird and extraordinary. . . ."

The cast did undergo changes, largely due to delays and demands by the studio. The most radical, however, was undoubtedly Robin Williams stepping in as the King of the Moon. Strangely enough, the actor originally signed for the part was Sean Connery (who portrayed King Agamemnon for Gilliam in *Time Bandits*)!

"People wouldn't necessarily cast those two people for the same part, now, would they?" Gilliam smiles.

"During the very bad days when everything was falling apart, Charles McKeown and I eventually capitulated and made some cuts in the film. One of those was cutting the moon sequence down from a world of two thousand people with detachable heads, down to a world of two people with detachable heads.

"The part was a bit dodgy anyway at that point. There was a certain grandioseness about it that appealed to Sean, and for that reason, he was perfect. But we chopped the part down to nothing, and he sensibly lost interest. So, we didn't have a King of the Moon, and we were wallowing around with nothing. I was very frustrated with the way we had rewritten it. I said 'Charles, we've got to do something else. Even though it's only two people, this is what I think we ought to do—' We started to work on this idea, and it became this vehicle for a very funny, comic part.

"Robin was a good friend of Eric, and Robin had actually been out to Rome; we had offered him the part of Vulcan at one point. He wasn't able to do it because he was promoting *Good Morning Vietnam,* but when Eric called him later about this, he said 'Yeah'!" says the director.

Gilliam had also planned to cast two actors from his previous films, Katherine Helmond and Bob Hoskins, for roles in his new production.

"Katherine was supposed to be the Queen of the Moon—she'd always intended to be there, and we wrote it with her in mind, but we couldn't make the schedules match. We wrote the part of Vulcan for Bob, and he couldn't do it because he was tied up with *Roger Rabbit.*

"So, two of the best bits of casting in the film were done at the last minute, with Robin and Oliver Reed, who plays Vulcan. Oliver is *brilliant.* Frankly, I can't imagine anybody doing it better, having gotten through it and seeing what he's done—he's absolutely extraordinary. Very, very funny and dangerous at the same time!" Gilliam enthuses.

In addition to personnel changes, the shooting itself underwent several adjustments along the way, although the director is hard pressed to cite specific instances.

"I would actually have to go back and look at what we started with, because I've forgotten—the whole process of making a film changes it. I have the script and I have the idea, and each thing that happens alters it slightly—some things more than slightly! There's time, money, not getting the right person, the location doesn't work, or the locations suggest different possibilities.

"Going to Rome affected the film enormously—it's much more baroque than it might have been if I'd done it in England, and I think it's more romantic. Everything affects everything else when I work on stuff," he explains, and points at the screen, where a seaside scene is running. "The main problem in getting these shots is there was a shipping lane in the background, and every time we'd want to shoot out there in that direction, there was a huge tanker sitting out on that horizon.

"That changes the way you work," he laughs.

Gilliam says they ended up using all manner of special effects.

"We used everything," explains Gilliam. "Models, blue screen*—basically every trick in the book. There was a lot more blue screen than I've ever done before—probably one hundred blue-screen shots in it."

One of the further complications of *Munchausen* resulted from Gilliam's rejecting the traditional show business axiom of not working with animals, children, or water.

"We were smart when we did *Monty Python and the Holy Grail* and used coconut shells for our horses. This had everything. Animals, small children, water FX—everything you should never do in a film, they're all in this one. Hopefully, I've gotten it out of my system now. The elephants were difficult. We trained the horses for months, and just before we went to Spain to shoot, there was an outbreak of horse fever in Spain, and the placed was closed. We couldn't bring in the horses that we had trained to do all these things. . . .

"There were two dogs used for the baron's dog, and they both came down with a liver complaint the same week the horses weren't allowed into Spain. A couple weeks before we would start, the horses couldn't go to Spain, the dogs came down with some disease, and David Puttnam [of Columbia] got the sack—all in three days. What a week!" Gilliam laughs.

The director says he had better luck with the eight-year-old newcomer, Sarah Polley, who plays one of the baron's companions, and had to hold her own on the screen with John Neville, Eric Idle, Oliver Reed, and Robin Williams.

*Blue screen is a process by which actors and scenery in the foreground are filmed in front of a blue screen, and a different background or effects are added later.

"She was fantastic, and professional. I treated her no differently than any of the others, and she was there all the time. She was amazing —quite frankly, we couldn't have done the film without her being as good as she is. The cast is brilliant."

Baron Munchausen contains elements of swashbuckling fantasy movies of the past, Gilliam explains, almost excessively so. "If this film suffers from anything, it's too much of everything.

"Americans are desperate for more and more and more, and this has got more than anything. On the one hand, it's like all the films that used to be made, all the great SFX-fantasy movies like *Sea Hawk* and *Thief of Bagdad*—it's like all of those films, and yet it's totally different," he explains.

"When we were making it, I kept going 'Wow!' because there was black-and-white video all the time we were shooting. I kept looking at the images, and it just kept reminding me of picture after picture that I'd grown up with."

In addition to the many SFX shots, Gilliam's project also involved extensive makeup.

"The makeup was the worst part about it for someone like John Neville, who was sixty-three—he had to play the baron at thirty-five, at sixty-five, and at eighty, so he had to go through all these different aging makeups. He was spending three to four hours a day in the makeup chair, which is murderous.

"We tried to make Robin Williams a floating head out of marble. The Queen of the Moon has got three violin necks sticking out the top of her head," he reveals.

"All the characters had to age and get young, and they're wearing false teeth. We shaved everybody's head, because they had to be old—rather than wearing bald caps all the time, which are very sweaty, and stain with makeup. Audiences can always see the joint. So, I convinced them all to shave their heads. They'd wear wigs when they were young and be naturally bald when they were old. There were a lot of sacrifices on people's parts."

Gilliam says making the film was not much fun and, in retrospect, claims that each scene was a nightmare to film; in addition to problems with the budget, pressures from the studios, and lack of preproduction time, he was forced to shoot under less than state-of-the-art conditions on location in Spain, and at Rome's Cinecitta Studios, where Fellini is based.

"I really didn't enjoy making this film, I hated it all the time when we were shooting it—I was just trying to survive. It wasn't about making the film, it was all about surviving! So, I have a strange lack of memory about the experience. . . ."

One day that Gilliam does remember is the sequence with the huge balloon, with a gas bag consisting of women's underpants sewn together, used to escape from the besieged city. In fact, the director says that day was the turning point of the entire film.

"Our finest day was the day the balloon flew in Spain. They were pulling us out of the country before we were finished and threatening to fire me. Everything was going wrong, the whole production. The day before, we had shot the death of the baron, and I thought that was it—it was all over, because just like *Brazil,* the making of the film followed the script itself," he recalls with a laugh. "We were shooting the baron's death when the film was falling apart and we were closing it down.

"We then had to shoot the balloon going up. The balloon, which cost a fortune and had to be supported by a three-hundred-foot crane, could only fly if there was no wind. There we were, on this hilly bit of Spain, where there was *always* wind. We got up in the morning, and of course the wind was blowing, so they couldn't get the balloon up. The day was ticking by while we were doing this, that, and the other thing, and the balloon wouldn't fly. I had said the night before that if the balloon goes, the film will be all right, and if the balloon doesn't go, we're dead—it's very simple.

"The sun set at five-thirty P.M., and at four-thirty we still hadn't gotten close to getting the balloon up and across the battlements. The clouds would come in, and every time we'd start taking the balloon across the battlements, it would turn in the wrong direction.

"The little gondola underneath would be pointing backwards and every which way. To get it the right way, we had to disconnect wires, turn the boat around, stick the wires back on and put it up—then it'd go the wrong way again!

"At five, everything was still going on, though luckily the wind had dropped. The line producer was saying 'What are we going to do?' I said I didn't know, and we couldn't decide which way to turn the balloon for the last time. I finally said 'I think

The book about the struggle to film Mun-chausen.

it ought to go that way—turn the wires that way.' He said 'Are you sure? Then let's do it that way—it's got to work that way.'

"We pulled the balloon up, and it was pointing the wrong way. Then it started to move. It turned. The sun came out in the late afternoon, and *the balloon flew*! It was stunning. Off across this battle below, and walls filled with people, the Turks going on and the cannons firing, and it went! It was just so amazing—everybody went crazy and started grabbing shots madly. The last shot we got is the flag flying over the town, with the last bit of sun catching the flag—it was a perfect day.

"I don't know if that was the turning point, I just knew the film would get finished," he says, laughing. "The filming got worse after that, but at least I knew secretly that it would get done."

Eric Idle looks back on the whole *Munchausen* experience as a survivor might.

"It was like being in the First World War, in the trenches," he jokes. "I think I'm glad to have done it. It was a fine film, somewhat *The Wizard of Oz.* And I felt that when they went to the moon, he had to put a killer song in there. Stop the whole thing, you put an 'Over the Rainbow' in, and you have a show. And I always kept trying to persuade him, but Terry never believed me. It just needed more of that, and it might well have worked, and less of the frenetic stuff. Because a lot of it's really good, and he really saved it—he worked and worked his butt off, and it's sort of tragic that it fell across the studio wars. But that's Hollywood—he got blamed for everybody else's vices. Whereas in fact, $45 million for that film is not at all a bad price, especially when you think of the prices now.

"Well, it's not all up there on the screen, some of it's in the drivers' pockets, because this is Italy, you know—a lot of money being quietly slipped into pockets, but not half as much as, say, Hollywood. They just steal big in Hollywood. Somebody will take four or five million—in Italy, at least, they split it up among everyone else," notes Idle.

When Terry Gilliam prepared *Munchausen* for its laser-disc release, he recorded his own running commentary on one of the soundtracks and also added an additional scene.

"It's a scene where soldiers are on the wall just before the baron's cannonball ride, and they're arguing about why they're not firing back—why the Turks are firing and the guys in the town aren't firing back. It's a long, complicated thing about `It's been half-day closing in this town since the Middle Ages'—all day Wednesday is half-day closing. It's a very silly scene that I shouldn't have cut out, but I did," explains Gilliam.

Ultimately, *The Adventures of Baron Munchausen* was sunk by Columbia Pictures, to Gilliam's frustration. As in *Brazil*, a book was written about the struggle to make and release *Munchausen* (*Losing the Light: Terry Gilliam and the Munchausen Saga,* by Andrew Yule, published by Applause Books).

The Adventures of Baron Munchausen was a success with critics, but very few people had the chance to see it, and Terry Gilliam is still angry that the movie fell victim to studio politics.

"I was disappointed that the studio didn't release the film," he explains. "They didn't distribute it. There aren't many films—especially films that big—that have been dumped so successfully by a studio. They did 115 prints—that's all that were made of that film. My mother lives out in the San Fernando Valley, and it never got out there. They spent on promoting it less than half of what we spent on *Time Bandits*, and that was ten years ago.

"The studio was basically being run by the accountants at that point, and they were trying to tidy it up for a sale to Sony. They made the books look good by spending absolutely no money on promoting, marketing, and distributing the films. I found out they spent more time trying to justify why they weren't putting money into the film than actually doing it. The actual distribution of that film was so terrible—in places like France and Australia and Spain, where the foreign guys actually got to work on it, it did fantastically well. I don't know if I'll ever get over that one, because it's a film that was really meant to be seen by the public. Columbia had convinced themselves that it would only work in sophisticated urban centers, and only the big ones, at that, which is just rubbish—totally untrue. They could not understand that it was also mainly for kids.

"Basically, they just put no money into it. They probably spent $2 million on the release of that film. The problem when you do that, when you've got a big film that has to be sold like an epic and you don't put money behind it, is that I think the public smells a rat. `Something's wrong here, this one has to be a stinker.'"

Munchausen got very respectable notices, but it wasn't enough to get Columbia to save the film.

"They had gotten the best notices they had gotten since *The Last Emperor*; they did the best business they had done since then too on the opening week. It did fantastic, it was great. Dawn Steel was on the phone to me, so excited about how well it had opened. The whole plan was that it would open as it did, and a couple of weeks later, go to five hundred prints, and on and on. They didn't do any of it. They just pulled the plug on it. It makes me angry, because as far as I'm concerned, it was just a total act of betrayal. We'd been told that if the film opened well, they'd be right in there. The problem was that Dawn Steel was, at the time, pretending to be president of the place. I foolishly believed she actually had some power, and she didn't. It was Victor Kaufman, the money man, who was really calling the shots at that point. That's the part that angers me—not that it didn't do well, but that the people didn't get a chance to go see it."

He admits that he inadvertently helped Columbia to sink the film by discussing the problems involved during the shoot, so that most of the press received by *Munchausen* concentrated on the problems attached to it rather than the movie itself.

"I should have kept my mouth shut. I was so brain-damaged by then that I couldn't *not* talk about the awfulness of making the thing, and again, people in this day and age are terrified of things that sound like they have problems attached to them. Twenty years ago that wasn't the case—people would rush out to see what it was about, but unfortunately, that's not the world we're living in now. I would get trapped by most of the interviews, because they would just want to talk about it going overbudget and all those thing, which is really beside the point. Nobody was talking about how good the film was, or how fantastic or whatever."

After it was too late to do anything about it, Gilliam discovered that the film had indeed been made a victim of studio infighting.

"It partly had to do with the backlash towards David Puttnam, because there were a lot of people who perceived this as a Puttnam film. They were really out to get him. There were so many reports coming in about this film in *Variety* when we were shooting in Rome, I couldn't work out where they were getting this information, because number one, a lot of it wasn't true, and number two, where were they getting it? It was being fed to them—I actually know how it got to them, but it was a way of beating Puttnam as well as me.

"I had a talk with Warren Beatty before I left L.A. after shooting the film, and I got a clearer picture of what was going on. He really felt it had been a way of getting at Puttnam."

 ## CRITICAL COMMENTS

"If this wildly ambitious film isn't always witty, it always looks witty, from its mad-architect sets to the portly maidens frolicking in a Turk sultan's pool. If its tone is so hopped-up that even Williams' unbilled cameo is half-again too much, there's also a gravity-defying dance between Neville and Uma Thurman that's as movie-magical as anything I've ever seen. That's no yarn—but the truth. Excesses or not, I'm rabid to see this again."

—Mike Clark, *USA Today*, March 10, 1989

"Much of *Munchausen* is truly astonishing, as was Gilliam's Orwellian fantasy *Brazil*. But like *Brazil*, *Munchausen* sometimes mistakes astonishment for delight. *Munchausen* lacks what one of Gilliam's models, the English classic *The Thief of Bagdad*, had—an enchanting balance of technical wizardry, narrative and character. Gilliam crams the screen with so many marvels that it's hard for his characters and the audience to breathe. Yet few movies contain the authentic prodigies in *Munchausen*; Terry Gilliam is one of the rare directors who can create an entire world. *Munchausen* is like a huge, flawed emerald, a real gem that has cracked under pressure."

—Jack Kroll, *Newsweek*, March 13, 1989

THE ADVENTURES OF BARON MUNCHAUSEN

BY CHARLES MCKEOWN AND TERRY GILLIAM. PUBLISHED BY METHUEN/MANDARIN BOOKS (1989), ISBN 0-7493-0017-5.

The novelization of the Terry Gilliam film.

THE ADVENTURES OF BARON MUNCHAUSEN: THE SCREENPLAY

BY CHARLES MCKEOWN AND TERRY GILLIAM. PUBLISHED BY APPLAUSE THEATRE BOOKS (1989), ISBN 1-55783-041-X.

The complete screenplay of the Terry Gilliam film, with photos and unused portions of the screenplay included.

LOSING THE LIGHT: TERRY GILLIAM AND THE MUNCHAUSEN SAGA

BY ANDREW YULE. PUBLISHED BY APPLAUSE THEATRE BOOKS (1991), ISBN 1-55783-060-6.

Terry Gilliam's fight to film and release *Munchausen*, told by all the participants.

THE ADVENTURES OF BARON MUNCHAUSEN

(1989) WARNER RECORDS 925826 (U.S.) SOUNDTRACK ALBUM OF THE TERRY GILLIAM FILM, BY MICHAEL KAMEN, WITH ADDITIONAL LYRICS BY ERIC IDLE FOR "THE TORTURER'S APPRENTICE," "A EUNUCH'S LIFE IS HARD," AND "PLAY UP AND WIN THE GAME."

NEARLY DEPARTED

STARRING ERIC IDLE. FIRST OF FOUR AMERICAN SHOWS BROADCAST APRIL 10, 1989

Grant Pritchard ....Eric Idle
Claire Pritchard...Caroline McWilliams
Mike Dooley...Stuart Pankin
Liz Dooley..Wendy Schaal
Derek Dooley ....Jay Lambert
Jack Garrett..Henderson Forsythe

Executive Consultant Eric Idle. Produced by Jack Seifert. Directed by John Rich.

SHOW 1:

(April 10, 1989, written by John Baskin and Roger Shulman) Adjusting to the afterlife, Grant wants to drive the Dooleys, the family now living in their house, out, but his wife Claire likes them. Grandpa comes over for dinner and brings his luggage, as he has just been evicted, which upsets Grant and Mike Dooley. Grant and Claire discover that Grandpa can see and talk with them.

Grandpa is upset at losing his driver's license, and therefore his job, and so Grant and Claire go down to the Motor Vehicle Department to help him pass; Grant forms the letters on the eye chart with his body.

SHOW 2:

(April 17, 1989, written by John Baskin and Roger Shulman) Grant is upset because Mike and Liz are going to the opening night of the symphony, and he and Claire aren't. Grandpa has to baby-sit Derek and make sure he does his homework, but when he has the chance to play poker, he gets Grant and Claire to do the baby-sitting. Derek calls his girl-friend over to study, and Grant tries to discourage their romantic designs by playing with the light and ringing the doorbell. His parents and Grandpa come home early; they're disappointed with Grandpa's dereliction of duty, and so Grandpa decides to leave in the middle of the night. Grant and Claire go to the bus station to retrieve him, and deal with a young punk.

SHOW 3:

(April 24, 1989, written by Sy Dukane and Denise Moss) Construction workers remodeling the house wake Grant and Claire early. The Dooleys find a box with items belonging to the Pritchards, including old pictures and love letters. Claire is upset to discover that Grant wasn't legally divorced when the two of them were married, and even finds a love letter he wrote to his first wife. Grant has to sleep on the pull-out bed with Grandpa, and the next morning Claire insists

they get married again by going to someone else's wedding, but the groom gets cold feet and a family fight breaks out.

SHOW 4:

(May 1, 1989, written by Neil Alan Levy) Derek's grades are falling, and his parents are concerned. Grant and Grandpa argue over TV, and Grant bribes Grandpa to let him watch *Masterpiece Theatre* instead of the Cubs game. Mike puts the TV in the basement because of Derek's grades. Grant and Claire go to school to find out how to improve Derek's grades and get the TV back, and help Derek deal with a bully who is stealing his homework.

 NOTES

It was NBC's confidence in Eric Idle and his work on *Around the World in Eighty Days* that led them to offer him a regular TV series of his own, which turned out to be *Nearly Departed*.

"NBC was very hot on me because I was in *Around the World,* and I was being cute as Passepartout, so they picked up the series," explains Idle. "Well, they didn't actually pick it up, they asked us to reshoot the pilot, because it was fairly lame. We got a very good director called John Rich, who is fabulous, and we went very well. That show started, and they said 'Okay, we'll do six,' and they ordered six. It was the classic American way—it took a year and a half on one script, the pilot, and then you've got three weeks to produce the next five scripts! It's a classic waste . . ." he laughs.

"So, we did pretty well, and it started to get good. We recast—we put in that very funny guy, Stuart Pankin, and the show was really starting to go. It was really getting together by the end. In fact, the last two are terrific. I did one where I played my own aunt. You never saw that one [in the U.S.]. The last two were very funny, and they should have put them on first. It got better and better, and we were nearly about to do a whole series, and then they just canceled us just before they were about to order another eighteen."

The experience left Idle frustrated with American network television.

"It would have been good, that series," he says regretfully. "I mean, it was getting to be

quite good, on everyone's terms, but they didn't allow it to grow. John Rich is still furious. He did *Dick Van Dyke* and *All in the Family* and he said both of them started the same way. Nowadays they don't develop, they won't go with a show and let it grow. So, you're straight on, and get results right away. And it didn't get bad results—it was like twenty-five, twenty-three, nineteen, twenty-two Nielsen ratings—it was up and down. I blame Lorne Michaels—he must have had a word with them. . . ." he laughs.

The first four *Nearly Departeds* aired in America, but Idle says he wasn't disappointed months later when the final two shows weren't aired in America, even though they were the best two of the series, because he had moved on to new projects.

"They pulled it off the air just like that. It was pointless—it wasn't like we were canceled, because we did them in January, and they aired in May, so it wasn't like it was any disappointment—I was in France at the time. I mean, why not just put out the next two—they were the funniest two. They aired here in England.

"As I say, we got better. That's what happens with comedy. But then they're mad, I mean, it's really impossible to do sitcom properly. We'd get notes from these twenty-three-year-old network people and they'd say 'Wear more green. Our research shows that people like people who wear green.' Really useful note, thanks a lot! I said 'Where's the exit?'"

 **CRITICAL COMMENTS**

"Nearly Departed has little going for it other than the always-enjoyable Idle, but even he can't deal with this sorry affair . . . the predictable, weary enterprise unleashes a tiresome pattern of `dead' jokes."

—Clifford Terry, *Chicago Tribune,* April 10, 1989

AROUND THE WORLD IN EIGHTY DAYS

FEATURING ERIC IDLE. FIRST BROADCAST APRIL 16, 17, AND 18, 1989, ON NBC-TV.

Phileas Fogg ....Pierce Brosnan
Passepartout ....Eric Idle
Princess ....Julia Nickson
Detective Fix ....Peter Ustinov

With cameo appearances by Jack Klugman, Roddy McDowall, Darren McGavin, Robert Morley, Stephen Nichols, Lee Remick, Jill St. John, Robert Wagner, plus Henry Gibson, John Hillerman, Christopher Lee, Patrick MacNee, Sir John Mills, and Pernell Roberts. Written for TV (from the Jules Verne novel) by John Gay. Produced by Renee Valente and Paul Baerwald. Directed by Buzz Kulik.

A mostly faithful adaptation of the Jules Verne novel. In order to win a bet, Fogg and his French servant, Passepartout, must travel around the world in the allotted time. Part one sees the wager and the trip through India, the second part follows their rescue of the princess in India through Burma to Japan, and the final part follows their journey through the American West and back to England; they are pursued all the way by a detective who is convinced Fogg robbed the Bank of England.

 NOTES

The six-hour adaptation of *Around the World in Eighty Days,* starring Eric Idle, was aired over three successive nights on American television. Strangely enough, Michael Palin set off to attempt a real-life version of the Jules Verne novel at about the same time Idle was filming. Idle says it was especially confusing to the viewers who often mistake him for Palin.

"It was just one of those strange coincidences that happens—`Is it Mike or Eric?' Now, we get totally mistaken for each other, so it doesn't really matter . . ." jokes Idle.

The film was actually shot in London and on location in Macau, Hong Kong, Thailand, and Yugoslavia, which was one aspect of the project that appealed to Idle.

"It was fun—again, it was a nice part. I loved Passepartout," notes Idle. "It was lovely locations, we went shooting all over. I love Pierce, I thought he was good, and Ustinov. It was a great acting part for me, because it wasn't entirely just silliness. It was a through part, and I played the same person. But it didn't quite work out. Pierce didn't quite make it, he didn't quite pitch his performance in the right way, I think he should have been funnier all the way through. I think they threw out a lot of comedy. It's the hit-and-miss stuff."

Around the World in Eighty Days was a learning experience for Idle in other ways, showing him the efficiency and speed with which TV films are done. "I was just amazed you could get through all that—how fast you could film, TV shooting. But it was phenomenal, I had a really great time. I loved it!"

 ## CRITICAL COMMENTS

". . . the whole thing lacks a feeling of joy and adventure. . . . A serviceable production, it is reasonably entertaining, but never seems to really make it, from the big events to the small touches. . . . Idle, who has made his reputation with an off-center brand of humor, is wasted in a conventionally comic role that requires him literally to take a roll in the hay."

—Clifford Terry, *Chicago Tribune*, April 14, 1989

THE BIG PICTURE

WITH A CAMEO APPEARANCE BY JOHN CLEESE. (1989) 100 MINUTES. STARRING KEVIN BACON, EMILY LONGSTRETH, J. T. WALSH, JENNIFER JASON LEIGH, MICHAEL MCKEAN, TERI HATCHER, DAN SCHNEIDER WITH CAMEO APPEARANCES BY EDDIE ALBERT, SR., RICHARD BELZER, JOHN CLEESE, JUNE LOCKHART, RODDY MCDOWALL, AND MARTIN SHORT. WRITTEN BY MICHAEL VARHOL, CHRISTOPHER GUEST, AND MICHAEL MCKEAN. PRODUCED BY MICHAEL VARHOL. DIRECTED BY CHRISTOPHER GUEST. RELEASED BY COLUMBIA PICTURES/ASPEN FILM SOCIETY. RCA-COLUMBIA HOME VIDEO #50263.

A young filmmaker faces a variety of personal and professional dilemmas as he tries to be a success in Hollywood.

 ## NOTES

John Cleese makes a brief appearance as a bartender named Frankie, first in a down-and-out fantasy sequence inspired by *It's a Wonderful Life,* shot in black-and-white, and in a quick, color, real-life shot. His screen time is just over a minute and a half.

The role is actually a serious, if slightly satirical, one for Cleese, and he doesn't have the chance to show off his talents to best advantage. He did the part as a favor to Jamie Lee Curtis and her husband, Christopher Guest, who directed.

"I got a call from Jamie, saying what about doing half a day's shooting to help her husband's pic, and I said I was absolutely delighted to do it," explains Cleese, but the actors' union stepped in to complicate the situation.

"Subsequently, I had to join Equity for some strange reason at that point," he explains. "Despite the fact that I'd already done *Silverado* and *Cheers.* One of those strange union regulations—you're allowed one or two appearances, and then you have to join. The only embarrassing thing was, no one in the American Equity offices recognized me or had any idea who I was! Consequently, they were all extremely kind and sympathetic to this fifty-year-old man who was coming in and deciding to try his hand at being an actor at this rather late stage of his life. It was, in fact, a humiliating experience in the Equity offices," he recalls with a laugh.

ERIK THE VIKING

WRITTEN, DIRECTED, AND CO-STARRING TERRY JONES. (1989) 104 MINUTES

Erik	Tim Robbins
Erik's Grandfather	Mickey Rooney
Freya	Eartha Kitt
King Arnulf	Terry Jones
Aud	Imogen Stubbs
Halfdan the Black	John Cleese
Slavemaster	Tsutomu Sekine
Loki	Antony Sher
Keitel Blacksmith	Gary Cady
Sven's Dad	Charles McKeown
Sven the Berserk	Tim McInnerny

Written by Terry Jones. Produced by John Goldstone. Directed by Terry Jones. Released by Orion Pictures/John Goldstone–Prominent Features, Orion Video #8748.

During a Viking raid on a village, a young Viking called Erik starts to question his life-style when he is supposed to rape a girl. Erik walks out on a drunken celebration in a pub afterward and tells his grandfather about his troubles. He goes to Freya for advice, and she tells him the Age of Ragnorrak is approaching. Erik decides to retrieve the Horn Resounding from the land of Hy-Brasil and go to wake the gods to prevent the end of the world.

Erik convinces a crew to come along on the journey. Loki convinces Keitel Blacksmith that Erik must be stopped, because if they are successful, his weapons-making business will collapse. As the crew says good-bye to the village and Keitel Blacksmith decides to go with them, several of the young ladies object. After Erik sorts out the seating arrangements, the ship sets sail.

Meanwhile, Loki visits Halfdan the Black, who is busy ordering his subjects tortured. Loki warns him that Erik wants to bring Ragnorrak to a close.

Erik's ship escapes a ship sent by Halfdan and passes through the Gates of the World, and

With Viking women in the foregroung, Jones prepares to shoot the Vikings' farewell to their village as they set out on their quest. Photo copyright Kim "Howard" Johnson

they see what they think is the sun for the first time in many years, but it turns out to be the Dragon of the North Sea. Erik causes the dragon to sneeze, blowing the ship many miles away. Their ship sinks in shallow water just offshore from Hy-Brasil.

They meet the princess and her father, the king, who welcome them, but warn if a sword spills any human blood, the land will sink. Everyone is very nice to each other there, and the king has his group sing for the visitors. Erik tells them he is looking for the Horn Resounding.

Erik goes to bed with the princess and has to hide when her father arrives using the Cloak Invisible. She promises to help Erik get to Asgard, but when they get on ship, Halfdan's ship arrives. They battle and defeat Halfdan's men, and the king gives them the Horn Resounding.

When Loki causes blood to be spilled, the country starts to sink, although the king refuses to accept the fact. The princess decides to travel with Erik and his men, but the rest of her people decline, and set sail. They blow the Horn Resounding and travel over the Edge of the World, arriving in Asgard. They blow the Horn Resounding a second time, and wake the gods.

Upon entering Valhalla, they find the gods are all children, and encounter the spirits of dead warriors. Odin is sending them all to hell, but

Harald the Missionary blows the Horn Resounding the third time, and the Vikings all arrive home, where Halfdan has captured the women and children. Halfdan is foiled when Harald lands on him in the returning ship.

 ## NOTES

The original drafts of *Erik the Viking* were actually based on Terry Jones's children's book *The Saga of Erik the Viking*, but the completed film has very little to do with the stories in his book.

"My book is actually twenty-eight separate stories about this Viking gang, and I sidetracked into a film. I saw a couple of sections of it and thought 'Hmm, good visuals there, going over the Edge of the World, and the Dragon of the North Sea. . . .' I started a script and got stuck about halfway through it.

"I thought it might help if I had somebody else involved, so I rang up Jim Henson. I asked him if he'd be interested in doing the monsters and things, and he said he was just about to ring me up, to ask if I'd be interested in writing a screenplay for this thing called *Labyrinth*. So instead of getting him involved in my film, I got involved in his!"

Subsequent attempts to redo the *Erik the Viking* screenplay, both alone and with others, proved unsuccessful. It wasn't until Jones found a Viking scene written by him and occasional partner Michael Palin (during a failed attempt to write another Monty Python film) that things began to click.

"I eventually decided I didn't want to make a film of the book. The book's the book, and I'd spend a year of my life setting up and making a movie of something I've already done—it's like retreading old material," relates Jones.

"I was about to chuck it all in, when I suddenly came across a scene that I had written, when Mike and I had been having a go at writing a Viking script. We had abandoned it—we actually produced a short screenplay, but neither of us liked it. I had written this scene for that. I suddenly thought 'Wait a minute, there's a story in this'—this Viking kills a girl and starts to think that maybe his way of life isn't right. So, I just started writing the script the way it is now. It wrote out very

quickly, in three or four weeks, and I decided to drag in anything from the book that was useful. The Edge of the World and the Dragon of the North Sea came in there, but nothing else is from the book—everything else is new."

Erik's home—a Viking village on a Norwegian fjord—was constructed down to the smallest detail in a huge sound stage at London's Shepperton Studios. The village itself was built upon a five-foot-high platform that extended over nearly all of the massive stage. This, in part, was to accommodate the man-made lake at one end of the building, where the dragon-prowed Viking ship was docked. Campfires were burning, a small duck pond was constructed in the center of the village, and pigs, ducks, and chickens roamed free; snowy mountain ranges appeared to veer off in all directions.

"I originally wanted to do it on location in Norway, but the way the film worked out, we couldn't—there was no daylight there at that time. To get both daylight and snow, it would have meant starting out there in the spring, and we couldn't have put the whole thing off for six months," reveals Jones, who says they were able to do a little exterior filming in Norway after the main production shooting had wrapped.

Most of the water sequences were shot in Malta, Jones explains. "We used Malta for Hy-Brasil, which is the Celtic version of Atlantis. So, we started off shooting in the court of the king of Hy-Brasil and then flooded the stage to shoot the Hy-Brasil sinking. We then got rid of that set and shot all of the water scenes—the battles, and things like that.

"In Malta, they've got this tank the size of a football pitch that we could flood up to four feet. It's built on the coast, so it looks out to sea, and has a spill wall on the sea side. So, when we chose the angle right, we were looking out to sea and an unbroken horizon. We could shoot our sea stuff in a tank, which is much more controllable. Actually shooting in the sea involves tides and weather conditions, and it gets a lot more tricky. Just shooting in a tank with four feet of water is much more controlled, and we could do it much quicker. We really wouldn't have been able to film it without that.

"Of course, we had snags. It's built right on the edge of Valletta Harbor, which must be one of the busiest harbors in the world!" he laughs. "We had a problem with boats on the horizon until we got it together. We eventually managed to reroute boats, but at first we'd sit there, waiting for the ships to go past."

The facilities at Malta allowed the crew to shoot some of their SFX there, including shots of the Viking ship going over the Edge of the World.

"They've actually got two tanks in Malta. They have their original tank, and then a deep tank, about thirty-five feet deep, which they built for the underwater sequences in *Raise the Titanic!* We used that as well.

"We built a ramp inside the deep tank and pumped up a huge quantity of water, to give us the Edge of the World waterfall. With various-sized models, it looked great. We actually did a lot of the model work out there," Jones says, explaining that a second unit directed by Julian (*Brazil*) Doyle was doing much of that filming.

"We had one go at the Edge of the World, but it didn't really work out the way we did it there. We shot it at night and lit it for day, so that when we crane up, we see it's daylight, with stars below—the stars didn't really work very well."

Another *Erik* effect shot in Malta was just as challenging for Jones the actor, in his role as the king of Hy-Brasil. When the last group of Hy-Brasilians are standing on the remaining roof as it sinks, the king is talking as he goes under.

"That was quite interesting to shoot. We were all sitting on this roof, and had these Maltese extras. It's quite tricky to stay underwater for that length of time, and the extras on the edge of the building were sinking underwater about thirty seconds sooner than me. They went under right at the beginning of this little speech, so they had to learn to hold their breath for quite a long time—and look unconcerned as they went down," he recalls with a laugh.

Terry Jones inside a London soundstage directing Erik the Viking. *Photo copyright Kim "Howard" Johnson*

"It was quite tricky. I had been practicing it and thought I wouldn't have any problem. The one thing I'd forgotten when we did the shot was that because I was talking the whole time—and it was essential for me to be talking the whole time I was going down—when I actually got underwater, I realized suddenly that I didn't have any breath left at all.

"I only managed to keep down for a couple of seconds. Fortunately, it was long enough for the shot. I didn't want to redo the shot, because I only had one wig, and it would take about an hour to get it all ready again!"

Not all of the challenging SFX shots were saved for Malta, though, including the battle with the Dragon of the North Sea. Jones explains that the creature is so huge, the whole thing is never seen on the screen; most of it was shot with models, but the eyes and nose were built life-size.

"The dragon was huge, vast—he took up the whole sea stage, and that was just the quarter-sized model! We never really see the whole dragon on screen, we only see bits of it. We did do some life-sized sections—its nose and eyes were life-sized, but those are the only things that weren't done as smaller models," he explains.

"Everything else was model-sized. At one point, Erik leaps onto its nose and goes into its nostril, so we had to build that life-sized," he laughs. "It's very big!"

Jones explains that he had to work with water, smoke, snow, and animals—traditional banes of all film directors. "The water's obviously a tricky thing—it slows everything up," he notes, and indicates that the use of smoke was also intended to disguise the fact that they were actually shooting in a studio.

"It was a wonderful set, but sets are always sets. When we saw the first day's rushes, the way we shot it still looked very `set-y' to me. So, we realized that we needed to keep it moving, keep it alive all the time. We always need wind and a bit of snow on everybody, and we had to break the background up a bit to keep it real."

Despite the workload involved for the film, Jones says he likes his job.

"I really enjoy directing." Jones smiles. "I always find it easier than *not* directing."

Erik the Viking marked his first attempt to direct his own non-Python script, which caused him to plan carefully during preproduction.

"I find I have to think it all out beforehand, and I have to have a storyboard. Even still, that just helps me keep my ideas straight. There are always unforeseen things happening—actors have different ideas of how to do things, and so they can change. But I wouldn't be able to do it if I hadn't really got tight storyboards. Sometimes we get away from the storyboards, and I suddenly realize there was a reason for having it like that on the storyboards. Then again, sometimes a storyboard is overelaborate—I'd think I needed all these shots, and we could cover it in one."

Jones says his approach to directing has mellowed over the last fifteen years, something he realized while shooting *Erik the Viking.* "I'm a lot more relaxed about it now. There's much less pressure, and I feel I tend to let things go a bit more—I don't want *everything* to be absolutely right.

"When we had some chickens up on a roof, they would *never* stay in the same place—but it's much more important to get all the sharp performances than to get the chickens in the right place. I wasn't going to hold the whole shot up just so we could have the chickens in the background—I know it doesn't matter in the end! So, I get less worked up about things like that.

"I'm also terribly lucky in having technicians around me who I really trust, so I can ease up on that. It's just wonderful to let George Akers, our editor, go off and edit, although I want to get my hands on the film at some point. I love cutting, actually, but I just have total confidence in George's cut, and he can do it so much quicker than I can! All I have to say is `I think we should do this with that,' and George can do it—generally, he comes up with ideas that are always improvements," Jones says.

Fellow Python John Cleese was invited along to play the villainous Halfdan.

"Actually, Halfdan the Black was one of the great kings of Norway. He was always reckoned to be a good bloke—until now!" Jones laughs.

In addition to Cleese, Python colleague Neil Innes scored the film for Jones and even did a bit of acting. "I wouldn't call it acting, though," he says, smiling. "Terry very kindly gave me some important parts with one or two lines, just because I happened to be in Malta. Supporting roles, like `Citizen at the Back,' `Man with Donkey,' and I think I'm `Third Drowned Hy-Brasilian.' They're always doing something to me. I got drowned in this film, though I wasn't alone—a lot of others got drowned too."

The critical reaction to *Erik the Viking* was generally negative, which Jones says was largely due to audiences expecting a Python movie.

"I was very upset by the critics' reaction to it, especially over here (in Britain)—it got annihilated by most critics. I think it was partly perception, and people were expecting something else. I knew it was dangerous starting with the rape scene, and I think it kind of set up the expectation of a Python kind of thing, which it isn't—the whole thing is basically a fairy tale. It's amazing, because it appeals like mad to ten-, twelve-, thirteen-year-olds, which really is who it was aimed at. Kids just love it, and that's what it was meant to be. I hoped adults would like it as well, but if you approach it as a Python film, you'll just say `What is this?'" he said, analyzing its reception from his London home.

"With Python, you're always telling people not to suspend their disbelief, but *Erik* was a fairy tale, so you *have* to suspend disbelief—if you don't, you don't get on to it. I should have done something else to get people to suspend their disbelief, whereas the first scene is actually more Pythonic, and you're led the wrong way."

Most upsetting to Jones was that his final cut of the film was not the one released in theaters in Britain and America.

"The worst thing for me was, both in the States and in England, was that the version that

Tim Robbins, Terry Jones, and Mickey Rooney watch a video monitor set up in the Viking village for a playback of the scenes just shot. Photo copyright Kim "Howard" Johnson

was released was not the final, best version. There was another one which was about ten minutes shorter, which I reedited with Julian Doyle, after it had been released over here, and I was wondering `Why did they go so against it?' One of the things I thought was the first location shot, which was Tim running over the mountain. I'd put this boiling sky onto it, and it hadn't quite worked. It was one of those opticals that arrived at the last moment, and we had to decide whether to put it in or not. I thought `I always wanted this boiling sky,' and what happened when I put this boiling sky on was, it made the mountains go flat. I don't know why, but they looked like they were cardboard. So, instead of being the first shot of actual location when he runs toward the mountains, it looked like he was in the studio again. And I thought, `It doesn't work. The first visual effect of the film, and it doesn't work.' So, I took that out and just put in the ordinary shot.

"We took out about ten minutes. The sinking's much better, and towards the end it goes a lot faster. Unfortunately, we weren't in time to get it cut for the American distribution, they'd already printed three hundred copies of the other one.

"But what *really* pissed me off was in the States, when they released it on video, despite everything we said and did, despite their assurances that they would release the right version on video, they released the same version. But in this country, the video is the proper version, the shorter one."

Still, Jones has hopes for the future of *Erik*.

"I think it's one of those things that will come back and be rediscovered someday. I got a card from Tim Robbins, and he said [reads] `People tell me how much they love *Erik*. He lives on!' People stop him in the street and tell him how much they really like it, where he probably thought it was a bit of a write-off," Jones declares.

"I find it too, especially when it was released on video. It did quite well over here on video. But I still wish we'd done it on location, rather than in the studio."

 ## CRITICAL COMMENTS

"Jones' yarn is good but its weave is laced with tired wit and half-hearted characterization. . . . This is a voyage to ho-hum land— pleasant to look at, expensively mounted, but bland as oatmeal."

—Johanna Steinmetz, *Chicago Tribune*, October 27, 1989

"*Erik the Viking* is an enjoyable romp of the imagination that will keep you smiling the whole way through.... Its humor takes the heroic grandeur of myth and shrinks it to an everyday level, even daring to poke fun at the Gods of Asgard themselves. Sweetened up with nice location shots and special effects, the movie moves into a very surreal view of history."

—Colin Brown, *Hesperia Resorter,* November 9, 1989

ERIK THE VIKING: THE SCREENPLAY

BY TERRY JONES. PUBLISHED BY APPLAUSE THEATRE BOOKS (1990), ISBN 1-55783-054-1.

The complete screenplay, credits, and over fifty stills from the Terry Jones film.

ERIK THE VIKING

BY TERRY JONES, ILLUSTRATED BY GRAHAM THOMPSON. PUBLISHED BY
ROBSON BOOKS (1989), ISBN 0-86051-631-8.

The comic-book adaptation of the Terry Jones film.

AROUND THE WORLD IN 80 DAYS

WRITTEN AND PRESENTED BY MICHAEL PALIN. FIRST OF SIX ONE-HOUR SHOWS
BROADCAST OCTOBER 11, 1989, ON BBC-1. WRITTEN BY MICHAEL PALIN. SERIES
PRODUCED BY CLEM VALLANCE. DIRECTED BY ROGER MILLS. BROADCAST IN
AMERICA ON ARTS AND ENTERTAINMENT CHANNEL IN JANUARY–FEBRUARY 1989.

"The Challenge" sees Michael accept the offer from the BBC to go around the world, retracing Phileas Fogg's journey and using only transportation available in Fogg's day. He packs and leaves from the Reform Club, where Terry Jones and Terry Gilliam see him and his BBC crew off. They take the Orient Express to Innsbruck and, because of a rail strike, have to take a bus to Venice. They take a garbage barge through the canals and catch a boat for Athens, Crete, and Cairo. They pass through the Corinth Canal and prepare to arrive in Egypt.

"Arabian Frights" sees a horse and driver deliver Michael to the station in Alexandria. When they arrive in Cairo, Michael goes to a football match. He plays a small role in an Egyptian movie, visits the pyramids, and rides a camel named Michael. Their original boat is canceled, throwing the schedule off, and they spend a day in Suez. They travel to Jeddah, Saudi Arabia, but their connecting boat is canceled. They have to drive to and transfer at Dubai, which will take longer, but is the only chance to complete the journey in eighty days.

"Ancient Mariners" follows Michael's drive across the Arabian peninsula to Dubai. They board a dhow—a medieval European trading ship, which only has two beds—to get to Bombay, and survive the six-day trip, though Michael is ill at one point. After a one-day delay at Indian Customs, they are a week behind schedule.

"A Close Shave" finds Michael pass through the Gate of India and get a shave from a blind street barber. They all board a train across India from Bombay to Madras. In Madras, they book passage on a Yugoslavian ship to Singapore, but the ship is late in leaving. They cross the Bay of Bengal to Singapore.

"Oriental Express" sees Michael and his crew barely make a modern ship in Singapore and then sail to Hong Kong. Only six days late on his arrival, Michael stays at a luxury hotel. While there, he visits the bird market, has a suit made, and visits a racetrack. He takes a three-hour ferry trip to Guangzhou, China. He orders snake at a restaurant, and the animal is killed and skinned at his table. They all take the train to Shanghai.

"Far East and Farther East" sees them in Shanghai, where Michael observes a jazz band in a coffeeshop. They board the ferry for Yokohama, a two-day journey. They then ride a bullet train into Tokyo, a fifteen-minute trip, and eat at a self-service sushi bar. After a stop at a karaoke bar, he sleeps at a capsule hotel. The next morning he boards a ship for America and crosses the international date line.

"Dateline to Deadline" finds him only two days late, with seventeen to go as he arrives in America. He stays in the Hotel Queen Mary and visits Venice Beach before boarding a train to Chicago. He stops in Aspen along the way and rides a dogsled and a hot-air balloon. After changing trains quickly in Chicago, he rides to New York and then crosses the Atlantic. He arrives in Liverpool, and the train into London is stalled by a bomb scare, but he finally arrives at the Reform Club to finish his trip.

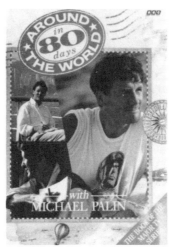

On September 25, 1988, Michael Palin left London with a five-man BBC crew to record his adventures on a round-the-world trip, a journey presented for a six-hour BBC documentary and in a full-length book that reprints Michael Palin's journal.

As it inspired him to go on a follow-up trip a few years later from North to South Pole, Palin says the first trip must have agreed with him.

"I can't have disliked it that much, because I'm off again!" he noted, shortly before embarking on the pole to pole trip. "It certainly didn't cure me of the travel bug—in fact, it stimulated me and made me more curious about what lies out there. Overall, you can't emulate the *Eighty Days* format, because a part of the fun of it was that it was a race against time, and I don't think you can do a travel series like that, with three days' break in eighty days of filming—you just can't do it. Physically, it's almost impossible. I was quite surprised that we got as much as we did out of it in the end.

"But when we hit somewhere like the dhow, it obviously struck a chord with people. A lot of people said that I made them feel as though they were on the journey with me, and they were very close to it all, and it made them want to travel the same areas. Also, the nicest thing of all, is I heard from people in the States who teach classes with kids, that it's not patronizing, and doesn't talk down, and doesn't try and seem that we're better than anyone else. That's high praise, and I'm flattered that people think that," notes Palin. "So, for all those reasons, I thought we ought to have a go at another one!"

AROUND THE WORLD IN 80 DAYS

BY MICHAEL PALIN. PUBLISHED BY BBC BOOKS (1989), ISBN 0-563-20826-0.

The detailed journal kept by Michael Palin during his around-the-world trip, copiously illustrated with photographs. The book is able to go into much more detail than the TV shows, and is much more than just a transcript of the series.

The Nineties

NUNS ON THE RUN

STARRING ERIC IDLE. (1990) 88 MINUTES

Brian ....Eric Idle
Charlie ....Robbie Coltrane
Faith ....Camille Coduri
Sister Mary of the Annunciation ....Lila Kaye

Cash Casey ....Robert Patterson
Sister Mary of the Sacred Heart ....Doris Hare
Father Seamus ....Tom Hickey
Morley ....Winston Dennis
Abbott ....Robert Morgan
Sister Superior...Janet Suzman

Written by Jonathan Lynn. Produced by Michael White. Directed by Jonathan Lynn. Released by Twentieth Century–Fox/Handmade Films. CBS/Fox Video #1830.

Brian and Charlie eat lunch in a café, complaining about their job robbing banks. They help their gang pull a clumsy bank heist in which one of the gang is accidentally shot by another member. Afterward, they complain about the new generation, and when a policeman tells them to move their car, Charlie picks his pocket.

Norm tells the pair he wants out of Casey's gang; they tell him Casey will kill him first. He says he also told Casey that both of them wanted out. Casey calls in Brian and Charlie and has them dispose of Norm's body in the river. They are still convinced Casey will have them killed.

Brian goes to a casino and gives Faith, a nearsighted waitress, his phone number. The next day Casey has Brian and Charlie follow the Triads, a rival gang. Brian suggests they steal the Triads' money for themselves and leave the country.

Out with Brian, Faith tells him she has a job dreaming for her school's psychology department, and they get acquainted. Brian admits to Charlie that he likes Faith. Charlie tells him he'll have to get rid of her soon. Faith overhears Casey say they're doing away with Brian and Charlie the next day during a theft from the Triads, and Faith tries to warn Brian away just before it happens. While Abbott and Morley, two of Casey's men, are holding up the Triads, Brian and Charlie hold up Abbott and Morley, and as they make off with the loot, the car bomb they planted goes off.

When Charlie's car is out of gas, they have to run off. Brian can't find Faith, who is slightly wounded by a gunshot. Brian and Charlie duck inside a convent to hide. They dress in nun's habits, but can't get away safely. After buying some makeup, they introduce themselves to the Sister Superior as Sister Inviolata of the Immaculate Conception and Sister Euphemia of the Five Wounds. She tells them the convent runs a college for eighteen- to twenty-two-year-old girls. Sister Mary of the Annunciation is called from an auditing meeting to show them to their rooms, and Brian and Charlie argue about staying.

Meanwhile, Faith assists the police but has broken her glasses. The other gang members report to Casey, who wants the money and wants Faith, to find out what she knows. Brian and Charlie are introduced to Father Seamus, who has eyes for Brian. Sister Superior enters with the police, who are investigating the robbery. Sister Superior has to question Sister Mary about missing funds and has Brian teach a religious studies class. Faith has stumbled into the convent, looking for Brian, but Charlie says she can't find out he's there. Charlie explains the Trinity to Brian, who has to teach it, while Charlie is assigned to the girls' physical education class.

Faith talks to the Sister Superior about joining the convent. When she isn't allowed to look around, she faints, and she is treated in the infirmary for the wound. Charlie teaches basketball, while Brian struggles through the religion class. Afterward, Brian retrieves the suitcase of money and goes to visit Faith, but tells her not to reveal that they're in the convent; he also tells her they can't get too involved with each other, and she says she's going to confession. Meanwhile, Charlie cowers in the girls' locker room after his class, and the two of them try to carry the two bags of money out, but Sister Superior insists they be locked in the storage closet.

Charlie realizes Faith may confess everything, so he has Brian hide and hear her confession. Faith says she loves Brian, and he cautions her to keep quiet about witnessing the crime. Charlie talks with the lewd Father Seamus. As Faith leaves the church, she is captured by the Triads.

Meanwhile, Brian hesitates about going to Brazil, because Faith loves him. Faith tells the Triads that Brian works for Casey, and they let her go, but she walks into a pole and is hospitalized. Charlie tries to make airline reservations on the phone, when Casey stops in and asks Sister Superior about the two men. The auditor tells Sister Superior they are missing £50,000, which Sister Mary has lost on the horses.

Brian and Charlie leave the convent to find Faith, but she isn't at her apartment, and they escape just as Abbott and Morley arrive to look for her. Escaping, they are pursued by Triads, and have to sneak back into the convent. They are spotted by Sister Mary, but after a thorough search in which they are not found, everyone thinks she's been drinking.

When Brian learns Faith is in the hospital, he insists on visiting, even though it's late. He meets Faith's father and brother there, and they threaten to kill the gangster she's been seeing.

The next morning Sister Mary spots Charlie's beard and discovers his and Brian's disguise, so they tie her up and break into the cabinet where their money is. Sister Superior asks them to explain, and they ask for absolution. They run off and steal a truck, pursued by Abbott and Morley and Sisters Superior and Mary, but make it to the hospital. Brian explains to Faith while Charlie dispatches the Triad spy, and they take Faith with them, with Abbott and Morley close behind. Dressed in nurse uniforms, Brian and Charlie make their escape, with Faith and one bag of money.

The sisters recover the other bag, the contents of which covers their deficit many times over, and Brian, Charlie, and Faith manage to make their flight to Brazil.

 NOTES

Nuns on the Run was strictly an acting job for Eric Idle, but proved to be his biggest film success in many years. He became involved with it through old friend Jonathan Lynn, and even though the Pythons' own film company, Prominent Features, didn't produce it, Idle still quickly agreed to be in it.

"Johnny Lynn came to me with it and asked me to produce it through Prominent. I tried to get it done through Prominent, but we didn't have our deal in place. So then Handmade picked it up while I was in Cannes. I was walking down the Croisette and I came face to face with Denis O'Brien, and he said `I really want to do *Nuns on the Run*—what do you think?' He took me out to dinner, and we had a three-minute business meeting, and he said `Will you do it? Will you be in it?' and I said `Yes.' He said `In that case, it's a movie.' So we did it, and that is truly the magic of cinema, *Nuns on the Run,* and the magic is that we took [in] three-and-a-half million pounds, and not a single penny went into my pocket! And that was just in England," declares Idle.

Although dissatisfied with the financial aspects, Idle says he enjoyed everything else about *Nuns on the Run.*

"A wonderful experience. I know Johnny Lynn, he directed my play, we were lads at Cambridge together, and we auditioned for the Footlights together with a script I wrote in 1963. He did *Yes, Minister*! and all that—he's wonderful," Idle notes, and says Lynn's intended cast was slightly different from the final result.

"He wanted me and Mike [Palin] to play it, and Mike was still trying to do *American Friends* at that time. So, I suggested Robbie Coltrane. We got Robbie, and Robbie's wonderful. He's fabulous—it was one of those great experiences, like `The Rutles' was a great experience. I really had a great time. It was the right team, all together, no shitty people intervening and trying to say `This is the way it should be done.'

"So, it was good fun. Then it went to Fox, and a very good man runs Fox, whose name escapes me—I must have show business Alzheimer's disease, I can't think of his name. Joe Roth. He loved it—still in love with it. He said it just needed a new ending, so he gave us another $500,000 to shoot a new ending and tighten it up, which was what it needed. They were really hoping for big things in America, and it didn't happen, and I felt rather sorry for him. But it did happen everywhere else—it happened in Europe, it was big in England, the video was big. It was nice, but they didn't make a killing in the States like they wanted to do."

The original ending for *Nuns on the Run* was actually more quiet and unexciting, notes Idle, before they were able to reshoot it. "We just left on a boat, and stood on the deck, and it was just like a nothing end. So, Jonathan Lynn, the writer, wrote much funnier stuff. I mean, it's nice to come back and write new stuff for a film when you get to do it. It's a good idea, it helps you a lot. 'I wish I'd done that scene.' And we did another of the love scenes, we retook, we did about three or four days more filming, and it really helped it."

Although they meant to promote *Nuns on the Run* well, Idle says they made mistakes in America.

"It was on the back of every bus, and they did a big television campaign, and they didn't open it wide until three weeks later. The American attention span is twenty minutes, and you've got to be on in the cinema if you're going to promote wide and spend all that money—it has to be there the next day. Otherwise, there's so much else intervening. So, I thought they didn't promote it very well, I thought they got it confused.

"They kept saying they wanted to do it like *Wanda*, put it in small theaters and build word of mouth—and then they didn't," he laughs. "They got confused and caught between two marketing plans. But, that being said, I think they never totally achieved it with that film, because Americans ultimately only want to see Americans in films—how can you blame them? So, you've got to have Americans in comedies. Python is only cult over there. You've got to make American films to be successful in America.

"It's a sweet film," sums up Idle. "One day I hope to get paid for it!"

 ## CRITICAL COMMENTS

"... a determinedly silly, wonderfully titled, and often very funny British import ... the tried-and-true proves surefire. The British have always had a way of pulling off such wacko fare, making it seem less weary or vulgar than it might in other hands. How they do it is something else. The seemingly effortless work of British comics seems part of the explanation. ... What also seems key is the movie's good-natured spirit: The church is kidded without an ounce of malice, and the comedy is witty and verbal, as well as physical. How can one resist a movie that not only features silly pratfalls and crazy chases but casually remarks of a recently deceased gangster: 'He never got last rites for his last wrongs.'"

—Joy Gould Boyum, *US*, April 2, 1990

AMERICAN FRIENDS

WRITTEN BY AND STARRING MICHAEL PALIN. (1990) 95 MINUTES

Francis Ashby	Michael Palin
Elinor	Trini Alvarado
Caroline Hartley	Connie Booth
Oliver Syme	Alfred Molina

Written by Michael Palin and Tristram Powell. Produced by Patrick Cassavetti and Steve Abbott. Directed by Tristram Powell. Produced by Millenium Films/Mayday/Prominent Features, presented by British Screen in association with the BBC. An MCEG Virgin Vision Release.

Francis Ashby is a senior tutor at Oxford who goes on holiday to the Swiss Alps. He relaxes his puritanical work ethic long enough to go skinny-dipping in a mountain stream, where he is observed through a telescope by Elinor. Lost along the trail, he meets Caroline Hartley and her seventeen-year-old ward Elinor, two American women vacationing in the Alps as well, and they make their way back.

Ashby rushes back to England suddenly when he hears that the

Palin, left, plays a character inspired by his own family history, with Trini Alvarado portraying the young object of his affections.

president of the college is dying; he tries to position himself as the next president but is challenged by young, worldly, modern Oliver Syme. While the two are jockeying for position, the two women arrive at the all-male college, and Ashby tries to discreetly show them around without jeopardizing his chances at the presidency. He has to fend off advances by Caroline, and in his struggle for the presidency and Elinor's affections, he wins one but loses the other.

 ## NOTES

American Friends was loosely based on the diaries of Michael Palin's great-grandfather, and it was a film he long attempted to make. Despite some lighter moments, it isn't a comedy, and is closer to a love story than any other genre, which may have made it difficult for him to raise the production costs. In fact, it took nearly five years from the first ideas to the final product, he says.

"It was the counterpoint to the last five years," notes Palin. "The initial idea came up in 1986, and I spoke to various people about it. Eric [Idle] encouraged me to have a go at writing it into a screenplay. It was different from what I'd usually done. It wasn't comedy; therefore, it was hard to know when it was right. In comedy, you read a page, and either it makes you laugh, or it doesn't.

With this, it was very difficult to know what to put in, what not to put in, how serious to be, how comic to be. . . ."

There were numerous interruptions along the way, but Palin never gave up; he says he was very happy with the final result.

"I was continually doing other things—I started writing in 'eighty-six, and along came *Wanda*, and then came *Around the World in 80 Days*, and I was still going in and out with this thing, doing rewrites. Although I lost heart occasionally, others, especially Steve Abbott and Patrick Cassavetti, said 'Right, we're going to go ahead, we're going to do this,' and they kept me at it, and I was very, very pleased with the result."

TOO MUCH SUN

STARRING ERIC IDLE. (1991) 98 MINUTES

Sonny	Eric Idle
Bitsy	Andrea Martin
Old Man Rivers	Alan Arkin

With Robert Downey, Jr. and Robert Downey, Sr. Directed by Robert Downey, Sr.

Sonny and Bitsy are the son and daughter of a dying millionaire, Old Man Rivers. He has left millions to his children, but one or the other must produce a child, or the money will all go to the conniving Father Patrick Kelly. Unfortunately, both Sonny and Bitsy are gay, and neither of them want to have a child, but to enjoy their luxurious life-styles, they must produce one.

Bitsy is convinced that she bore a child when she was sixteen, and tries to find her son, Frank Della Rocca, who is now a two-bit real estate swindler. Meanwhile, Sonny attempts to reproduce on his own with a woman, while Father Kelly schemes to divert the money to his own pockets.

 NOTES

Although the film was unreleased for over two years—and eventually premiered on Cinemax in America—Eric Idle is rather proud of his work in *Too Much Sun*.

"I like my character, who is a gay guy who has to jump on women. That, essentially, is a comedy idea. What you need is to bring the ideas into collision, but not extend it and go off into other little areas that he tended to ramble off in. You've got to face all the problems, and bring them in and try to address them honestly, and address them in the comedic fashion—which is essentially funny. I mean, how do two gay couples have a baby? It's almost a Shakespearean idea, but it needs far more skill on the text, and that, ultimately, is where it was just a drag. I made that film for nothing—we ended up shooting eighteen-hour days," Idle remarks.

Too Much Sun appealed to him initially because of the opportunity to play an American and to work with his friend Jon Lovitz.

"I quite liked Sonny, the character I chose, and I also wanted to play an American. That, for me, was the key thing—I wanted to see if I could play an American. It's easier to play a gay American, because they're more stereotyped in the gay roles, because they're sort of playing a role anyway, which is forced on them by society or whatever," he says. "It's easier to latch onto as an actor, because it's a slight parody of behavior anyway, so it's easier to act. It's much more extravagant and outrageous, and therefore interesting as an acting attempt.

"So, I enjoyed the moments of acting Sonny—it was interesting to me. I don't think it

was entirely wasted from my point of life. It was certainly wasted financially," he laughs. "And frustrating in a comedy sense. It was typical Hollywood. They call up and say 'Will you be in this film with Jon Lovitz and Alan Arkin?' Okay, yeah, that sounds like a fun cast. You get there, and it's not Jon Lovitz, because he backs out, and it's not Alan Arkin, because he hasn't finished his other movie.

"The producers sued Lovitz—I'm glad to say I defended him in court. I had to sit here, and they phoned me up, and they were saying 'You are now in the Court of California, your voice is now coming from a box in the court. Do you swear to tell the truth, the whole truth, and nothing but the truth?' and I'm sitting in my living room. Cleese is arriving for dinner, and I'm giving evidence! They were trying to blame Lovitz for all the overspends," explains Idle.

"Silly piece of shit . . . and you can quote me! I'll never work for that bunch of no-paying [inaudible expletives]. I worked for scale, and my expenses were more than my salary."

Idle looks at *Too Much Sun* as a great story for a film with enormous potential, which was ultimately wasted.

"The people that are best in comedy have no certainty about it, and are open to anything that is said. Whereas I find more and more that people who do not have any idea about comedy are very dogmatic about it," he notes. "That was a sort of sad film, because it could have been good, or at least interesting, because it was on that dangerous nerve area. But ultimately, it became about nothing. It just waltzed out of control. It was a nice idea—two gay couples had to produce this child. A simple, classic problem."

Idle says he overheard one exchange between Robert Downey, Jr., and his father that almost summed up his attitude on the filming. "I heard his father say to him 'When do you learn your lines?' Junior says 'Usually about the third take!'"

GBH

STARRING MICHAEL PALIN. FIRST OF SEVEN SHOWS AIRED JUNE 6, 1991, ON CHANNEL FOUR. STARRING MICHAEL PALIN AS JIM NELSON, ROBERT LINDSAY AS MICHAEL MURRAY, AND JULIE WALTERS AS MRS. MURRAY. WRITTEN BY ALAN BLEASDALE.

This eleven-hour drama of political corruption is based loosely on the events surrounding the Liverpool Militants in 1985. Michael Murray is the newly elected leader of the local Labour Council, a wisecracking, sunglasses-wearing urban politician who wants to use the council as a launching pad for his own high-profile career; he relishes sweeping aside the old order and bringing in his left-wing cronies. Jim Nelson, headmaster of a school for children with special needs, stands against him as a high-principled accidental tabloid hero, when inefficient picketing leaves him as the only council employee working during a day of labor action.

Murray decides to crush Nelson, but his mission of revenge, revealed in a number of flashbacks, is not as easy as he thinks.

 ## NOTES

Michael Palin was happy to play such a different role in *GBH*, which he said was unlike anything he'd ever done before. He was convinced by the Alan Bleasdale script, which ended up being much more than the standard good versus evil story it first appeared to be, and he got good critical notices for the dramatic part.

"Alan Bleasdale isn't known in the States, but he's one of the most respected and successful television dramatists we have here," explains Palin. "He's also written stuff for the theatre. His work is very British and local, in a way, and deals with situations from a fairly critical and usually left-wing perspective.

"He got in touch with me and said he'd written this character of a charismatic council leader who's gone completely mad, and it's set up in the north of England. It's really an examination of what happened in political life in Liverpool in the last years of the Thatcher administration," he says, explaining that it was a a drama with elements of comedy.

"It tells of this council leader trying to terrorize this schoolmaster into toeing the party line. The schoolmaster is a sort of a stroppy, independent-minded character who fights against this, and the two of them go through a lot of adventures, dragging themselves down as they go.

"He offered me the part of council leader. It was a huge work, ten hours of television. I was very flattered to be asked to do it and agreed. Then, for various reasons, he changed the casting around, and I played the stroppy schoolmaster, Jim Nelson, who is also cracking up! It was a seven-part series of ninety-minute films. There was a lot of comedy in it, and I suppose it was a meaty acting role—a chance to see if I could do some meaty acting."

Palin wasn't involved in any of the writing, and says he was glad to be able to limit his participation to acting in *GBH*.

"I was able to concentrate purely on acting. After doing *American Friends*, where I felt responsible for writing and many other aspects of the production, it was a relief to do a purely acting role."

JACK AND THE BEANSTALK

TOLD BY MICHAEL PALIN. (1991) 30 MINUTES. WRITTEN BY ERIC METAXAS. MUSIC BY DAVE STEWART. DRAWINGS BY EDWARD SOREL. PRESENTED BY RABBIT EARS PRODUCTIONS/ DISTRIBUTED BY UNI DISTRIBUTION CORP. VIDEOCASSETTE REV 10260.

Michael Palin reads the traditional story of "Jack and the Beanstalk" on this videotape, which is illustrated with a variety of color drawings in this entry in the Rabbit Ears "We All Have Tales" series of thirteen stories.

 NOTES

"Rabbit Ears Productions, an American outfit, approached me to read the 'Jack and the Beanstalk' story for a series of videos for children," explains Palin.

"There was going to be a series of videos, compact discs, and pictures; they were trying to provide it in these different forms. They also wanted well-known actors and musicians together. At one time, it was going to be George [Harrison], but that didn't work out, so Dave Stewart did the music. I just went into Pinewood Studios one day for an hour and a half and recorded the story."

THE FISHER KING

DIRECTED BY TERRY GILLIAM. (1991)

Jack Lucas	Jeff Bridges
Parry	Robin Williams
Anne	Mercedes Ruehl
Lydia	Amanda Plummer
Aging Chorus Boy	Michael Jeter
Parry's Trio	Bradley Gregg
	William Jay Marshall
	William Preston
Young Punks	Jayce Bartok, Dan Futterman

Written by Richard Lagravenese. Produced by Debra Hill and Lynda Obst. Directed by Terry Gilliam. Released by Tri-Star Pictures. Also on videocassette and laser disc.

(Gilliam notes that when *The Fisher King* was released on laser disc, all of the scenes that were cut out of the final print were restored, scenes that were printed in the script book.)

The hottest D.J. in New York, Jack Lucas finds out that one of his regular callers has just massacred a number of people at a trendy New York bar, apparently as a result of a conversation with Jack.

A year later the broken, melancholy Jack is working at a video store run by his girlfriend Anne. One night after a drinking bout, two punks try to beat him and douse him with gasoline; he is rescued by the homeless Parry and three of his friends.

The following morning Jack wakes up in the boiler room where Parry lives. Parry fears the evil Red Knight, and tells Jack that the Little People say Jack is the man who will help him find the Holy Grail, which Parry believes is in the home of billionaire Langdon Carmichael. As Jack rushes away, the building superintendent tells him that Parry was once a college professor whose wife was killed a year ago in a massacre at a trendy New York bar. Parry became catatonic for months and is still unable to remember his past.

After telling Anne that helping Parry may be the way to help himself recover, Jack tracks down Parry. He tries to give him money, but Parry is more interested in watching over the awkward, gawky office worker Lydia, with whom he is in love. Parry says the only way Jack can help him is by recovering the Holy Grail; when Jack tries to help him recover his memory, Parry sees the Red Knight being frightened off by Jack. They chase the Red Knight to Central Park, where they help an aging, drunken chorus boy to the emergency room.

Parry takes Jack along to Grand Central Station, where he watches Lydia go to her train;

Jack meets all of Parry's friends, and all of the commuters break into a waltz during rush hour.

Jack tracks down Lydia, and he and Anne devise a plan to get Parry together with her, with the assistance of the aging chorus boy and a free video membership. With Parry posing as an employee, the four of them go out for Chinese food; Parry adores Lydia, and she starts to fall for him. By the end of the evening, Jack slips Parry his wallet so he can cover expenses and goes home with Anne. After Parry kisses Lydia good night, he is confronted by his past, represented by the Red Knight, and a trio of street punks beat him severely.

The next morning Jack feels vindicated, and tells Anne he's ready to get back to work, but thinks they should cool their relationship. Suddenly they get a call. Jack's wallet has been found on Parry, who has been beaten back into catatonia. The doctor says he's in the state he was in after his wife died. After the doctor leaves the room, Anne walks out of Jack's life.

Six months later, Jack is rich and successful again, but suddenly realizes he is becoming what he used to be. He tracks down Parry, still catatonic; Lydia has been looking after him. He decides to recover the Holy Grail for Parry.

Jack scales Carmichael's mansion and finds the "Grail," saving Carmichael from near suicide in the process. After he returns the cup to Parry, he begins to recover, to Lydia's joy, and Jack reconciles with Anne.

 NOTES

For as long as Terry Gilliam has been making movies, he always said he would never do a project like *The Fisher King*, but after his battles over *Brazil* and *Baron Munchausen*, he admits he was tired of fighting studios. The script for *The Fisher King* arrived at a time when he was finally willing to shoot a movie in Hollywood and direct someone else's screenplay.

"It's funny that this particular script turned up when I was feeling rather shagged out after *The Adventures of Baron Munchausen*, and pretty depressed. It was just a funny script, and easy reading. It was one of those scripts that I wished I

had written, because I understood the attitudes and the characters totally.

"The fact is, it really involved four characters, and it didn't involve special effects. I'd really been thinking after *Munchausen* that I wanted to do something small, so there it was."

At the time, Gilliam was going to make another attempt to write a project with Michael Palin, but schedule conflicts and other problems prohibited that work.

"The project that I'd been working on at the time, which was *The Minotaur*, was going rather slowly, and the actual script really wasn't coming together properly. This thing popped up and I thought I'd better think about it. Then the producers and a studio executive flew over here and I talked to them, I said 'Why not do the very thing I said I would never do?' The important thing about making rules is to then break them, it seems!" he says, laughing. "So, there we did it!

"I always said I wouldn't work in the States, I said I wouldn't do somebody else's script, and I said I wouldn't work for a studio, *especially* I wouldn't work in Los Angeles—and I did all of those things. The extraordinary thing is, it's actually proved to be the easiest film I've ever made."

Gilliam and his crew did have to contend with a number of problems, most related to filming exteriors on location in New York.

"Shooting in New York is extremely difficult, to say the least—it's nonstop noise. The city just would not stop to let us get on with what we were doing. It obviously thought its business was more important than ours!" he jokes.

"We made it difficult for ourselves, too, by choosing locations like Park Avenue and Fifth Avenue and Madison Avenue, so that doesn't help. On Madison Avenue, we were trying to make it appear to be Fifth Avenue—this particular building we were shooting around beyond Fifth Avenue, facing the park. Well, Fifth Avenue goes the opposite direction of Madison Avenue, and that meant we had to turn the traffic around, which isn't the easiest thing to do. On Fifth Avenue, we were busy shooting the Red Knight—this Knight with all this smoke and flame on his horse, and we were doing it at rush hour. So, when you're doing things like that, you're asking for trouble.

"That was the rough stuff. Basically, it was straightforward, because it wasn't complicated special effects work. It was about four people. It was nice just to be able to concentrate on the acting, and bringing the characters out and trying to keep my imagination in check."

Gilliam's imagination, which made studio accountants cringe on *Baron Munchausen*, was much easier to hold back on *The Fisher King*, he explains.

"Every time I started to elaborate or make things more complicated or fantastical, I kept checking with [screenwriter] Richard Lagravenese. I'd say 'What do you think? Am I pushing too far?' I kept him around the whole time, because it's his script—as far as I was concerned, it's his film, and I

wanted to make sure I wasn't violating it. I kept him there as my conscience. . . .

"There are certain things that weren't in the original script that I now have in there, like a thousand commuters during rush hour at Grand Central Station, all waltzing. That was never in the original script," Gilliam reveals. "Things like that were my additions, just because it seemed like a good idea at the time. That was the thing that just worried me the whole time, though—I didn't want the characters to get lost or pushed into the background by big ideas. The Knight is pretty spectacular, and that was one of the things I was worried about.

"First of all, to get a horse painted red is harder than you'd think. And to get a Knight with smoke pouring out of its armor everywhere, and flames shooting out of its helmet—this proved to be a bit more difficult than we had envisaged, because it all had to be able to work in New York City, not out in the protected environment of a studio. We were right in the heart of the city! That ended up consuming so much time and energy, I was beginning to think the film was about the Red Knight. Once you've expended that kind of energy, you want to shoot it for all it's worth. And I thought 'Uh, oh, I'm getting in trouble here . . .' But in the end, I don't think it overbalanced the original material."

Shooting some of the quieter scenes between the actors was one of the most enjoyable parts of *The Fisher King* for him, even though Gilliam has built much of his reputation on flashy visuals.

The Fisher King *Criterion laser disc has material cut from the final release, as well as a running commentary by Gilliam*

"It's the first film where I haven't done a storyboard. I decided to test myself and see if I can do it without a net," he says with a laugh. "I really enjoyed the acting. In a way, it's just me showing to people that I've always been directing actors. People are often confused by the visuals and other stuff in my films and a lot of times I don't think they notice that there are a lot of terrific performances going on. So I thought okay, this time we'll show people that I've been doing it from the beginning—it's nothing new.

"It was nice. I really enjoyed it. I felt really confident, and I know the actors have given the best performances they've ever done on film, all four of them. It's a phenomenal cast. Everyone who sees it agrees that it's a terrific cast, and they all give amazingly wonderful performances."

The only actor Gilliam had worked with before was Robin Williams, who played the King of the Moon in *Baron Munchausen*; Gilliam says he and his star are alike in many ways.

"Robin, in a way, suffers from the same problems I do. One always goes straight for the over-the-top, biggest, most spectacular, and feels comfortable doing funny things. When we first met and talked about it, I said that everything about the part of Parry, no matter how funny it is, has really got to be based on the pain of his particular tragedy—the loss of his wife. If that's solid, we can be as silly as we want, but it's got to come from that.

"One of the reasons I wanted Jeff was because I knew Jeff would ground both of us, and stop us from going the cheap and easy routes that we were comfortable with," he explains.

"Like any comedian, Robin is more nervous about really exposing himself than most actors, because almost every comedian uses comedy as a defense mechanism, so they can avoid revealing what they really are and what they're really feeling. I just had to keep making sure Robin was feeling confident and secure so that he could actually open up the wounds as much as they needed to be opened up for this thing. He's nonstop inventive, and in a sense I was always pulling him back, trying to stop him from doing that, because he doesn't need to. He does it because he feels comfortable doing it."

Still, Gilliam says he allowed for Williams's input in *The Fisher King,* largely because he would have been foolish not to.

"There would always be at least one take that was just for him to ad lib whatever he wanted to, to come up with anything that might happen. He never felt comfortable unless he was given that opportunity to go at it. I didn't use many of those takes, though—we pretty much stuck to the original script. But there are several ad-libbed moments that are wonderful, and you gain, so it's silly not to use Robin for that."

Williams was actually involved with *The Fisher King* before Gilliam, and indirectly led to the director getting the job.

"The whole thing was a bit weird, a bit chicken-and-eggy, because Robin was interested

Terry Gilliam poses with a friend in his office. Photo copyright Kim "Howard" Johnson

in it, and the studio was interested in him," reveals Gilliam. "Apparently, there were only a handful of directors that he was interested in working with, and I was on that list, so I think the studio then approached me as a way of securing Robin. So, once I said yes, I had to go through it with Robin and convince him. I did actually have to spend a fair amount of time with him and his managers and agents to secure the whole thing."

Gilliam says their work on *Munchausen* was one of the things that led to their collaboration.

"We had a really good time on that one. We got on really well and it was great fun, so he felt comfortable," he explains.

He says he cast Jeff Bridges in part because audiences like him so much.

"That was definitely one of the reasons. I knew we could make him a real asshole and the audience would still stay with us, because Jeff is likable—they just go for him. It's a strange bit of casting for the part of a New York, smart-ass D.J. The first person you would think of is not Jeff Bridges. It was the thing that excited me the most, because it was the scariest part of the casting. It was so much of a leap into areas that Jeff had never really dealt with. I got a glimpse of it in *Baker Boys*, enough to get me excited.

"In a strange way, I also like Jeff doing it because it's really a fairy tale, and Jeff is the representative of America, and where it's got to. It starts out with this D.J., and his smart-ass, sarcastic attitude—he's got everything in the world, it's like a dream come true. He's clever, rich, and successful, and it's totally empty. It's more interesting than taking some street-smart New York guy and turning him into this kind of D.J.—if you take a guy from the heart of America and turn him into that, he's got further to fall than another guy who's already started that way. I quite liked the idea of coming out of the heart of America and aspiring to being this kind of person. I don't know if any of that's in there. . . ."

The part of the fast-talking disc jockey sounds, on the surface, like Williams's role in *Good Morning, Vietnam*; when the project was first announced, Gilliam says many people thought Williams would play the D.J., but he's happy with his decision.

"I actually think it works best this way. The thing about Robin and Parry is that Parry is totally vulnerable and crazy, and Robin is that. Robin is so vulnerable—and it shows—that you get much more out of him being Parry. I don't know if Jeff would make a good Parry, frankly. I think the way we did it was right. When we were getting together a list of people to play the part of Jack, a page-and-a-half list that the casting director came up with, strangely enough, all the names were there in capital letters and lower casing, except for one name that was in all lower casing, and it was Jeff Bridges. Which is wonderfully odd," he recalls with a smile.

"He was not the first choice. We were going a much safer route to begin with. Billy Crystal was actually involved before I got involved—there was talk of a package of him and Robin, and I didn't want two comedians in it. I thought that was wrong. From the beginning when I talked to Robin, I said I wanted a really solid actor who would ground it all."

Even though he didn't write the screenplay, Gilliam still managed to make the film his own.

"Unfortunately, I have this tendency," he laughs. "But that's why I was drawn to it. I read it and I thought `I understand all this stuff. . . .' On one hand, it was easier doing it because it hadn't sprung from my brain initially, and it wasn't something that I'd spent a lot of years working on and then tried to raise the finance. In that sense, it was much easier, and I could play the trick with my own mind, saying that it was Rich Lagravenese's film, and I was just the director, just trying to get his film on film. Doing that actually relaxed me a lot, and so the whole thing was less pressured, and I never felt the panic of not being able to achieve what I had been thinking of for a year or two."

The Fisher King didn't disappoint his fans, critics, or the public in general, and it proved to be the award-winner many thought it might. Mercedes Ruehl won the Best Actress Oscar, and the same award from the L.A. Film Critics. Robin Williams was nominated for the Best Actor Oscar (and won the Golden Globe), while *The Fisher King* won the highest award at the Toronto Festival of Festivals. Gilliam's response to the latter: "Thank you for justifying my decision to sell out."

Despite its accolades, the director says he still isn't sure if *The Fisher King* is a "Gilliam film."

"I don't know what it is," he laughs. "It's `Gilliam Sells His Soul and Goes to Hollywood.' In a strange way, it's clearly my film somehow, and yet it isn't my film. That's the odd thing. I think you can actually say it's a Gilliam film, and yet there's nothing in there that makes it a Gilliam film—it's written by somebody else, it was somebody else's idea.

"It's kind of intriguing, that one. . . . I suppose this is what happens with directors. `Is this an Oliver Stone film?' I mean, it's what you choose to do as director. You're still always the filter. Whether it's the script, originally, that you're choosing to do, because it's what you're about—it works that way, I think. You don't *have* to write the stuff. When you're making the film, the actors are doing things all the time. I'm not doing them, they're not my ideas—all I do is be the filter, I say `That stays' or `That goes.' In that sense, you always make the choice toward what your own sensibilities are."

Prior to *The Fisher King*, Gilliam admits that he felt he had to write the script in order for a film to really be his, but says this film changed his mind.

"I just wanted to make the other films totally mine. It's like a painting—it's having an idea and carrying it through all the stages. You may hire a lot of assistants along the way who can paint grass or trees better than you can paint them. To me, the reason for making films was always that I had an original thought, and I wanted to carry it through. It's a great relief not to have to do it all," he says with a giggle. "I quite liked this way of making films."

Gilliam has always talked about his three previous films as constituting a fantasy trilogy, with *Time Bandits* portraying the fantasist as a boy, *Brazil* showing the fantasist as a young man, and *Munchausen* viewing the fantasist as an old man. *The Fisher King* doesn't have a place in that trilogy, he explains.

"I think it's my 'Mature Film,' is what it is—'the one where he at last comes of age,'" he laughs. "I think we can safely say it's my Hollywood Film, since I did make it there, and it's for a studio, and all that stuff. . . . What's nice about it is because I was more relaxed and less frenetic about all this, I think it actually does have a certain 'relaxed maturity' about it, or 'confident maturity.' I've maintained a much cooler attitude toward this film through all the stages, and it's interesting to see how it works.

"The themes are similar—there's still the elements of fantasy and reality, and madness and sanity, materialism and romance—they're all there. And there's definitely the search for the Holy Grail in there! It fits in the same themes. I want to think of *Jabberwocky*, I see some similarities there. . . ."

The Fisher King is actually different from all of his prior movies, he feels. "It's not really like any of them—that's what's intriguing. I actually don't know how to compare it to anything—I don't even know how to describe the film very well. I was looking at it yesterday, and it's like three films all put together—it shifts gears and styles, and somehow it all holds together and seems to work. It's the most eclectic film I've done. It's like several different ones all strung together somehow."

One of the most interesting shots in *The Fisher King* sees Parry lying on his back in Central Park, telling Jack the legend of the Fisher King. Essentially a long monologue, Gilliam decided to take a chance when filming it.

"I actually did it in one shot," he explains. "We ended up cutting, because it ran about five minutes long! There are actually two cutaways from it. Robin and Jeff are lying on the ground, with Robin in the foreground and Jeff behind him—the camera is right on the ground, so it's basically a huge profile of Robin's head and chest, and then you see Jeff behind him. The only cutaways are to Jeff, reacting twice. We just play it on that one shot.

"I'd had all sorts of plans—I was going to be craning here and there, and I said 'No, no—I'm just going to be bold here.' One shot. I covered myself with the closeup of Jeff, which gets us through the cuts in the speech, but there's no trickery or cleverness there.

"It's right in the middle of the film, it's exactly halfway. We've been going with one kind of thing, and from then on, it's actually trying to get this date together, trying to get the girl for Robin. It's really weird, it moves into this completely different gear. It's even a different style at that point, it just feels different. Then it seems to tie itself up, you think it's all over, happy ending, and then it all completely unravels. Most people say it keeps twisting and turning, and think it's completely unpredictable.

"All four of the main characters really are great. I certainly think these are their best performances."

There are also some fantasy elements in *The Fisher King* for most fans of his previous films as well.

"There's the Red Knight. We gave 'em the best knight ever seen on film," he laughs. "We also have the wonderful scaling of a castle in New York, Carmichael's place. For Carmichael's town house, where the Grail is kept, we found this armory up on Ninety-fourth and Madison. It's a medieval tower, and we made it into a town house. It goes into the wonderful Indiana Jones sequence. There's a wonderful Holy Grail story with the Fisher King speech—the search for the Holy Grail in the late twentieth century."

Shooting the Red Knight sequences was more difficult than they had anticipated, says Gilliam.

"We got a big Clydesdale, a Percheron stallion, to be the horse. What I was trying to do with the Red Knight was to make a suit of armor that looked like it had been left under the ocean for several years, rusted with coral growing out of it—it was all ripped apart. I'm not sure if that's what we got, but that's what we set out to do," he says with a laugh.

"It actually ended up more beautiful than I was hoping. I actually wanted to do him more visually horrifying, but he was actually quite a beautiful knight. He also looked like a cross between a knight and one of those scorpion fish in the South Pacific, with all these beautiful fins and spines coming off—he looked kind of good, actually.

"We wanted the horse to be this flame-red, and that seems to be the one color horses don't grow in. We had this white one that kept growing pink on us, and the more we painted him, the pinker he got—he went magenta for a while! We finally managed to get enough on him. We actually had two horses, so the one could be worked on while the other was being used. . . .

"I didn't actually shoot him in slow motion as much as I'd done in the past—I always used that to make the thing feel bigger and weightier. There are some shots where he's in slow motion; in others he's just rocking along. He ends up being pursued through Central Park, which is quite nice. Central Park becomes like a medieval kingdom for a brief moment."

Although it couldn't compare to *Baron Munchausen*, Gilliam says *The Fisher King* still had some tough scenes to shoot. "Physically, the most difficult scene was climbing this tower, because we were working on Madison Avenue, and we had to bring in all these cranes to put the camera on. That was a slow and tedious process."

"The one that came closest to almost not working was the big waltz at Grand Central Station, where we had a thousand extras trying to learn to waltz. We had supposedly gone to all these dancing schools for people who would know how to waltz, and we got 'em down there, and most of 'em didn't know how to waltz. We were sitting in Grand Central Station with a thousand extras and a choreographer trying to train them, and we've got to be out of there by dawn, when the trains start arriving. The

Between films, Terry Gilliam designed the poster for the 1991 London Film Festival—his first commissioned work in years.

camera finally started turning about four-thirty in the morning, and we had to be out of there at six! That was a close one. We just started rolling cameras, we were pushing and shoving. . . .

"There's shots at the end of it where people are getting off the first trains, and we're still shooting. I said `Robin, just go in there,' and we had everybody walking back and forth in circles, I had the crew going in there just to make the scene look busy as the first commuters were coming off the train. We were not very popular at Grand Central Station!"

Gilliam compares the waltz sequence here to the raising of the hot-air balloon in *Munchausen*, in that both of them were do-or-die attempts at grabbing shots. Fortunately, he says there were very few problems compared to his previous experience.

"That's what was nice about this film. Whatever problems we had, they were *nothing* to what I had been through in the past. I was able to float rather balloonlike through the whole thing."

Despite his headaches and hassles, Gilliam says he'll probably always go on making films, because he has little choice.

"I like movies. I hate the process, I hate all the bullshit, but I still like movies. My skills apply very nicely to films. It's very perverse. That's what's so funny about going after *Munchausen* and doing *Fisher King*, because it's basically the same studio, Columbia/Tri-Star. The irony of going right back into the lion's mouth after *Munchausen* when a lot of people said `The guy will never work again' is too good to miss," Gilliam laughs.

"There are so many people who are so keen to count you out—I never felt like that. I didn't have a problem. I know I'll keep making films, and I can continue if there's enough people to get the money from. I just thought it was interesting to go into Hollywood and see if I could actually get my hands on a bit more of their money!"

 ## CRITICAL COMMENTS

". . . The latest mad epic from ex-Monty Pythonite Terry Gilliam is more accessible than either *Brazil* or *The Adventures of Baron*

Munchausen. It is, however, an indisputable mold-breaker—an oft-beguiling but squirrelly mix of fantasy and reality. Robin Williams has some touching scenes and gets to cut up. Yet *King* belongs to second-billed Jeff Bridges—arguably the role of his career. . . . *King* is 2 1/4 hours of darkness and sun, and at times I thought Gilliam might lose control. He doesn't (quite), and given the ambitious material, that's saying something."

—Mike Clark, *USA Today*, September 20, 1991

"How the lives of Jack, Parry and the women they love are intricately interwoven keeps *Fisher King* soaring through one surreal scene after another. . . . *Fisher King* bypasses easy formula moviemaking to score as a bold, unique and exhilarating cinematic trip."

—Bruce Williamson, *Playboy*, November 1991

". . . The swoops and dives into compromise don't affect the rush you get when the film is flying high with Gilliam's visionary inventiveness. *The Fisher King* restores our belief in the power of movies to transform reality, even temporarily. So what if it's not perfect? It's magic."

—Peter Travers, *Rolling Stone*, October 17, 1991

THE FISHER KING

PUBLISHED BY APPLAUSE THEATRE BOOKS (1991), ISBN 1-8362-4213-0.

The complete screenplay of the Terry Gilliam film, with an appendix of deleted or altered scenes and illustrated with 200 photos. "The script book is a very confusing thing," says Gilliam, "because it's not the final script, and it's not the film. It was one of the later scripts, but it's not the finished film, so there's stuff in there that will be included on the laser disc."

THE FISHER KING

A NOVEL BY LEONORE FLEISCHER, BASED ON THE RICHARD LAGRAVENESE SCREENPLAY. PUBLISHED BY SIGNET AE 7222 (1991) ISBN 0-451-17222-1.

The novelization of the Terry Gilliam film.

AN AMERICAN TAIL 2: FIEVEL GOES WEST

FEATURING THE VOICE OF JOHN CLEESE. (1991)

JOHN CLEESE PROVIDES THE VOICE OF CAT R. WALL, THE VILLAINOUS CAT. WRITTEN BY FLINT DILLE. PRODUCED BY STEVEN SPIELBERG AND ROBERT WATTS. DIRECTED BY PHIL NIBBELINK AND SIMON WELLS. RELEASED BY UNIVERSAL PICTURES/AMBLIN ENTERTAINMENT.

The story involves the further adventures of Fievel the Mouse in the late 1800s. He and his friends are attacked by Cat R. Wall and his evil cats, who trick them into going West by using a mouse puppet. On the train, Fievel spots Cat R. Wall and learns of his scheme.

When they reach the Western town of Green River, Cat R. Wall gains the trust of the other mice. Fievel and his friends have to rescue the town from Cat R. Wall's giant mousetrap.

 ## NOTES

John Cleese has done voice-over acting in commercials and radio shows; *An American Tail* marked his first extensive voiceover work for an animated feature.

"I met one of the producers at the Italian Oscars when I got my Oscar (for *A Fish Called Wanda*). He mentioned this animated film coming up, and would I do a voice, and I said 'Sure, ask me close to the time.' I enjoyed the first *American Tail*, and so I was very pleased to do it. I said sure, a couple of days in the studio should be great fun. I love sound studios anyway—there's none of the hassle and boredom and time-wasting you get in television. The

only shock was the size of the fee, which was probably the smallest fee I've been paid in ten years. But I decided to do it anyway," explains Cleese.

"Apparently, Spielberg is famous for his tightfistedness, but it's the smallest fee I can remember earning in recorded history. I was a little bit ticked, because I was asked about publicity, and I said I was busy and couldn't help. Then I got another more official request. I sent back a message saying 'Tell Mr. Spielberg that I always make it a point not to publicize my charitable activities!'"

SO THIS IS PROGRESS

WRITTEN AND PRESENTED BY TERRY JONES. FIRST BROADCAST DECEMBER 7, 1991, ON BBC-TV.

Terry Jones turned his love of history into a BBC documentary with this one-shot special that spawned talk of a regular series.

"It's just looking at history with a kinder eye, saying 'What can we learn from the past?'"

Jones notes. "We're always assuming we do everything better than they did back then!"

THE YOUNG INDIANA JONES CHRONICLES: SPAIN 1917

DIRECTED BY TERRY JONES. (1992) ABC-TV. WRITTEN BY GAVIN SCOTT. PRODUCED BY RICK MCCALLUM AND GEORGE LUCAS. DIRECTED BY TERRY JONES.

Terry Jones hadn't planned to do any TV directing, even for George Lucas, when he was approached about directing the tenth episode of *The Young Indiana Jones Chronicles*.

Even though he was finishing up a screen-play called *Mirrorman* and had been writing heavily for the past year, Lucasfilm was still able to convince Terry Jones to take on Indiana Jones.

"They just rang me up and asked me if I was interested in directing one. I said I wasn't." He laughs. "It was like writing *Labyrinth*—it went on from there. I enjoyed the script, and it also fit in with *Mirrorman*. I'd been writing quite a lot for the last year, so it's nice to get out and run a little bit of film through a camera."

The script for episode 10 was set in 1917 Spain and involved the teenage Indy, played by Sean Patrick Flanery, on a spy mission. Terry says he didn't need to worry about making revisions. "I worked with Gavin Scott on a little bit of it, but not much—it was all there. I just made a few suggestions after seeing the locations," reveals Jones.

Before shooting it in Spain and Czechoslovakia in July 1991, Jones was enthusiastic about the project.

"It's a good story—a good yarn, basically. I originally thought it would be a two-and-a-half-week shoot, but it actually looks now like it will be a three-and-a-half-week shoot. It's such good fun, and there's such a great lot of people doing it. It involves the *ballets russes*, who are performing in Barcelona at the time—it all takes place in Barcelona, which is where we're shooting it. Then there's a lot of theater, and we're shooting that up in Prague."

Jones says he was a fan of the films, and he was particularly excited about the historical underpinnings of the series.

"I enjoyed the films, and I liked George Lucas's idea for the series, which was to take this Indiana Jones character, who must be one of the most popular imaginative characters around at the moment, and use him in a kind of semieducational way. They're not just educational, they're great stories as well, but the idea is, he's traveling the world with his father, and it's a way of putting kids nowadays in touch with world history and culture. When they're in Paris, 1910, he encounters Picasso and Degas."

His own story involved a period that many viewers weren't familiar with, which made it even more interesting.

"The episode involves spying, a vague history of the First World War, the *ballets russes*, and the idea of the excitement of the culture in those days. The ballet wasn't a bunch of people in tutus dancing around, it was actually very raunchy and sexy and exciting, and created a great uproar at the time," explains Jones.

"I was resisting it for a while, but I finally thought it would be a nice thing to do—and it would be nice to work with George Lucas."

Jones says he had a wonderful time during the filming, although it wasn't an easy shoot.

"It was good fun, and everybody seems to be happy with it," he relates. "There was a little bit of action, and it was quite funny—there was a lot of fun in it, and a bit of chasing around. It was nice to do something that was different and lighthearted."

MOM AND DAD SAVE THE WORLD

CO-STARRING ERIC IDLE. (1992)

Marge Nelson	Teri Garr
Dick Nelson	Jeffrey Jones
Tod Spengo	Jon Lovitz
Sibor	Wallace Shawn
Emperor	Eric Idle
Rebel	Kathy Ireland

Written by Ed Solomon and Chris Matheson. Produced by Michael Phillips. Directed by Greg Beeman. Released by Warner Bros.

Dick and Marge are a middle-age couple living in Woodland Hills; at the opposite side of the galaxy is a very tiny planet called Spengo, named after its ruler. Jealous because Earth is so much larger, Spengo is about to destroy the planet when he sees Marge exercising by the pool. He falls madly in love with her and decides he must have her.

As Dick and Marge are driving to Santa Barbara in hopes of rekindling their romance on their twentieth anniversary, Spengo uses his Magno-Ray to pull their 1989 Ford Crown Victoria to his planet. Dick is thrown in a dungeon, where he meets the former emperor, while Marge is taken away to luxury.

Dick finally escapes through the sewers, where he encounters the Lub-Lubs. He teams up with rebels he encounters in the desert. The inhabitants of the planet are apparently the stupidest people in the universe, and so Dick is a sexy, heroic genius to the natives, and organizes the rebels.

They construct a huge statue of Spengo, with the motto "In Tod We Trust," in a Trojan Tod plan. Dick finally fights a duel with Spengo to prevent his wedding to Marge, and Dick and Marge do indeed save the world.

 NOTES

Although he didn't spend a great deal of time on the set, Eric Idle says he enjoyed filming his dungeon scenes.

"It was nice. I knew some of the people, like Teri Garr and Jon Lovitz and Wallace Shawn, so it was a very pleasant day's shooting with them. And a very pleasant day being chained by the throat filming with Jeffrey Jones, who is very funny—I liked him a lot.

"But the best thing about the main day was that I fell totally in love with Kathy Ireland's legs," he laughs. "She does have, outside of my wife, the best legs in America. It was the high point of my career, really, and I hope she felt the same way about my legs, although mine were not so exposed as hers. The great thing about all planets, as we know, is that all girls with lovely bodies tend to wear little fur bikinis. . . .

"It is odd, isn't it? Because you look at the space programs, and they tend to be wearing a lot of clothes. But, when the girls get up there, little fur bikinis are the order of the day. . . . I don't know why this is Hollywood's view of the future."

His own role in *Mom and Dad*—also known as *Dick and Marge Save the World*—was rather limited, Idle notes. "My perspective is, I was king of this planet, who was deposed and put in jail by Jon Lovitz, whose film it is—I spend most of the film in jail. The people in the film who are funny are Lovitz, Teri Garr, and Jeffrey Jones—my take on it is very limited, which is why I talk about Kathy Ireland's legs," he jokes.

"The basic scene that I'm in is that Jeffrey Jones is on this planet, in the midst of rebellion, and he finds me chained to the wall of a dungeon. He finds this strange creature covered with cobwebs just going `Waugghhh. . . .' He keeps telling him something very important, but keeps forgetting it. . . ."

In a welcome contrast to his work with Terry Gilliam on *Baron Munchausen*, Idle notes that his part was relatively free of special effects. "I have done my days with SFX. No actor likes working with SFX, no actor in the world. It's just the pits—it's just there to annoy you and make you suffer.

"My particular part was not full of SFX—it was very Python. It was chained to the wall of a dungeon, a lot of facial hair, and smoke blowing in your face. Instead of Graham Chapman, it was Jeffrey Jones. Normally, it would have been Graham going `What?!' and doing all those reactions. I had to go `Now, this is very important. . . . Did I say we are idiots?' It wasn't different or difficult for me to play that part! Then at the end, I'm freed from prison and brought out, because Mom and Dad save the planet, or the universe, or whatever it's called."

Although he isn't certain why he was approached about the project, Idle has his suspicions.

"I think Lovitz got me into it, but I'm not sure entirely. Michael Phillips, who's the producer, just asked me. It was a nice role, they sent it along, and it fit in nicely with my schedule. It was fun to do, really," he recalls.

He notes that his character was not too great of a departure from characters he has played in the past.

"It was very Pythonic, really—it was a character that could easily have been in a Python movie. So, it was kind of not hard to play. He was just a guy who keeps forgetting things—he just constantly has amnesia, which I'm getting very close to having myself lately," he laughs.

"So, it was fun, really except for one line which I had to say. Teri Garr ripped me unmercifully afterwards when she saw me at a party: `I have reversed the polarity on the magno-beam, you are now safe to return.' A very hard line to have to deliver, because you haven't got any idea what you're talking about," he says, laughing. "I hope I managed to pull that line off, or else they cut it—one way or another!"

Idle, who wrote his own science fiction musical called *Outta' Space* (formerly *The Road to Mars*), says *Mom and Dad Save the World* is quite different from his movie, even though they both involve outer space.

"This is a SFX movie. They have enormous, clever, complicated creatures with heads that move and eyes that roll—it's that kind of space, as opposed to *Road to Mars*," he says.

"I was trying to make a thirties film of the future—nostalgia for the future is my key. I personally believe the future will be much more about human beings than about little furry creatures. I was trying to go for a non–*Star Wars* look of the future, reality from a show business perspective. It's like a Bob and Bing *Road* picture, it's two comedians in the future. The only thing you can be certain of about the future is, there *will* be show business in it. And we'll be the same kind of assholes!" he laughs.

Working on an American film like *Mom and Dad* doesn't require much adjustment for English actors, notes Idle.

"The difference is in the script. I think that Brits tend to rewrite more deeply into the script, and the Americans tend to just put alternatives in. Something like *A Fish Called Wanda* had four drafts by the same author, whereas in America you'd have had eight drafts by twelve different authors. The advantage is that themes and characters emerge better. Of course, the advantage of the American way is that they still have a film industry."

"I was having tea with somebody who observed that American humor was getting tougher, and he observed conversely that English humor was much tougher, but was now getting weaker," he comments. "I think that's true. By weaker, I mean more sentimental, much more television-type humor, blander, and much less sure. I think you have to be sure of where you are in the world to be tough about things. American humor is actually getting tougher, I think. People are no longer content with bland sitcoms all the time."

POLE TO POLE

WRITTEN AND PRESENTED BY MICHAEL PALIN. WRITTEN BY MICHAEL PALIN. SERIES PRODUCED BY CLEM VALLANCE. DIRECTED BY ROGER MILLS. BROADCAST OF EIGHT ONE-HOUR SHOWS AUTUMN 1992 ON BBC-1, AND U.S. PREMIERE ON ARTS AND ENTERTAINMENT CHANNEL JANUARY 10, 1993. PRODUCED BY THE BBC/PROMINENT FEATURES (1992).

Michael Palin and a BBC crew set out from the North Pole and travel down to the South Pole; they travel through Finland and Russia, into Africa, go down the Nile and into Antarctica.

 NOTES

Michael Palin's first global journey for the BBC, *Around the World in 80 Days*, was so successful that he was asked to make another trip; since he had already traveled west to east, the north-to-south route seemed appropriate.

The biggest reason Palin wanted to make the polar journey, however, was the overwhelmingly positive response he received to the first shows.

"I thought we ought to have a go at another one, partly to satisfy my own curiosity, and partly because of the very, very different route, down through Finland and Russia, and right through Africa—from Cairo to the Cape, the historic route down the Nile. . . .

"My director, Clem Vallance, was looking at what journey, what *epic* journey we could do, and decided 'We've done across, let's go *down*.' The thirty-degree line of longitude goes through land almost all the way, and quite interesting, varied land."

A few weeks before he was set to depart, Palin discussed his preparations for the trip eagerly.

"I'm terrified!" he laughed. "Well, I am now. A couple of months ago, I was saying 'Oh, I'll be going from pole to pole, pretty cool, this is my next job,' blasé, blasé. Now I'm beginning to think of the realities of it and bringing back all the film, and it's quite terrifying. But it'll be great. Mentally, I think I'm ready for it now.

"*80 Days* was an unknown quantity, I just didn't know what it was going to be like, *how* it was going to be like, what *tone* we were going to adopt, how it would work. In the end, the people we met made the show—it just wrote itself as we went 'round. That was just a basic fear of the unknown," Palin recalls.

"This isn't quite so unknown. The technique we now know. Roughly, the sort of tone of it, we know. So, it's really just the places we go through that are going to be different—but they're *very* different, and there's less time for luxury. A lot of it will be much rougher."

His trip was actually begun in July of 1991 at the northern tip of Norway, and he spent the rest of the year travelling to the South Pole; due to climatic conditions, he had to complete the beginning of the journey in April of 1992.

"We hadn't completed it, because owing to the vagaries of climatic conditions in the north, we had to go to the North Pole at a time when it was safe to land there. That's only a short period of the year, late April and early May," he explains.

Palin explains that having done most of the trip and having to go back months later to do the "beginning" is a little frustrating.

"We went from the north of Norway, the first bit of land in Europe, to the South Pole. It took us about five months. We traveled overland and didn't catch any major diseases, though I cracked a rib white-water rafting in the Zambesi," Palin notes.

"Apart from that, there were no great problems as far as I was concerned. Some of the crew got sick, but we managed to film every day, despite the extremes of heat and cold, and the film all came out. It makes a pretty rich series, much different in content from *80 Days*."

The main difference from his trip *Around the World in 80 Days* is that the polar voyage involved very little sea travel.

"It was nearly all overland," he reveals. "Instead of going from city to city, which we tended to do in *80 Days*, we went across a lot of bare, difficult country terrain. We also went through a lot more different climatic extremes than we did in *80 Days*. It was even hotter than *80 Days*, and of course we also had extreme cold. I think that the overland journeys through the countries were more difficult, but in the end, more rewarding, because the scenery that we saw and the beauty of the countries was much greater than we really had time to see in *80 Days*."

There were some problems along the way, of course, but Palin says the trickiest area of the journey was traveling through the Sudan.

"It's not an easy country to work in, for many reasons," he notes. "It was very, very hot. It's largely desert, and its government is xenophobic in the sense that they're not very keen on the West. There's an Arab fundamentalist government and life is quite hard there for Westerners. Also, they are very bureaucratically obstructive, which again meant that just getting through it was difficult—you have to have papers and permissions, and lots of queueing up at offices.

"To compound all that, it is an *enormous* country," Palin says with a laugh, "so it takes a long time to get through anyway. The final section of that was to cross the border into Ethiopia along what appeared on the map was a road, but in fact turned out to be nothing but a track which had been heavily indented by trucks. We got stuck, and it took us hours longer than we intended to get across. It was undoubtedly the most difficult place."

Palin and his BBC crew actually avoided the turmoil in the Soviet Union during late 1991, though he takes the credit for having instigated it all.

"We started it all. I think we finally precipitated the total collapse of the Soviet Union," he laughs. "Within forty-eight hours of our intensive, searching documentary, literally as we were crossing the Black Sea, the coup happened, and we heard a few days later that it had collapsed and Gorbachev was back. The major change happened about forty-eight hours after we left!"

By the time they arrived in Antarctica at the end of the trip, Palin says they were all rather tired.

"We were airlifted out from the southern part of Chile to the central part of the Antarctic plateau, looked after on a small base there, and then flown to the Pole. If you've got a fear of flying, it's a difficult place to be, because there's just this emptiness below, and even though it was summer, the temperatures were very low.

"But we were well looked after there. We got to the Pole, and there was an American base there. It was rather like going to a Python fan convention. The most remote part of the earth, and there are people there with copies of *Wanda* that they want you to sign. That didn't happen to Captain Scott!"

POLE TO POLE

BY MICHAEL PALIN. PUBLISHED BY BBC BOOKS (1992).

The day-to-day diary of Michael Palin kept during the voyage. "I wanted to call it *Jules Verne's Pole to Pole*, since I took all the credit from him for *80 Days*," he jokes.

Pole to Pole is also fully illustrated with photos from the journey.

SPLITTING HEIRS

WRITTEN BY AND STARRING ERIC IDLE. (1993). STARRING ERIC IDLE, RICK MORANIS, BARBARA HERSHEY, JOHN CLEESE, AND A PUMA. WRITTEN BY ERIC IDLE. PRODUCED BY SIMON BOSANQUET AND REDMOND MORRIS. DIRECTED BY ROBERT M. YOUNG. RELEASED BY UNIVERSAL PICTURES AND PROMINENT FEATURES.

Eric Idle, who also served as executive producer, penned this comedy, shot in May, June, and July of 1992. This is a "bloody buddy film about greed and riches and killing people," according to Idle. Set in England, he says it's actually a buddy picture "Where one buddy tries to kill the other buddy."

Part Four

GRAHAM REMEMBERED

GRAHAM CHAPMAN

January 8, 1941– October 4, 1989

$\mathcal{B}$efore he became ill in late 1988, Graham Chapman was hard at work on several projects. In addition to the previously mentioned *Jake's Journey* and the film he was planning on The Dangerous Sports Club, he also served as executive producer on a British film called *Love Potion Number Nine,* directed by Python film editor Julian Doyle. He was also going to star in a black comedy film called *Stiff,* to be shot in North Carolina. Even during his final illness, he had negotiated a development deal with Imagine Entertainment to come up with story ideas for possible TV shows and films.

Perhaps the biggest project that didn't happen was *Ditto,* a screenplay Graham had originally written in the late 1960s with John Cleese. It was going to star Peter Sellers and Sophia Loren, with her husband Carlo Ponti producing it, when Ponti backed out. (Graham alleged that Sellers and Loren were becoming too friendly to suit Ponti.)

"We wrote it and never heard a word back from the person who commissioned it," recalls John Cleese. "Apparently we never even got the second half of the fee or anything like that. We'd forgotten all about it, but it was always a very good idea."

Graham revived the science fiction comedy years later, and began rewriting it with David Sherlock.

"I always thought it was a good script," says Cleese, "but I made the decision not to get involved. Graham asked me if I wanted to rewrite it and I thought no, it's going into the past. It was actually quite a good script."

A film deal was nearly set up several times, but after his experiences on *Yellow-beard*, Graham insisted on retaining as much control as possible. Just before he became ill, he had arranged to shoot it on a smaller budget, but retaining creative control. His death put a temporary end to the comedy, which involves cloning, but Sherlock resolved to continue attempts to get the film made.

Graham intended to do all this and more when cancer was first detected on his tonsil in November 1988, beginning his long battle with the disease. He was in and out of the hospital for the next year. The cancer spread to his spine, but his determination to beat the disease never wavered. It even looked as if he had succeeded by the following September, when he was discharged from the hospital and began making plans to resume his career as he was undergoing physical therapy. After he had been home a short time, however, he was rushed to the hospital, wracked with pain, and doctors discovered the cancer had spread too far for hope of recovery.

For three days Graham held on, with friends and family, including his fellow Pythons, at his side. During that time his son, John Tomiczek, was able to fly in from America in time to visit with him. Terry Jones kept a bedside vigil and left early on the morning of October 4; Michael Palin and John Cleese were at his side when he died a few hours later.

"I just talked to him—and then he died!" Palin said later.

"We were always getting on to Michael for talking too much," quipped Eric Idle. "When we talked later about Graham's death, we were able to have a laugh and a weep."

Dying on the eve of the twentieth anniversary of the first *Monty Python's Flying Circus* broadcast prompted Terry Jones to call it "The worst case of party-pooping I have ever come across."

Cleese and Palin each wrote tributes to Graham for London newspapers; Cleese's appeared in the October 6, 1989, *Independent* as follows:

Graham Chapman and I wrote together almost full time between 1966 and 1973, while producing sketches for The Frost Report, The 1948 Show, *and* Monty Python, *as well as several film scripts, none of which made their way intact to the silver screen.*

As a writing partner he had two rare gifts: the ability to get us un-stuck with some inspired off-the-wall conceit when I was enmeshed in very on-the-wall musings; and in addition, the priceless talent of knowing whether something was funny or not. I noticed this early and relied upon it shamelessly. In fact the Cheese Shop Skit—my all-time favorite—owes its life to him. Every dozen or so cheeses, I'd sigh and say "Gra, is this really funny?" and he'd puff on his pipe calmly and say "Yes, get on with it."

I wished he'd had the same confidence in front of audiences because he was probably the most talented actor of us all. But, he found the Python TV recordings a terrible strain, and some of his drinking was an attempt to dampen that fear. After he gave up the booze at Christmas 1977—for good—he gave us his splendid Brian, which is as clever and well-judged a piece of comic acting as you'll see.

Of course, he'd given up medicine to pursue comedy, but he was absolutely at his best when caring for others. He looked after the entire film unit practically single-handed while we were filming in Tunisia and I was reminded of this again in recent months when we visited him in hospital. I think he was just as keen to look after us then, and his optimism, cheerfulness and absolute lack of self-pity made me, for one, feel very, very small. We all bought his optimism, of course. We wanted to. But his elder brother John thinks that he knew better what the score was than he ever let on.

That his bravery was ended so abruptly and unexpectedly seems very cruel.

Graham Chapman at one of the early Monty Python writing sessions, circa 1969. Photo copyright Terry Jones

Michael Palin's lengthy tribute, which follows, first appeared October 6, 1989, in *The Guardian*:

I first heard of Graham Chapman as one of that pool of ex-Oxbridge revue talent that sloshed around the BBC in the mid-1960s.

I use the word sloshed advisedly, for many of our best times were had propping up the various bars of the Corporation. Graham was like a figure out of a Biggles story. Strong, finely-chiselled features, pipe at a jaunty angle in his mouth, pint in one hand and progger in the other. A progger was Graham's name for the flat-ended instrument which he used to bed down the tobacco in his pipe. I never knew whether it was a real name or not. Graham liked words and used them well, but if he felt the right one didn't exist he'd invent another one.

In the post-Cambridge days he was a journeyman writer, like us all. One day he would be working with John Cleese to produce a dazzling succession of successful sketches for The Frost Report, *the next he would be writing filler jokes for the Petula Clark show.*

He kept a low profile as a performer until At Last the 1948 Show *in which he revealed a talent for playing intense, rather serious characters hilariously. He was a charismatic performer, drawing the eye to himself, as much for the originality and un-showbizziness of his approach, as for the likely detectable hint of unpredictability. An audience was never quite sure what he would do next. Nor I think, as a performer, was Graham. During a singing court scene in one of the early Python shows he quite inadvertently substituted 'window dresser' for 'window cleaner' in his song. A Freudian slip at which we all fell about, especially Graham.*

In 1969, when the mutual admiration society which became known as Monty Python assembled, Graham met David Sherlock and embarked on one of the many radical changes in his life, when they decided to live together. It was a courageous decision, which shocked some of his friends at the time but was borne out triumphantly by the fact that they shared the rest of their lives. David, together with their adopted son John Tomiczek, nursed and cared

for him with stoic patience and quiet strength throughout his final illness.

Graham's need to relax himself with a dram or two took a disproportionate hold on his life as the pressures of a heavy Python schedule grew. Drink was not always the friend he thought it, affecting his performances and occasionally doing a great disservice to a much underrated natural acting talent.

His writing contributions to Python were of quality rather than quantity. Whilst all around were scratching their heads for inspiration. Graham would puff his pipe and glance sideways at the Times *crossword and be quite silent for 30 minutes or so before coming out with a single shaft of inspiration that would transform a mundane sketch into something very mad and wonderful.*

Such surreal flashes were the very essence of Python as were his memorable performances as the Colonel, as the Hostess in the Eurovision song contest, Raymond Luxury-Yacht and others.

His off-stage performances included collecting an award from the Sun *newspaper by leaping high in the air, emitting a loud squawk and crawling all the way back to his table with the award in his mouth, leaving Lord Mountbatten, who had given him the award, looking very confused.*

But Graham's most memorable performances were sustained and demanding—as King Arthur in Monty Python and the Holy Grail *and Brian in the* Life of Brian.

Around the time of the filming of Life of Brian, *Graham made a conscious effort to free himself from the dependence on the large G and Ts—after that "ice but no lemon please." His restless ever-inquisitive need to be freed from the boring and the conventional had led him to the brink, but his cautious disciplined rational side saved him at the last minute from toppling over. He gave up drinking and later, with immense difficulty also laid aside his pipe.*

Perhaps Graham too easily overestimated the talents of others while underestimating his own and, as a result, his ventures outside Python—Out of the Trees for the BBC and his two films, Odd Job and Yellowbeard—were full of good ideas badly resolved. The commercial failure of Yellowbeard depressed him.

His recent illness was another in a series of mountains which Graham had to climb. He always regarded death as highly overrated and could never understand why anybody made such a fuss about it. Despite great physical discomfort he remained alert, informed, articulate and humorous.

He hated to be bored which is why he joined the Dangerous Sports Club and once hurled himself into thin air attached to a length of rubber . . . "I was high for two weeks after that."

I suspect he would have enjoyed an old age of increasing eccentricity, dispensing his considerable wisdom and hospitality, occasionally leaping in the air and shouting "Eeke!"

A small funeral service was held for the family a few days later, the Rolling Stones sent flowers, and the other Pythons were responsible for a floral arrangement in the shape of a huge foot.

Two months later a celebration of Graham's life was held in London, followed that evening by the delayed Python anniversary party. A variety of Graham's friends spoke at the celebration, including Douglas Adams, Tim Brooke-Taylor, John Cleese, and Michael Palin. Neil Innes performed (wearing his duck hat), and the Fred Tomlinson Singers led the crowd in singing a Chinese version of "Jerusalem." The festivities wrapped up with Eric Idle leading the group in "Always Look on the Bright Side of Life," and sherry was passed around at the conclusion so that everyone could toast to Graham's memory.

John Cleese and Michael Palin addressed the crowd in a manner that Graham certainly would have loved. Cleese's opening comments were as follows:

Graham Chapman, co-author of the "Parrot Sketch," is no more. He has ceased to be, bereft of life, he rests in peace, he has kicked the bucket, hopped the twig, bit the dust, snuffed it, breathed his last, and gone to meet the Great Head of Light Entertainment in the sky, and I guess that we're all thinking how sad it is that a man of such talent, such capability

and kindness, of such unusual intelligence should now be so suddenly spirited away at the age of only forty-eight, before he'd achieved many of the things of which he was capable, and before he'd had enough fun.

Well, I feel that I should say, "Nonsense. Good riddance to him, the freeloading bastard! I hope he fries." And the reason I think I should say this is, he would never forgive me if I didn't, if I threw away this opportunity to shock you all on his behalf. Anything for him but mindless good taste. I could hear him whispering in my ear last night as I was writing this, "Alright, Cleese, you're very proud of being the first person ever to say `shit' on television. If this service is really for me, just for starters, I want you to be the first person ever at a British memorial service to say "fuck"!"

In late January 1990 another memorial was held for Graham in Los Angeles, hosted by the British Academy of Film and Television Arts L.A. chapter. Guests included David Sherlock and Harry Nilsson.

During the course of preparing this book, I uncovered a lengthy interview I had conducted with Graham in early 1983. Much of the discussion involved *Yellowbeard* (those comments can be found in the appropriate chapter); however, I was startled to discover that toward the end of that interview, Graham had talked for several minutes about his thoughts on life, death, and growing old, comments particularly poignant after his death five years later.

We began by briefly discussing his childhood, which he regarded as normal, "Apart from the Second World War. It didn't happen to everybody, but it happened to a lot of people. It was very normal, apart from people throwing bombs made in Germany outside our house," he said. "My father was a policeman; I suppose I did get to meet quite a variety of odd characters because of that. But it was startlingly normal, really."

Graham said he occasionally liked to watch his old films and TV shows, though he was watching them more infrequently.

"I do for a short time. For instance, for about three or four years after the Python TV shows, I enjoyed watching them—not all of them, as there were some I was not so keen on. And I did enjoy that. I find I do that less and less, though," he noted in 1983. "Now, I suppose I feel a little more like once a thing is done, it's done. I'm probably a little more critical now before a thing happens than I was—of course, now there's more time to be so, because I'm dealing with movie scripts.

"I'm a little more tolerant of past errors now than I was. I used to find them more irksome, and I wouldn't want to look at them again for that reason, things that I knew that weren't my best. No, that worries me less, I'm less easily embarrassed from that point of view. There are quite a few little moments like that, where one looks back on a history of alcoholism too," he said, laughing. "Moments that are actually recorded on tape when one was not at one's best. That, perhaps, makes me more tolerant than most."

Although he had many shaky moments during the Python TV shows as a result of his drinking, he was never surprised while watching the old shows by a sketch he had forgotten he had done.

"I can't think of anything offhand, but I'm sure there were moments. I have seen one or two old Python TV shows where I can definitely tell that I was a little more worse for wear than I should have been, the timing is a little slower. It's a very strange experience talking of this . . ." he said.

Graham said he had never planned out his life with long-term goals when he was starting his career.

"I don't think I did then—there were very vague ones. My progress toward medicine wasn't really with the set aim of doing that—it was sort of vaguely 'Oh, I'll do some research eventually that will be of immense benefit,' that sort of thought. But it was all really quite vague. I don't have any set goals as such, just as long as everything's going in the general direction of progress," he laughed.

In 1983, having made it through five years without alcohol, he could start looking forward in a way that he hadn't been able to before. He preferred not to think about what he'd be doing twenty-five years in the future, but remained optimistic.

"Up until five years ago I thought my future was more limited than that, but now it seems to stretch out more endlessly than I expected," he said with a laugh. "If someone could tell me what I'd be doing in twenty-five years, I wouldn't really want to know. I'd like it to be a surprise when it happens. I think that's one of the best things about life—it can be a complete surprise. I kind of like to think that by that age, I might have taken yet another switch in some strange direction—maybe ten years in movies, then a few years as a biochemist. Or becoming a beach bum! It's quite farfetched, but I don't know. . . ."

Without question, it was giving up alcohol that accounted for his positive feelings at the time. "The biggest change was the spirit of optimism that overcame me when I'd stopped drinking. It took time to emerge, really."

The one incident that made him decide to give up alcohol occurred in 1974.

"I've pinned it down rather accurately now. I think the precise moment of decision to really do something about it was on the first day of filming *Holy Grail*. That's when I resolved to do something about it as soon as I could.

"We were filming the Bridge of Death sequence over the Gorge of Eternal Peril. We happened to film it the first morning of the whole shoot up in Scotland. I hadn't gotten myself organized, and we were up on the mountainside at seven A.M., and of course I had taken no drink along with me at all. I hadn't gotten myself organized yet, and no one else had anything, either. I couldn't believe that out of an entire crew, *no* one there went without a little nip of scotch or anything. I was stuck and began to go through DTs on the mountainside *during* that sequence. Each time after we'd do a take, I'd go off and moan in the heather and the drizzle and have a good shake, and try to get myself back together again to go back and do it next time. That was *really* miserable!

"There is, in fact, a photograph of me in one of the Python books. I'm sitting down on the hillside with a white cap on, rather than the crown, and I'm looking fairly miserable. John Cleese assigned the total blame for that to the miseries of filming. In actual fact, it's quite a different story."

He explained that his shyness was one of the principal reasons for his alcohol abuse. "That was part of it, yes. I make a more ebullient, sociable person than an antisocial person because of it, I suppose. . . ."

Graham said he didn't fear death, although he planned to avoid it as long as possible.

"Like most people, I think it would be very pleasant not to have to go, but one accepts that.

It's more or less inevitable. We try to do what we can to avoid the ravages and to keep your faculties about you, and if there is anything like an advance in health care, I'll be the first to take it.

"But it doesn't actually worry me a great deal, because I've been impressed by some wonderful old people, and not just great ones like J. B. Priestley and Bertrand Russell and George Bernard Shaw. . . . So, I don't think there's any real fault that one should let one's brain give up easily. I have every intention of trying to remain as twinkly as I can until I feel like retiring, really. I think you could quite easily reach a point where people say to themselves `Perhaps it's about time I turned a little off, you know, I've done just about everything I can think of—tried this, tried that—oh, I think I'll just retire and—oops, I'm dead!' I think it's important to go on living until something catches you.

"I don't really look back with regret on any feelings or problems I've had in the past. I think I'm more able to accept that kind of thing now as being part of the rough and tumble of life. There are bound to be ups and downs. In retrospect, when you've gotten past a rough period, it makes the good things that much better. Sort of a trite thing to say, but it doesn't seem to worry me that much!"

Besides keeping his regrets in check, Graham said he didn't attach too much importance to his successes, either.

"I'm a little more moderate on those now as well than I used to be. I don't get too elated—there's a more satisfying inner elation, and much less leaping up and down. From my own point of view, my life used to be very black and white in many ways. Now I appreciate tones of gray. That was really a coincidence with drinking too—I think my philosophy changed a little bit afterwards. Before, I had very little patience and had to do things *now*, and if someone annoyed me, I'd tell them. Now I can wait until they annoy themselves!"

The interview concluded with my asking Graham how he wanted to be remembered after he was gone. His words speak for themselves.

"I think I would like to achieve something lasting. Most people like to feel that they're a little unique—as everyone is—and I suppose that's it. If there's any vague ambition, it is that eventually, there will be something I've done which would be worth remembering, that I've done something that people can look back on and say `Ah, he was good at that,' or `At least he did *that*, that was good!'"

Graham Chapman Photo copyright Kim "Howard" Johnson

AFTER MONTY PYTHON:
THE THIRD 200 YEARS

*W*hen I began work on this book, I felt I was aware of the talents and abilities of the six members of Monty Python.

Once I had nearly completed the project and began an overview of all the material, however, I was amazed at the scope, variety, and quality of their works.

Terry Gilliam has become one of the most acclaimed directors in film, while the quality of Eric Idle's writing and performing (everything from sitcoms to opera) is apparent. John Cleese may work more slowly and meticulously, but whether he is involved in a book, a film, or a commercial, he gives it everything he's got.

Michael Palin's career has seen him writing everything from children's books to film scripts and travelogues, winning acclaim for his performing. Terry Jones's talents are every bit as broad; in addition to acting and directing, he has written everything from children's books and filmscripts to scholarly texts and poetry. And obviously, Graham Chapman has left behind a large body of work that will long be remembered.

What began as a low-budget, throwaway late-night TV series has resulted in a legendary comedy group and six individual careers whose output continues to impress and astound, with upcoming films like Gilliam's *A Connecticut Yankee in King Arthur's Court,* Cleese's apocryphally titled *Death Fish II,* and all sorts of projects that have yet to be created. And their work will continue to entertain, inform, influence, and amuse for many years to come.